HERODOTUS

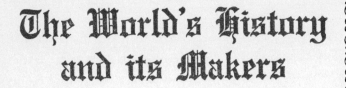

The World's History and its Makers

BY

EDGAR SANDERSON, A.M.
JOHN PORTER LAMBERTON, A.M.
CHARLES MORRIS, A.M.

AND

A CORPS OF EMINENT WRITERS

REVISED

VOL. I.
Ancient and Mediæval History

WASHINGTON, D. C.

HAWKINS & UPHAM

1915

Editors, Writers, and Contributors

EDGAR SANDERSON, A.M.
Author "Ancient Empires and Modern Europe," with special relation to the History of Civilization," "History of England and the British Empire," "Hero Patriots," "Historic Parallels," etc.

JOHN PORTER LAMBERTON, A.M.
Collaborator with A. R. Spofford, Late Librarian of Congress, on "Historic Characters and Famous Events," "Literature of all Nations," etc.

CHARLES MORRIS, A.M.
Author "Historical Tales," "Half-Hours with the Best American Authors," "Students' Universal History," etc.

JOHN McGOVERN
Author "Famous American Statesmen."

OLIVER H. G. LEIGH
Collaborator on "Library of American Literature," etc.

JOSEPH M. ROGERS
Formerly Managing Editor New York Sunday Herald.

M. A. LANE

G. SENECA JONES, A.M.

FREDERICK LOGAN

WILLIAM MATTHEWS HANDY

Introduction by
MARSHALL S. SNOW, A.M.
Professor of History, Washington University.

CONTENTS

ILLUSTRATIONS

INTRODUCTION

ADVANTAGES AND PLEASURES TO BE DE-RIVED FROM A STUDY OF HISTORY

In laying before our readers the present series of ten volumes, it seems fitting not only to describe the general character of the work, but to dwell for a few moments on the study of history as an important part of a useful and well-spent life.

History is the written record of the past; it is also such written study of the present as enables us to reveal the unwritten past. The great pyramid is not history, and until Herodotus wrote and Champollion deciphered, it was but an artificial mountain. The mounds in the region of Nineveh were only heaps of sand whose excavation would have added little to history, had not Grotefend, by years of diligent study and shrewd conception, happily found a key to the translation of the cuneiform writings of the Assyrians that lay buried in the libraries of Mesopotamia.

History, again, beside its function of unequaled dramatic entertainment, gradually amasses the informing facts concerning man's action in his environment. Scholars for centuries have been striving to acquire the philosophy of history, in order to predetermine the destiny of their race. Man, physically a compound of many elements, stands in the midst of more than seventy things also called elements, arranged into one thing called the Universe. It has been the dream of philosophy since the days of Pythagoras first to demonstrate that man acts in accordance with the laws of his environment, and next to reach the plane of scientific prophecy as to his future actions. In this series, one volume has been apportioned to the recent history of the triumph of man over the forces of a nature that once seemed rude and unfertile, but now teems with interest more startling than the boasts of necromancers.

History, to the living, is not the chief function of language, but to the unborn the handing down of history will be by far the most notable of our deeds. Whoever, then, adds to this heritage that is to be transmitted to the future, throws himself wisely upon the gratitude of a race which will rapidly grow more generous and appreciative. As we may easily perceive the desirability of stores of knowledge for the future, so we may by that measure also value our own opportunities of peering into the past. By means of history, we who are limited in life to a few decades may dwell upon the experience of our own kind for sixty centuries.

The earliest poets in the Aryan languages of Europe wrote what was then looked upon as history. Homer, Hesiod, Virgil, Tasso—history is the kernel of their song. The early balladists are tellers of legendary story. The favorite short poems of the world are more often history than sentiment—"Alexander's Feast," "Hohenlinden," "Scots Wha Hae," "The Charge of the Light Brigade"—the more stirring the lyric, the more of history it recalls.

There is no theatrical drama that is not the mimic of that imposing stage which we here place before the reader. To this, his own theater, he may enter at all hours; these actors are always at his bidding. From his almost royal divan in this arena, he may summon before him a glittering pageant of patriarchs, kings, queens, conquerors, captives, statesmen, philosophers, inventors, magicians. All will obediently play their parts; no poet, however godlike his imagination, has wrought with such skill of plot, as time has wrought.

On this stage walk Adam (Manu, Menu, Menes, Minos, Man) and his nine descendants; Noah and his nine descendants. Here is unrolled the chapter of the tenth of Genesis, that gives a geography to the world. Here rise Egypt and the pyramids; Tyre and her dark daughter Carthage; Greece and her white statues; Rome and her short sword; here comes Mohammed out of his cave, with his scimitar, and here flashes the panoply of ten crusades to the Holy Sepulcher; here sleeps Europe through a devout siesta of ten centuries; here again upspring art and architecture, freedom of thought and science; intercourse, knowledge, and progress.

What tragedian of the imagination has even mimicked the drama of Napoleon's life? Here the reader may see the carnage of Wagram or Borodino, and may thrill with the early dreams of the Corsican soldier, or sadly ponder with him at St. Helena. He may tremble with Louis XI before Charles the Bold. He may build the long bridge with Alexander at Tyre, or peer with covetous eyes on the Persian treasure at Susa. He may watch the building of the pyramids, and set up the tall columns at Karnak. He may enter Granada with Isabella, or see Christina laying down her Northern crown. He may watch the world-beleaguered Frederick, now floundering in blood to immortality, now turning a verse to meet the tuneful ear of Voltaire. What stage-played scene shall so excite him again, after he has beheld the earth-enacted plot of the French Revolution, where tragedies crash upon each other like glaciers falling into Arctic seas!

We love Herodotus because he is old and honest; Tacitus, because he is brilliant; Gibbon, because he is great. These are but brighter stars in the firmament; innumerable are the lesser lights that twinkle. Hardly a novelist but if he did his work with probity, he filled in the arabesquerie which the more stately historian must forego. We know more of old Paris when we read Hugo's "Hunchback of Notre Dame;" more of later Paris when we read Dickens' "Tale of Two Cities;" more of modern Paris when we read Daudet's "Immortals."

A love of History, early instilled, will not only acquaint the child with human life, but elevate the taste, to demand a high standard of entertainment. These volumes are the in-

dex to all that has been genuinely exciting and instructive.
Three of the series cover the general History of the World.
Seven other volumes, again, tarry to give detailed studies of
exceedingly valuable parts of the panorama.   The series has
been compiled with a view of itself acting as a pleasant and
effective stimulus to the receptive powers of the mind, in
order that the reader may move into a position to scan the
entire history of our race.

So far we have spoken largely of the history of deeds;
more should be said of the history of thought—a world of
delight equally keen, a study no less beneficial.   Through this
lens of knowledge, guided by such seers as Lenormant, we
look upon the stars, and in the names of the constellations
we read the prehistoric ideas of men.   We consider the naming of the days after the seven planets; we read the ancient
names of the months and gather meanings new to us; we
consider the sacred numbers of twelve and sixty—the sixty
shekels, manehs, talents; the sixty seconds, degrees, circles
or hours.   We see the struggles of Light and Darkness; the
grasping of the cycles of eclipse and Sirian star.   We see in
geometry the magic results of study of the circle and its
diameters; Ptolemy hanging the orbs in the sky; Copernicus
rearranging them; Columbus, their pupil, sailing into the
abyss of the sunset.   We see Napier consolidating our figures into logarithms, and Linnæus, by similar methods, naming all organic things.   We see Darwin successfully offer to
man a hypothesis of animal variation and form, and Faraday
hard after an equally successful hypothesis for Matter and
Motion.   Man, who has harnessed Niagara, and liquefied the
air, stands at the seaside, bridle in hand, ready to ensnare the
tides and banish manual labor from the world.   If philosophers have written about the philosophy of history, they in
turn must peruse the history of philosophy, which already
far surpasses the wonders of Oriental fable.

It is the duty of those who have lived many years to
guide the footsteps of those who with glad countenances are
eagerly pressing upon the scene.   Their advent becomes

more and more interesting and optimistic.   At the portal we
should stand, offering, as our most precious possession, the
History that we received from our ancestors, the History that
our own generation has increased with its deeds and adventures; the History into which each coming year must add
even more remarkable chapters.

ANCIENT AND MEDIÆVAL HISTORY

IMPORTANCE OF HISTORY

History is a record of the doings of civilized mankind, in its progress toward the greatest of political and social blessings—a rational freedom of thought and action. History deals with the life only of political communities, or nations, and not with races of men who have made little advance from a primitive state. The special duty of history is to sketch the career and describe the condition of those great nations whose ideas and institutions, or whose achievements in art, science, politics, literature, and war were remarkable in their own epoch, or, by influencing other nations, helped to make the civilized world what it is now.

The Eastern nations did not reach to the height of the idea that mankind is, and ought to be, free; they only knew of freedom for one—the despot—to whose caprices they became victims and slaves. The Greeks first became conscious of freedom as the right of mankind, but they, as well as the Romans, knew only of freedom for a part of mankind—their own citizens, and so had a system of slave-holding bound up with the free constitution which those citizens enjoyed. The Teutonic nations, aided by Christianity, first became conscious that man, as such, is free, and by slow degrees slavery was abolished, and constitutional freedom was established in modern states, organized in a rational way. The history of the world is an account of the growth among mankind of this consciousness of freedom for the race. This is the grand aim which the world's history has seen, at least in part, attained—the acquirement of freedom for the heaven-born spirit of man. On this altar have been laid the sublime sacrifices of patriots and heroes; to this pole-star, amid the constant change of conditions and events, the magnet guiding the track of this great laboring sorrow-laden bark of humanity has been, on a wide view, ever true. The springs of action in history are the various needs, characters, passions, and talents of men. Passing to the picturesque view of this great subject, we find that "the world's history is a grand panorama of events and changes, the sight of which calls into play all the emotions of the soul of man—love of goodness, enjoyment of beauty, admiration of greatness; hope and fear for the results of struggles in which human action and suffering are involved; pity for the fallen greatness both of men and of empires; joy in the issuing of new life from the ashes of the funeral-pile of nations that have consumed themselves away."

The grand crisis in the history of the world is the contest between freedom and despotism which was, in Grecian history, decided on the plain of Marathon, where the Greeks overthrew the power of Persia, and saved Europe from falling under the rule of an Eastern despot. From that hour it was possible for Europe to work out and to enjoy true liberty and civilization in the combination of the personal freedom of the private citizen with a willing submission to the supremacy of public law. In the Roman Empire we have the spectacle of almost the whole civilized world ruled by one state, upon a system adapted with consummate skill for the maintenance of law and order throughout. When the Roman Empire perished under the pressure of foreign influence, aided by internal corruption and decay, the vigorous races of northern and central Europe began a new development of civilization which, combined with Christianity, by slow degrees made Europe what we see it now. The shattered fragments of the Roman Empire, under the pressure of the conquering tribes, assumed new forms, and new nations arose to become the founders of the state-system of Modern Europe.

The political and social life of Greece and Rome have directly influenced all European nations down to the present hour. The present character of the English-speaking race is closely connected with the facts that, at Athens, a citizen enjoyed absolute political and social freedom, and that in the Roman system all personal feelings and tastes were subjected to the rigorous supremacy of absolute law. All ancient history leads up, through Greece, to Rome triumphant; all modern history comes down to us from Rome beaten and broken. This is the ample vindication of the claims of Greek and Roman history to the study and regard of modern readers. How stands the case with India and China, as contrasted with Greece and Rome? The Chinaman was, and is, a pedant; the Hindoo was, and is, a dreamer; the Greek was a thinker and an artist; the Roman was a man. For European civilization, the pedant could teach nothing; the dreamer has done nothing; the thinker and artist developed, molded, and improved himself and all around him, and all that came after him; the man conquered and governed the world.

It is interesting and important to notice the geographical conditions under which great nations have arisen. This has always occurred either in valley-plains, the regions traversed and watered by some great river and its tributaries, or on a coast which has afforded the means of commercial intercourse with other nations. Thus

India and China consist of valley-plains, and have given rise to great nations, lying beyond the scope of the general history of the world, though curious and interesting in themselves.   Babylonia, which had the Euphrates and the Tigris for its rivers, was one of the great empires of old. Egypt was watered by the Nile.   In all these regions, agriculture provided plenteous food for man, and soon gave rise to property in land; this property was the origin of legal relations, and so we have the basis of a state.   The chief seat of the history of the ancient world was the great Mediterranean Sea.   "On its shores," says Hegel, "lie Greece, a focus of light; Syria, the center of Judaism and of Christianity; southeast, not far away, are Mecca and Medina, cradle of the Mussulman faith; Rome, Carthage, Alexandria, lay all on the Mediterranean, mighty heart of the old world.   Around this great uniting sea, a bond between the three great continents of the eastern half of this our globe, all ancient history of the higher value gathers."   Nations really great in arts and arms, in polity and learning, have arisen only in the temperate zone of the earth.   The reason is that there alone has nature allowed man to devote his time and powers to self-culture. In the torrid and the frigid zones, the struggle with the forces of nature is too fierce and constant to allow men to do more than reach a certain point of civilization.

THE FAMILIES AND RACES OF MANKIND.

Ethnologists have divided mankind into five leading families—the Caucasian, Mongolian or Tartar, Negro or Ethiopian, Malay, and American—or, according to color, the white, yellow, black, brown, and red races.   The epithet Caucasian is taken from the mountain-range between the Black and Caspian Seas, near to which region the finest specimens of man—regarded physically—have always been found. Mongolian is derived from the wandering races who inhabit the plateaux of Central Asia. Negro is the Spanish word for black. Malay is connected with the peninsula of Malacca, where some of the race founded a state in the Thirteenth Century. American is applied to the copper-colored race found in that continent when it was discovered.

The Caucasian race has now spread, through colonization, over the whole world, but its proper region is Europe, Western Asia, and the northern strip of Africa. Nine-tenths of the people of Europe belong to the Caucasian family, the other tenth consisting of the Turks, the Magyars (in Hungary), the Finns, the Laplanders, and the pagan tribe called Samoyeds in the extreme northeast of European Russia. In Asia, the Caucasians include the Arabs, the Persians, the Afghans, and the Hindoos. In Africa, the Caucasians are spread over the whole north, from the Mediterranean to the south of the Sahara Desert, and to the farthest border of Abyssinia. In North and South America two-thirds of the people are now Caucasian. In Australia and New Zealand the Caucasian colonists have almost extinguished the native races.

The Mongolian family includes the Mongols proper, or the wandering and settled tribes between China and Siberia; the Japanese, Chinese, Burmese, Siamese, and other peoples in the southeast and east of Asia, and the native tribes of the Siberian plains. The Turks, Magyars, Finns, Laplanders, and Samoyeds, in Europe, and the Esquimaux, in America, are all Mongolian.

The proper home of the Negro race is Africa, to the south of the Sahara. The Malay tribes inhabit the peninsula of Malacca and the adjacent islands, and include also the people of Madagascar, the New Zealanders, and the dwellers in most of the Polynesian archipelagoes. The American or red variety of mankind includes the native races of North and South America.

Of all these races of mankind the only one whose history is important for us is the Caucasian or white race, to which belong the people of those states and empires of old—the Egyptian, the Assyrian, the Babylonian, the Hebrew, the Phœnician, the Hindoo, the Persian, the Greek, and the Roman. This race is historical, because it displays the most highly civilized type of mankind—that type whose progress and achievements are the true province of history. This grand stock—the Caucasian race—has been classified into three main branches—the Aryan, or Indo-European, the Semitic and the Hamitic. The term Aryan is derived either from one ancient word implying that they were "cultivators of the soil," or from another meaning "worthy, noble." The earliest known home of the Aryan people was the high table-land of Central Asia, near the sources of the Oxus and Jaxartes. The great philologist Max Müller says that "the parent-stock (from whom all the Aryan tribes have sprung) was a small clan settled probably on the highest elevation of Central Asia, speaking a language not yet Sanskrit, or Greek, or German, but containing the dialectic roots of all. There was a time when the ancestors of the Celts, the Germans, the Slavonians, the Greeks and Italians, the Persians and Hindoos were living together, separate from the ancestors of the Semitic race." The Semitic branch is so called from Shem, son of Noah, described in the Bible as ancestor of some of the nations which it includes. The Hamitic branch is named from Ham, the son of Noah, and ancestor of some of its peoples. The Aryan branch includes nearly all the present and past nations of Europe —the Greeks, Latins, Teutons or Germans (including the

English race), Celts and Slavonians, as well as three Asiatic peoples—the Hindoos, the Persians, and the Afghans. The Semitic branch includes, as its chief historical representatives, the Hebrews, Phœnicians, Assyrians, Arabs, and Babylonians. The Hamitic branch is represented in history by one great ancient nation—the Egyptians.

A leading part in the history of the world has been, and it still, played by the Aryan nations. The only great Hamitic nation—the Egyptians—became highly civilized at a very early time, and exerted a marked influence on others, and so on the civilization of succeeding ages. The Semitic race is highly distinguished in the records of religious belief, because with them originated three faiths whose main doctrine is that there is but one God—namely, the Jewish, the Christian, and the Mahometan. Apart from this, and with the special exception of the ancient Phœnicians, the Semitic nations have not done so much for mankind as the Aryan. They have not been generally distinguished for progress and enterprise, but have mainly kept to their old home between the Mediterranean, the river Tigris, and the Red Sea. It is the Aryans that have been the parents of new nations, and that have reached the highest point of intellectual development, as shown in their political freedom, and in their science, literature and art.

The glory of the Aryan element is shown in the fact that the ancient Greek and Roman, the modern German, Englishman, American and Frenchman are all of Aryan race. The Caucasian presents us with the highest type among the five families of man: the Aryan branch of the Caucasian family presents us with the noblest pattern of that highest type. The Aryan in history shows all that is most worthy of renown in energy, and enterprise, and skill, and claims of right the foremost place on history's page.

At some remote period of the past the forefathers of the Hindoos and the Persians were one people, living together on the plateau north and northwest of the Himalaya Mountains. Under the pressure of numbers, and spurred onward by their enterprising nature, these Aryan peoples began a movement of migration from their ancestral seat, a portion of them going southward into Hindostan, another portion westward into Persia, where they developed into the Hindoo and Persian nations. Some philologists maintain that this was the seat of the fathers of the whole Aryan race, but later authorities place them in eastern or northern Europe. Of them the Celtic branch was the first to invade the west. They appear to have spread themselves over a great part of the continent; but as a distinct people they are now only found inhabiting parts of the British Isles and France. Later came the Italic—Latin—tribes, who drove the Celts out of the peninsula now known as Italy; the Hellenic—or Grecian—tribes, who occupied the peninsula of Greece; the Teutonic tribes, who drove out the Celts from Central Europe, and finally occupied Denmark—Sweden and Norway. The last comers of the Aryans were the Lithuanians and Slavonians—the Slavonians being now spread over Russia, Poland, and Bohemia, while the Lithuanians settled on the Baltic Coast, partly in Prussia, partly in Russia. The greatest part of these movements took place before the dawn of history, and thus was Europe gradually overspread by successive waves of Aryan settlement.

The proof is here simple and decisive. The comparison of words in Sanskrit, the ancient language of the Hindoos; Zend, the olden speech of Persia; Greek, Latin,

English, and other tongues, has shown that all these languages come from a distant common original, spoken by some race yet unparted by migration.   In all, or nearly all, these tongues, the names of common things and persons, the words expressing simple implements and actions, the words for family relations, such as father, sister, mother, brother, daughter, son, the earlier numerals, the pronouns, the very endings of the nouns and verbs, are substantially the same.   Accident could not have caused this phenomenon; and, since many of the nations speaking thus have for long ages been parted from each other by vast stretches of the earth's broad surface, they could not learn them, in historic times, one from another.   Borrowing and imitation being thus excluded, the only possible account is that these words and forms were carried with them by the migratory Aryan tribes as part of the possessions once shared by all in their one original home.   The study of these Aryan tongues has also told what progress had been made by this, the king of races, before the time arrived for starting south and west, to fill, to conquer, and to civilize the Western world.   Whatever words are alike in all or nearly all these Aryan tongues, must be the names of implements, or institutions, or ideas, used, started, or conceived before the first wave of migration made its way. We thus learn that, at that far-distant time, the Aryans had houses, ploughed the earth, and ground their corn in mills.   The family life was settled—basis as it is of all society and law.   The Aryans had sheep and herds of cattle, horses, and dogs, and goats, and bees; they drank a beverage made of honey; knew and could work in copper, silver, gold; fought with the sword and bow; had the beginnings of kingly rule; looked up and worshiped either the sky itself, or One whom they regarded as the God who ruled there.   Thus far above the savage state the Aryan race had risen.

All history is really one unbroken whole, but for practical convenience it has been divided into Ancient History, ending with the breaking up of the dominion of Rome in the Fifth Century (A. D. 476) ; Mediæval History, from the downfall of Rome to about the middle of the Fifteenth Century; and Modern History, from that part of the Fifteenth Century to the present day.

CHINA

China is one of the oldest and strangest of nations.   At a very early period she advanced to the state in which she now is, with the exclusion of all change in her system, and with an apparent incapacity for vital progress.   China has always been a subject of marvel to Europeans, as a country which, self-originated, appeared to have no connection with the outer world.   Recently some eminent scholars have maintained that by researches into the most ancient writings of the Chinese they have been able to discover an early communication or connection between China and Western Asia, and that the culture of China must have borrowed various elements from an earlier civilization in Babylonia.   The people belong to the Mongolian family of man.

China proper, sloping eastward from a mountainous interior, sinks by successive terraces into a vast level tract of unequaled fertility, formed by the alluvial deposits of its great rivers, the Yang-tse ("Son of the Ocean"), and the Hoang-ho ("Yellow River," from the color of its mud).   Its temperate climate and rich soil, productive in wheat, barley, rice, roots, and green crops, favored the early and rapid growth in numbers of a people distinguished by skill and industry in agriculture.

The traditions of China, setting aside fabulous absurdities, go back to 3,000 years before Christ, and one of their sacred books, the Shu-king (treating of history and of the government and laws of the ancient monarchs), begins with the Emperor Yao, 2357 B. C. About 600 B. C. the philosopher Lao-tse was born. He is famous as the founder of a part of Chinese religion, called "Taou-tse" or "Worship of Reason," and as the author of the "Tao-te-king" or "Book of Reason and Virtue." He teaches a kind of Deism in theology, and a sort of Stoicism in practical philosophy.

About 550 B. C. the great philosopher Confucius was born. His name is a Latinized form of the Chinese word "Kong-fu-tse, i. e., "the teacher, Kong." This great teacher of religion and morals is still venerated by his countrymen. He was of royal descent, and held high office at court, which he left to become the founder of a philosophical sect and an earnest instructor of the people. After his death, about B. C. 480, the Chinese worshiped him as a god. He taught that there was but one God and one Emperor, to whom all rulers of other nations are as vassals. His moral teaching dwelt on reverence for ancestors, benevolence, justice, virtue, and honesty, the observance of all usages and customs once introduced, reverence for old age, and strict discipline for children. He inculcated the peaceful virtues of domestic life, and justice and humanity as duties of monarchs. He praises also the delights of friendship, and teaches the forgiveness of offences. He revised the five Kings or sacred books of the Chinese, documents similar, as regards the estimation in which they are held in China, to the Mosaic records of the Jews, or to the Vedas of the Hindoos, and the

Homeric poems of the Greeks.   These old books are the foundation of all Chinese studies.   Besides the Shu-king, there are the Y-king, a metaphysical work; the Shi-king, a book of ancient poems; the Li-king, dealing with the customs and ceremonial observances connected with the Emperor and the state functionaries; and the Tshun-tsin, a history of China in the time of Confucius.

In the Third Century B. C. the Great Wall of China, 1,500 miles in length, was built on the northern frontier, to defend it against the inroads of the Huns, who, however, broke through the wall at the beginning of the Second Century B. C. and overran the country.   The Chinese Emperors bought off the barbarians by a regular tribute of money and silk, as in England Ethelred II paid Danegeld to his foes.

The famous Mongol Emperor Jenghis Khan, who reigned from A. D. 1206 to 1227, invaded China, took the royal city of Pekin, and annexed some of the northern provinces.   In A. D. 1260 the Mongol Emperor Kublai Khan, a grandson of Jenghis, conquered the whole of Northern China, to which, in 1279, he added Southern China, and so became the ruler of the whole country. Kublai Khan thus founded the Mongol dynasty of China, and removed the capital from Nankin to Pekin.

At this time an interesting connection between China and Europe arose.   The celebrated Venetian traveler, Marco Polo, explored the strange Eastern land for the first time, and lived for seventeen years at the court of Kublai Khan, about whom he gives some interesting information in the trustworthy book of travels which his own age rejected as fabulous.

About the middle of the Seventeenth Century the Manchoos, from the northeast, invaded and conquered the country and established the Manchoo dynasty, which still reigns there, the language of the conquerors being that used at court and for official documents.

In recent times the East India Company established a trade with China, and in 1793 Lord Macartney was sent by George III as Ambassador. He had several interviews with the Emperor, but the mission had no result beyond the insight it gave into Chinese character and customs. In 1816 Lord Amherst's embassy tried to obtain permission for a British Minister to reside at Pekin, and sought the opening of ports on the northern coast to British trade. Lord Amherst did not even succeed in seeing the Chinese Emperor, owing to his refusal to perform the ceremony of Koutou, or prostration at the Celestial ruler's feet, and returned to England with a letter to the Prince Regent, which contained the words, "I have sent thine ambassadors back to their own country without punishing them for the high crime they have committed" (in approaching me). This revealed the secret of China's failure to make real advances from her stationary condition—the insanity of self-conceit and the stolid refusal of intercourse with other nations. The overcoming of that reserve by force and the political and commercial encroachments of the Caucasian race will be treated in its proper place in modern history.

If the state and the upper classes of China can be said to have any religion at all, it is Confucianism, a system of morality and philosophy which has little or nothing to do with a creed in the true sense. The lower classes believe to some extent in the religion called Buddhism, introduced from India in the First Century A. D. It is called in China the "religion of Fo," another name for Buddha, and is a system of materialism which teaches the annihilation of man after death, mixed with gross idolatry and superstition. There is also a sect devoted to the worship of

Lao-tsze. China has thus three religious faiths, of which two have degenerated into superstitions, while the third is simply a code of ethics.

In China a patriarchal despotism is the system of rule. The laws of the state are partly civil ordinances and partly moral requirements reaching to the inner self of every citizen. The state is treated as virtually one great family, and the people regard themselves as children of the state. The whole development of the civil and social polity is a grotesque mixture of reason and absurdity. An exaggerated filial reverence causes the merits of a son to be attributed to his dead father, and ancestors have titles of honor bestowed upon them for the good deeds of their posterity. The Emperor is supposed to direct the whole business of the state, for which end the Imperial Princes are educated on a strict system that has furnished China with a succession of pedantic Solomons. There is no proper nobility—official station, based entirely upon competitive examinations, being the only rank recognized outside the Imperial family. The administration of the government is exercised, under the Emperor, by the high officials called Mandarins, of two classes, learned (the civil officers) and military. The highest administrative body is the Council of the Empire, composed of the most learned and able men. There is a permanent board of Censors, who exercise a strict supervision in all matters of government and over the public and private conduct of the Mandarins, reporting thereon direct to the Emperor. The monarch is the center round which everything turns, and as the well-being of the state is made to depend on him, the succession of a slothful and unprincipled ruler is the signal for an all-pervading corruption. The officers of government are supposed to have no conscience or honor of their own to keep them to duty, but only external Mandates, which, even with the highest officials, are enforced by the use of the stick. Every mandarin can inflict blows with the bamboo, and Ministers and Viceroys are punished in this way. At every turn, in a system in some points excellent, but the product of a prosaic understanding, without regard to sentiment, honor, or free-will, we are met in China by pedantic pettiness and degrading folly.

In respect of civilization the Chinese have ever been a nation of ingenious and precocious children who have never succeeded in growing up. They are said to have known the art of making paper as early as the First Century A. D., and to have practiced printing from wooden blocks, which they still continue to do, as early as the Seventh or Eighth Century. They were famous at a very early period for the porcelain, which has made the name of their country a generic term for all such fine and beautiful earthenware. Their robes of woven silk were worn by the luxurious Roman ladies under the early Empire, and they have been long noted for their skill in lacquered ware and their delicacy of carving in wood, ivory, tortoise-shell, and mother-of-pearl.

They profess to hold the sciences in great honor, and one of the highest governmental boards is the Academy of Sciences. What they call science, however, is merely a collection of ill-arranged facts and beliefs; it is pursued without regard to intellectual ends, and hindered in progress to what is higher by a curious, cumbersome, and clumsy language. The Chinese tongue has never attained to the possession of an alphabet, which, with nations of the higher development, has always been the first step toward the acquirement of a rational instrument for the expression of thought. Each Chinese character represents a word, and in writing and printing the characters are not arranged horizontally either from left to right as in Euro-

pean languages, or from right to left as in Hebrew and the
cognate languages, but in vertical columns, to be read
from top to bottom.   China's want of scientific attainments in astronomy is attested by the fact that for hundreds of years the Chinese calendars have been made by
Europeans; and in medicine, by the theory that the beating
of the pulse alone can tell the physician the cause and
locality of the disease.

It is clear enough that Europe and true civilization
had nothing to gain, and have gained nothing, in culture,
from a country where 400 millions of people are treated
like children; where there is no originality and no free-
will; where no progress, save from outward impulse, is
possible.   The outcome of the elaborate and minute regulations, of the severe and constant competitive examinations, of the Chinese system is simply, that after the lapse
of 4,000 years, they still have no convenient written
language; that, pretending to be astronomers, they know
not how to use the telescope; that the medical art is a mere
ignorant superstition; and that the artist cannot shade a
drawing, and has no notion of perspective.   The superficial cleverness of handiwork displayed by Chinese artisans
serves but to heighten the effect of the ludicrous produced
on the European mind by the paltry results of a preten-
tious, antiquated, and inherently unprogressive order of
civilization.

INDIA

Indian civilization, like that of China, has contributed
little or nothing to the culture of the Western world.
From the prosaic pedantry of China, however, we pass,
in India, to a region where fancy and sensibility have held
sway, though the absence of energy, and of true human
dignity and freedom, has prevented the people from

exhibiting historical progress of the highest order. Indian
records present us with no political action; the people
have achieved no foreign conquests, and have repeatedly
succumbed to foreign invasion. They are a people of
dreams, not of deeds.

In regard to general history, India has been an object
of desire to other nations from very early times, as a land
teeming with riches and marvels; the treasures of nature,
such as pearls, perfumes, diamonds, elephants, gold; and
treasures of wisdom in her sacred books. Alexander the
Great was the first European recorded to have arrived
there by land; in modern times the European nations first
made their way to India by sea round the Cape of Good
Hope. The Hindoos are one of the two Aryan races of
Asia, and probably crossed the Indus into the rich alluvial
river-plain of the Ganges about 2,000 years B. C. They
dispossessed the peoples, probably of Tartar origin, to the
north of the River Nerbudda, and gradually penetrated
the great southern peninsula known as the Deccan. The
dark-skinned aboriginal natives were by no means exterm-
inated, and their descendants, in the persons of the hill-
tribes and others, amount to many millions.

India first came into historical connection with Europe
at the invasion of Alexander the Great in B. C. 327. The
Macedonian conqueror did not go far beyond the Indus,
and, after defeating a king named Porus, returned to Persia by way of the Indus and the sea.

Early in the Tenth Century A. D. Mohammedan invasions of India, through Afghanistan, began, and early in
the Thirteenth Century an Afghan dynasty was established at Delhi, and northern India was subdued.

During the Thirteenth Century the Mongols of the
Empire of Jenghis Khan invaded India and met with
many successes and defeats. In 1398 the great Tartar

conqueror, Tamerlane, took and sacked Delhi, and, after overrunning the land to the mouths of the Ganges, retired and left anarchy and misery behind him.

In 1526 Sultan Baber, a descendant of Tamerlane, founded the Mogul Empire in India. His grandson, Akbar, reigned from 1556 to 1607, and extended his power over most of the peninsula, being distinguished by his justice and his tolerance in matters of religion. Akbar's son, Jehanghir, received in 1615 the English Ambassador, Sir Thomas Roe, despatched by James I; Jehanghir's son, Shah Jehan, displayed great architectural magnificence, culminating in the exquisite Taj Mahal ("Crown of Empires") at Agra, a mausoleum of white marble built for the remains of his favorite wife. During his reign, which ended in 1658, the Mahrattas began to be formidable in Southern India. The history of British presence in India begins at about this time, and the commercial connection of other European nations with the Hindoos will be noticed in its proper place.

In India we see an essential advance, in theory, from the Chinese state of a dead-level of equality for all below the Emperors. In spite of the despotic power of the ruler are found also different ranks and orders of men. These distinctions are the Castes, established in accordance with religious doctrine, and viewed by the people, at last, as natural distinctions. The very ancient book of Hindoo laws, called the Institutes of Menu, regulates these class-divisions of society. In later times many minute subdivisions of caste have arisen, but there were originally four only: The Brahmins, the order of men devoted to religion and philosophy; the Shatryas, or military and governing class; the Vaisyas, or professional and mercantile class; the Sudras, or lower-class traders, artisans, and field-laborers. The rigid stereotyped character of these orders caused the people of India to be spiritual slaves. Into his caste a man was born, and bound to it for life, without regard to poverty or riches, talents, character, or skill. Thus life and energy were fettered; the individual could not make his own position. Nature had for ever settled it for him. Human dignity and human feeling were bound up in the separate castes, and so true expansive morality was unknown; the spirit of man wandered into the world of dreams, and political progress was impossible.

Government in India, before its conquest by the English, was nothing but the most arbitrary, wicked, and degrading despotism, unchecked by any rule of morality or religion—a condition worse than that of China under the worst of Emperors. The people were degraded even below a feeling of true resentment against oppression; much less were they capable of any manly attempt to throw off the yoke.

The prevailing religions of India are Brahminism, Mohammedanism, and Buddhism. More than two-thirds of the people are supposed to hold the Brahminical creed, more than one-fourth are Mohammedans, and the rest are mainly Buddhists, with a small fraction of Christians.

Brahminism is the oldest religion, and its tenets are contained in the sacred books called Vedas, of which the oldest, the Rig-Veda, is certainly one of the most ancient literary documents in existence. The pure Deism of the older form of this religion had for its leading doctrine that of an all-pervading mind, from which the universe took its rise. Then came a belief in three deities, or diverse forms of the same universal deity, viz., Brahma, or the Creator; Vishnu, or the Preserver; and Siva, the Destroyer. This was further corrupted into a pantheism, which sees a god in everything—in sun, moon, stars, the Ganges, the Indus, beasts and flowers. In its higher development, Brahminism holds that the human soul is of the same nature with the supreme being, and that its destiny is to be reunited with him. This led to the great doctrine of metempsychosis, or transmigration of souls, which is necessary to purify the human soul for union with the divine. According to this view, man's soul in this world is united to the body in a state of trial, which needs prayer, penance, sacrifice, and purification. If these are neglected, then the human soul, after death, is joined to the body of some lower animal, and begins a fresh course of probation. In popular practice, the grossest idolatry and superstition, with a cowardly and selfish disregard of human life, have largely prevailed alongside of the philosophical tenets of the educated class. Mohammedanism was introduced by conquering armies of Islam's prophets early in the Tenth Century A. D.

Buddhism arose about 550 B. C., and derives its name from Buddha, or the Buddha ("the enlightened one"), a surname bestowed upon its founder Gautama, a Hindoo of high rank, who developed his creed in retired meditation, and began to teach it in opposition to Brahminism. This religion recognizes no supreme being; it insists on practical morality; teaches the transmigration of souls, and regards annihilation as the good man's final reward.

The Sanskrit tongue was spoken by the ancient Hindoos, but has been in disuse, save as a literary language, for over 2,000 years. From it most of the numerous Hindoo dialects are derived. Its condition is a testimony to the high intelligence of the Aryans who peopled India. The name of this elder sister of the Greek, Latin, Persian, Slavonic, Teutonic, and Celtic tongues is derived from sam, "with," and krita, "made," meaning "carefully constructed" or "symmetrically formed." It is rich in inflectional forms and very flexible, and it has a boundless wealth of epithets. The alphabet is a very perfect instrument for representing the sounds of the language. A vast religious, poetical, philosophical, and scientific literature is written in Sanskrit.

The Hindoos, at the time of Alexander's invasion, had reached a high point of development. They were good astronomers and mathematicians; had great skill in logic and philosophy; manufactured silk and cotton in beautiful and costly forms, and worked rich ornaments in gold and silver. The chief artistic works of India have been architectural. Many splendid buildings are scattered over the country, displaying a variety of styles in which the pyramidal form is very prevalent, a profusion of sculptured ornamentation being also a marked feature. Remarkable works of a somewhat different kind are the rock temples of Ellora in the Deccan, near Aurungabad, and of Elephanta, a small island near Bombay. These stupenduous and magnificent works have massive pillars and display very rich and elaborate carving.

The Phœnicians were probably the first of the nations dwelling round the Mediterranean to enter into commercial relations with India, the trade being carried on both by sea and land. In later times some of the products of India were also known to the Greeks, while among the Romans they were not uncommon, and fetched very high prices.

As illustrating the character of the Hindoo intellect it is remarkable that their literature possesses no historical works. Their minds seem to have been unable to regard events in their true light, and they have had no love of veracity to induce them to record facts as they occurred. The Hindoos exhibit a state of mind in which a sensitive and imaginative temperament turns all outside them into a feverish dream, and so, with all their intelligence and taste, they have had slight influence upon the progress of other nations.

GREAT ORIENTAL PEOPLES

The old Eastern monarchies, with the sole exception of Hamitic Egypt, all arose in Asia. The truly historical nations of olden Asia are the Assyrians, Semitic; Babylonians, Semitic; Hebrews, Semitic; Phœnicians, Semitic, and Persians, Aryan. All these had their career in Southwestern Asia. This great area of early history may be divided into three regions: That west of the Euphrates; the valleys of the Euphrates and the Tigris; the region from the Zagros Mountains, east of the Tigris, to the Indus.

West of the Euphrates were the peninsula of Asia Minor, containing the important Lydian nation and Greek colonies connected with the later Oriental history; Syria, on the eastern shore of the Mediterranean Sea, divided into three distinct parts—Syria proper; Phœnicia, or the strip of coast between Mount Lebanon and the sea; and Palestine, south of Phœnicia; the peninsula of Arabia, extending southeastward, and having little to do with ancient history.

In the basin of the Tigris and the Euphrates were several distinct territories: Armenia, or the mountainous region between Asia Minor and the Caspian Sea; Assyria proper, lying between the Tigris and the Zagros Mountains; Babylonia, the great alluvial plain between the lower courses of the Tigris and of the Euphrates, and extending westward to the Syrian Desert; Chaldæa (in the narrower sense, as a province of the Babylonian Empire), west of the Euphrates, at the head of the Persian Gulf; Mesopotamia, or the district between the middle courses of

the Tigris and the Euphrates; Susiana, the country east
of the Tigris and at the head of the Persian Gulf.

In these territories, the valleys of the Tigris and the
Euphrates, arose the three great monarchies of Chaldæa,
Assyria, and Babylonia, afterward absorbed in the Sixth
Century B. C., by the mighty Empire of Persia, extending
almost from the Indus to the Mediterranean, Ægean,
Euxine, and Caspian Seas, when it had reached the summit
of its power.

East of the Zagros Mountains lay Media and Persia
proper—Media, northeastward, towards the Caspian Sea,
and Persia, on the table-land southward, stretching to the
Persian Gulf.

Before the rise of an extensive commerce by sea or
land, it is possible for great communities to gather and
continue to exist only in those regions where a rich soil
provides plenteous food. No soils exceed in fertility the
alluvial deposits of great rivers, and among such soils the
valleys of the Nile and of the Tigris and Euphrates have
ever been famous for their wonderful productive power.
Nature herself provides man with that delicious and most
nutritious food the date, and as for rice and other grain
crops, the earth has fatness such that "if she be but tickled
with a hoe, she laughs with a harvest." In pastoral lands
the people wander, and must wander, with their flocks and
herds, to find fresh grass; they cannot settle down into a
polity or state; the agriculturists, who stayed to reap where
they had sown the seed, became progenitors of mighty
nations, founders of great empires famous through all
regions and all ages of the civilized world.

Here then, in such a territory, on such a soil—here, in
Egypt, and in Southwestern Asia, the true history of the
civilized world begins, with those nations that had historic
records of their own, that rose to a highly-civilized con-

dition; and, more than all, that brought their culture, with more or less of permanent effect, to bear on nations whom they conquered, or who subjugated them. As it comes forth from the gloom of a past before all records, we turn our gaze to greet the rising sun of history, disclosing to our view two grand developments of human culture— Egypt and Chaldæa.

EGYPT

The people of Egypt are one of the earliest nations of whose government and institutions we possess any certain record, their only rivals being the Chaldeans and possibly the Hittites, a nation but recently discovered. Long before the Hebrews came into possession of their promised land Canaan, Egypt had Kings, and priests, and cities, and armies; laws and ritual and learning; arts and sciences and books. Egypt is at this day, beyond all other lands, the land of ruins, surpassing all other countries in gigantic and stately monumental remains, the result of boundless human labor. In these great memorials of Egypt we have expressed for us the character of the people, a half-fettered spirit, whose favorite symbol was the Sphinx—a half-brute, half-human form. This human head looking out from the brute typifies the intellectual and moral part of man—the human spirit— beginning to emerge from the natural, striving to get loose and to look freely around, but still restrained by the de- based original state of existence. The edifices of the strange people who dwelt of old in this land of wonders are, as it were, half under and half above the ground, so that the kingdom of life seems ever in contact with the silent realm of death.

Egypt is a land that has been created out of the desert by the alluvial deposits of her mighty river, the Nile.

Flowing down from the mountains of Abyssinia in its eastern branch, the Blue Nile, it unites at Khartoom, in Nubia, with the western and longer branch, or White Nile, which is now known to issue from the great equatorial lake, Victoria Nyanza. The river then flows, northward mainly, to the Mediterranean, and provides a rich soil of muddy deposit in the yearly overflow caused by the great rainfalls of the Abyssinian mountains. Egypt is thus composed of a highly fertile strip of territory inclosed by hills and sandy wastes on each side. The Delta of the Nile was ever noted for its rich soil and teeming population; the water of the river was always famous for its wholesomeness and pleasant taste.

The chief mineral products of Egypt were the beautiful granite of Philæ, Elephantine and Syene, whose quarries furnished the huge masses used for obelisks and statues; the whitish or grayish sandstone of the hills north of Syene, which supplied the masonry for the temples; and the limestone of the hills northward again to the Delta, which last chain furnished the material for the Pyramids. The climate of Egypt is remarkably dry, and to this is due the wonderful state of preservation seen in many of the monumental remains, which display a sharpness of outline in the stone and a freshness of color in the painting that are like the work of yesterday. The vegetable products of Egypt, due in their great abundance to a hot sun acting on the thick fertile layer of fresh soil yearly bestowed by the river, were varied beyond all example in the ancient world. The olive and pomegranate, the orange and the vine, the citron, the date-palm and the fig, all yielded their delicious produce for the use of man. The vegetable gardens teemed with cabbages and cucumbers, onions, leeks, garlic, radishes, and melons. Rice and a species of millet called doora grew in great crops. The fir, the cypress, and the cedar furnished valuable timber.   The papyrus of the marshes by the river gave the material for writing which we call, in a different substance ,"paper."   The same plant furnished sailcloth, cordage, and baskets.   Cotton and flax gave raw material for manufacturing skill.   Medical science went to Egypt for its drugs, and in her later days Rome was largely fed by Egypt's corn.

To the abundant food was due the plenteous population, and to that again the mighty architectural works raised by the toilsome efforts of cheap and well-fed labor. The country abounded, too, in animals and birds.   Sheep, goats, and oxen swarmed; geese and ducks, and quails and widgeons flew in countless numbers.   Egypt was famous for the horse as used in war in early times; the scarabœus, or sacred beetle, is known to all from its sculptured semblance on the monuments; and the white ibis, among birds, migrating into Egypt along with the rising of the Nile, became sacred in the eyes of those to whom the rising river gave their bountiful subsistence.   Rain scarcely ever falls in Lower Egypt, or in the part nearer to the Mediterranean Sea.   The inundation of the Nile begins early in August, turning the valley of the river into a shallow inland sea, and subsides by the end of October.

Until the present Century, what was known about ancient Egypt was mainly got from the narrative of Herodotus, the great Greek, the father of history, who traveled in Egypt about the middle of the Fifth Century B. C., and made careful inquiries of the people and the priests; from Manetho, an Egyptian priest about 300 B. C., who wrote in Greek a lost work on the history of Egypt, of which the lists of dynasties of kings have been preserved by other writers; and from Diodorus Siculus, who wrote (in the time of Julius Cæsar and Augustus) a universal history, of which the portion about Egypt

remains entire. During the present Century knowledge
of the history of the "land of Pyramids and priests" has
been greatly increased by the deciphering of the inscriptions on the monuments, and by extended observation of
the countless sculptures in which the olden Egyptians have
recorded their ways of life, their arts and arms and sciences
and ritual and faith.   In carving or in painting, or in both
combined, the obelisks, the temple walls and temple columns, the inner walls of tombs, the coffins of the dead,
utensils, implements, artistic objects, all are covered with
the strange characters known as hieroglyphics.   This
word, of Greek extraction, means "sacred carvings," and
the name was given to the sculptures in the supposition that
all such characters were of religious import, and known
only to the priests of ancient Egypt.   The meaning of the
characters had been utterly lost for many hundreds of
years, and the word "hieroglyphics" had long become
proverbial for mysteries and undecipherable puzzles, when
a keen-eyed Frenchman found and put into the hands of
scholars the clue that was to guide them within the
labyrinth for ages inaccessible and unexplored.   An
artillery officer of Napoleon's army in Egypt, named
Bouchart, discovered near Rosetta, in 1799, an oblong
slab of stone engraved with three inscriptions, one under
the other.   The upper one (half of which was broken off)
was in hieroglyphics, the lower one was in Greek, and the
middle one was stated in the Greek to be in enchorial characters (i. e., characters of the country, Gr. chora, country),
otherwise called demotic or popular (from the Greek,
demos, the people).   The victories of the British army
in Egypt put the English government in possession of
this celebrated and interesting relic, which George III presented to the British Museum, where it stands now in the
gallery of Egyptian sculpture.

The Greek inscription at once told scholars that all three inscriptions expressed a decree of the Egyptian priests, sitting in synod at Memphis, in honor of King Ptolemy V (Ptolemy Epiphanes, who reigned B. C. 205-181), to commemorate benefits conferred by him upon them. To the efforts of two men chiefly the world was indebted for the deciphering of the two forms of Egyptian writing found on the Rosetta stone. These were Dr. Thomas Young, an eminent linguist and natural philosopher, who was foreign secretary to the Royal Society, dying in 1829; and the great French orientalist, Jean François Champollion, superintendent of Egyptian antiquities in the Louvre Museum, and member of the Academy of Inscriptions. M. Champollion died in 1832. By careful study and comparison, firstly of the Greek with the enchorial inscription, and then of both with the hieroglyphic characters, combined with the study of similar inscriptions on other monuments, a key to the mystery was at last obtained, and a flood of light thrown on the olden history and civilization of Egypt. Their work has been continued by the Egyptian Exploration fund established in 1881, under whose direction Petrie, Naville and others have discovered ancient Egyptian cities buried under the earth but which, excavated, confirmed the tales told by the hieroglyphics and have added new and interesting details to the world's knowledge of the wonderful civilization of the extinct race. Hieroglyphics are representations of objects or parts of objects, including heavenly bodies, human beings in various attitudes, parts of the human body, quadrupeds and parts of quadrupeds, birds and parts of birds, fishes, reptiles and parts of reptiles, insects, plants and parts of plants, buildings, furniture, dresses and parts of dresses, weapons, tools and instruments, vases and cups, geometric forms, and fantastic forms, amounting in all to about a thousand different symbols. Of these more than six hundred are ideographic (idea-writing), i. e., the engraved or painted figure, either directly or metaphorically, conveys an idea which we express by a word composed of alphabetic signs. Thus, directly, the figure of a man means "man;" metaphorically, the figure of a man means "power." About one hundred and thirty of the hieroglyphs are phonetic (sound-conveying), i. e., the engraved or painted figures represent words (which are nothing but sound with a meaning attached thereto), of which the first letter is to be taken as an alphabetic sign, and thus phonetic hieroglyphics answer the same end as our letters of the alphabet. An example of each will clearly show what is meant. In ideographic writing, a bird, a mason, a nest, mean "birds build nests;" in phonetic hieroglyphs the figures of a bull, imp, rope, door, and ship would give the word "birds," and the words "build" and "nests" would be expressed in the same roundabout and clumsy fashion. The difficulty of deciphering the inscriptions on monuments was increased by the fact that both ideographic and phonetic hieroglyphs, along with certain mixed signs, or phonetic followed by ideographic, occur in the same inscriptions.

The first inhabitants of Egypt came from the north by the Isthmus of Suez, and not from the South, descending the Nile, as was supposed until recently. They belonged to the race known in Genesis as the Sons of Ham, whom the Arabs called the "red." Temples have been discovered built 1600 B. C., upon the ruins of buildings still more ancient. Egyptian chronology is not yet fixed with certainty, but the dates given by Mariette Bey, founder of the Museum of Boulak at Cairo, may be accepted. Under the name of Cushites, the Hamitic race constituted the basis of the population along the shores of the Indian

Ocean, Persian Gulf and Red Sea. These Cushites formed little states, which existed for many centuries, before the powerful chief, Menes, made himself master of all the valley from the sea to the cataracts of Syene, and founded, at least 5000 B. C., the first royal race of which we have any knowledge. Tradition is that at first gods reigned, and then demi-gods, represented by priests, but these were forced to yield to a warrior chief. Little has yet been discovered of these three first dynasties, the rule of which for eight centuries extended as far as to the peninsula of Sinai. But it is known that under the fourth dynasty, which began about 4020 B. C., there existed a civilization unparalleled at the period. The arts gained a development which is scarcely excelled by the most brilliant epoch. The building of the Great Pyramid at Gizeh, near Cairo, is ascribed by Herodotus to King Cheops, otherwise called Suphis, according to the hieroglyphic royal name found inside the structure. This early King is believed to have reigned about the middle of the Twenty-fifth Century B. C. Cheops was the second and most celebrated monarch in the fourth of the dynasties of Manetho, which ruled at Memphis as the capital. The third King in this list, Cephren, also founded a pyramid, as did the fourth, Mencheres, a sovereign beloved and praised in poetry for his goodness. His mummified remains are now in the British Museum. In the sixth dynasty was a female sovereign noted for her beauty, named Nitocris, who also built a pyramid and reigned at Memphis. The monarchy appears to have been for some time divided, the chief power being held by the Kings ruling at Thebes, in Upper Egypt. To about 2050 B. C. is ascribed the invasion and conquest of the country by the Hyksos or Shepherd-Kings, said to be the Hittites. They conquered Lower Egypt first, and then subdued the kingdom of Thebes, ruling the whole land, as is supposed, from about B. C. 1900 to 1500. It is probably to this period that the story of Joseph belongs. Amenophis seems to have expelled the Shepherd-Kings, with the aid of the Ethiopians from the South, and then came the great period of Egyptian history, from about 1500 to 1200 B. C. During this time Egypt was a great empire, having Thebes for its capital.

The greatest monarch of this or perhaps any age of Egypt's history was Rameses the Great, called by the Greek writers, Sesostris. To him have been attributed many of the monuments and pictures which represent triumphal procession and the captives taken in war. Rameses the Great reigned for nearly seventy years in the Fourteenth Century B.C. Among his many monuments two are chiefly remarkable, the Memnonium or palace-temple at Thebes, and the great rock-cut temple of Aboosimbel in Nubia. These great architectural works possess an interest more historical than that of the pyramids. Their sculptures and inscriptions tell us the chief events of the reign of Rameses, and even suggest some idea of his personality. His portraits show a face of partly Semitic type, and indicate a strong but gentle character of unusual cultivation for the times. This great conqueror is said to have subdued Ethiopia, to have carried his arms beyond the Euphrates eastward, and among the Thracians in southeast Europe. The monumental sculptures and paintings tell us of war-galleys of Egypt in the Indian seas, and of Ethiopian trib-ute paid in ebony and ivory and gold, in apes and birds of prey, and even in giraffes from inner Africa. Other sculp-tures display the Egyptians fighting with success against Asiatic foes. To this monarch was due a vast system of irrigation by canals, dug through the whole of Egypt for conveying the waters of the Nile to every part. After the great Rameses we find no sovereign of note until we come to Shishak, who, in the year B. C. 970, took and plundered Jerusalem.   The empire continued to decline, and latterly it was attacked by Sennacherib, King of Assyria, who, however, accomplished little.   By Esarhaddon and Assurbanipal, however, Egypt was entirely reduced, and became for a time tributary to the Assyrian monarchs.   This was in the early part of the reign of a King named Psammetichus, who reigned from B. C. 671 to 617.

Then Egypt was in connection, for the first time in her history, with foreign countries, otherwise than as conquering or conquered.   Psammetichus had in his pay a body of Greek mercenaries, and sought to introduce the Greek language among his subjects.   In jealousy at this, the great military caste of Egypt emigrated into Ethiopia, and left the King dependent on his foreign troops, with whom he warred in Syria and Phœnicia.   Egyptian policy at this time, and in succeeding reigns, seems to have aimed at the development of commerce, and the securing for Egypt of the routes and commercial centers for the trade, by the Red Sea, between Europe and Asia.   Necho, son of Psammetichus, succeeded his father, and reigned from B. C. 617 to 601.   He was an energetic, enterprising prince, who built fleets on the Red Sea and the Mediterranean, and strove to join the Nile, by a canal, with the Red Sea.   Africa was circumnavigated by Phœnicians in his service, who sailed from the Arabian Gulf, and passed round by the Straits of Gibraltar to the mouths of the Nile. He was the King who fought with and defeated Josiah, King of Judah, sustaining afterwards defeat from Nebuchadnezzar, King of Babylon.

In B. C. 594 came Apries, the Pharaoh-Hophra of Scripture, who conquered Sidon, and was an ally of Zede-

PYRAMID OF CHEOPS, FROM THE DESERT.

kiah, King of Judah, against Nebuchadnezzar. After being repulsed with severe loss in an attack on the Greek colony of Cyrene, west of Egypt, Apries was dethroned by Amasis, who reigned from B. C. 570 to 526. His long and prosperous rule was marked by a closer intercourse than heretofore with the Greeks.

Psammenitus, son of Amasis, inherited a quarrel of his father with Cambyses, King of Persia, who invaded and conquered Egypt in B. C. 525. For nearly two hundred years afterward the history of Egypt is marked, disastrously, by constant struggles between the people and their Persian conquerors, and, in a more favorable and interesting way, by the growing intercourse between the land of the Nile and the Greeks. Greek historians and philosophers—Herodotus and Anaxagoras and Plato—visited the country and took back stores of information on its wonders, its culture, and its faith.

In B. C. 332 Egypt was conquered by Alexander the Great, and with this event, and the foundation of the new capital, the great city of Alexandria, destined to a lasting literary and commercial renown, the history of ancient Egypt may end.

At an early period the form of government in Egypt became a hereditary monarchy, but one of a peculiar kind. The power of the King was restricted by rigid law and antique custom, and by the extraordinary influence of the priestly class. In his personal life he was bound by minute regulations as to diet, dress, hours of business, of repose, and of religious worship, and submitted to a daily lecture from the sacred books as to the duties of his high office. Under the Kings, governors of the thirty-six nomes or districts held sway, and these high officials were invested with large powers over the land and the levying of taxes. The soil was held by the priests, the warriors, and the King.

The Egyptian monarchs appear, as a rule, to have used their authority well and wisely; there was seldom insurrection or rebellion, and many received divine honors after death for their beneficence and regal virtues. The common title, "Pharaoh," is derived from the Egyptian word "Phra," the sun. The body of the people was divided into castes, concerning the number and nature of which the accounts differ. It seems, however, that they were not rigidly separated, as in India, and that the members of the different orders might intermarry, and the children pass from one caste to another by change of their hereditary occupation. The castes are, perhaps, most correctly given thus: 1st, priests; 2nd, soldiers; 3rd, husbandmen; 4th, artificers and tradesmen; 5th, a miscellaneous class of herdsmen, fishermen, and servants. The priests and warriors ranked far above the rest in dignity and privilege. The hierarchy was the highest order in power, influence, and wealth. To the priestly caste, however, many persons belonged who were not engaged in religious offices. They were a landowning class, and they were, emphatically and solely, the learned class, like the clergy of the Middle Ages. In their possession were all the literature and science of the country, and all employments dependent, for their practice, on that knowledge. The priesthood thus included the poets, the historians, the expounders and administrators of law, the physicians, and the magicians who did wonders before Moses. They paid no taxes, had large landed possessions, exercised immense influence over the minds of the people, and put no slight check even on the King. History discloses a powerful and excellent military organization in Egypt. An army of over 400,000 men was mainly composed of a militia supported by a fixed portion of land (six acres per man), free from all taxation. The chariots and horses of Egypt were famous; the foot-soldiers were variously armed with helmet, spear, coat of mail, shield, battle-axe, club, javelin, and dagger, for close fighting in dense array; and with bows, arrows and slings for skirmishing and conflict in open order. The soldier was allowed to cultivate his own land when he was not under arms, but could follow no other occupation. The castes below the warriors and priests had no political rights, and could not hold land. The husbandmen who tilled the soil paid rent in produce to the King or to the priests who owned it. The artisan-class included masons, weavers, sculptors, painters, embalmers of the dead, and workers in leather, wood, and metals, whose occupations are recorded upon the monuments. The herdsmen were the lowest class, and of these the swineherds were treated as mere outcasts, not permitted to enter the temples, or to marry except among themselves.

The land of Egypt, teeming with population, abounded in cities and towns. Of these the greatest were Thebes, in Upper Egypt, and Memphis, in Middle Egypt, whose site was near the modern Cairo. Thebes is the No or No Ammon of Scripture, and was at the height of its splendor as capital of Egypt about B. C. 2000. Its vastness is proved by the existing remains known (from the names of modern villages) as the ruins of Karnak, Luxor, etc. They consist of obelisks, sphinxes, colossal statues, temples, and tombs cut in the rock. These mighty monuments, with their countless sculptured details and inscriptions, are themselves the historians of the Egyptian Empire of 3,000 years ago. Memphis, after the fall of Thebes, became the capital of Egypt, and kept its importance till the conquest of the country by Cambyses. It was superseded as capital by Alexandria, and finally destroyed by the Arabs in the Seventh Century A. D. The desert sands have overwhelmed its famous avenue of sphinxes, and the great pyramids of Gizeh, and the colossal Sphinx, are the chief memorials of the past in its vicinity.

The chief feature of Egyptian architecture is its colossal, massive grandeur, derived from the use of enormous blocks of masonry, and from the vast extent of the buildings in which these blocks were employed.   Towering height and huge circumference in the pillars; length and loftiness in the colonnades, and avenues, and halls, produce in the beholder an unequaled impression of sublimity and awe.   The approaches to the palaces and temples were paved roads lined with obelisks and sphinxes, and the temples and the palaces themselves surpassed in size and in elaborate ornament of sculpture and of painting all other works of man.   There are about forty pyramids now left standing, all in Middle Egypt, and of these the most remarkable are the group of nine at Gizeh, near the site of ancient Memphis.   The Great Pyramid, that of King Cheops, covers an area of more than twelve acres, and exceeds 450 feet in height.   An outer casing of small stones has been removed, and, instead of showing a smooth and sloping surface, the sides have now a series of huge steps.   A narrow passage, fifty feet above the base of the structure on its north face, leads to the sepulchral chambers, of which that called the King's chamber is lined with polished red granite.   The wooden coffin with the King's mummy was long since removed from the red granite sarcophagus which held it.   The second large pyramid, that of King Cephren, is somewhat smaller.   A third, that of Mycerinus, is far smaller than the other two.   The removal of the vast blocks of stone from distant quarries, and their elevation to heights which have puzzled the heads of modern engineers, were effected not by the ingenuity of mechanical contrivance, but by the labor of human hands. Thousands of men, employed for months in moving single stones, regardless of expense, might well effect results startling to modern ideas of economy in toil.

Egyptian sculpture displays size, simplicity, stiffness, and little of what modern art calls taste or beauty. Statues are made either standing quite upright, or kneeling on both knees, or sitting with a rigid posture of the legs and arms. In the work of the tombs and temples a bolder and more varied style is often found. The work is remarkable for clean execution and fineness of surface, showing an excellent edge and temper in the tools employed. It is likely that improvement in the forms of Egyptian art was hindered by religious scruple, confining the artist to the limits of traditional example. In Egypt, life was the thing sacred. Hence all that had life was in a way divine; the sacred ibis, crocodile, bull, cat, snake. All that produced and all that ended life. Hence death, too, was sacred. The Egyptian lived in the contemplation of death. His coffin was made in his lifetime; his ancestors were embalmed; the sacred animals were preserved in myriad heaps, through generations in mummy-pits. The sovereign's tomb was built to last for, not centuries, but thousands of years.

Hegel declares that in the religion of Egypt are united the worship of Nature and of the spirit which underlies and animates Nature. The physical existence of the Egyptians depended on the Nile and the Sun; from those forces only could come the vegetation needed for the food of the people. This view of nature gives the principle of the religion, in which the Nile and the Sun are deities conceived under human forms. From the observation of the constant course of nature, on which the Egyptian rested as his sole hope for the bread of life, arose the mythology of Egypt. In the winter-solstice the power of the sun has reached its minimum, and must be born anew. And so, according to the legend, the god Osiris, representing both the Nile and the Sun, is born; but he is killed by Typhon, the burning wind of the desert, which parches up the waters of the Nile. Isis, the goddess representing the Earth, or the receptive fertility of Nature, from whom the aid of the Sun and of the Nile has been withdrawn, yearns after the dead Osiris, gathers his scattered bones, and with all Egypt bewails his loss. Osiris becomes judge of the dead, and lord of the kingdom of spirits. To Osiris and to Isis were ascribed the introduction of agriculture, the invention of the plough and the hoe, because Osiris—the Nile and the Sun—not only makes earth fertile, but gives the means to turn its power of reproduction to account. He also gives men laws, and civil order, and religious ritual; he thus places in men's hands the means of labor, and secures its result. Isis and Osiris were the only divinities that were worshipped throughout Egypt. It was in later times that they came to be regarded as divinities of the sun and the moon. Another god, Anubis, worshipped in the form of a human being with the head of a dog, is represented as an Egyptian Hermes, and to him was ascribed the invention of writing, grammar, astronomy, mensuration, music, and medicine. The highest form of the religious belief of this strange people appears, beyond a doubt, to have included the idea that the soul of man is immortal.

Whatever higher religious ideas may have been held by philosophical and learned priests, the worship of the common people was chiefly a zoölatry, or adoration of animals. The sacred bull, called Apis, was worshipped at Memphis with the highest honors, and at his death was replaced by another, searched for until they found one with certain peculiar marks, and this was then pretended

to be miraculously born as the successor. All Egypt
rejoiced on his annual birthday festival, and there was a
public mourning when he died. The dog, the hawk, the
white ibis, and the cat were also specially revered. The
sparrow-hawk, with human head and outspread wings,
denoted the soul flying through space, to animate a new
body. Thus in the religion of Egypt, gross superstition
in the masses of the people was mingled with the spiritual
conceptions of cultivated minds.

A papyrus-book discovered in the royal tombs of
Thebes has revealed to the world some curious matter concerning the funeral ceremonies of the Egyptians, and their
belief, as expressed in those rites, as to a future life. In
this book, called the Book of the Dead, we read in pictured
writing of a second life, and of a Hall of Judgment, where
the god Osiris sits, provided with a balance, a secretary
and forty-two attendant-judges. In the balance a soul
is weighed against a statue of divine justice, placed in the
other scale, which is guarded by the god Anubis. The
assistant-judges give separate decisions, after the person
on trial has pleaded his cause before them. The soul
rejected as unworthy of the Egyptian heaven was believed
to be driven off to some dark realm, to assume the form of
a beast, in accordance with a low character and sensual
nature. An acquitted soul joined the throng of the blest.

With the religion of the people, it is thought, was
connected the practice of embalming the bodies of the
dead. This was performed by the use of drugs and spices
stuffed within the head, and by the baking of the body,
followed by steeping for seventy days in a solution of salt-
peter. It was then closely wrapped in linen bandages
soaked in resinous and aromatic substances. The next
thing was to place the swathed form in the mummy-case,
which was then laid in a sarcophagus of stone or in a

coffin made of sycamore-wood. If the origin of this practice was not a belief that at some period after death the
soul would rejoin the body, it may have been occasioned
by the fact that the yearly inundation made burial impossible for weeks over so large a portion of the land.

As the Egyptian columns were formed by their architects on the model of the palm-tree, whose feathery crown
of foliage was ever before their eyes, or of the full-blown
or budding papyrus, so in the mural decorations the figure
of the famous lotus-plant, or lily of the Nile, is found constantly.   The lotus was beheld by the Egyptians with
veneration, and was used in sculpture and in paintings
as no mere ornament, but as a religious symbol.   It occurs
in all representations of sacrifices and other holy ceremonies, in tombs, and in all matters connected either with death
or with another life.   This water-lily of Egypt was the
emblem to the people of the generative powers of the
world.   It was consecrated to Isis and Osiris, and typefied
the creation of the world from water.   It also symbolized
the rise of the Nile, and the return of the sun in his full
power.   The lotus of Egypt must not be confounded with
that of the fabled "lotus-eaters," which was probably the
shrub called jujube, growing still in Tunis, Tripoli, and
Morocco.

Their monuments prove that the Egyptians practiced
the arts of the potter, glass-blower, carpenter, boat-build-
er, and other mechanics; that they used balances, levers,
saws, adzes, chisels, the forceps, syringes, and razors.
They were adepts at gold-beating, engraving, inlaying,
casting, and wire-drawing.   They grew and prepared flax,
which they wove into fine linen.   The sailcloth of the boats
on the Nile was often worked in colored and embroidered
patterns.   Bells, crucibles, and surgical instruments were
all in use.   From the papyrus the Egyptians made excel-

lent paper, and the present freshness of the writing on it proves their skill in the preparation of colors and inks. They could dye cloth in fast hues, and engrave precious stones with great delicacy. They were skilled in veneering and inlaying with ivory and precious woods. There is thus ample proof that the ancient Egyptians were a highly ingenious, artistic, tasteful and industrious race. The women adorned themselves with bracelets, anklets, armlets, finger-rings, ear-rings, and necklaces; they always wore their own hair, which it was the fashion to have long and braided; the service of the toilet brought into use highly-polished bronze mirrors, large wooden combs, perfumes, and cosmetics, which included a preparation for staining the eyelids and the eyebrows. The women joined the men at dinner, where all guests sat, instead of reclining in the usual Eastern fashion; and at the meal the wine was cooled in jars and handed round in cups of bronze, or porcelain, or silver. Before the feast was over, an attendant carried round a figure of a mummy, bidding the guests enjoy the present hour, for mummies after death they all should be. The music at dinner came from the lyre, tambourine, and harp; and dancing, tumbling, and games with dice and with ball helped frivolity under the Pharoahs to pass its hours of idleness away.

Such was the land of Egypt, the wonder of the nations of old, and a marvel to us in this age. Among all nations, for the massive and sublime, for the quaintly picturesque, it stands unrivalled in the world. An Arabian conqueror describes the land as "first a vast sea of dust; then a sea of fresh water; lastly, a sea of flowers," and, in the time of inundation, as "a sea of islands." When the waters cover the valley of the Nile, the villages and towns and scattered huts rise just above the level of the lake, and Virgil sings of how in the Delta, at that season, the farmer "rides his fields in painted bark around." In the time when vegetation is luxuriant, the contrast of the greenery by the river, with the yellow sand of the desert and the red granite of the rocks and ruins, is very striking. So unlike all the rest of the world was Egypt in her nature and her art, that the mere names of things found there, and there alone, or there in hugest or in strangest form, call up the image of the whole strange land with magic power. Temples, rock-tombs, gigantic ruins; the ibis, crocodile, ichneumon, asp; the pyramids, the sphinx, the obelisks; the mummy, scarabæus, hieroglyph, papyrus—these were the products of the region where the Pharaohs reigned, where Moses grew from birth to manhood, where Joseph came forth from a dungeon to rule in wisdom at the King's right hand, and whence the chosen people of God went out into the wilderness toward the promised land.

HITTITES, CHALDÆANS, ASSYRIANS, AND BABYLONIANS

In the basin of the Euphrates and the Tigris we find a civilization which may be more ancient than that of Egypt. To explorations made during recent years we owe the discovery of this very ancient empire, that of the Babylonians or Chaldeans.

Modern research has greatly added to our knowledge of the history of this region. In 1843 M. Botta, French consul at Mosul, on the Tigris, discovered at Khorsabad, twelve miles northeast of Mosul, and beyond the river, an Assyrian palace which had been buried for perhaps two thousand years. Austin Layard, then a traveler in the East, was hereupon incited to make excavations in the lofty mounds of Nimrud, eighteen miles southeast of Mosul, and also beyond, i. e., east of the Tigris. The enterprise was rewarded with immediate

and brilliant success. From the labors of Mr. Layard
at Nimrud and at Koyunjik, on the Tigris, opposite to
Mosul, came the slabs covered with cuneiform (wedge-
shaped) or arrow-headed inscriptions, the huge winged
bulls and lions, with human heads, bas-reliefs, figures, and
ornaments, which are now to be seen, as one of its most
valuable collections, in the British Museum. These objects themselves gave instant and abundant information
as to the state of art and the progress of civilization at the
time when they were made, but the cuneiform inscriptions
were a different matter. For these the penetrative power
of superior intellects was needed, and the researches of
numerous archæologists have resulted in the deciphering
of a vast number of the inscriptions containing the history
of ancient Babylonia and Assyria and their Kings.

Late research and the study of Egyptian and Assyrian
inscriptions and of Biblical statements have unfolded to
us the existence of a powerful people of the far past, long
lost to history, yet seemingly great among the early nations. These were the Hittites, who were the rivals of
the Pharaohs in peace and war from the twelfth to the
twentieth Egyptian dynasty, and concerning whom there
are references in the Bible extending over a thousand
years. Their country, known as Khita, extended from
the Euphrates on the east to far in Asia Minor on the
west, having two capitals, Kadish and Carchemish. They
pushed a wave of invasion southward as far as Hebron
and Egypt, proving unpleasant neighbors to the Israelites,
and stubbornly resisting the forces of the warlike Pharaohs, until an alliance, offensive and defensive, was made B.
C. 1383 between them and the great Pharaoh, Rameses II,
who, in token of amity, married a daughter of Khitasire,
King of Khita. Full account of this treaty and of the
marriage are given on tablets discovered by recent Aus-

trian Egyptologists, and by a papyrus in the British Museum. The inscriptions on the walls of Thebes and the monuments found at Aleppo show the Hittites to have been of the Mongolian or Tartar race. They wore boots with long toes turning upwards, after the fashion revived during the Middle Ages, a short-skirted tunic, and gloves without fingers. The two-headed eagle of Austria occurs frequently upon Hittite monuments many ages before it was used by the Turcoman chiefs. The relics left by these mighty people prove them to have been fully equal in civilization to the ancient Egyptians and to the Babylonians. Indeed, it was their wealth and luxury which made them the objects of attack by the Assyrians. Apparently their history is that of Egypt, Greece, Rome and all other nations that have grown great and luxurious and then been scattered because of their luxury. The Assyrians invaded Khita for the sake of spoil, returning with treasures of gold, copper and iron, of wood and ivory, slaves, and rich stuffs, as duly chronicled upon stones from Nineveh. They occupy an important place in Assyrian inscriptions, beginning in the reign of Sargon I. Under that of his sons they were finally subdued and their empire brought to an end by the capture of Carchemish and the defeat of Pisiri. Over 300 geographical names mentioned in these inscriptions show how extensive their empire was. Professor Sayce, the distinguished philologist, is of the opinion that the civilization of the Greeks was largely due to Hittite influences. Herodotus, Thales, Pythagoras, and Homer were all born in Asia Minor, and the Kiteians of whom Homer speaks in the Odyssey were supposed by Gladstone to be the Khetans or Hittites.

The work of the Hittites seems, however, to have been carried on by the Chaldæans. Chaldæan is a word of several meanings, being applied to the early Babylonian empire; to a province of the later Babylonian empire; to a learned class, a priestly caste, at the court of Nebuchadnezzar, King of the later Babylonian empire. In a sense similar to the last the word was familiar to the Romans. Philip Smith, in his "Ancient History," says: "The Chaldæans at the court of Nebuchadnezzar are classed with the astrologers and magicians, had a learning and language of their own, and formed a sort of college. Those who acquired their learning, and were admitted into their body, were called Chaldæans, quite irrespective of their race, and thus Daniel became the master of the Chaldæans."

The Chaldæan, or Old Babylonian, Empire was founded in the south of Mesopotamia, the alluvial plain between the Tigris and Euphrates. This country was, like Egypt with the Nile, the creation of these rivers by their deposits of rich mud. The waters were supplied for cultivation partly by the natural inundations, partly by artificial irrigating canals. The fertility of the district was famous in ancient times, producing wheat as an indigenous crop, and other kinds of grain, with dates, grapes and other fruits. The rivers and the marshes supplied huge reeds, which were used to make houses and boats. The chief building material was bricks made from the clay found on the spot, and springs of bitumen furnished a strong cement. In this region, as told in Scripture, Nimrod, the "mighty hunter," of the race of Ham, founded a kingdom which included four cities named Babel (Babylon), Erech, Calneh, and Accad. The land of Shinar was the name used in the Hebrew Scriptures for the country called Babylonia. In the inscriptions it is known as Shumer and Accad, the southern and northern sections of old Babylonia. Babylon was the late capital and the ruins of various other cities have been identified.

The inhabitants of Chaldæa of whom most is known, were undoubtedly of the Semitic race, and spoke a Semitic language closely akin to Hebrew. But the study of cuneiform inscriptions has revealed that there was here an earlier race as well as an earlier civilization than that of the Semites. This race, that of the Sumerians and Accadians, was conquered by the Semites and disappeared from history. But it formed for several thousand years the literary people of the land, the inventor of the cuneiform system of writing and of much pertaining to the useful arts. It was a people of authors and libraries, who strongly influenced the civilization of the later nations.

The beginnings of civilization in Babylonia are now held to date back to about 7000 B. C. In the cuneiform inscriptions there is an account of a great flood, strikingly similar in details to the flood in the time of Noah. At some time, perhaps two or three hundred years, before 2000 B. C., the Kings of Elam invaded Babylonia, and for a time established themselves as rulers over it and Mesopotamia, and their supremacy lasted several centuries. Elam was a mountainous country to the eastward of Chaldæa, its capital being Susa. It is to this period of Chaldæan history that Abraham's connection with the country belongs. It has been supposed that in Abraham's time, about 2100 B. C., Chaldæa contained a Semitic population professing a pure form of religion, in the midst of idolaters, and that Abraham, who was of Semitic race, was called to emigrate to the land of Canaan, with a view to the preservation of the pure faith. Chedorlaomer, King of Elam, invaded the land of Canaan soon after Abraham had migrated there, and, in his retreat with booty, was pursued and beaten by the brave patriarch.

The period 2000-1000 B. C. was the most flourishing period of the monarchy, and Chaldæa was then the foremost state of Western Asia in power as well as in science, art, and civilization. The rule of its princes extended to the mouth of the Euphrates and over Mesopotamia and the Upper Tigris. The rise of the powerful Assyrian Empire was what brought the downfall of Chaldæa, though it was able to maintain its independence against this rival down to the Ninth Century B. C. Indeed, it does not seem to have been thoroughly subdued, though greatly reduced from its former extent and power, till nearly two centuries later.

With the Chaldæans, as with the Egyptians, the art of writing, at first in the pictorial or hieroglyphic form, was early developed. Cuneiform, or wedge-shaped, writing is a later stage of the pictorial, and the Chaldæans may thus claim to be one of the nations that invented alphabetical writing. The contents of their tombs prove that they had much skill in pottery, and could make in various metals such articles as bracelets, ear-rings, fishhooks, nails, bolts, rings, and chains. Philip Smith says: "It is, however, by their cultivation of arithmetic and astronomy, and the application of these sciences to the uses of common life, that the Chaldæans have left the most permanent impress upon all succeeding ages. . . . All the systems of weights and measures used throughout the civilized world, down to the present time, are based upon the system which they invented. . . . Astronomical science seems to have been the chief portion of the learning handed down by the Chaldæan priests as an hereditary possession. . . . There is reason to believe that they mapped out the Zodiac, invented the names which we still use for the seven days of the week (based on the idea that each hour of the day was governed by a planet, and each day by the governor of its first hour, and from this one the day received its name) . . . and measured time by the water-clock. . . . Connected with their astronomy and star-worship they had an elaborate system of judicial astrology." The importance attributed to astronomy is attested by the fact that there were astronomers-royal in several of the cities, who had to send in reports regularly to the King. The towers, such as that of Babel, were probably both temples and observatories. The clearness of the sky and the levelness of the horizon on all sides favored the study of astronomy, which was, moreover, connected with religion. It is known that Chaldæans worshiped the heavenly bodies. When Babylon was taken by Alexander the Great in B. C. 331, there was found in the city a series of observations of the stars dating from B. C. 2234.

The Assyrians were a Semitic people, like the Chaldæans, Hebrews, Arabs, and Phœnicians, and first acquired power in the district called Assyria, between the Upper Tigris and the Zagros Mountains. Assyria was in all probability peopled from Chaldæa, as the language, writing, and religion of both peoples exhibit the closest relationship and agreement. At an early period the Assyrians were subject to the Chaldæan monarchy, but their warlike spirit enabled them to become independent and to effect conquests among their neighbors, gaining at last the ascendency over Babylonia. Toward the end of the Fourteenth Century B. C., Shalmaneser is said to have founded the city of Calah on the upper Tigris, and to have restored the great temple at the ancient city of Nineveh.

The early history of the Empire is still obscure, and no attention need be paid to the legends of Greek writers about Ninus, and the warrior-Queen Semiramis, and the voluptuous King Sardanapalus. About 1120 B. C., Tiglath-Pileser I conquered nations to the west and north of Assyria, and to the borders of Babylonia on the south. He made his dominions stretch from the Mediterranean

to the Caspian, and was the greatest monarch of the earlier Assyrian period, but was not able to subdue the Chaldæans.

After the death of Tiglath-Pileser I comes a long time
of obscurity. Asurnasirpal carried on extensive warlike operations and made important conquests in the West.
To him are attributed many of the great architectural
works which have been lately discovered.   He reigned
from B. C. 884 to 859, and under him Assyria became the
leading Empire of the world.   He built afresh the city of
Calah, then in ruins.   The magnificent palaces and temples built during this reign, with the sculptures and paintings that adorn them, prove the existence of great wealth
and luxury, and the development of much artistic ability.
His son Shalmaneser II, was successful in war against the
monarch of Babylon, Benhadad, King of Damascus, the
rulers of Tyre and Sidon, and Jehu, King of Israel.   In
B. C. 745 Tiglath-Pileser II became King of Assyria.   He
made himself master of Babylon, and had great successes
in war against Syria and Armenia, extending the Empire
from Lake Van on the north to the Persian Gulf, and from
the borders of India to those of Egypt.   Sargon reigned
from B. C. 722 to 705, and was engaged in war against
Samaria, which he captured, carrying the people into captivity; against King Sabako, of Egypt, whom he defeated;
and the revolted Armenians, whom he thoroughly subdued.   He then turned against Merodach-Baladan, King
of Babylonia, and drove him from his throne, and, after
a period spent in internal reforms, was succeeded by his
son, the famous Sennacherib.   This warlike monarch
marched into Syria in B. C. 701, captured Zidon and As-
kelon, defeated the forces of Hezekiah, King of Judah,
with his Egyptian and Ethiopian allies, and made Hezekiah pay tribute.   In B. C. 700 Sennacherib marched into

Arabia, where he defeated Tirhakah, King of Egypt and Ethiopia, and then his army perished before Libnah, in the south of Judah, by the catastrophe recorded in the Hebrew Scriptures.   Sennacherib was engaged, on his return to Assyria, in crushing rebellions of the Babylonians, constructing canals and aqueducts, and greatly adding to the size and splendor of Nineveh.   In 681 he was murdered by two of his sons, and another son, Esar-haddon, became King in 680.   Esar-haddon made successful expeditions into Syria, Arabia, Egypt, and as far as the Caucasus Mountains, and after the erection of splendid buildings at Nimrud and other cities, was succeeded in 667 by his son, Asurbanipal (the origin of the Greek "Sardanapalus").

The Assyrian Empire was at its height of power under the Kings Sennacherib, Esar-haddon, and Asurbanipal. The states nominally subject to the Assyrian King, paying tribute and homage, extended from the river Halys, in Asia Minor, and the sea-board of Syria, on the west, to the Persian Desert on the east, and from the Caspian Sea and the Armenian Mountains, on the north, to Arabia and the Persian Gulf, on the south, and latterly included Egypt.   But these states were held together by a very loose bond of connection, and we read in the Assyrian history, on the monuments, of constant wars, revolts, crushings of rebellion, and rebellion renewed.   The risings of tributary states were put down with great severity, which included the carrying of whole peoples into captivity, and the destruction of cities, but no effectual measures were taken to secure allegiance in subjugated nations, and the Empire was doomed to be the victim of the first really powerful assailant.

Asurbanipal inherited Egypt as part of his dominions, but his power was not firmly established in that country until he led an expedition there and sacked the city of Thebes. He erected splendid buildings at Nineveh and Babylon, and did much for literature and the arts, so that under him there was a great development of luxury and splendor. He died in B. C. 625, and soon afterwards Babylonia, for the last time, and now successfully, revolted. The Babylonians marched from the south against Nineveh, under their governor Nabopolassar, and the now powerful Medes, from the north, came against it under their King, Cyaxares. Nineveh was taken and given to the flames, which have left behind them in the mounds the calcined stone, charred wood, and statues spilt by heat, that furnish silent and convincing proof of the catastrophe. Thus, about B. C. 625, warlike, splendid, proud Assyria fell.

Modern research has unearthed much of the remains of Nineveh from beneath the mounds that for many miles are found along the eastern bank of the Tigris. We are not to think of it as being like a city of modern times, composed of continuous or nearly adjacent buildings. The city was a large expanse, supposed to be at least sixty miles in circuit, containing temples, palaces, pasture-lands, ploughed fields and hunting-parks, as well as the dwellings of the people, built of sun-dried bricks. It thus resembled a modern suburban district, but included the stately structures for the uses of religion and of royalty, which in modern cities usually hold a central place amongst dense masses of connected streets and squares. At the time of Alexander the Great, in the Fourth Century B. C., almost every trace of the great city in which Jonah preached repentance had vanished, save the shapeless mounds of earth.

The Assyrian language was much like the Hebrew and Phœnician, and had a literature comprising hymns to the gods, mythological and epic poems, and works on astrology, law, and chronology. The religion of Assyria was a worship of various gods, representing the powers of nature, and especially the heavenly bodies. The great national deity was Asur, appearing in the nation's name and in those of many of the Kings. All religion was connected with royalty, and in the pure despotism of Assyria the King was himself a deity, a type of the supreme being. All his acts in peace or war, were divine acts, and his robes and ornaments all have embroideries and figured animals of mystical religious import.

Assyrian art must be considered great in architecture and sculpture. The emblematic figures of the gods show dignity and grandeur. The scenes from real life, of war, and of the chase, are bold and vivid; and in succeeding ages marked progress is shown in the acquirement of a more free, natural, lifelike, and varied execution, though the artists never learnt perspective and proportion. The Assyrians, as the sculptures and other remains prove, constructed arches, tunnels, and aqueducts; they were skilled in engraving gems, and in the arts of enameling and inlaying; they made porcelain, transparent and colored glass, and even lenses; ornaments of bronze and ivory, bells and golden bracelets, and earrings of good design and workmanship, were all produced. In mechanics, and for measuring time, they used the pulley, the lever, the water-clock, and the sun-dial. Their astronomical science was that of the Chaldæan philosophers.

The implements and methods used in war, as the monuments show, included swords, spears, maces, and bows and arrows, as weapons of offence; cavalry and chariots for charging; movable towers and battering-rams for sieges; and circular entrenched camps as quarters for a military force. The one thing wanting in Assyria, as in other Eastern Empires, for continued sway, was the genius for government which could at least make subject nations satisfied to serve, if it could not mould them into one coherent whole.

The history of the later Babylonian Empire begins with the year 625 B. C., and ends in 538 with its subjection to Persia. The founder of the Empire was Nabopolassar, the Assyrian general who joined the Medes in the destruction of the Assyrian power. Babylon then became an independent Kingdom, extending from the valley of the lower Euphrates to Mount Taurus, and partly over Syria, Phœnicia, and Palestine.

Nabopolassar was succeeded by his son, the famous Nebuchadnezzar, who reigned from B. C. 604 to 561, and carried his arms with success against the cities of Jerusalem and Tyre, and even into Egypt. The Empire was at its height of power and glory under him, and extended from the Euphrates to Egypt, and from the deserts of Arabia on the south to the Armenian Mountains on the north. Nebuchadnezzar's chief work in home affairs was the renovation and decoration of the great city Babylon, capital of the Empire. This famous place was built on both sides of the Euphrates, and, on its completion by Nebuchadnezzar, formed a square said to have been sixty miles in circuit. The clay of the country furnished abundant and excellent brick, and springs of bitumen supplied a powerful cement. The walls of the city were of immense height and thickness, surrounded by a deep ditch, and having a hundred brazen gates. Like Nineveh, the city included large open spaces, some being parks and pleasure-grounds of the King and the nobles. The architectural wonder of the place were the temple of Belus, a huge eight-storied tower, the remains of which are believed to be identified at Birs Nimrud, "the tower of Nim-

rod," on the west side of the Euphrates, six miles southwest of the town of Hillah; and the "hanging gardens"
of Nebuchadnezzar, which consisted of a series of terraces
rising one above another, supported by huge pillars and
arches, and covered with earth, in which grew beautiful
shrubs and trees.

The carrying into captivity of the Jews by Nebuchadnezzar, and the pride of his heart, his image of gold in the
plain of Dura, his fiery furnace, his strange madness,
recovery, and repentance, are well known from the interesting and eloquent account in the Hebrew Scriptures, as
written by the prophet Daniel.

Nebuchadnezzar was succeeded by his son, Evil- Mero-
dach, the friend of Jehoiachin, captive King of Judah. He
was followed by Neriglassar, a successful conspirator
against his power and life, who, after some years, was
defeated and slain in battle against the Medes and Persians. After a few months of tyranny, ended by assassination, under the cruel and sensual Laborosoarchod, the last
Babylonian monarch, Nabonadius came to the throne, in
B. C. 555. The Medes and Persians to the north had now
become a formidable power, and in 540 the Babylonians
came into collision with them. The Persian King, Cyrus,
marched against Babylon, and under its walls defeated
Nabonadius, who fled to Borsippa, a city to the south of
Babylon. The capital was held by a son of Nabonadius,
who had been made co-king with his father, and is known
to us by the name of Belshazzar. The revelries of this
sovereign during the siege, the handwriting on the wall,
and his death on that same night, are given in the Scriptural narrative of Daniel. According to Herodotus, the
army of Cyrus entered the city along the bed of the river
Euphrates, which they had drained off into canals, and
thus the Babylonian Empire fell in B. C. 538, and became

a province of the Persian Empire. Recently deciphered inscriptions, however, would seem to prove that this account is erroneous, and that the city was surrendered without any siege. The site of the great city of Babylon is now a marsh formed by inundations of the river, due to the destruction of the embankments and the choking up of the canals.

The Assyrians were, pre-eminently, a warlike, the Babylonians a commercial and luxurious people. The position of the great city on the lower Euphrates, near to the Persian Gulf, made it a great emporium for the trade between India and Eastern Asia and Western Asia, with the nearest parts of Africa and Europe. From Ceylon came ivory, cinnamon, and ebony; spices from the Eastern islands; myrrh and frankincense from Arabia; cotton, pearls, and valuable timber, both for shipbuilding and ornament, from the islands in the Persian Gulf. There was also a great caravan trade with Northern India and adjacent lands, whence came gold, dyes, jewels, and fine wool. The wealth of Babylon became prodigious and proverbial, and her commerce was in large measure due to ingenious and splendid manufactures. Carpets, curtains, and fine muslins, skillfully woven and brilliantly dyed, of elegant pattern and varied hue, were famous wherever luxury was known. The Babylonian gems in the British Museum display art of the highest order in cutting precious stones.

The system of government was a pure despotism, with viceroys ruling the provinces under the monarch, who dwelt in luxurious seclusion from his people. The fall of Babylon was a proof that the real power of nations does not reside in trade and luxury and wealth, but in the spirit, equal to the occasions both of peace and of war, developed in a people by the possession of freedom.

THE ISRAELITES

The Hebrews were a pure Semitic race, akin to the Phœnicians, Chaldæans, and Assyrians. The founder of the nation was Abraham, who in the Twentieth or Twenty-first Century B. C., removed from the plains of Mesopotamia to the land of Canaan, on the south-eastern coast of the Mediterranean Sea.

In this people we have the worship of the one spiritual God—Jehovah—the purely One. In the Jewish idea He was the God of a family that became a nation—the God of Abraham, of Isaac, and of Jacob, He who commanded them to depart out of Egypt and gave them the land of Canaan. With the other Eastern nations, the primary and fundamental existence was Nature; but that, with the Hebrews, becomes a mere creature, and Spirit is foremost. God is the creator of Nature and all men, the only first cause of all things. The great element in the Jewish religion was exclusive unity—only one people, only one God. All other gods were regarded as thoroughly false; nothing divine was admitted to exist in them. In the religion of the Hebrews, Spirit became the one great truth, and true morality appeared; God was honored, and could be honored, only by righteousness, the reward of which was to be happiness, life, and temporal prosperity.

Their earliest history, as told in the Bible, that of Abraham and his first descendant, is merely a family history, and the Jewish nation begins with the departure from Egypt perhaps about B. C. 1320.

The interval between that time and the conquest of Judæa by the Romans may be divided into four periods.

From the departure out of Egypt to the establishment of the monarchy under Saul, about B. C. 1320-1067;

From the establishment of the monarchy to the sepa-

ration into the two kingdoms of Israel and Judah, about
B. C. 1067-975;

From the separation of the kingdoms to the Babylonian captivity, B. C. 975-588;

From the Babylonian captivity to the conquest of
Judæa by Rome, B. C. 588-63.

The first period opens, on the departure from Egypt,
with the theocracy or government by God in revelations
of His will to the people, through laws directly given from
Sinai, and communications made to the high-priest. This
lasted, during the wanderings in the wilderness under
Moses, and the conquest of Canaan under Joshua, until
perhaps B. C. 1250. Then came the tribal federation,
for some two centuries, under which the tribes were sep-
arately governed, subject to the divine laws, by their own
patriarchs, but were all united in one state and one common bond by the worship of Jehovah. As the people
from time to time fell off into idolatry, they suffered at the
hands of neighboring tribes, and rulers called "Judges"
were given by divine appointment to deliver the people,
governing according to the divine laws, and having no
royal prerogatives. Of this line of rulers the last was
the Prophet Samuel, and the misconduct of his sons
caused the people to ask for a King.

The time of the sole monarchy includes three reigns,
those of Saul, David, and Solomon. Saul reigned for
a period of unknown duration, and, after wars with various neighboring peoples known as Moabites, Edomites,
Amalekites, etc., was defeated and driven to suicide by
the powerful Philistines. Saul's son-in-law, David, the
son of Jesse, reigned also about forty years, from B. C.
1056 to 1015, and having conquered Jerusalem from the
Jebusites in 1048, made it the capital of his kingdom, the
seat of the national government and religion. David was

a warlike monarch, and conquered the Philistines, Moabites, Edomites, and Syrians, extending his power from the Red Sea to the Euphrates. His son Solomon succeeded him in B. C. 1015, and also reigned forty years, from 1015 to 975. Under him the Jewish nation attained the height of its power, and he confirmed and extended the conquests of David. Solomon married a daughter of a Pharaoh, King of Egypt, formed an alliance with Hiram, King of Tyre, built the magnificent temple at Jerusalem, and made his kingdom the supreme monarchy in Western Asia. An extensive commerce was carried on by land and sea. Solomon's ships, manned by Phœnician sailors, traded to the furthest parts of the Mediterranean westward, and from ports on the Red Sea to Southern Arabia, Ethiopia, and perhaps India. From Egypt came horses, chariots, and linen; ivory, gold, silver, peacocks and apes from Tarshish or Tartessus, a district in the south of Spain; and gold, spices, and jewels from the place called Ophir, variously placed in Southern Arabia, India, and Eastern Africa, south of the Red Sea. The corn, wine and oil of Judæa were exchanged by Solomon for the cedars of Lebanon supplied by Hiram, King of Tyre.

On the death of Solomon, in B.C. 975, the temporal glory of the Hebrews was eclipsed. Ten of the twelve tribes revolted against Solomon's son and successor, Rehoboam, and formed a separate Kingdom of Israel, with Samaria as capital, while the tribes of Judah and Benjamin made up the Kingdom of Judah, having Jerusalem for the chief city. The Syrian possessions were lost; the Ammonites became independent; commerce declined; idolatry crept in and grew; the prophets of God threatened and warned in vain; gleams of success against neighboring nations were mingled with defeat and disgrace suffered from the Edomites, Philistines, and Syrians, until, in B.C.

740, Tiglath-pileser II, King of Assyria, carried off into captivity to Media the tribes east, and partly west, of the Jordan—Reuben, Gad, and Manasseh. In B.C. 721 Sargon, King of Assyria, took Samaria, and carried away the people of Israel as captives, beyond the Euphrates. The Kingdom of Israel thus came to an end after a duration of about 250 years. In B.C. 713 Judah, under King Hezekiah, was attacked by Sennacherib, King of Assyria, and relieved by the destruction of the Assyrian army. A time of peace and prosperity followed, but in 677 the Assyrians again invaded the country, and carried off King Manasseh to Babylon. In B.C. 624 the good King Josiah repaired the temple and put down idolatry, but was defeated and slain by the Egyptian King, Pharaoh-Necho, in 610. In B.C. 606 Nebuchadnezzar, King of Babylon, took Jerusalem, and made the King, Jehoiakim, tributary; on his revolt Jerusalem was again taken, and 10,000 captives of the higher class were carried off to Babylon, with the treasures of the palace and temple, in 599. In B.C. 593 the Jewish King, Zedekiah, revolted from Nebuchadnezzar, who now determined to make an end of the existence of the rebellious nation. In B.C. 588 Jerusalem was taken and plundered; the walls were destroyed, and the city and temple burnt, and nearly the whole nation was carried away as prisoners to Babylon. For over fifty years the land lay desolate, and the history of the Hebrew nation is transferred to the land where they mourned in exile.

The history of the Jews during the Babylonish captivity is contained chiefly in the book of Daniel, and includes the episodes of Shadrach, Meshach, and Abednego, the faithful Jews thrown into the furnace by order of Nebuchadnezzar, and of Daniel's deliverance when he was thrown into a pit containing lions by order of Darius the

Mede, or Cyaxares II, who was placed by the success of his nephew Cyrus on the throne of Babylon after the death of Belshazzar.   In B.C. 537 Cyaxares II died, and Cyrus became monarch of the Persian Empire.   He issued an edict in B. C. 536, by which the Jews were allowed to return to Jerusalem and rebuild their temple.   Nearly 50,000 Jews, chiefly of the tribes of Judah and Benjamin, went to the old home of their race under the command of Zerubbabel and Jeshua, taking with them many of the vessels of silver and gold carried away by Nebuchadnezzar.   Zerubbabel was appointed Governor of the land, now a dependency of the Persian Empire.   In B.C. 519 the Persian King, Darius Hystaspis, confirmed the edict of Cyrus, and in 515 the temple was completed and dedicated.   The ten tribes disappear at this time from history, such of them as returned to their land having united themselves with the tribe of Judah, and henceforth the Hebrews are called Jews and their country Judæa.   In the reign of the Persian King, Artaxerxes Longimanus, more of the Jews emigrated from Babylonia to Judæa under the command of Ezra, B.C. 458, and Ezra was Governor of the land until 445.   Nehemiah was Governor, (with an interval), from 445 to 420, and under him the walls and towers of Jerusalem were rebuilt, and the city acquired something of its ancient importance.   With B. C. 420 the history of the Jews ends, as far as the Scriptural narrative goes in books esteemed to be of sacred authority.

From 420 to 332 Judæa continued subject to Persia, paying a yearly tribute, and being governed by the high-priest, under the Satrap of Syria.   In B.C. 332 Alexander the Great, then engaged in conquering the Persian Empire, visited Jerusalem, and showed respect to the High-priest and the sacred rites of the Temple.   In 330 the Persian Empire fell under the arms of Alexander, who

died at Babylon in B. C. 323. Judæa was taken possession
of by Alexander's General, Ptolemy Lagus, and from 300
to 202 B.C. was governed by the dynasty of the Ptolemies,
ruling Egypt, Arabia Petræa, and Southern Syria. The
Government was administered by the High-priest under
the Ptolemies, whose capital was at the new city of Alexandria in Egypt. At this time the Jews began to spread
themselves over the world, the Greek language became
common in Judæa, and the Septuagint (or Greek version
of the Hebrew Scriptures), was written during this and
the following Century. In B.C. 202 Antiochus the Great,
King of Syria (including in its empire Asia Minor, Mesopotamia, Babylonia, etc.), conquered Judæa from Ptolemy
V. Antiochus Epiphanes, one of the sons and successors
of the great Antiochus, drove the Jews to rebellion by
persecution and profanation of their Temple and religion.

Under the great patriot and hero, Judas Maccabæus,
the Jews asserted their religious freedom in B.C. 166.
Antiochus Epiphanes died in 164, and Maccabæus fought
with success against the Idumæans, Syrians, Phœnicians,
and others, who had formed a league for the destruction
of the Jews. In 163 Judas Maccabæus became Governor
of Judæa under the King of Syria, but fell in battle, in
161, while he was resisting an invasion of his country by
the troops of Demetrius Soter, new ruler of the Empire.
His brother, Jonathan Maccabæus, ruled from B.C. 161 to
143 amidst many troubles from Syria, and was succeeded
by his brother, Simon Maccabæus, who strengthened the
land by fortifications, was recognized by the Romans as
High-priest and ruler of Judæa, and fell by assassination
in B.C. 136. His son, John Hyrcanus, threw off at last
the yoke of Syria, and made himself master of all Judæa,
Galilee, and Samaria,, reigning then in peace till B. C. 106,
when the line of the greater Maccabæan Princes ended.

A miserable time of civil wars and religious and political faction followed. These ended in the interference of Rome, and in B.C. 63 Pompeius Magnus took Jerusalem after a siege of three months, and entered the "Holy of Holies" in the Temple, with a profanation before unheard of in Jewish history.

From this time the Jewish state was virtually subject to Rome, and became in the end a part of the Roman province of Syria. The turbulence of the Jews under Roman rule is well known, and a general rebellion ended, after fearful bloodshed and misery, in the capture and destruction of Jerusalem by Titus, A. D. 70. The history, as a separate political body, of the chosen people of God, unequaled in the annals of our race for sin and suffering, ends with the dispersion of their remnant over the face of the civilized world.

The Hebrew language, in the antiquity of its literary remains, surpasses all the other Semitic tongues, and in the importance of its chief treasures, the books of the Old Testament canon, outweighs all other languages. The country of the Hebrew nation was of very limited extent; the political value of the race, as compared with that of the great Eastern empires, was trifling; the contributions of the Jews to art and science, until the downfall and dispersion of the people, were yet more insignificant. It was their mission to conserve and to convey to future ages that deposit of moral and spiritual truth which, combined with its development and exaltation in the form of Christianity, was to influence mankind in all time to come.

THE PHŒNICIANS

The Phœnicians were the people most distinguished in the most ancient times for industry, commerce, and navigation. They were of pure Semitic race, closely connected with the Hebrews in blood and language, and became a separate nation so early that they are found to have settled on the southeastern coasts of the Mediterranean before the arrival of the Israelites in Canaan, in the Fifteenth Century B. C. The distinctive character of the Phœnicians among the nations of the most ancient world is, that they were colonizers, not conquerors; peaceful merchants, not fighting meddlers; intrepid and enterprising seamen, not bold and ambitious soldiers; industrious and ingenious workmen and creators, not ruthless and wanton destroyers of the labors of their fellow-men.

A high place in the history of ancient civilization is held by the Phœnicians, for their diffusion of commodities and of culture partly produced at home, in part received from abroad. They present a new principle of development in civilization, that of a nation relying solely on the activity of industry, combined with the careful bravery which dares the deep, and devises means of safety thereon. Man's courage, energy, and intelligence is brought into play mainly for the benefit, not the bane, of mankind. Foremost in Phœnicia are human will and work, not Nature's bounty, as in the fertile valleys of the Nile, Tigris, and Euphrates. In Babylonia and Egypt, human subsistence depended largely upon Nature and the sun; in maritime Phœnicia, on the sailor's skill and courage. Valor gives way to intelligence, and warlike ferocity to ingenuity, in this sea-faring and manufacturing life, and thus the nations were freed from a bondage to Nature and from fear of her powers upon the ever-flowing sea.

Phœnicia was a narrow strip of country on the southeastern coast of the great inland sea of antiquity, lying chiefly between Mount Lebanon and the Mediterranean shore, and extending for about 120 miles north of Mount Carmel, the scene of the contempt poured on her great god Baal by the prophet Elijah.   Here lay the cities Tyre and Sidon, Byblus and Berytus, Tripolis and Ptolemais. The land was fertile, and rich in timber-trees and fruits, such as the pine, fir, cypress, sycamore, and cedar; figs, olives, dates, pomegranates, citrons, almonds.   Here was material for trade abroad, and comfort and prosperity at home, and the coast was so thickly studded with towns as almost to make one continuous populated line.

Phœnicia's history is peculiar in that it is a history of separate cities and colonies, never united into one great independent state, though now and then alliances existed between several cities in order to repel a common danger. When the Israelites conquered Canaan in the middle of the Fifteenth Century B. C., they interfered but slightly with Phœnicia, and the two peoples dwelt side by side in friendship nearly always undisturbed.   Each city of Phœnicia was governed by a King or a petty chief, under or with whom an aristocracy, and at times elective magistrates, called in Latin suffetes, appear to have held sway. But Phœnician government is an obscure and unimportant subject; the genius of the race cared little for political development, and was one-sided in its devotion to commercial matters, regardless, in comparison, of freedom from inward or external domination.   The two chief cities in the history are Sidon and Tyre.

Of these, Sidon was probably the more ancient, being named in the Pentateuch as chief of the Phœnician cities, while its richly embroidered robes are mentioned in the Homeric poems.   It was the greatest maritime place until its colony, Tyre, surpassed it, and it seems to have been subject to Tyre in the time of David and Solomon.   About 700 B.C. it became independent again, but was taken by Nebuchadnezzar, King of Babylon, about B.C. 600, and became subject to Persia about B.C. 500.   Under the

Persian rule, it was a great and populous city, and, coming into the hands of Alexander the Great in B.C. 333, helped him with a fleet in his siege of Tyre. Its history ends with submission to Roman power in the last Century, year 63 B.C. Tyre was a powerful city as early as 1200 B.C. The friendship of her King Hiram with Solomon (reigned B.C. 1015-975) is well known from the Hebrew Scriptures, and at this time the commerce of Tyre was foremost in the Mediterranean, and her ships sailed into the Indian Ocean from the port of Elath on the Red Sea. Tyre is celebrated in history for her obstinate resistance to enemies. Sargon, King of Assyria, besieged the city in vain for five years, B.C.721-717. Nebuchadnezzar took thirteen years, B.C. 598-585, to capture the place partially, and it was only taken by Alexander the Great after a seven months' siege, in B.C. 332. The old glory of Tyre departed with the transfer of her chief trade to her conqueror's creation, Alexandria, though the indomitable energy of the Phœnician race had again, in Roman times, made her a great seat of trade.

Phœnicia was at the height of prosperity from the Eleventh to the Sixth Centuries B.C. As a colonizing country she preceded the Greeks on the shores and islands of the Mediterranean, and sent her ships to regions that the Greeks knew nothing of, save by report of the bold mariners of Tyre. Until the rise of Alexandria, about B. C. 300, the sea-trade of Phœnicia was rivaled only by that of Carthage, her own colony, and she still kept up her great land-trade by caravans with Arabia, with Central Asia and Northern India (through Babylonia), and with Scythia and the Caucasian countries, through Armenia. Their colonies were planted on the coasts and islands of the Mediterranean, in Cyprus, Rhodes, the Islands of the Ægean Sea, Sardinia, Sicily, the Balearic Islands, Cilicia (in southeast of Asia

Minor), and in Spain. Westward, they even passed out of the Mediterranean, and were the founders at an early period of Gades, the modern Cadiz. They first in all the ancient world pushed out into the Atlantic Ocean, crossed the stormy region of the "Bay of Biscay," and traded to the British coast for tin from the Scilly Isles and Cornwall. Tradition tells of their mariners reaching sunny fertile shores in what must have been either the Canary Islands or the Azores. Under the patronage of Necho, King of Egypt, Phœnician sailors went round Africa from the Red Sea to the Nile. In the Eastern seas, they had establishments on the Arabian and Persian Gulfs, from which they traded to the eastern coast of Africa, to Western India, and to Ceylon. By far the most renowned of all Phœnician colonies—famous in poetry for Dido's hopeless love and hapless death, in history for Hannibal's heroic hate of Rome and warlike skill—was Carthage, in the center of the northern coast of Africa. The date of her foundation is put about 850 B.C. At Utica and Tunis, to the north and south, Phœnician settlements were already existing.

The trade of Tyre and her sister-cities reached almost throughout the then known world. They exported wares and manufactures of their own; they imported and re-exported products of every region east and south of their own land, that had anything of value for the markets of nations dwelling round the great central sea. Thus to Phœnicia came the spices—notably myrrh and frankincense —of Arabia; the ivory, ebony, and cotton goods of India; linen-yarn, and corn from Egypt; wool and wine from Damascus; embroideries from Babylon and Nineveh; pottery, in the days of Grecian art, from Attica; horses and chariots from Armenia; copper from the shores of the Euxine Sea; lead from Spain; tin from Cornwall. From

Phœnicia went to foreign ports, not only these articles of food and use and luxury, but the rich purple dyes made from the murex (a kind of shell-fish) of her coast, the famous hue of Tyre, with which were tinged the silken costly robes worn by the despots of that time. From Sidon went the not less famous glass produced in part from fine white sand found near the headland called Mount Carmel. So great and so important was the trade by caravans through Babylon with the interior of Asia that the great town Palmyra (or "Tadmor in the desert") was founded or enlarged by Solomon to serve the traffic on its route through Syria to the valley of the Tigris and Euphrates. With lawful trade these ancient merchants, like the English in the reign of Queen Elizabeth, combined a taste for piracy and for indulgence in a slave-trade which included the kidnapping, at times, of Hebrew victims to the lust of gold.

As a money-making race the Phœnicians were skilled in arts by which the grand aim of its life could be attained. Phœnician drinking-cups of silver and of gold, and Sidon's works in brass, were famous, and her weavers were skilled in making cloth of flax and of cotton, grown and spun in Egypt. Great as they were at the dyeing-vat and loom, adepts in working metals and in fabricating glass, they were also the best shipbuilders, and the most famous miners of their time. Their energy and enterprising character are beyond dispute, but much has been ascribed to their invention, in the sciences and arts, which they received from nations further East. Their greatest service to civilization seems rather to have been in appropriating, developing, and spreading the ideas of others, especially in forming an alphabet for the Western world.

Although the story about the mythical Cadmus taking his sixteen letters from Phœnicia into Greece must be rejected, the European world owes to this race of traders the alphabetic symbols now. in use.   The Greeks and Romans from the Phœnicians, and most of modern Europe from the Romans, acquired these precious and indispensable rudiments of learning.   The gradual change of shape is easily traced in most of the signs.   The simple and ingenious device by which each sign stands for one elementary sound of human speech is largely due to the Phœnician people, as an improvement on the cumbrous hieroglyphs of Egypt.   Of literature they have left nothing whatever recognized by scholars as really theirs.

In morals, they had a name for craftiness in trade, and wealth led to worse than luxury—to soft licentiousness and flagrant vice.   Their religion was a kind of nature-worship, which adored the sun and moon and five planets, the chief deities being the male Baal, and the female Ashtoreth, or Astarte.   The worship itself was a sensual excess and revelry, combined with cruelty.   Children were offered in sacrifice to idols, and the foulness of the rites is known by the denunciations of the Hebrew prophets Jeremiah and Ezekiel.   At Tyre a deity was worshipped with the attributes of the Greek god Hercules.   The worship of Adonis, under the name of Thammuz, in the coast-towns, included a commemoration of his death, a funeral-festival, at which women gave way to extravagant lamentations.   It was Phœnician women, fair of face, that tempted Solomon the wise to foul idolatry; it was a Princess of Phœnicia, Jezebel, that brought Ahab, her husband, King of Israel, to ruin, that slew the prophets of God, and left a name proverbial for infamy in life, and for ignominious horror in her death.   The work done by Phœnicia in the cause of human progress was important and interesting in material things, but not, with one great exception, leading to intellectual ends or moral and political improvement.

THE MEDES AND THE PERSIANS

The last of the great Oriental empires was that of the Medes and Persians, commonly known as "the Persian Empire," which absorbed all the territories of Western and Southwestern Asia (except Arabia), as well as Egypt and a small portion of Europe. The Medes and the Persians are treated of together, because of their intimate connection in race and the fact that Media was conquered by and included in Persia, as the latter empire rose into power and importance in the Western Asiatic world. Media occupied the table-land south of the Caspian Sea, east of Armenia and the Zagros Mountains, and north and west of the mountains of Persia Proper and the great rainless Persian desert or desert of Iran. The mountain ranges inclosed fertile valleys, rich in corn and fruits, and the Zagros Mountains had on their pastures splendid horses of the breed famous as the Nisæan, which supplied the studs of the King and nobles of Persia. Persis, or Persia Proper, was a mountainous district between the desert of Iran and the northeastern shore of the Persian Gulf. The country contained, amongst its hills, fertile plains and valleys abounding in corn, pasture, and fruits.

The Medes were of Aryan race, and, like the Persians, called themselves "Aryans." Their close connection, in origin and institutions, with the Persians is shown in the famous expression, "The law of the Medes and Persians, which altereth not." The people began to migrate into Media at an early period, of which we have no record, from the original abode of the Aryan race. By degrees they overcame the Scythian races whom they found in possession of the land. The Medes were a warlike race, strong in cavalry and archers. Their language was a dialect of the Zend, the ancient tongue of Persia, and their religion was the Magian, which involved the worship of a good principle or deity called Ormuzd, and the practice of divination of his will by dreams and omens. The Median tribes, who seem to have been in part subject to the King of Assyria, began toward 700 B. C. to be cemented together under a chief named Deioces, who chose as his capital Ecbatana, identified with the modern Hamadan. Under his son Phraortes their power grew stronger, and that monarch subdued the Persians, but perished in war with the Assyrians. Cyaxares, son of Phraortes, renewed the war against the Assyrians. Cyaxares extended the Median Empire westward, by conquest, through Armenia to the River Halys in Asia Minor. His great achievement was the capture of Nineveh about B.C. 620, in alliance with the revolted Babylonians, and the consequent overthrow of the Assyrian empire. Cyaxares reigned forty years and died about B.C. 593. He was succeeded by his son Astyages, who reigned for over thirty years, and seems to have been a despot of quiet life and peaceful disposition, enjoying what his father had acquired. Against him the Persians, under their Prince Cyrus, revolted about 558 B.C., and, being joined by a portion of the Median army under a chief named Harpagus, they took Ecbatana and deposed the Median ruler. From this time the two nations were spoken of as one people. Ecbatana became the summer residence of the Persian Kings. After the death of Alexander the Great, 324 B.C., the northwest portion (Atropatene) of Media became a separate kingdom, which existed until the time of Augustus.

In race, language, and religion, the Persians were closely connected with the Medes. Of their early migration to the home where history finds them, little is known. They appear first in human records as hardy and warlike mountaineers, noble specimens of the great Aryan race.

They were simple in their ways of life, noted for truthfulness, keen-witted, generous, and quick-tempered. The language which they brought with them when they migrated is known as the Zend, closely allied to the Sanscrit, and now only existing in the sacred books of the Zendavesta, containing the doctrine of Zoroaster, King of Bactria, founder of the Magian religion in 2115 B.C.

The peculiarity of Persia, in the political history of Eastern empires, is that monarchy appears in an empire ruling over many peoples differing widely from each other. The several members of the state are allowed a free growth, and we find roving nomades existing in one part, whilst in other territories commerce and industrial pursuits are in full vigor. The coasts of the empire are in communication with foreign lands, and the Israelites, amidst all the diversities of races and creeds, are allowed the free exercise of their own religion.

Persia was an empire displaying a period of historical transition, at the time when the Persian world came in contact with the Greek. The Persian could conquer, but could not fuse into one harmonious whole the diverse nationalities that fell under his sway. The monarchy was thus a loose aggregate of peoples spread over three different geographical regions, the highlands of Media and Persia, the valley plains of the Euphrates, Tigris, and Nile, and the maritime districts in Syria, Phœnicia, and Asia Minor. In developing civilization Persia's mission was that of bringing to an end the barbarous feuds between the nations of the western world of Asia. With a settled dominion, comfort, and happiness were diffused, and with the growth of wealth, culture, and luxury, the military prowess of ruder times declined. Of the calm courage of well-ordered civilization the Asiatics had little. Effeminacy relaxed their energies as opulence grew, and sensual indulgence, along with unwieldiness and want of organization in such elements of strength as they possessed, made them succumb, when the time came, to the superior skill and vitality of Greece. The Persians were, in their early history, subject to the Medes, but governed by their own native princes, called the Achæmenidæ, who began to reign as semi-independent rulers about B. C. 700. The founder of the Persian Empire was Cyrus, who began his career of conquest by the defeat and dethronement of Astyages, King of Media, in B. C. 558. The Median supremacy thus passed to the Persians.

Master of Media, Cyrus came next into collision with the great kingdom of Lydia, in Asia Minor. With its capital at Sardis, and extending from the coast of the Ægean Sea eastwards to the River Halys, Lydia was one of the most powerful monarchies of the second class in Asiatic history. The Lydians were a highly civilized, wealthy, and energetic people, great in agriculture, manufactures, commerce, and the arts. In music and metallurgy their names are famous as inventors or improvers; they were proverbial in the ancient world for luxury and the softer vices that attend it. Crœsus was King of Lydia when Cyrus met his attack and conquered him in B. C. 546. The rising Empire of Persia was thus extended to the western sea-board of Asia Minor. The Greek colonies on the coast next fell a prey to the arms of Cyrus, and in B.C. 538 he got possession of Babylon, and added the provinces of the later Babylonian Empire to the Persian. Before this he had conquered the territory eastwards between Media and the Indus. The power and life alike of Cyrus came to an end in his expedition against the Scythian people, called the Massagetæ, by whom he was defeated and killed in B.C. 529. Cyrus, the greatest King among all the Persian monarchs, had spread the Persian sway from the Hellespont on the west to the Indus on the east.

Cyrus was succeeded by his son Cambyses, who reigned from B.C. 529-522, and is distinguished by his conquest of Egypt in 525. According to the common account he was guilty of ferocious and wanton cruelty toward the Egyptians and his own family and subjects. He stabbed with his own dagger the sacred calf Apis, to the horror of the Egyptians; murdered his own brother Smerdis, and in several acts displayed something like insanity. Recent researches, however, have shown that the character and acts of Cambyses have been greatly misrepresented; and instead of outraging the religious feelings of the Egyptians he was himself initiated into their religion and buried the sacred calf with the usual honors. He died in 522, on his march from Egypt against a Magian pretender to the throne, who declared himself to be the Smerdis put to death by Cambyses. The usurper reigned for a few months, and was then dethroned and slain in an insurrection headed by Darius Hystaspis, one of the royal line of the Achæmenidæ.

Darius Hystaspis, or Darius I, who reigned from B. C. 521 to 485, finished the work which Cyrus had begun, by setting in order the affairs of the vast Empire which Cyrus and Cambyses had conquered. The whole territory was divided into twenty satrapies or governments, and a fixed payment was the contribution of each province to the expenses of administration. The satrap, or governor, represented the royal authority, and was charged to remit to the King the fixed tribute of the province which he ruled. Justice was administered by independent officers, called Royal Judges, and a watch was kept upon the conduct of the viceroys (satraps) by officials appointed for the purpose. The Governors, however, often oppressed the provinces and intrigued against each other. The "Great King," as the Persian monarch was called, was held to be the lord of all the land and the water. Thus Darius Hystaspis and Xerxes demanded "earth and water," in token of submission, from the Greeks. Tyrannical Governors were extortionate in money-matters, but there was a general tolerance of all religious faiths, and no systematic or outrageous oppression.

Darius I is credited with the establishment of high-roads and swift postal communication between the provinces and the court. The Kings of Persia resided in the winter at Susa, a warm place in the plain east of the lower Tigris; in the summer at Ecbatana, in Media, by the mountains; and Babylon was a third capital of occasional residence in winter. From these different centers of power the Persian monarchs watched, and, according to their measure of energy and resolution, controlled the conduct of the satraps in every quarter of their wide-spread dominions.

About B. C. 508 Darius invaded Scythia, and, crossing the Danube, marched far into the territory which is now European Russia, but the expedition ended in a retreat without encountering the enemy, and with great loss of men from famine. On his return his generals subdued Thrace and Macedonia, north of Greece, and added them to the Persian Empire. His famous war with the Greeks arose out of the revolt of the Ionian Greek cities in Asia Minor in 501, and the burning of the city of Sardis by their Athenian allies. An expedition sent against Greece under the General Mardonius in B. C. 492 was defeated by the Thracians on land, and frustrated by a storm in the Ægean Sea. In 490 a great armament was sent by Darius under Datis and Artaphernes and then was fought the decisive battle of Marathon. Darius' proposed and long-prepared revenge upon the Greeks was baffled by a rebellion in Egypt, and he died in 485, leaving the task to his son and successor, Xerxes.

Xerxes reigned from B. C. 485 to 465, and he began with the suppression of the Egyptian revolt in 484, devoting the next four years to preparations against Greece. The grand effort was made in 480, and has been ever famous in history for the magnitude of the host of men and ships employed, for the insane display of vanity and pageantry by Xerxes, for the heroism of the resistance on the one side and the completeness of the final disaster on the other. Xerxes himself returned to Sardis, after the destruction of his fleet at Salamis, toward the end of the year 480. The defeat of his General Mardonius at Platæa in 479 ended the war in Greece, and in 478 the Persians lost their last foothold in Europe by the capture of Sestos on the Hellespont. Of Xerxes little more is known; he was assassinated in 465, and left behind him a reputation that is proverbial for Oriental vanity and the total failure of prodigious efforts.

After a short usurpation by Artabanus, the assassin of Xerxes, the Persian throne was filled by Xerxes' son, Artaxerxes I, surnamed Longimanus, who reigned B. C. 464-425. The only notable matters in his reign are a revolt in Egypt, in which the Athenians assisted the Egyptians, and Athenian defeats of the Persians by land and sea in and off Cyprus. Darius II, surnamed Nothus, son of Artaxerxes I, who reigned B. C. 424-405, was a weak personage, who was subjected to constant insurrections by his satraps, and lost Egypt in 414. His son, Artaxerxes II, surnamed Mnemon, reigned 405-359. The period of his rule was eventful. At the beginning occurred the revolt of his younger brother Cyrus, satrap in Western Asia, who marched against Babylon, and fell

in the battle of Cunaxa, B. C. 401.   He was supported by
a body of Greek mercenaries, whose retiring march to the
Black Sea over the mountains of Kurdistan has been
immortalized by Xenophon's description in his Anabasis,
and is known as the "Retreat of the Ten Thousand
Greeks."   After many conflicts between the Persians and
Greeks, the peace of Antalcidas, concluded in B. C. 387,
gave to the Persians all the Greek cities in Asia Minor.
The Persian Empire, however, was now going to decay.
Artaxerxes failed to recover revolted Egypt, and was constantly at war with tributary Princes and satraps.   The
want of cohesion in the unwieldy ill-assorted aggregate
of "peoples, nations, and languages" was being severely
felt.   Artaxerxes III, son of the former, succeeded in
B. C. 359, and reigned till 338.   He was a cruel tyrant,
who did nothing himself for his Empire; but Greek troops
and generals in his pay reconquered Egypt and other lost
territories.

In B. C. 336 the last King of the Persian Empire,
Darius III, surnamed Codomannus, succeeded to power.
His struggle with the Greeks is given in the notice of
Alexander the Great.   With the great battle in the plains
of Gaugamela, in Assyria, known as the battle of Arbela,
from a town fifty miles distant, where Darius had his headquarters before the struggle, the Persian Empire came to
an end in October, B. C. 331.   The defeat of Darius was
decisive; and in 330 he was murdered in Parthia by one
of his satraps named Bessus.   Asiatic Aryans had succumbed at last to their kinsmen of Europe, who, after
repelling Oriental assaults upon the home of a new civilization, had carried the arms of avenging ambition into Asia,
and struck a blow to the heart of the older system of polity,
culture and power.

In the doctrine of Zoroaster, pure spirit was worshiped

under the form of light.   There was no adoration of individual natural objects, but of the universe itself.   Light
is the form of the good and the true; it enables man to
exercise choice, which he can only do when he has emerged
from darkness.   Light involves its opposite—darkness,
as evil is opposite to good.   Among the Persians,
Ormuzd (called also Auramazda and Oromasdes) and
Ahriman were the two opposed principles.   Ormuzd was
the lord of the kingdom of light, or good; Ahriman, king
of the realm of darkness, or evil.   Ormuzd is represented
as to be finally conqueror in contest with Ahriman.
Ormuzd, as lord of light, created all in the world that is
beautiful and noble, the world being a kingdom of the
sun.   He is the excellent, the positive, in all natural and
spiritual existence.   Light is the body, or essence, of
Ormuzd, and hence came the worship of fire, because
Ormuzd is present in all light; but he is not represented as
being the sun or moon itself, and this shows the spiritual-
ity of the Persian belief.   In the sun or moon the Persians
worshipped only the light, which is Ormuzd.   He was
held to be the ground and center of all good existence—the
highest wisdom and knowledge—the destroyer of the ills
of the world, and the maintainer of the universe.   On the
contrary, the body of Ahriman is darkness, and the per-
petual fire was burned to banish him from the temples.
The chief end of every man's existence was held to be to
keep himself pure, and to spread this purity around him.
The sacrifices offered were the flesh of clean animals, flowers, fruits, milk, perfumes.   Such was the interesting and
spiritual form of belief held by the best of the ancient
Persians who extended their sway over so many nations
of divers faiths and degrees of civilization.   The popular
creed throughout the Empire appears to have been the

religious system of the Magians, referred to in the account of the Medes. The priests, or Magi, had great power, from the reverence of the people for them. The great objects of worship were the heavenly bodies. This national priesthood, like the Chaldæans in the Babylonian Empire, formed a caste to whom belonged all mental culture, and all knowledge of art, science and legislation. The modern term of reproach "magic," in its superstitious sense, is connected with their professions of divination and pretence at acquirement of hidden knowledge by the raising of the dead and by juggling with cups and water.

In science, art and learning the Persians developed little or nothing that was new, except in architecture. In the conquest of the Assyrians, Babylonians, Phœnicians, and Egyptians, the Persian King and nobles came into possession alike of the scientific acquirements and learning of those peoples, and of the products of the mechanical arts which are concerned in the luxuries and comforts of life. The Persians were soldiers, and not craftsmen, and had no need to be producers, when they could be purchasers, of the carpets and muslins of Babylon and Sardis, the fine linen of Egypt, and the rich variety of wares that Phœnician commerce spread throughout the Empire. In architecture they were at first pupils of the Assyrians and Babylonians. The splendid palaces and temples of Nineveh and Babylon had existed for centuries before the Persians were anything more than a hardy tribe of warriors, and it was only after the acquirement of Imperial sway that they began to erect great and elegant buildings for themselves. When that time came, the Persians showed that they could produce, by adaptation of older models, an architectural style of their own. This style was one that comes between the sombre, massive grandeur of Assyrian and Egyptian edifices and the perfect symmetry and beauty of the achievements of Greek art. Palaces and tombs, not temples, were the masterpieces of Persian building, as the outdoor worship of the sun, or of the sacred fire kindled on some lofty spot, required no gorgeous "temples made with hands" for the indwelling of the God who was adored either in spirit or in the luminous manifestations of his power in the heavens above. The ruins of the city of Persepolis, in the province of Persia, are the most famous remains of Persian architecture. Here, on a terraced platform, stood vast and splendid palaces, "with noble portals and sweeping staircases, elegant fretted work for decoration, rows of massive pillars, and sumptuous halls." The doorways are adorned with beautiful bas-reliefs, and the great double staircase leading up to the "Palace of Forty Pillars" is especially rich in sculptured human figures. The columns are beautiful in form, sixty feet in total height, with the shaft finely fluted, and the pedestal in the form of the cup and leaves of a pendent lotus. Throughout the ruins a love of ornament and display is visible. In the bas-reliefs are profuse decorations of fretwork fringes, borders of sculptured bulls and lions, and stonework of carved roses. The ruins, as a whole, present a complicated spectacle of fallen magnificence.

Ecbatana, formerly the capital of the Median Empire, called Achmetha in the book of Ezra, and supposed to be the modern Hamadon, was a very ancient city, surrounded by seven walls, each overtopping the one outside it, and surmounted by battlements painted in five different colors, the innermost two being overlaid with silver and with gold. The strong citadel inside all was used as the royal treasury. Susa, called Shushan by the Hebrew writers Daniel and Nehemiah, was a square-built city unprotected by walls, but having a strongly fortified citadel, containing a royal palace and treasury. The only remains of the place are extensive mounds, on which are found fragments of bricks and broken pottery with cuneiform inscriptions. Persepolis was one of the two burial-places of the Persian Kings, and also a royal treasury. Darius I and Xerxes greatly enlarged and adorned the place, and it retained its splendor till it was partially burned by Alexander the Great. Pasargada, the other royal place of burial, its site having still the tomb of Cyrus and a colossal bas-relief sculpture of the great founder of the monarchy, was either southeast or northeast of Persepolis, the tomb of Cyrus appearing to settle the site as at Murghab, in the northeastern position. Sardis, in western Asia Minor, once the capital of the Lydian monarchy, was the residence of the satrap of Lydia, and often occurs in history in connection with the presence of the Persian Kings. It had an almost impregnable citadel placed on a lofty precipitous rock.

Of ancient Persian literature there are scarcely any remains except the sacred books in the collection called the Zendavesta. The splendor of Persian life at court and abroad is known to us from many sources. The sculptures of Persepolis show something of the state and ceremony attendant on a Persian King. In the book of Esther we read of King Ahasuerus (who is identified as Xerxes) entertaining all "the nobles and Princes of the provinces" for "a hundred and fourscore days," of his making a feast for seven days "in the court of the garden of the King's palace" for all the people of Susa; of pillars of marble, silver curtain-rings, beds of gold and silver, pavements of marble that was red, and blue, and white, and black; of drink in vessels of gold diverse in shape and size, and "royal wine in abundance, according to the state of the King;" of garments of purple and fine linen; and of the absolute power of a Persian despot in his caprices and his wrath, with his "seven chamberlains that served in his presence," and with the lives of men and women of all ranks held in the hollow of his hand.

HISTORY OF GREECE

The part played by Greece in the great drama of Universal History makes her a connecting link between East and West, the Asiatic and the European, the enslaved and the free. Grecian history is one of the greatest phases of the question between East and West, alive in the politics of the present day, when the recovery of Constantinople for Europe is a great matter for European diplomacy.

A review of Greek history from the earliest times, including a period legendary in detail, but having a basis of fact, will enable us to judge of the place of Greece in history, and the vital connection existing between the ancient and modern worlds. The story of the war of Troy, embellished by poetry with marvels, is a legendary version of some part of the contest between East and West. After this comes the colonial period, when the Greek makes inroads on the commercial dominion of Phœnicia and a part of Asia practically becomes Europe by the settling of Greek cities on the coasts of Asia Minor. Then the powers of the East, embattled by Persia, advance in their turn. Asiatic Greece is conquered, European Greece is threatened, and at last has to fight for life on her own soil. By sea and by land Greece is triumphant, and the future of cilivilization is settled. Whatever the fate of Europe is to be she is not to be handed over to the grasp of Oriental despotism, but is to be left to struggle forward in a career uninfluenced by Eastern control. Then Greece, after reaching the highest point of culture in art and literature, is weakened by internal dissensions, and loses ground both in East and West. Her old foe, Persia, regains some of her former power on the seaboard of Asia Minor; in the West, Greek dominion is lessened by the rising power of Carthage and Rome, and the last effort of Greece for political dominion there fails when the phalanx of Pyrrhus succumbs to the Roman legion. Then the Macedonian King, Alexander the Great, reconquers the East and spreads Greek culture and an artificial Greek nationality over a large part of the world. Into this new Greek world Rome forces her way, and at once secures political supremacy. Rome, however, never supplants the tongue and culture of Greece, but largely accepts them herself until much of her own power is transferred to a Greek city, Constantinople. Hence, at the revival of learning, the products of the old Greek mind come forth to transform the Western world.

The interest of the great story of ancient Greece is really inexhaustible. It has been well said that "of all histories of which we know so much, this is the most abounding in consequences to us who now live. The true ancestors of the European nations are not those from whose blood they are sprung, but those from whom they derive the richest portion of their inheritance. The battle of Marathon, even as an event in English history, is more important than the battle of Hastings. If the issue of that day had been different, the Britons and the Saxons might still have been wandering in the woods. The Greeks are also the most remarkable people who have yet existed." This high claim is justly made on the grounds of the power and efforts that were required for them to achieve what they did for themselves and for mankind. With the exception of Christianity, they were the beginners of nearly everything of which the modern world can boast. By their own unaided exertions they, alone among the nations of the earth, emerged from barbarism. It was they who

originated political freedom and first produced an historical literature, and that a perfect one of its kind.   The same
wonderful race rose to the height of excellence in oratory,
poetry, sculpture, architecture.   They were the founders
of mathematics, of physical science, of true political
science, of the philosophy of human nature and life.   In
each of these departments of skilled and systematic
acquirement they made for themselves those first steps on
which all the rest depend.   Freedom of thought they bestowed on the world, a heritage for all ages to come.
Unfettered by pedantries or superstitions, they looked the
universe in the face, and questioned nature in that free,
bold spirit of speculation which has worked with so powerful an effect in modern Europe.   All these things the
Greeks achieved in two centuries of national existence, and
the twenty Centuries that have passed away since the
Greeks were the most gifted of the nations of the world
have added little, in comparison, to human attainments and
human development on the intellectual side of our nature.
Such, in its extreme form, is the claim advanced for the
Greeks of old.   What is certain is, that, even if they
received the rudiments of art and literature, and the germs
of political and social organization, from Eastern nations
—from Asia Minor, Egypt and Phœnicia—they impressed
a new and original character on that which they received.

The Greeks would not endure absolute monarchy;
from constitutional Kings they passed to republican institutions in an infinite variety of forms as compounded in
various degrees of democratic or oligarchic elements.   In
literature and science the Greek intellect followed no beaten
track, and acknowledged no limitary rules.   The Greeks
thought their subjects boldly out, and the novelty of a
speculation invested it in their minds with interest, and
not with criminality.   Versatile, restless, enterprising, and

self-confident, they presented the most striking contrast to the habitual quietude and submissiveness of the Orientals. Such was the people whose history we are now to deal with in a rapid summary of their rise, their fortunes, their institutions, and their political decline and fall. We pass from the Oriental history of dynasties and barren conquests to the history of a free nation exercising, through her intellectual triumphs, an enduring dominion over Europe and the whole civilized world.

The Greeks belonged to the great Aryan branch of the Caucasian race—to the stock that includes all the historic nations of Europe, the Latins, Teutons or Germans, Celts, and Slavonians, as well as the Persians and Hindoos of Asia. The Aryan migration from Asia into Europe, brought the forefathers of the Greeks into the farthest east of the three Mediterranean peninsulas. It is in the southern part of this peninsula, in the Peloponnesus, called in modern geography the Morea, and in the territory immediately north of the Peloponnesus, that we are to look, in ancient history, for the people who were strictly and truly Greeks, apart from the colonies which were settled on various parts of the islands and coasts of the east and central Mediterranean, and of the neighboring seas, the Propontis (Sea of Marmora), and the Euxine (now Black) Sea. The name Greece was almost unknown by the people whom we call Greeks, and was never used by them for their own country. It has come to us from the Romans, being really the name of a tribe in Epirus, northwest of Greece, the part of the country first known to them. The Greek writers and people called their land Hellas, the term meaning, however, all territory in which their own people, whom they called Hellenes, were settled. Hellas, therefore, included not only the Greek peninsula, but many of the islands of the Ægean Sea, and the coast settlement and colonies above referred to.   Hellas was originally the name of a district in Thessaly, in northern Greece, the people of which gradually spread over the neighboring territory, and the name was in time adopted by the other tribes.

Greece consisted, geographically, of many islands, and of a peninsula much indented by bays.   It was thus broken up into many small divisions, connected by the sea.   There were numerous mountains in ridges, off-shoots, and groups; there were plains, valleys, and small rivers.   All was diversified; there was no great feature.   The position and conformation of the country undoubtedly helped to render the Greeks the earliest civilized people in Europe, both by developing, in a life of struggle with nature on land and sea, their special and innate character, and by bringing them into contact with the older civilizations, in Egypt and Phœnicia, on the eastern shores of the Mediterranean.   The mountains that divided the country into small isolated districts had a great political importance in giving rise to many separate and independent states, the rivalries and conflicts of which favored the working out of political problems and the growth of political freedom. Greece naturally divides itself into Northern, Central and Southern.   Northern Greece extends from the northern boundary line in about 40 degrees north latitude to a line drawn from the Ambracian Gulf on the west to Thermopylæ on the east.   Central Greece stretches from this point to the isthmus of Corinth.   Southern Greece includes the Peloponnesus and adjacent islands.   Northern Greece contained two principal countries, Thessalia and Epirus, though the Greeks themselves did not regard the inhabitants of Epirus as being of real Hellenic race.   It was only in later times that Macedonia, north of Thessalia, was considered a part of Hellas.   Central Greece had nine separate states—Acarnania, Ætolia, Doris, Eastern Locris, Western Locris, Phocis, Bœotia, Attica and Megaris. The most important of these was Attica, the peninsula jutting out southeastward from Bœotia, and renowned for evermore through its possession of the city of Athens. Southern Greece, or the Peloponnesus, meaning "island of Pelops," a mythical King of Pisa, in Elis, contained seven principal states—Corinth, Achaia, Elis, Arcadia, Messenia, Argolis, and Laconia. Of these the most important was Laconia, equally famous as Attica for Athens in containing the city of Sparta, capital of the state called Lacedæmon, forming the southern part of Laconia. Islands formed a considerable and famous part of ancient Hellas. The largest of the islands on the coast was Eubœa, about ninety miles in length, noted for good pasturage and corn. On the west coast was the group known to modern geography as "the Ionian Isles." To the south lay Crete, 160 miles in length, noted for the skill of its archers. In the Ægean Sea were the two groups called the Cyclades and Sporades. The Cyclades, or "circling isles," as lying round the chief one, Delos, are clearly shown upon the map. The Sporades, or "scattered isles," lay to the east, off the southwest coast of Asia Minor, northward in the Ægean, in mid-sea, or on the Asiatic coast, were Lemnos, Scyros, Lesbos, Chios, and Samos.

Of the date when the Aryan tribes first made their way into the Greek peninsula and islands we know nothing, from the lack of records. As a prehistoric people in that region, we hear of the Pelasgi, akin to the Greeks in language and in race, so far as we can judge, and said to have known agriculture and other useful arts. The Aryans, before they set out on their migrations into Europe from their primeval home in Asia, possessed a certain degree of culture, and the Pelasgi, being Aryans, would have carried those acquirements with them to their new abodes. The Pelasgians formed the basis of the older population both in Italy and Greece, according to the evidence of language and the researches of scholars. The so-called Pelasgic, or Cyclopean, remains at Mycenæ and at Tiryns, both in Argolis, consisting of huge rude masses of stone, piled on each other in tiers, without cement, resemble the Stonehenge in the mystery existing as to their real authorship and age. As with the Pelasgi, so with the Hellenes —of the date when, and means by which, they became predominant in the land which they called Hellas, we know nothing. The safest conjecture is that the Hellenes were the flower for enterprise, ability, and courage, of some section of the Aryan immigrants into Europe, just as the Normans were the choicest specimens of Scandinavian tribes in mediæval Europe. These superior qualities gave the Hellenes possession, at an early date, of the territory in which they found established the Pelasgians, really akin in blood and language to themselves, but men whom the Hellenes, innocent of ethnology and comparative philology, called "barbarians," or men of different language to themselves. It is certain that, as far back as history or even legend can carry us, we find the land of Greece in the occupation of a branch of the Aryan family, consisting, like all other nations, of various kindred tribes.

Of these Hellenes, then, who occupied the land, and made it famous for all time, there were four chief divisions, the Dorians, Æolians, Achæans and Ionians. At a date probably as early as 1200 B. C., the Dorians are found in the northern part of Central Greece, in and about Doris, on the southern slope of Mount Œta; the Æolians mainly in Thessalia; the Achæans in the west, south and east of Peloponnesus, where the Arcadians, probably descendants of the Pelasgi, occupied the center of the territory; and the

Ionians in the northeastern Peloponnesus and in Attica.
The Dolopes, Ænianes, Magnetes, Dryopes and Danai,
are the names of tribes, Pelasgic and otherwise in origin,
occupying parts of the territory of Greece at the same early
date.

We are dealing with history, not legend, and therefore
with the mythical exploits of the so-called Heroic Age we
have nothing to do, except so far as those legends may be
considered to embody a real kernel of historical truth.
We have space here to allude only to two, and those the
most famous, of these legends—the Argonautic Expedition and the Siege of Troy.   The Argonauts are represented as a body of heroes who went in a ship called the
Argo, under the command of a prince named Jason, to
fetch from Colchis, a district on the eastern coast of the
Pontus Euxinus, a golden fleece hung on an oak tree in
the grove of Ares, Greek god of war, and guarded there
by a dragon.   After many adventures, losses and dangers,
the fleece was carried off.   The kernel of truth here is
that in very early times navigators went to the coasts of
the Euxine and there made money by trade with wild
inhospitable tribes.

The Siege of Troy or Trojan War is known to all the
civilized world from Homer's poem called the Iliad.
Paris, the son of Priam, King of Troy, is represented as
having carried off from Greece, Helen, the wife of his
entertainer, Menelaus, King of Lacedæman.   Helen was
the loveliest woman of her time, and all the Grecian princes
took up arms and sailed for Troy, under command of Agamemnon, King of Mycenæ, in Argolis.   The greatest hero
on the Greek side was Achilles, on the Trojan, Hector.
After a ten-years' siege and much slaughter Troy is taken
by a stratagem and burned, and the remaining princes and
their peoples return to Greece.   The Iliad deals only with

the events of the last year of the war, "the wrath of
Achilles" and its results, when Achilles, offended by Agamemnon, for a long time refuses to fight, and leaves the
Greeks a prey to the prowess of Hector. When Patroclus,
a friend of Achilles, is slain by the Trojan hero, the Greek
warrior takes up his spear again, slays Hector, and the
story ends, in Homer's poem, with the delivery of his body
to the sorrowing father, Priam. How much of this is
fact and how much fiction is not known. The matter long
has been, and it remains, a battleground of angry and
bewildered critics. The truth contained in the Homeric
poems, the Iliad and the Odyssey is this, that they give
a real and valuable picture of the state of civilization in
the Grecian world at the time when the poems were written or otherwise composed and preserved, which we may
take to be about 1000 years B. C.

The form of government was that of a hereditary
King, acting as priest, general, judge, and president of the
popular assembly, supported and guided by a council of
elders. The tribe or nation appears as more important
than the city, which, in historical Greece, is found to be
itself the state. We find existing a landed aristocracy, an
elementary middle class of bards, priests, prophets, sur-
geons, and skilled artisans, a class of hired workmen, and
another class of mildly-treated slaves. A state of warfare
was almost constant between some two or more of the various tribes, and military prowess was the virtue most
esteemed. There was no polygamy, and woman, and
especially the wife, was held in high regard. Care for the
young and reverence for the old were practiced. A general sobriety in drink and bodily indulgence, and a chivalrous feeling of respect for self and others, are found to
exist. The belief in various deities, whose attributes were
those of a glorified humanity, and in fatalism, was strong.

Sacrifices of slaughtered animals, and of outpoured wine, were offered to the gods.

The artistic works described were not of Grecian execution, but Phœnician chiefly. Men's chief occupations in the Homeric times were in agriculture, as ploughmen, sowers, and reapers; and in pastoral life, as cowherds, shepherds, swineherds, and goatherds. There were wagons drawn by mules, and chariots drawn by horses, as appliances of war. The weapons, defensive and offensive, were the shield, the helmet, the breastplate, and greaves, or metal leggings, from the knee to the ankle; the sword, the spear, the javelin, ax, and huge stones hurled by mighty arms at the oncoming foe. We read of coppersmiths, carpenters, and shipbuilders; eating of beef and mutton, bread and cheese; of spinning and weaving of flax and wool for clothing, carpets, coverlets, and rugs. Such is the state of things represented to us in the poems which enshrine the legend of the tale of Troy—that legend which, "set forth in the full blaze of epic poetry, exercised a powerful and imperishable influence over the Hellenic mind."

There is another class of legends concerning the earlier times of Greece, in which we find asserted the reception by the Greeks of foreign immigration from Egypt and Phœnicia. The element of truth contained in these traditions is that early Greece did receive something from Egypt, and much, perhaps, from the Phœnicians, when Greeks began to spread themselves over the isles and coasts to east and south and west of their own land, and thus came into contact with those great traders, the Phœnicians, who preceded Greece in spreading culture and commerce on the coasts of the great inland sea. What rudiments of art, or science, or religion Greece may have got from Egypt is matter of conjecture only; certain it is that Greece owed infinitely more to native genius than to any outward sources of civilization.

Grecian history may be divided into four periods. From the Dorian migration to the First Olympiad, the beginning of the authentic history of Greece, B. C. 1104-776.

From B. C. 776 to the beginning of the Persian Wars, B. C. 500.

From the beginning of the Persian Wars to the subjugation of Greece by Philip of Macedon, B. C. 500-338.

From the subjugation of Greece by Philip of Macedon to the Roman conquest, B. C. 338-146.

THE GREEK CITY-STATES

Leaving the dim twilight of legendary Greece, we come to a period when there took place those movements of tribes that resulted in settling the Hellenes in those parts of Hellas in which we find them during the times of authentic history. The chief of these movements was that known as the Dorian Migration or Return of the Heraclidæ, this latter name following the legend that the descendants of the demigod Heracles (Hercules), called Heraclidæ, after being driven from the Peloponnesus, returned thither in alliance with the Dorians. The event thus referred to is really the Conquest of the Peloponnesus by the Dorians, and the date assigned to it is B. C. 1104, about eighty years after the supposed date of the legendary Trojan War. The germ of historical truth in the matter is that, about B. C. 1100, the Dorians, under various leaders, made their way from their abodes in Central Greece into the Peloponnesus, and conquered the greater part of the peninsula after a long and severe contest with the Achæans and others who were established there. All

Peloponnesus, except Arcadia and the part called afterward Achaia, became Dorian, including the Kingdoms of Sparta, Argos, and Messenia, Elis being occupied, it is said, by Ætolian allies of the Dorians. This great movement led to other changes in the Hellenic world. Of the Achæans in the Peloponnesus some were subdued and remained in the land as an inferior class, tilling the soil as tenants under Dorian lords. Other Achæans, expelled from the south and east of the peninsula, fell back upon the northern coast, inhabited by the Ionians, whom they drove out into Attica and other parts of Central Greece. From this time the Peloponnesus was mainly Dorian, the Ionians being dominant in Central Greece and many islands of the Ægean Sea.

The Dorian conquest was succeeded by the planting of numerous colonies on the west coast of Asia Minor and in the neighboring islands of the Ægean Sea. These colonies were settled by the three races, the Æolians, Ionians and Dorians. The Æolians colonized the northwestern part, the coast of Mysia, and the island of Lesbos. Of their confederation of twelve cities in that region the chief were Methymna and Mytilene, Cyme and Smyrna, which last was, early in the historical period, taken by the Ionians. The Ionians settled in the central part, on the coast of Lydia, and in the islands of Chios and Samos. Of their powerful confederation of twelve cities the chief were Phocæa, Miletus and Ephesus. The Dorians occupied the southwest corner of Asia Minor and the adjacent islands. Of the six Dorian states the chief were the islands of Cos, Thera, and Rhodes, and the cities of Cnidus and Halicarnassus. Of all these confederations by far the most important, wealthy and powerful was the Ionian.

Gradually the Greeks spread themselves in settlements along the northern coast of the Ægean Sea and the Propontis, in Macedonia and Thrace, so that the whole Ægean became encircled with Greek colonies, and its islands were covered with them. The need of room and the temptations of commerce drew colonists even to the northern and southern shores of the Euxine Sea, the Ionians of Miletus being the founders of many settlements in that region, including the greatest of them all, Sinope. The tide of emigration flowed westward also in great strength. The coasts of Southern Italy were occupied by Dorians, Achæans, and Ionians in settlements which grew to such importancce that the region took the name of Magna Græcia, or Greater Greece. The cities of Tarentum, Croton and Sybaris became famous for their wealth, the latter giving rise to the proverbial name for a luxurious liver. On the southwestern coast of Italy was Rhegium, and further north came Pæstum, Cumæ and Neapolis, Naples. In Sicily flourishing Greek settlements abounded, the chief being Messana, Syracuse, Leontini, Catana, Gela, Selinus and Agrigentum. Farther west still a colony from Phocæa, in Asia Minor, founded the city of Massilia, known now to all the world as Marseilles. On the southern coast of the Mediterranean, westward from Egypt, the Greek colony of Cyrene became the chief town of a flourishing district called Cyrenaica. It must be understood that the establishment of the later of these colonies brings us down well within authentic historical times, and that the whole period of Greek colonization extends from about B. C. 1100 to 600, the colonies being in many cases offshoots of colonies previously established and risen to wealth and over-population. In all these movements and settlements the enterprise and ability of the Greeks made them great commercial rivals to, and, in a measure, successors of the Phœnicians.

The two leading races of Greece were the Ionians and

the Dorians, and they stand to each other in a strong contrast of character which largely affected Greek political history. These prominent points of difference run through the whole historical career of the two chief states, Ionian Athens and Dorian Sparta, and were the cause of the strong antagonism that we find so often in action between them. The Dorian was distinguished by severity, bluntness, simplicity of life, conservative ways, and oligarchic tendency in politics; the Ionian was equally marked by vivacity, excitability, refinement, love of change, taste in the arts, commercial enterprise, and attachment to democracy. The Dorian, in the best times of his history, reverenced age, ancient usage, and religion; the Ionian, at all periods of his career, loved enjoyment, novelty and enterprise.

In the kingly government of the Heroic Age—the monarch was "the first among his peers, the small rude noble of a small Hellenic town." His power was preserved by respect for his high lineage, traced to the gods in legendary song, and by the warlike prowess which he knew how, on occasion, to display. At about 900 B. C. an important change had taken place in the form of government of most of the states. Kingly rule had passed into republican, and the people were gathered into little separate states enjoying various degrees of freedom according to the aristocratic or democratic nature of the constitution, though at first these commonwealths were mostly aristocracies, in which "only men of certain families were allowed to fill public offices and to take part in the assemblies by which the city was governed." In the democracies all citizens could hold offices and speak and vote at the assemblies for legislative and executive business. In Sparta alone did the office and title of King remain.

The Greeks were, politically, parcelled and divided into

many different states, but there existed still a national bond of union. All were of Hellenic race—Ionians, Dorians, Æolians—and, in certain dialectic varieties, they had a common speech which distinguished them at once from the "barbarians" of strange and unintelligible tongue, as well as a common literature, religion, rites, temples, and festivals equally open to all. The great feeling of every Greek, however, was for his native city, and the bane of the Hellenic race was the political dissension existing between the rival parties in the same state, and the jealous antagonism rife between different states endowed with different forms of republican constitution. The only system which can bind together firmly into one great state a number of independent smaller communities of democratic government is that of Federal Union, with which modern times are familiar both in Europe and America. In Greece the principle was discovered and acted on too late to have a chance of saving her from the overwhelming power of Rome.

The Dorian conquest of the Peloponnesus had made Dorians supreme, in three states of that peninsula—Argos, Messenia and Laconia, about 1100 B. C., and in time the Spartans, or the people of Lacedæmon, properly the southern half of Laconica or Laconia, became the dominant nation in that part of Greece. Of Spartan doings and fortunes we know almost nothing until the time of the great legislator Lycurgus, whose date cannot be put later than B. C. 825. The state of things in Laconia established by the Dorian conquest was a very peculiar one. The population included, when Sparta was settled into a regular political community, three distinct classes. There were the Spartiatæ or Spartans, the Dorian conquerors residing in Sparta, the chief city of the land; the Periœci, "dwellers-round," who were old Achæan inhabitants, trib-

THE VICTORIOUS GREEKS RETURNING AFTER THE BATTLE OF SALAMIS

Painting by F. Cormon

utary to the Spartans, forming the free dwellers in the provincial towns, having no political rights or share in the government; and the Helots, who also were a part of the old Achæans, but such as had been made into slaves, to till the soil for the individual members of the ruling class or Spartiatæ, to whom they were allotted, paying a fixed rent to their masters. The Periœci paid a rent to the state for the land which they held, but were, personally, free members of the community. There was a large number of the Helots, and they were constantly treated by the Spartans with a harshness and a cruelty (extending to the frequent infliction of death) which have made the word "Helot" proverbial for a downtrodden miserable outcast. The Spartans were thus in the position of a powerful garrison in a hostile country, being surrounded, in the Periœci, by those who had no political interest in the maintenance of Spartan supremacy, and, in the Helots, by those whom fear and force alone restrained from rising to massacre their oppressors. Considering these circumstances, we can well understand the growth in the Spartan citizens of that hardness of character and hardihood of temperament for which they became a byword through all ages.

Lycurgus, of whom, as a personage, nothing certainly historical is known, was the legislator who, about 850 B. C., organized the existing elements of society into the famous Spartan constitution, though all parts of the system must not be attributed to a man whose existence has been denied by some historians. The probability is that he altered and reformed existing usages, and that the reverence of after-ages ascribed to him the promulgation and establishment of a full-grown brand-new set of institutions which must have been, in many points, of gradual growth.

The government was that of an aristocratic republic under the form of a monarchy. There were two Kings, whose powers were nominally those of high-priests, judges and leaders in war, but in the two latter capacities their functions were in time greatly restricted and almost superseded. The chief legislative and judicial, and much of the executive, power lay with the Senate, or council of twenty-eight elders. No citizen could be a member of this body until he had become sixty years of age, and the office was held for life. The popular assembly, open to every Spartan citizen over thirty years old, really handed over its powers to a board of five commissioners, officers called Ephors (meaning "overseers"), whom it annually elected. These high officials had a secret and irresponsible control over the executive power, both at home and abroad, and in military enterprises, where the Kings were the nominal leaders, the two Ephors who accompanied the army exercised much influence. The whole body of Spartan citizens was an aristocracy, as regarded their subjects, the Periœci, and amongst themselves entire political equality existed.

The object of the peculiar institutions of Sparta and of the peculiar training of Spartan citizens, ascribed to Lycurgus, was the maintenance of Spartan supremacy over the subject population. It was necessary for safety that the small body of men, said to have numbered 9,000 in the days of Lycurgus, surrounded by enemies in their own land, should be ready at all points, in complete efficiency, against every attempt at opposition or rebellion. Sparta, against the rest of Laconia, and against the outside world, if need were, had to be "all sting," and at this result the Spartan institutions aimed, with eminent success.

As every man had to be a soldier, and the citizen existed only for the state, the state took the Spartan citizen in hand at his birth, and regulated him almost from the cradle to the grave. Weakly and malformed infants were at once exposed and left to die of hunger. Up to the age of seven the male children were left to their Spartan mothers, who were not likely to treat them with overmuch indulgence, and were then taken from home and trained to the hardiest of lives by educators appointed by the state. The Spartan citizen was regarded as nothing but a tool of the state, and every means was used to give the instrument the finest temper, in a physical sense, and to bring it to the sharpest edge. The system was that of a huge public school or university in which nothing was cultivated except the body, and nothing esteemed except athletic sports and military training. The frugal fare provided was eaten in messes or companies at public tables, for which each citizen contributed a share of the expense. This training lasted till the sixtieth year of life, when the Spartan became qualified by age, if not by wisdom, for election to the Gerousia, "assembly of old men," or Senate. To bear extremes of hunger and thirst, and heat and cold, and bodily torture, and to steal without detection, under certain license and regulation, were the virtues of youthful Spartans. The girls were trained in athletic exercises like those of the youths, and all was done, that could be done, to rear a race of vigorous women, hardy in frame and stern of mood, prepared to gladly see their sons die on the battlefield for Sparta. Thus were created in the citizens unrivaled habits of obedience, self-denial, hardihood, and military aptitude; complete subjection on the part of each individual to the local public opinion, and preference of death to the abandonment of Spartan maxims; intense ambition on the part of everyone to distinguish himself within the prescribed sphere of duties, with little ambition for anything else. It is needless to say that at Sparta we look in vain for any attainments in literature and the arts; the genius of the Dorian race lay in a different direction, and the Spartan training would have stifled any abilities or aspirations that might have existed for a higher culture than that of the gymnasium and the drill-ground. Oratory was despised, and Spartan wisdom and philosophy had for their only vent the utterance of the sayings called, in their blunt brevity, laconic. The Spartan citizen was not allowed to work at any handicraft, to till the ground, or to practice commerce, and the money used was made of iron, in order to confine trading to transactions of absolute necessity. The result of all was that the Spartans became a race of well-drilled and intrepid warriors, but a nation basely distinguished in the history of Greece for the display, in other countries, of a domineering arrogance, a rapacity, and a corruption, which contributed not a little to her downfall. It must be admitted, however, that the Spartan institutions were very successful in giving her security at home and success in war abroad. Sparta was free from domestic revolutions, and the spectacle she presented of constancy to her maxims of policy gave her a great ascendency over the Hellenic mind.

The Athenians became by far the most famous, in political ascendency and in artistic and intellectual eminence, of all the Ionian race to which they belonged, and it was in Athens that democratic freedom was ultimately carried further than in any other state of Greece. Little that is certain is known of her earlier history. We hear of a King named Theseus as having, in the Thirteenth Century B. C., united the various townships of Attica into one state, making Athens the chief seat of government, and establishing, as a religious bond of union, the Panathenæa, or general festival of the great goddess Athena, the patron divinity of the land. He is also said to have divided the four original tribes of Attica into thirty clans, and each clan into thirty houses, an arrangement which tended to level distinctions and to increase the power of the mass of the people. At first, then, the Athenians were under Kings, like the other Hellenes, but about 1050 B. C. the title of King seems to have been changed to that of Archon, "ruler," though the office was still held for life, and continued in the same family. The Archon was responsible for his acts to a general assembly of the people, in which, however, the nobles had the chief influence, and down to long after the time of the first Olympiad, Athens may be regarded as an oligarchic republic, in which the supreme office, the Archonship, was confined to one family, and members of the chief court of justice, called Areopagus, "hill of Ares," from the place of its assembly at Athens, were elected only from the noble houses. In the year B. C. 776 the chronology of Grecian history becomes consecutive, and dates are reckoned by Olympiads. These were the periods of four years each which elapsed between the successive celebrations of the Olympic games in honor of the Olympian Zeus, the chief Greek deity, in the plain of Olympia in Elis. The First Olympiad began at midsummer 776 B. C., the Second Olympiad at midsummer 772 B. C., and so on—any event being dated by the statement that it occurred in a particular year of a specified Olympiad.

In B. C. 752 the office of Archon became decennial. In 714 is was thrown open to the whole body of the nobles instead of being confined to the family of the legendary King Codrus. In 683 the office became annual, and its duties were divided among nine Archons, discharging the different functions which had pertained to the King as general guardian of the rights of citizens, as high-priest, as the general-in-chief, and as judicial interpreter of the

unwritten traditionary law.   The people were still without a substantial share in the government, and popular discontent at oligarchical oppression caused a demand for a
written code of laws.   The legislator Draco, one of the
Archons, enacted laws in B. C. 621, the severity of which
has become proverbial, and which were intended, by their
rigor, to check the growth of the democracy that was
clamoring for a change.   The penalty of death assigned
to all offenses, great and small, would enable the nobles to
get rid of dangerous leaders of the people, but such a system could not, and did not, long continue.   Anarchy prevailed in Attica, caused by the various factions of the
oligarchs, the democrats, and a middle party (the "mod-
erates"), and a wise reformer was greatly needed by the
distracted community.   This reformer was found in Solon,
who was chosen as an Archon in B. C. 594, and invested by
his fellow-citizens, for the special purpose of restoring
tranquillity, with unlimited power to change the constitution.   He was already distinguished as a poet and as a
general in the war of Athens against her neighbor,
Megara.   He made it his great object to put an end to the
oppressive and excessive power of the aristocracy without
introducing anything like pure democracy.   A truly conservative reformer, he proceeded on the principle that
political power should reside mainly with those who are
possessed of means and have something to lose in case of
violent changes.   Draco's statutes were abolished, except
that involving the penalty of death for murder, and with
his celebrated disburdening ordinance for the relief of
debtors.   The precise details of this measure are uncertain; but Solon appears to have shown great skill in making arrangements fair to all parties concerned, and he thus
won the complete confidence of the people for the funda-

mental changes in the constitution of the state which he next took in hand.

Democratic character was given at the outset to the constitution of Solon by the division of the people into four classes, according to property, which was now substituted for birth as a qualification for the higher offices of state. The nine Annual Archons were continued; state offices could be filled only by citizens of the three higher classes. A council of state, or senate, called the Boule, was chosen annually by lot, to prepare measures for submission to the popular assembly, or Ecclesia, in which the citizens of the fourth or lowest class (who could hold no state office) had the right of voting. The Ecclesia included all classes of the citizens, who there legislated, elected the magistrates, decided on peace or war, and dealt with other matters sent down to it for discussion and decision by the council of state. For the courts of justice below the Areopagus, a body of 6,000 jurors, was to be annually selected by lot from the popular assembly, and the causes were tried by divisions of the whole body. Solon was also the author of many laws which regulated private life and private rights, public amusements, slavery, marriage, and other matters. He appears then to have left Attica for a prolonged period of travel abroad.

A renewal of faction followed Solon's departure, and the struggle of parties ended in the seizure of power by the "tyrant" Pisistratus, in the year 560 B. C. In this connection the word "Tyrant" means simply an absolute ruler, in the first instance as an usurper of power, and not necessarily a cruel misuser of power, as our use of the word implies. The Greek "Tyrants" were aristocratic adventurers who took advantage of their position and of special circumstances to make themselves masters of the government in their respective countries. They are found in power from about 650 to 500 B. C., and their rule was in several instances highly beneficial to the states which they governed. Being carried into power by the confidence of the people over the ruins of a defeated aristocracy, they established order for the time, and in some cases their dynasties lasted for over a Century. In the Peloponnesus a succession of such rulers governed with justice and moderation for 100 years at Sicyon. At Corinth, Periander, succeeding his father Cypselus, ruled for forty years, from B. C. 625 to 585, and under him Corinth became the leading commercial state in Greece. Polycrates, tyrant of Samos, was the most distinguished of all these rulers in the period of transition from oligarchy to democracy. He was in power in the latter half of the Sixth Century B. C., and under him Samos became a powerful and wealthy commercial state. These despots were often patrons of literature and the arts, and the oppression which was sometimes exercised was relieved by brilliant episodes of prosperity and culture.

The constitution of Solon had not yet entered into the political life of the community and made itself felt as the habit of civil existence, when Pisistratus (B. C. 560), in the lifetime of the great legislator and against his opposition, acquired supreme power. The legislation of Solon, however, virtually continued in force under the rule of the dictator, who, after being twice expelled and twice regaining his position, maintained order and held his power till his death in B. C. 527. It is to Pisistratus that the world owes the preservation in their present form of the poems of Homer, which he caused to be collected and edited in a complete written text. He was succeeded, as joint-rulers, by his sons Hippias and Hipparchus; but the severity of Hippias (after the murder of Hipparchus by the famous

Harmodius and Aristogeiton) caused his expulsion by the people, and the end of the tyranny at Athens, B. C. 510.

The government at Athens now (B. C. 507) became a pure democracy under the auspices of Cleisthenes, of the noble family of the Alcmæonidæ. He put himself at the head of the popular party and made important changes in the constitution. The public offices of power were thrown open to all the citizens, the whole people was divided into ten tribes or wards, and the senate now consisted of 500 members, fifty from each ward or tribe. Cleisthenes also introduced the peculiar institution called ostracism (from ostrakon, the voting tablet on which the name was written) by which the citizens could banish for ten years, by a majority of votes, any citizen whose removal from the state might seem desirable. This device was intended to secure a fair trial for the new constitution by checking the power of individuals when they might appear dangerous to popular liberties, and by putting a stop to quarrels between rival politicians. Athens had at last secured a republican government of the thoroughly democratic type, and from this time she began to assume a new and ever-growing importance in Greece, and was soon regarded as the chief of the Ionian states. The people, through their assembly, the Ecclesia, became thoroughly versed in public affairs, and practically, as well as legally, supreme in the state. Internal quiet was secured and new vigor was seen in the whole administration.

Under the system established by the legislation of Lycurgus, Sparta became a thoroughly military state, and in two great wars (743-723 and 685-668 B. C.) she conquered her neighbors on the west, the Messenians, reducing them to the condition of the Helots and taking full possession of their land. By this and by successful war against her northern neighbors, the people of Argos,

Sparta became the leading Dorian state of Peloponnesus. and of the Grecian world.

THE PERSIAN INVASIONS

The great Persian monarchy, founded by Cyrus and extended by Cambyses, was consolidated by Darius I, who became King of Persia in B. C. 521.   By the conquest of Lydia, Persia had become master of the Greek cities on the coast of Asia Minor, which Crœsus, King of Lydia, had subdued.   In B. C. 500 a general revolt of the Ionian cities took place, and the Athenians sent a force of ships and soldiers to help their kinsmen.   The united force of Ionians and Athenians took and burned Sardis, the capital of Lydia, in 499, but, after a six-years' struggle, the power of Darius conquered the whole sea-board of Ionia, and left Persia free to punish the audacity of the Athenians in interfering between the great Eastern Empire and her revolted subjects.   The exiled Hippias fanned the flame of the anger of Darius, and the wars between Persia and Greece began.

The first Persian expedition under Mardonius, in B. C. 492, failed, and the grand attempt was made two years later, after many of the Greek islands in the Ægean, and some of the states on the mainland, had given in their submission to the envoys of Darius, sent to demand the token of "earth and water."   The two great states, Athens and Sparta, treated the Persian despot with contemptuous defiance.

A second expedition, commanded by Datis and Artaphernes, in 490 B. C., crossed the Ægean Sea, guided by the traitor Hippias.   Naxos was sacked and Eretria was betrayed.   It seemed hardly possible that Athens could be saved.   The Persians disembarked 100,000 soldiers near Marathon, in Attica, avoiding the dangers of a voyage around the rocky coast. An appeal was made to Sparta for help, but the Spartans, because of religious scruples, would not march before the full moon. So 9,000 Athenians, with slaves to carry their shields, went forth to meet the mighty army of the Persian King. On the way they were joined by a thousand Platæans—the whole force of that city—who came to stand by their old protectors. Miltiades, formerly ruler of the Chersonese, was one of the ten Athenian generals. Five of these voted for awaiting Spartan help, while the other five, led by Miltiades, were for giving battle at once. Miltiades' counsel prevailing, under his command the Greeks charged down the hillside upon the Persians. The Greek center was driven in, but the Greek wings prevailed and then closed upon the Persian center. The Persians fled to their ships. Six thousand Persians fell, while the Greek loss was only 192. By their heroic courage the Athenians saved their country, liberty and the civilization of the world. Hippias was left on the field of battle and the Persian fleet sailed away to Asia in shame. The hero of this great victory, Miltiades, undertook to conquer the Cyclades, but failing before Paros was accused of treason and condemned to a fine which he was unable to pay. He died in prison from the effect of wounds received at Marathon.

The victory at Marathon, in which the Spartans had no part, in its immediate moral result, encouraged further resistance to a power hitherto deemed invincible, and gave Athens a position in Greece which she had never yet held. She was released from fear of the return of her tyrant Hippias, who fell in the battle: her soldiers had caused themselves to be regarded as the equals in valor of the famous Spartans: she had won a hard-fought day to be commemorated in painting, and poetry, and oratory as long as Athens should endure—a glory to be enshrined for evermore in the proud hearts of her free and patriotic people. The death of Darius in B. C. 485 prevented him from renewing the Persian attack on Greek liberties, and the task was bequeathed to his son Xerxes.

A respite of ten years was granted to Greece before she was again called on to meet Asiatic aggression. The leading men in Athens at this time were Themistocles and Aristides. Aristides, famed for his justice, was a man of the purest patriotism, and of conservative politics, which caused him to oppose the measures of Themistocles, the champion of the democracy. The sagacious Themistocles foresaw the need of a powerful navy to resist the coming onslaught of Persian power, and the Athenians, by his advice, used the income derived from the silver-mines at Laurium, a mountain in Attica, for the purpose of building and equipping a fleet of 200 triremes, war-galleys propelled by three banks of oars on each side. While the great preparations of Persia went on, Aristides was banished, by the operation of ostracism, in B. C. 483, but was recalled when the invasion took place. As the time for the great conflict drew near, a general congress of the Greek states was summoned by Athens and Sparta and held at the Isthmus of Corinth. At this national meeting Sparta was placed, by the voice of Greece, at the head of the patriotic league against Persia.

Early in the spring of B. C. 480 Xerxes set out from Sardis for Greece with a host such as the world has never seen gathered before or since. Allowing for exaggeration, it seems probable that it exceeded one million of men, including camp-followers, a throng representing more than forty different tribes or nations, in all their varieties of complexion, language, dress, and fighting equipment. This huge force passed into Europe by a double bridge of boats across the Hellespont, and marched through Thrace, Macedonia, and Thessaly, with the view of coming down from the north upon Attica. The Persian fleet, of 1,200 triremes and many transports, kept its course along the northern shore of the Ægean Sea, and then southward, in communication with the land-force.

The Greeks had resolved to make their stand at the Pass of Thermopylæ, in Eastern Locris, a narrow way between the eastern spur of Mount Œta and the marsh on the edge of the Gulf of Malis. It was now midsummer, and the Olympic games and a great Dorian festival being at hand, the Greeks had decided to solemnize these, in the hope that a small force could hold the pass against the Persians till the whole Greek army was gathered. The Spartan King, Leonidas, with 300 Spartans, and a total force of about 7,000 men, was charged with the defence of the position. For a whole day's desperate fighting the Greeks held their ground against the Persians, slaughtering them in heaps, and, to the wrath and astonishment of Xerxes, who sat on his throne and watched the conflict, they even repulsed the Persian guard, the ten thousand "Immortals," as Oriental vanity named them. During the second day the Greeks still kept firm, but on the third a traitor, named Ephialtes, of accursed memory, showed Xerxes a path across the hills by which the Greek position could be taken in the rear. Then came the end, of undying fame for Greek valor. The main Greek force retreated when the position was seen to be turned, but Leonidas and the survivors of the three hundred Spartans and seven hundred Thespians charged desperately into the thick of the Persians on the open ground to the north of the pass, and were killed to the last man, after slaying two brothers of Xerxes and many Persian nobles. Thus did the Spartans act up to their country's laws, bidding them die on the ground they occupied rather than yield, and the brave Thespians shared their fate. The history of the world has nothing finer or more famous than this act of self-devotion "for altars and hearths" against overwhelming force. The Battle of Thermopylæ took place in August, B. C. 480.

The naval force of the Greeks was posted to the north of the island of Eubœa, and fought smartly, though indecisively, against the superior Persian fleet, about the time of the fight at Thermopylæ. Themistocles was directing the operations of the Greeks, and when he learned that the pass was carried and the Persians were marching on Athens, he withdrew the Greek fleet southward to the Bay of Salamis, southwest of Attica. Resistance to the Persian force on land was hopeless, and Themistocles, as the enemy approached, put the whole population of Athens on shipboard, transported them to Salamis and to the Peloponnesus, and prepared to encounter the enemy's fleet again. The Persian army occupied and burnt Athens; and by this time the Persian fleet, after severe losses by storms off the coast of Eubœa, was face to face with the Greek ships near Salamis. The Greek fleet numbered about three hundred and fifty vessels, of which nearly two hundred belonged to Athens, to encounter three times the number on the Persian side. On the shore of Attica sat Xerxes to watch the result. The Persian ships, crowded in a narrow sea, could not maneuver, and the skill of the Greek sailors in rowing and steering made the victory, won by "ramming" the enemy, easy and complete for the inferior force. The Persians were routed with the loss of over two hundred ships. The battle of Salamis occurred in September, B. C. 480.

The Oriental vanity and overweening confidence of Xerxes were beaten down by this disaster, and the sea being closed to him, he made his way back to Persia by the land-route which had brought him to the scene of an anticipated triumph over his hereditary foes. He quitted Greece in October, leaving his general Mardonius behind him, with a force of 300,000 men, to winter in Thessaly, and prosecute the war in the spring of the next year. Early in B. C. 479 Mardonius marched through Bœotia into Attica and retook Athens, again abandoned by its inhabitants and again burnt by the Persians. He then returned into Bœotia, and in September was fought the great, final, and decisive battle of Platæa. There an army of 70,000 Greeks thoroughly defeated the Persian host. The Athenians and their allies were commanded by Aristides; and the Spartans, with their confederates, were under the Spartan Prince Pausanias, who also held the command-in-chief. The Greeks slaughtered the Persians like sheep, and stormed their camp, in which was taken a great and magnificent booty, displaying in a striking form Oriental wealth and luxury. From part of the plunder the Greeks fashioned a golden offering for the Delphian Apollo, supported by a three-headed brazen serpent, still to be seen in the Hippodrome at Constantinople. The Persian fleet had retreated, after Salamis, to Asia Minor, and in the autumn of B. C. 479 a combined naval and military force of Spartans, Athenians, and their allies encountered them on the coast of Ionia. On the very same day at Platæa, in September, the Perisans were defeated, both by land and sea, at and off Mt. Mycale opposite the island of Samos.

Thermopylæ, Salamis, Platæa, Mycale—these four glorious conflicts had decided, and for ever, the contest between Asiatic despotism and Greek freedom, the East

and the West, the old civilization and the new; between
darkness and light, between self-indulgence and self-culture, between effete Orientalism and the magnificent pos-
sibilities of a future reserved now for Athens, Europe, and
the world.   At Thermopylæ the Greeks had shown matchless, though for the moment ineffective heroism; at
Salamis they had won the mastery of the sea; at Platæa
and Mycale they had completed the destruction of the
forces of the foe that should nevermore attempt to med-
dle, uninvited, with the destinies of Europe.   To Athens,
the chief victor at Salamis—to Athens and to Themistocles, the great leader who had abandoned a city to save a
world, the chief thanks were due, and they have been amply
paid by posterity.   The immediate consequences were that
within two years from Salamis and Platæa the Persians
were driven from all the points held by them on the northern coast of the Ægean, and many of the maritime states
of Greece had ranged themselves under the general leadership of Athens.

The half-century following the battle of Salamis
(B. C. 480-430) forms the most brilliant period of
Athenian history, and one of the greatest eras in the history of the world.   About B. C. 470 Pericles, the illustrious man who gives his name to this age, began to be distinguished in Athenian politics as leader of the democratic
party.   In the constitution of Athens a wide scope was
given for the development of great political characters,
because the system not only allowed the display of a man's
powers, but summoned every man to use those powers for
the general welfare.   At the same time, no member of the
community could obtain influence unless he had the means
of satisfying the intellect, taste, and judgment, as well as
the excitable and volatile feelings, of a highly cultivated
people.   Such a man, in an eminent degree, was Pericles.

From the grandeur of his personality he has been called "the Zeus of the human Pantheon of Athens." His stature was majestic, his aspect stern, his voice sweet, his manners reserved, his courtesy princely, his self-possession imperturbable, his oratory studied, measured, overpowering in its awful splendor and effect. For over thirty years (B. C. 461-429) Pericles swayed the policy of Athens with an influence and authority derived from his personal character, and the impression which he produced on the minds of his fellow-citizens that he was a thoroughly noble man, exclusively intent upon the weal of the state, and superior to all around him in native genius and acquired knowledge.

After the fall of the sagacious, subtle, prompt, energetic, and resourceful Themistocles, banished by ostracism in B. C. 469 at the instance of the aristocratic party in Athens, the wealthy, able, and popular Cimon was at the head of affairs. In B. C. 466 he gained a great victory, both by land and sea, over the Persians, at the mouth of the river Eurymedon, in Pamphylia, on the south coast of Asia Minor. A part of the value of the plunder taken was devoted to the adornment, with splendid porticoes, groves, and gardens, of the city of Athens, which Themistocles had rebuilt and fortified. Cimon spent large sums of his own on the city, and under his direction the defences of the famous Acropolis (the citadel of Athens) were completed. He was the son of Miltiades, the victor of Marathon. In B. C. 461 the democratic party at Athens banished Cimon by the ostracism, and Pericles, who had been for some years his rival, came to the front.

To strengthen the power of the democracy Pericles had caused his partisan, Ephialtes, to bring forward a measure, which was carried, for abridging the power of the aristocratic stronghold, the court of Areopagus, by withdrawing

certain causes from its jurisdiction. This was severely
felt by the oligarchy, and henceforward, on the fall of
Cimon, the power of Pericles was paramount at Athens.
He had already gained popular favor by an enactment
that the citizens should receive from the public treasury the
price of admission to theatrical performances, and also
payment for attendance as jurors in the courts before
described, and for service as soldiers. He gave especial
attention to the strengthening of the Athenian navy, and
to him is due, in the largest measure, the adornment of
Athens with those triumphs of sculpture, those eternal
monuments of architecture, whose remains astonish posterity, and have made Grecian art famous in all after-ages
of the world.   Pericles was at once a statesman, a general,
a man of learning, and a patron of the fine arts.   He recovered for Athens (B. C. 445) the revolted island of Eubœa;
he was the friend of the great sculptor Phidias, and in his
age the great dramatic compositions of Sophocles were
presented on the Athenian stage.

The development of Athenian intellect at this time is,
indeed, astonishing, and unequaled in the history of the
world as the display of a possession belonging, in a measure, to the whole body of citizens in a state.   In the
Ecclesia, or popular assembly, the men of Athens met to
deliberate upon matters of the highest importance and of
the most varied interest.   The number of their warships,
the appointments of a stage-play, the reception of ambassadors, the erection of new temples, all these and many
other matters—intrusted in modern times to committees
and to boards composed of men of special knowledge, to
elected parliaments, to sovereigns and statesmen, to private enterprise and professional skill—were discussed and
decided, in that wonderful democracy of Athens, by those
who, with us, are privileged only to drop a voting-paper

into the ballot-box at an election. Thus taking a lively and unceasing interest in all that arouses the mind, or elevates the passions, or refines the taste; supreme arbiters of the art of the sculptor, as of the science of the lawgiver; judges and rewarders of the painter and of the poet, as of the successful negotiator or the prosperous soldier; we see at once the all-accomplished, all-versatile genius of the nation, and we behold in the same glance the effect and the cause: everything being referred to the people, the people learned to judge of everything. They had no need of formal education. Their whole life was one school. The very faults of their assembly, in its proneness to be seduced by extraordinary eloquence, aroused the emulation of the orator, and kept constantly awake the imagination of the audience. An Athenian was, by the necessity of birth, what Milton dreamt that man could only become by the labors of completest education—in peace a legislator, in war a soldier—in all times, on all occasions, acute to judge and resolute to act. All things that can inspire the thoughts or delight the hours of leisure were for the people. Theirs were the portico and the school of philosophy —theirs the theater, the gardens, and the baths; they were not, as in Sparta, the tools of the state—they were the state! Lycurgus made machines, and Solon men.

In Sparta the machine was to be wound up by the tyranny of a fixed principle; it could not dine as it pleased —it was not permitted to seek its partner save by stealth and in the dark; its children were not its own—even itself had no property in self. Sparta incorporated under the name of freedom the most grievous and the most frivolous vexations of slavery. And therefore was it that Lacedæmon flourished and decayed, bequeathing to fame men only noted for hardy valor, fanatical patriotism, and profound but dishonorable craft—attracting, indeed, the wonder of the world, but advancing no claim to its gratitude, and contributing no single addition to its intellectual stores. But in Athens the true blessing of freedom was rightly placed in the opinions and the soul. Thought was the common heritage, which every man might cultivate at his will. This unshackled liberty had its convulsions and its excesses, but, producing, as it did, unceasing emulation and unbounded competition—an incentive to every effort, a tribunal to every claim—it broke into philosophy with the one, into poetry with the other, into the energy and splendor of unexampled intelligence with all. More than four-and-twenty centuries after the establishment of the Athenian constitution, we yet behold, in the labors of the student, in the dreams of the poet, in the aspirations of the artist, and in the philosophy of the legislator, the imperishable blessings which we derive from the liberties of Athens and the institutions of Solon. The life of Athens became extinct, but her soul transfused itself, immortal and immortalizing, through the world.

Athens had first acquired ascendency by her achievements as one of the champions of Greece against Persia, and her maritime power gave her command of the islands of the Ægean, containing the allies whom she transformed by degrees into subjects. In B. C. 461 the treasury of the confederacy, to which the allies paid tribute, for the maintenance of a naval force against Persia, was transferred from Delos to Athens, and she then, with full command of the joint purse, pursued her policy of aggrandizement in the Ægean. The jealousy of Sparta was aroused, and in B. C. 457 and 456 fighting occurred in Bœotia between the forces of Sparta with her Bœotian allies, and the Athenian army. Athens, on the whole, prevailed in this contest, and most of the Bœotians and Phocians joined the Athenian confederacy. In B. C. 447 the aristocratical party in Bœotia got the upper hand, and the Athenian troops, after a defeat, were withdrawn. From time to time states subject to Athens revolted and were reduced, as Eubœa in B. C. 444 and Samos in B. C. 440. All this tended to produce the conflict between Athens and Sparta, with their respective allies ranged on their sides, known as the Peloponnesian War, which had so disastrous an effect on the fortunes of Greece.

DOWNFALL OF ATHENS

The immediate occasion of the Peloponnesian War was a quarrel between Corinth and Corcyra, the large island (now Corfu) west of Epirus. The Athenians interfered on the side of the Corcyræans, the Spartans took up the cause of Corinth; and in B. C. 431 the long-impending struggle came on. The real causes of the war were the discontent of the allies of Athens with her arbitrary treatment; the rivalry of the democratic principle in the Ionian states, headed by Athens, with the aristocratic spirit in the Dorian states, of which Sparta was the champion; and the jealousy—deep-seated, long-brooding, at last irrepressible—existing between the two great powers—Athens and Sparta—of the Greek world. The strength of the Ionians was mainly on the sea, of the Dorian states in their land forces. The allies of Athens were: Nearly all the islands of the Ægean Sea, with Corcyra and Zacynthus to the west; the Greek colonies on the shores of Thrace, Macedonia, and Asia Minor, with Platæa and a few other cities on the mainland of Greece. With Sparta were: All the Peloponnesus, except Achaia and Argos, which held aloof, Locris, Phocis, Megara, and Bœotia, the island of Leucas and a few cities in northwestern Greece. The contest lasted, with a short interval, for twenty-seven years—

from B. C. 431-404, and ended in a general weakening of Greece, and in the absolute loss of the Athenian supremacy. The gain to the world was the noble work of the historian Thucydides, in which he has described, with masterly power and fidelity, the changeful course of the struggle which he witnessed.

During the first period—ten years, from B. C. 431-421 —success was, on the whole, evenly balanced. The Athenians lost their great leader, Pericles, in B. C. 429, carried off by the plague which then ravaged Athens. The Spartan army, which the Athenians could not cope with in the open field, regularly invaded and devastated Attica; the Athenian fleet, which the Spartans could not rival, regularly made descents on the coast of Peloponnesus, and was engaged in the defense of the colonies and allies of Athens in the Ægean, and in conveying troops to assailable points on the mainland, wherever the cause of Sparta was favored. After the death of Pericles, the people of Athens gave their confidence to unworthy demagogues, of whom the most notorious was Cleon. The chief generals on the Athenian side were Demosthenes (to be carefully distinguished from the great orator of a later time) and Nicias; the chief on the Spartan side was the famous Brasidas, who had much success against the Athenian colonies on the coast of Thrace. Before the end of this period the brilliant Alcibiades began to display his powers as a statesman at Athens. In B. C. 422 a battle near Amphipolis, on the coast of Thrace, ended in the defeat of the Athenians, and the deaths of Cleon and of Brasidas, the latter an irreparable loss to Sparta. On the death of Cleon, the mild and cautious Nicias became one of the leading statesmen at Athens. His efforts for peace resulted in the conclusion of a truce between Athens and Sparta in B. C. 421.

F. A. HEULLANT, PINX

ALCIBIADES AND ASPASIA

The complaints of bad faith as to keeping the terms of truce, and the distrust and jealousy of each other felt by Sparta and Athens, soon led to a renewal of hostilities, instigated by the chief Athenian statesman, Alcibiades. Nothing decisive occurred until the Athenians, turning their attention westward, resolved to send an expedition against Syracuse, the great Dorian settlement in Sicily, with a view to the reduction of that fertile and wealthy island, and the acquirement of a great dominion in the west.   Athens, the great repeller of Eastern invasion, appeared now as the assailant of others.   She had become the mistress of the sea, and was hoping now to gain possession of such sway in the Mediterranean from end to end as might enable her, with the resources of Sicily and of Magna Græcia at command, to crush Sparta and become the foremost power of the world.

It was in the year B. C. 415 that Athens entered on this bold enterprise for conquest, which was to bring her to ruin as a state holding a great place amongst the nations of the world.   A powerful expedition sailed in the summer of that year, under the command of Alcibiades and Nicias.   With suicidal folly, the Athenians recalled, on a fanatical and probably false charge of insult to the national religion, the one man—Alcibiades—who might have made the great effort succeed.   He fled to Sparta, and by his assistance and advice there given contributed much to the downfall of his country.   The Spartans, in B. C. 414, sent a brave, politic, and skillful man named Gylippus to assume the command of the forces at Syracuse; and Nicias, a weak, overcautious, and irresolute general, was completely overmatched.   After Athenian repulses at Syracuse, the Athenians made a grand effort, and in B. C. 413 sent out a second powerful armament of ships and men, commanded by Demosthenes and Eurymedon.   It was the last throw of Athens for the Empire of the world, and it was decisively and irretrievably lost. In a grand land-fight, and in a series of sea-encounters, in which the Syracusan confederate force of galleys was headed by the Corinthian squadron, ably led, the Athenian military and naval force was utterly vanquished; Nicias and Demosthenes were taken and killed; the whole expedition, to the last ship and man, was annihilated.

Henceforward Athens could only fight, not for conquest, but for her life as a great independent state of Greece. In B. C. 412 many of her allies or subject states revolted, including the wealthy Miletus, on the coast of Asia Minor, and the islands of Chios and Rhodes. Sparta now formed an alliance with Persia, and used Eastern gold to furnish ships and mercenary soldiers against Athens. Alcibiades had quarreled with the Spartans, and, rejoining his country's side, conducted the war for Athens, in some of its closing years, with brilliant success. In B. C. 411 a revolution took place at Athens, which really amounted to a sweeping away of the old democratic constitution of Solon, and the substitution of an oligarchical faction in power.

The war was chiefly carried on in Asia Minor, where Alcibiades and others defeated the Spartans and their allies by land and sea; but in B. C. 405 the tide of success for Athens turned again, and the Athenian fleet was captured by the Spartan admiral, Lysander, at the so-called battle of Ægospotami in the Hellespont, the Athenian galleys being seized, by surprise, on the beach, where they had been carelessly left by the crews with an insufficient guard. In B. C. 404 Athens, blockaded by the Spartans both by land and sea, surrendered to Lysander after a four months' siege, and the war ended in the downfall of Athens, and the formal abolition of the great Athenian democracy, seventy-six years after the battle of Salamis, which had given to Athens her place of pride and power. Henceforward Athens was a subordinate power in Greece; Sparta was, for a time, supreme; a Spartan garrison held the Acropolis; Alcibiades, who might have restored Athens, was assassinated in Persia through the influence of Lysander; and though, after a brief period of rule by the Thirty Tyrants, set up by Lysander, a counter revolution restored in part the constitution of Solon, the political greatness of Athens had departed, and there remained for her only her undying empire in art, philosophy and literature.

Sparta, on the decline of Athenian power, became the leading state in Greece, and held that position for thirty-four years, from the capture of the Athenian fleet at Ægospotami (B. C. 405) to the defeat of the Spartan army at Leuctra by the Thebans (B. C. 371). This period was one of warfare carried on by the Spartans with the Persians in Asia Minor (B. C. 399-395); with a confederacy against Sparta, composed of Corinth, Athens, Argos, Thebes, and Thessaly (B. C. 394-387); and with Thebes, as she rose in strength under Pelopidas and Epaminondas (B. C. 378-362). During this time we find both Sparta and Athens intriguing with the old enemy, Persia, in order to obtain her aid, for Greeks against Greeks, in their international contests—so low had Greece fallen, so devoid of national spirit had she become, since the days of Salamis and Platæa. The chief incidents of the first part of the period are the defeat of the troops of the above-named confederacy at Coronea in Bœotia by the Spartan King, Agesilaus (B. C. 394); the destruction of the Spartan fleet at Cnidus in Asia Minor by a combined Persian and Athenian fleet under Conon (B. C. 394); and the disgraceful Peace of Antalcidas (the Lacedæmonian gen-

eral who arranged it), concluded in B. C. 387. By this
treaty of peace, (which Sparta brought about in order to
break up the alliance between Athens and Persia), the
Greek cities in Asia Minor, and the island of Cyprus, were
given up to the Persian King; the Athenians were to keep
only the islands of Scyros, Imbros, and Lemnos, and all
the other Greek states were to be independent both of
Athens and Sparta. Greek disunion had thus brought it
to pass that the Oriental enemy over whom, a century
before, Greece had so gloriously triumphed, was dictat-
ing terms of settlement in Greek domestic strife.

The power that the Spartans had acquired among the
Greek states was abused by them quite as much as the
Athenians had ever abused theirs; and thus they had
quickly aroused the hatred and jealousy of the other states.
Their interference in the internal affairs of Thebes led to
a war between the two states, which speedily resulted in
the defeat of Sparta, and the downfall of her supremacy.
The war between Thebes and Sparta, in the second part
of this period, began in B. C. 378. Thebes, long undis-
tinguished (since the death of the great poet Pindar, about
B. C. 440) in purely intellectual matters, had been giving
great attention to warlike training, evolutions, and tactics,
and in her two great statesmen and soldiers, Pelopidas and
Epaminondas, she had found the men to direct her newly
acquired powers to successful achievements on the field
of battle. Epaminondas is one of the greatest characters
in Grecian history. He made Thebes great, and, with his
death, Theban greatness died. A most skillful general
and a good man, he was well supported by his close friend
Pelopidas, who was in all ways worthy of the association
of their names in recounting the brief glory of Theban
history. Athens joined Thebes in the contest, and the
doings of her fleet revived the memory of her old renown,

and gave back to her for a time her supremacy over the
maritime states of Greece. In B. C. 376 the Athenian
fleet, under Chabrias, severely defeated the Lacedæmonian
off Naxos. In B. C. 371 the Spartan army invaded Bœotia, and was utterly defeated by the Thebans, under
Epaminondas and Pelopidas, at the great battle of Leuctra.
The moral influence of this victory was very great; the
name for invincibility, so long possessed by Sparta, passed
away from her, and henceforward she held but a secondary
position amongst the states of Greece. The victorious
Thebans now invaded Peloponnesus, formed an alliance
with Argos, Elis, and Arcadia, and warred against Sparta
with success enough to render Messenia independent in
B. C. 369, after she had been under Spartan dominion for
350 years. In B. C. 367 Sparta had some success against
Argos, Arcadia, and Messenia, and in B. C. 364 the Thebans lost Pelopidas, killed in action in Thessaly. In B. C.
362 Epaminondas, with a Theban army, invaded Peloponnesus, and gained his great victory at Mantinea, in
Arcadia, over the Spartan army, dying gloriously of a
wound when the battle was won. In B. C. 361 a general
peace was made, when Greece was for the time exhausted
by international fighting; the supremacy of Thebes came
to an end with the loss of Epaminondas, and as Greece
proper, politically corrupt and greatly weakened by long
warfare, declined in moral and military strength, a new
era began with the accession of Philip II to the throne
of Macedon in B. C. 359.

Macedonia, to the north of Thessaly, was not considered by the Hellenes as a part of Hellas, though some
connection in point of race undoubtedly existed. The people seem to have been composed of Thracians and Illyrians
with a large mixture of Dorian settlers amongst them.
The country had no political importance till the time of

Philip.   The line of Macedonian Kings claimed to be of Hellenic descent, and Greek civilization had been cultivated by some of them.

Philip of Macedon was a prince of great ability, educated at Thebes during the time of Theban supremacy, and trained in war by Epaminondas, on whose tactics he founded his famous invention, the "Macedonian phalanx." He was a master of the Greek language, and a diligent and acute observer, for future use, of the condition of Greece and of the character of the degenerate politicians of Athens.   His fame has been overshadowed by that of his illustrious son, but he made Macedonia the leading power in Greece, and gave Alexander the basis for his great achievements.   He was a man of unscrupulous character, determined will, prompt action, and patient purpose; and when he became King of Macedon in B. C. 359 he had formed the plan of making his country supreme in the Hellenic world, as Athens, Sparta, and Thebes had successively been.   He partly bought and partly fought his way to the end he had in view, bribing the Greek politicians to further his designs in their respective cities, and wielding the phalanx with irresistible effect, when force, instead of fraud, was the weapon to be employed.

From B. C. 356 to B. C. 346 a war called the Phocian or First Sacred War was waged between the Thebans and the Phocians, with allies on each side, the origin of the war being a dispute about a bit of ground devoted for religious reasons to lying perpetually fallow.   The end of it was that Philip of Macedon was called in to settle matters, and his ambition had secured a firm foothold in Greece.   He possessed himself by force of the Athenian cities of Amphipolis, Pydna, Potidæa, and Olynthus, being vigorously opposed throughout by the great Athenian orator and patriot, Demosthenes, who strove to rouse his countrymen against Philip's dangerous encroachments, in the famous speeches known as the Olynthiac and Philippic orations.

The political career of Demosthenes extends from about B. C. 355-322, and was marked by patriotic fervor and matchless eloquence. In B. C. 338 he brought about an alliance between Athens and Thebes, and their armies met that of Philip on the fatal field of Chæronea, in Bœotia. There Greek independence perished—sapped by Greek folly, selfishness and sloth—overthrown by the Macedonian phalanx and Philip's warlike skill. This renowned military formation consisted of men ranged sixteen deep, armed with a pike extending eighteen feet in front of the soldier when it was held ready for action, and clad in the usual defensive armor. It thus presented a weighty mass, bristling with deadly points, to the onslaught of the foe.

The battle of Chæronea, fought in B. C. 338, closes the third period of Greek history. Philip had already formed and taken some steps toward carrying out the design of subjugating the Persian Empire. This task was left for his son, Alexander, to undertake, as Philip was killed by an assassin in B. C. 336. At a congress held at Corinth, after Chæronea, Philip had been appointed, by the voice of united Greece (save Sparta), commander-in-chief of the national confederate forces against Persia, and Alexander naturally succeeded to the enterprise on becoming monarch of Macedon.

ALEXANDER'S CONQUESTS

Alexander of Macedon was one of the supremely great men who have been called "world-historical," because of the great influence which their achievements have exercised upon the world as they found it, and have continued to exert long after they had passed away.

Alexander, who was educated by Aristotle, the most intellectual man of his time, and one of the most intellectual men of all time, was not only a soldier of consummate ability, but a statesman of large and comprehensive ideas, as displayed in his schemes of commerce and of culture, and of the union of the nations into a great Empire conterminous with the known and civilized world. Of his military abilities it is enough to say that Napoleon selected Alexander as one of the seven greatest generals whose noble deeds history has handed down to us, and from the study of whose campaigns the principles of war are to be learned. He is celebrated in Grecian history as being, next to Pericles, the most liberal patron of the arts, and, in short, there was no department in which the greatness of his character, either in personal achievement or in his appreciation of others, was not shown forth for the admiration of mankind.

Alexander's exploits were all performed in the short space of thirteen years, his rule lasting from B. C. 336-323. Coming to the throne of Macedon at the age of twenty, he had to deal with enemies on every side. After putting down rebellion in his own Kingdom, he marched into Greece, overawed Thebes, which had been intriguing against him, and in a congress of Greek states at the Isthmus of Corinth, he was unanimously appointed the representative of Greece in command of the great expedition against Persia. In B. C. 335 he made a successful expedition against the barbarians of the North and West, the Thracians, Getæ, and Illyrians, and on his return found Thebes in revolt against him. He dealt with the matter in a sharp, short, and decisive way. Thebes was taken by storm; the inhabitants were all slain or sold as slaves; and all the buildings, except the temples and the house which had been that of Pindar, the poet, were razed. The capital of Bœotia had defied Alexander, and had ceased to exist. In B. C. 334 Alexander crossed the Hellespont at the head of an army of 30,000 foot-soldiers and 5,000 cavalry, and first met the foe at the river Granicus, in Mysia. The result was a Persian defeat, which cleared the way through Asia Minor, and brought the Macedonians to the borders of Syria. The second battle (B. C. 333), and a great one, was fought at Issus, in the southeast of Cilicia. There Alexander met the King of Persia himself, Darius III, and gained a complete victory over a vastly superior force. Darius fled, leaving his wife and mother prisoners in the conqueror's hands. They were treated by him with courtesy and kindness.

The Persian resistance disposed of for a time, Alexander turned southward, in order to do his work thoroughly as he proceeded, and leave behind him nothing unsubdued before his advance into the interior of Asia. He made an easy conquest of the cities of Phœnicia, except Tyre, which resisted obstinately for seven months, and was taken in the summer of B. C. 332. After taking Gaza, Alexander marched into Egypt, which received him gladly, from hatred of her Persian rulers. Early in B. C. 331 the Macedonian King handed down his name to future ages by founding, at the mouth of the western branch of the Nile, the city of Alexandria, which was destined to become so famous for commerce, wealth, literature, and learning.

In the spring of B. C. 331 Alexander set out again for Persia, where Darius had been gathering an immense force with which to make a last struggle for the Empire of the world. After traversing Phœnicia and Northern Syria, Alexander crossed the Euphrates and Tigris, and came out on the plain near the little village of Gaugamela, to the southwest of the ruins of Nineveh. The great and decisive battle that ensued with the Persians was fought in October, B. C. 331, and has been called the battle of Arbela, from a place many miles to the east, across the river Zabatus, where Alexander had his headquarters on the day after the battle.

The battle of Arbela was a miracle of heroism and generalship on the part of the victor. With a force of less than 50,000 men, Alexander met at least six times the number of warlike, well-trained troops, on ground admirably suited for the action of their formidable cavalry, almost equaling in numbers the whole Greek army. Taking his life in his hand, and risking all to win all; trusting to his own skill and to the courage and devotion of his troops; calculating on the moral effect to be produced by a suc‹ cessful assault on that part of the Persian host where Darius himself was posted; confident in the power of the phalanx, and yet taking every precaution that skill and foresight could suggest—Alexander gained for himself, by his dispositions and conduct on this great day, a place among the foremost tacticians and heroes in the history of the world. The phalanx forced its irresistible way through the Persian center, moved nearer and nearer to Darius, shook his strong nerves at last, and sent him fleeing, fast as horse could bear him, from the field of, not merely a lost battle, but a ruined Empire. A few days afterward Alexander entered Babylon, far to the south, as virtual master of the Eastern world, at the age of twenty-five. In the following year (B. C. 330) Darius was murdered by his satrap Bessus, governor of Bactria.

After receiving the surrender of the other two capitals, Susa and Persepolis, Alexander spent the year B. C. 330 in conquering the northern provinces of the Persian

THE BATTLE OF ARBELA
Painting by Giuseppe Sciutti

Empire, between the Caspian Sea and the Indus. In B. C. 329 he marched into Bactria, over the mountains now called the Hindoo Koosh, caught and slew the traitor Bessus, and advanced even beyond the river Jaxartes (the Sir or Sihon). In B. C. 328 he was engaged in the conquest of Sogdiana, between the Oxus and Jaxartes, the country of which the capital was Maracanda, the modern Samarcand. In the spring, B. C. 327, Alexander marched through what is now Afghanistan, crossed the Indus, and defeated an Indian King, Porus, on the banks of the Hydaspes. He was thus the first European sovereign to conquer the Punjaub, which he restored, in honor of a gallant resistance, to his prisoner Porus. Beyond the Hyphasis the now war-worn Macedonian soldiers declined to march, and Alexander determined to go back, by a new route, to Persia. On his way to the Indus he stormed the capital of an Indian tribe, now Mooltan, and was himself severely wounded in the assault. In B. C. 326 he sailed in a fleet, built on the spot, down the Indus, into the ocean; despatched a part of the army on board the ships, under his admiral Nearchus, by sea coastwise into the Persian Gulf, and marched himself with the rest through Gedrosia (now Beloochistan), reaching Susa early in B. C. 325.

During the rest which the troops took here, Alexander, many of his generals, and many thousands of his soldiers, married Asiatic women, and, with the same view of bringing Europe and Asia into one form of civilization, great numbers of Asiatics were enrolled in the victorious army, and trained in the European fashion. For the improvement of commerce, the Tigris and Euphrates were cleared of obstructions. From Susa, in the autumn of B. C. 325, Alexander visited Ecbatana, in Media, and thence proceeded to Babylon, which he entered again in the spring of B. C. 324. He received on the way ambassadors from almost every part of the world which he had awed and astonished by his exploits.   In the tenth year after he had crossed the Hellespont, Alexander, having won his vast dominion, entered Babylon; and, resting from his career, steadily surveyed the mass of various nations which owned his sovereignty, and revolved in his mind the great work of breathing into this huge but inert body the living spirit of Greek civilization.   In the bloom of youthful manhood, at the age of thirty-two, he paused from the fiery speed of his earlier course, and for the first time gave the nations an opportunity of offering their homage before his throne. They came from all the extremities of the earth to propitiate his anger, to celebrate his greatness, or to solicit his protection.

It was the intention of Alexander to make Babylon the capital of the Empire, as being the best means of communication between East and West; and among the great schemes which he meditated are said to have been the conquests of Arabia, of Carthage, of Italy, and of Western Europe.   For commercial and agricultural purposes he intended to explore the Caspian Sea, and to improve the irrigation of the Babylonian plain.   All his plans were made vain by his sudden death of a fever at Babylon in the summer of B. C. 323, after a career of which the bare recital is, perhaps, the best eulogium.   His wisdom as a statesman, concerned in retaining what he had subjugated as a general, was strikingly shown in the policy which he pursued toward the conquered.   With enlightened and prudent toleration, he protected them from oppression; he respected their religion, and left the civil administration to their native rulers; his great principle being to alter as little as possible the internal organization of the countries subdued by his arms.   In the plans of Alexander, the union of the East and the West was to be brought about in the amalgamation of the dominant races by intermarriage, by education, and, more than all, by the ties of commerce. In nothing, probably, is the superiority of his genius more brilliantly displayed than in his exemption from all national prejudice.

Alexander the Great left no heir to his immense Empire; but the Greek Kingdoms which arose after him in Asia and in Africa are the dynasty which he founded. The territory which he had subdued was divided amongst many successors, but the Greek culture which his arms conveyed with them endured for many generations. In Bactria (the modern Bokhara), Asia Minor, Armenia, Syria, Babylonia and above all in Egypt, Greek Kingdoms were established as centers of science, art, and learning, from which Greek light radiated into the world around them. In Europe, besides that of Macedon, a Kingdom in Thrace, stretching beyond the Danube, another in Illyria, and another in Epirus, were under the rule of Greek princes. The general knowledge of mankind was greatly increased by Alexander's conquests, which opened up the Eastern world fully to Europeans, and penetrated into countries, such as Bactria and Sogdiana, which were previously almost unknown to them. The sciences of geography and natural history thus received great additions, and so Asia made some return for the boon which she was receiving from Europe. To Alexander the world owed, amongst other great cities built by him or his successors, Alexandria in Egypt, and Antioch in Syria.

The Greek language became the tongue of all government and literature throughout many countries where the people were not Greek by birth. It was thus at the very moment that Greece began to lose her political freedom that she made, as it were, an intellectual conquest of a large part of the world. In the cities and lands which in this way became partially Hellenized, that is, imbued with Greek ideas and civilization, learning and science flourished as they had never flourished before. The Greek tongue became the common speech of the civilized world. Throughout Asia Minor, Syria, and Egypt, the Hellenic character that was thus imparted remained in full vigor down to the time of the Mahometan conquests. . . The early growth and progress of Christianity were aided by that diffusion of the Greek language and civilization.

On the death of Alexander in B. C. 323 a struggle of more than twenty years' duration ensued among his principal generals and their heirs—Perdiccas, Ptolemy, Antigonus, his son Demetrius Poliorcetes, Cassander, Seleucus, and others. At last, in B. C. 301, a great and decisive battle was fought at Ipsus, in Phrygia, between Antigonus (with his son Demetrius) and a confederacy of his rivals. The result was to distribute the provinces of Alexander's Empire in the following way: Lysimachus got nearly the whole of Asia Minor; Cassander was left in possession of Greece and Macedon; Seleucus took Syria and the East; Ptolemy had Egypt and Palestine. Of all these we can here notice only the two most important Kingdoms— that of the Ptolemies in Egypt and that of the Seleucidæ in the East.

Ptolemy I, surnamed Soter, the Preserver, who had really become King of Egypt on Alexander's death, was the founder of a line of monarchs who governed for 300 years, until the conquest of Egypt by Rome. His administration of the country was successful and enlightened, and he raised Alexandria to the highest place amongst commercial cities. It was he who founded there the colony of Jews, to whom the subsequent fame of Alexandria in philosophy and literature, as well as in politics, was largely due. He was a great patron of science, art and literature, and founded the museum and library of Alexandria. The great mathematician, Euclid, flourished in his reign. He was succeeded in B. C. 285 by his son Ptolemy II, surnamed Philadelphus, brotherly. This King is renowned as a munificent patron of science and literature, and raised to the greatest splendor the institutions founded by his father. The library of Alexandria was enriched with the treasures of ancient literary art. He was the builder of the famous lighthouse on the island of Pharos at Alexandria, which was one of the "seven wonders of the world," and he greatly promoted commerce in the Red Sea, and the caravan trade with Arabia and India. Ptolemy Philadelphus died in B. C. 247. He was succeeded by his son, Ptolemy III, surnamed Euergetes, or "benefactor," by his Egyptian subjects, because he brought back, on his return from an Eastern expedition, the statues of their gods carried off by Cambyses, and restored them to their temples in Egypt. Under the Ptolemies generally, the Egyptians were treated with mildness; the civil administration was much left to native rulers, and the ancient religion was respected; all this was in accordance with the principles of the great Alexander. The patronage of literature was continued, and the court of Ptolemy Euergetes was the resort of the most distinguished men of the day, including the celebrated grammarian and poet, Callimachus, who was chief librarian of the famous Alexandrian institution, and the founder of a great school of grammarians. Ptolemy III died in B. C. 222, leaving the Græco-Egyptian Kingdom in the highest prosperity at home, and with the widest dominion abroad, which it ever attained. Under his vicious son, Ptolemy IV, surnamed Philopator (filial), who reigned till B. C. 205, the Kingdom declined in political power; but even this Ptolemy was the supporter of literature, and dedicated a temple to Homer as a divinity. Under Ptolemy V, surnamed Epiphanes (illustrious), who reigned B. C. 205-181, nearly all the foreign possessions of Egypt were permanently lost to Antiochus of Syria and others, and Roman influence in Egypt began in the form of an alliance for her protection. Under the successors of this monarch the Egyptian Kingdom gradually declined, and Roman influence increased, until, with the death of the famous Cleopatra, in B. C. 30, Egypt became a Roman province.

While the Ptolemies held sway, the city of Alexandria was not only the chief center of the commerce of the world, but the point of union for Eastern manners and tradition with Western civilization. Like Alexander the Great, the best of the Ptolemies, amidst all military enterprises, and in all civil administration, paid great regard to the spread of civilization by the furtherance of commercial intercourse and of literary and scientific research. The peculiarity of the culture which prevailed during this period at the literary capital of the world, Alexandria, was the contact and mutual reaction of the ideas of the Jew, the Egyptian, and the Greek. The intellectual friction caused hereby resulted in great mental activity, especially in mathematical science, cultivated with distinguished success by Euclid the geometrician, founder of the Alexandrian mathematical school; Apollonius, the inventor of conic sections; Hipparchus, the father of astronomy and of scientific geography; and Eratosthenes, the learned astronomer, geometrician, geographer, and grammarian. What the Pharos of Alexandria was to the ships that used her harbor, that was Alexandria herself, with her schools of learning, to a great part of the civilized world—a light shining, not into utter darkness, but so as to guide men past the shoals of error into the haven of the truth as then known and understood. The Hebrew Scriptures were translated into Greek (the Septuagint version, or version of "the seventy") by learned Jews; the great Homeric poems, the "Iliad" and the "Odyssey," were revised and critically edited by the celebrated grammarians Zenodotus, his pupil Aristophanes, and the greatest critic on antiquity, Aristarchus, whose edition of Homer has been the basis of the text to the present day.

The Syrian monarchy of the Seleucidæ began in B. C. 312, with Seleucus I, surnamed Nicator, one of Alexander's generals, and under him was extended over much of Asia Minor, including also the whole of Syria from the Mediterranean to the Euphrates, and the territory eastward from the Euphrates to the banks of the Oxus and the Indus. Seleucus I was an able and energetic monarch, and sedulously carried out the plans of Alexander the Great for the spreading of Greek civilization, establishing in nearly every province of his great Empire Greek colonies for that purpose. He died in B. C. 280, having founded the city of Antioch in Syria as the capital of his Kingdom. His successors, the dynasty known as the Seleucidæ, or "descendants of Seleucus," ruled for about two centuries. The most notable of these monarchs were named Antiochus. The third of the name, Antiochus the Great, reigned from B. C. 223 to 187, and was the monarch at whose court Hannibal, the great Carthaginian, took refuge. Antiochus invaded Greece in B. C. 192, and there came into collision with the Romans, who defeated him both by land and sea, and compelled him to yield a large part of his dominions in Asia Minor. Much of the eastern territory had been lost before this time, as well as Phœnicia, Palestine, and Western Syria, conquered by Ptolemy Philopator, King of Egypt. Antiochus Epiphanes (reigned B. C. 175-164) was the King who oppressed the Jews, and tried to introduce the worship of the Greek divinities; it was against him that the brave Maccabees rose in rebellion. The Syrian Kingdom came to an end in B. C. 65, conquered by the Romans under Pompey.

THE PERIOD OF DECLINE

The last period in the history of Greece presents a spectacle dreary and degraded, affecting and instructive. Long wars were carried on, amongst different successors of Alexander, in contention for the sovereignty of the Greek states. Factions and intrigues were rife in and between the different communities. From time to time great and patriotic men arise, making a struggle glorious for themselves, vain in its issue, for the restoration of political freedom and of the spirit of the olden time that could return no more. "Leagues" and confederations were formed in order to resist, if possible, by combination, and by the resources of diplomacy, the coming doom of political extinction. Greece was, last of all, brought into contact with the guile and power of Rome, her great successor in the world's history, and absorbed into her growing Empire.

An effort to free Greece from the Macedonian supremacy was headed by Athens in B. C. 323. The renowned Athenian orators, Demosthenes and Hyperides, were the political heroes of the occasion, opposed by Phocion, a man of pure character, but one who despaired of a successful rising against Antipater, ruler of Macedonia before and after Alexander the Great's death. Athens was joined by most of the states in Central and Northern Greece, and the war derives its name from the town of Lamia in Thessaly, where Antipater, after being defeated by the confederates, was besieged for some months. The war ended in B. C. 322, by Antipater's complete victory at the battle of Crannon, in Thessaly. Demosthenes ended his life by poison in the same year; Hyperides was killed by Antipater's orders; Phocion died by the hemlock at Athens in B. C. 317, on a charge of treason.

A distinguished character of this period of Greek decline was Demetrius Poliorcetes ("besieger of cities"), King of Macedonia B. C. 294-287. His life was passed in fighting with varied success, and he was driven from the throne of Macedon at last by a combination of enemies, including the famous Pyrrhus, King of Epirus. Demetrius was a man of wonderful energy, promptitude, daring, and fertility of resource, deriving his surname from the enormous machines which he caused to be constructed for the siege of Rhodes, one of his warlike enterprises. He was of service to Athens, and freed her for a time from Macedonian domination before he became himself ruler of Macedon.

Epirus, in the northwest of Greece, was inhabited by descendants of the old Pelasgians and Illyrians. The first King was Alexander, the brother of Olympias, mother of Alexander the Great. He ruled from B. C. 336 to B. C. 326. Pyrrhus became King in B. C. 295, and reigned till B. C. 272, and is renowned in history as the greatest warrior of his age. His career resembles that of Charles XII of Sweden in its warlike activity and adventurous character, and in its failure to leave any enduring result of ambitious enterprise and brilliant achievement. Pyrrhus seems, says Mommsen, to have "aimed at doing in the Western world what Alexander the Great did in the East; but while Alexander's work outlived him, Pyrrhus witnessed with his own eyes the wreck of all his plans." According to the great historian of Rome, Dr. Arnold, Pyrrhus aimed at foreign conquest as a means of establishing his supremacy over Greece itself.

He hoped that after being victorious over the Romans he should then, passing over into Sicily, assail thence effectually the dominion of the Carthaginians in Africa, and return home to Epirus with an irresistible force of subject-allies, to expel Antigonus from Thessaly and Bœotia, and, making himself master of Macedonia, to reign over Greece and the world, as became the kinsman of Alexander and the descendant (as he claimed to be) of Achilles.

This affable, generous, daring, and popular prince fought with great bravery at the decisive battle of Ipsus in B. C. 301. He had been driven by his subjects from Epirus; but, assisted with a fleet and army by Ptolemy I of Egypt, returned thither and began his actual reign in B. C. 295. His first efforts were turned against Macedonia; but, after much fighting, he lost his hold there in B. C. 286. It was in B. C. 280 that he began his great enterprise by crossing over into Italy, to aid the Tarentines against the Romans. In his first campaign he defeated the Romans in the battle of Heraclea in Lucania. The skill of Pyrrhus was aided by a force of armored elephants and by the Macedonian formation of the phalanx, both novelties in war to the Romans.

In the second campaign (B. C. 279) Pyrrhus gained a second dearly-bought victory over the Romans at Asculum in Apulia, but there was no decisive result, and in B. C. 278 he crossed over into Sicily, to help the Greeks there against the Carthaginians. At first he was successful, and defeated the Carthaginians, taking the town of Eryx; but he failed in other operations, and returned to Italy in B. C. 276, again to assist the Tarentines against the Romans. In B. C. 275 his career in Italy was closed by a great defeat inflicted by the Romans at the battle of Beneventum in Samnium, and Pyrrhus returned to Epirus

with the remnant of his army. In B. C. 273 he invaded
Macedonia with such success as to become King, and his
restless spirit then drove him to war in Peloponnesus. He
was repulsed in an attack on Sparta, and, after entering
the city of Argos to assist one of its factions, was knocked
from his horse, stunned by a heavy tile hurled from a
house-top by a woman's hand, and killed by the soldiers
of the other party. Thus died Pyrrhus, in the forty-sixth
year of his age and the twenty-third of his reign, a man
coming nearer than any other in the olden time to the
character of one of the chivalrous fighters of the Middle
Ages—a Cœur de Lion, and something more—a man of
the highest military skill, capable of conceiving great
enterprises, but without the steady resolution and the practical wisdom to bring them to a successful issue.

An interesting occurrence of the time was an invasion
of Greece by the Gauls, in B. C. 280. After penetrating
through Macedonia and Thessaly, they were defeated under their leader Brennus (to be carefully distinguished
from the captor of Rome a century earlier), near Delphi,
in Phocis. Some of the Gauls in this irruption made their
way into Asia Minor, and ultimately gave their name to
the province called Galatia, adopting the Greek customs
and religion, but keeping their own language.

In B. C. 284 Ætolia, a large territory in the west of
Central Greece—many of the tribes of which were barbarians (i.e. did not speak Greek) at the time of the
Peloponnesian war—formed against the Macedonian
monarchy a powerful league, which included Acarnania,
Locris, and part of Thessaly, and had many allies in
Peloponnesus. This and other such federal unions of different states had for their object the restoration and maintenance of Greek independence, the control of questions of
peace and war being left to certain high officials and a com-

mittee appointed by the different states.   They were serv-
iceable for a time against Macedonia, but all succumbed at
last to the power of Rome.   Most of Greece was included
in one or other of these confederacies, while Macedonia
in the North was ever striving to recover and to maintain
her influence, and Sparta in the South kept her usual position of sullen isolation.

The Achæan League was founded, in its new form,
in B. C. 280, consisting of the towns in Achæa, and afterward including Sicyon, Corinth, Athens, and many other
Greek cities, so that it became the chief political power in
Greece.   In B. C. 245 the able and patriotic Aratus (sometimes called the "last of the Greeks"), became general or
head of the league, and much extended its influence, being
especially skillful in diplomacy.   Philopœmen, an Arca-
dian, was another distinguished man of this period, and
became general of the league in B. C. 208, and again in
B. C. 201 and B. C. 192.   He was successful in battle
against the Spartans when they made war on the League,
and in B. C. 188 took Sparta, leveled the fortifications,
and abolished the institutions of Lycurgus, introducing in
their stead the Achæan laws. He died in B. C. 182, a great
man, worthy of a better age and of a better fate, having
been taken in battle by the revolted Messenians, and poisoned in prison.

In B. C. 244 Agis IV, one of the associate Kings of
Sparta, tried to reform the state by a revival of the decayed
institutions of Lycurgus, Sparta having fallen away into
luxury and vice, which had sapped national and social
strength.   His colleague, Leonidas II, assassinated him by
command of the Ephors, to please the corrupt Spartan
aristocracy.   Cleomenes III was King of Sparta from B.
C. 236-222, and his period of rule throws a last gleam of
olden glory over the gloom of his country's inevitable

decay. He was a Spartan of the olden type, modified by the age in which he lived, and strove with great energy and temporary success to regenerate his country. He was successful in war against the Achæan League, and in B. C. 226 effected a revolution at home. He overthrew the Ephors, and restored the ancient constitution on a new and wider basis by admitting to Spartan citizenship many of the Periœci, while he enforced the regulations of Lycurgus bearing on simplicity of life and manners. His power was ended by an alliance between his old enemy, the Achæan League, and the Macedonians, whose united forces completely defeated him at the battle of Sellasia, in Laconia, B. C. 222. He fled to Egypt, and died there by his own hand in B. C. 220. With him the day of Sparta was done as a free state, and she sank into insignificance, forced at last to join the Achæan League in B. C. 188, by Philopœmen.

Macedon was brought into collision with the growing power of republican Rome during the reign of King Philip V, B. C. 220-178. He was an able monarch, skilled in war, but was totally defeated by the Roman general Flamininus, at the battle of Cynoscephalæ, in Thessaly, in B. C. 197. In the following year, by authority of Rome, Greece was declared free and independent by a herald at the Isthmian Games, which were celebrated at Corinth. The power of Macedon thus virtually came to an end, but, as regarded the Greeks, this proclamation was really a transfer of supremacy from Macedon to Rome, and henceforward Rome constantly interfered in Greek affairs. Domestic faction helped Roman intrigues, ambition and arms, and the battle of Pydna, in Macedonia, gained by the Romans in B. C. 168 over Perseus, the last King of Macedon, formally ended the dominion established by Philip

II nearly two centuries before. Macedonia was made a Roman province in B. C. 147.

The Achæan League had gradually declined in power, and in B. C. 150 war with Rome began, as a last effort on behalf of Greece. It ended in the defeat of the forces of the League by the Roman general Mummius, under the walls of Corinth, B. C. 146. The city was taken, plundered, and burned to the ground; the Achæan League was formally dissolved, and Greece was made into a Roman province under the name of Achaia in B. C. 146. Amongst others, the city of Athens was allowed to retain a kind of freedom, and she became, along with Alexandria, a university town of the civilized world, in which students of art, philosophy, and literature found the best models and the best instruction, and were inspired by memorials of the past in a land that was politically dead, but was living with an imperishable life in all that pertains to the highest forms of intellectual culture.

GREEK COLONIES

By the peace of Antalcidas, concluded in B. C. 387, the Greek cities in Asia Minor were ceded to Persia, and on the fall of the Persian Empire they were incorporated with Alexander's, and followed the fortunes of some of the Kingdoms formed out of the fragments of his vast dominion. Cyprus and much of the south coast of Asia Minor came under the Ptolemies of Egypt; nearly all the west coast was governed by the Seleucidæ of the Syrian Kingdom; the coast opposite to Lesbos became in B. C. 280 the independent Kingdom of Pergamus, lasting till B. C. 133, when its King, Attalus III, bequeathed his territory to the Romans. Pergamus was a splendid city, with a library and school of literature rivaling those of Alexandria, and interesting in the history of books for the invention of parchment as a writing material, the prepared skin of sheep and goats there introduced being called by the Romans Charta Pergamena, or paper of Pergamus, whence (through the French parchemin) our word is derived. Smyrna is remarkable as the only great city on the west coast of Asia Minor which has survived to the present day, where it remains the greatest commercial town of that quarter of the Mediterranean. The ancient city was abandoned and a new one founded near it on the present site by Antigonus, one of Alexander's generals. It has a splendid harbor, and soon attained great prosperity, which it kept through the Roman times, being famous also as one of the "seven churches of Asia," addressed by St. John in the Apocalypse, and as the scene of the martyrdom of Polycarp, its bishop. Ephesus, chief of the Ionian cities, was celebrated for its temple of Artemis (Diana), built in the Sixth Century B. C., and burnt down by the incendiary Herostratus on the night on which Alexander the Great was born, B. C. 356. It was splendidly rebuilt, and was the chief ornament of the magnificent city, of which many ruins are still visible. Ephesus flourished through the time of Alexander's successors, and became under the Romans the capital of the province of Asia, and the greatest city of Asia Minor, being well known also in connection with early Christianity and St. Paul. Halicarnassus, the Dorian city in Caria, was taken by Alexander the Great and destroyed, in B. C. 334. It had a worldwide reputation through its Mausoleum (the origin of the name of all such splendid tombs), the edifice erected by Queen Artemisia II (who reigned B. C. 352-350), in honor of her husband, Mausolus. The greatest Greek sculptors of the age adorned this building by their art, and some splendid relics of it are in the British Museum.

The island of Rhodes early became a great maritime state, and founded many important colonies in Sicily, Southern Italy, and elsewhere.   The city of Rhodus (Rhodes) was built in B. C. 408, and the island, after subjection both to Sparta and to Athens, became an independent republic in B. C. 355.   After Alexander the Great's death, Rhodes was in alliance with the Greek Kingdom in Egypt (the Ptolemies), the city acquiring great fame by its successful resistance in B. C. 305 to the efforts of Demetrius Poliorcetes.   After this even the famous Colossus (one of the "seven wonders") was erected at the mouth of the harbor, but not with its legs extended across, as commonly supposed.   Greek taste would be a guarantee against an attitude so absurd and inelegant, and there is no authority for the statement.   It was a huge bronze statue of the Sun-god, 105 feet in height, and remained there for 56 years, being overthrown and shattered by an earthquake in B. C. 224.   Rhodes remained a great commercial state and maritime power till the time of the Roman emperors, but the city was completely ruined by an earthquake in A. D. 155.

In Italy Tarentum, founded in B. C. 708 by Lacedæmonian settlers, became the greatest city of Magna Græcia, and had a large commerce, war-fleet and army.   The citizens were wealthy and luxurious, and at last sought aid from Greece against Italian foes.   They were helped for a time by Pyrrhus against the Romans, but after his defeat the city of Tarentum was taken by the latter in B. C. 272, and its prosperity departed after the second Punic war, in which it revolted to Hannibal, being retaken by Rome in B. C. 207.   Croton or Crotona was a powerful commercial city, famous for the school of the philosopher Pythagoras, and, in a different way, for the possession of the greatest athlete of all Grecian history, Milo, a man

GRECIAN ACROPOLIS AT ATHENS.

of prodigious strength and activity, six times victorious in wrestling at the Olympian and as many times at the Pythian games. It destroyed the wealthy and luxurious city of Sybaris in B. C. 510, and sank itself to decay in its wars with Syracuse and with Pyrrhus. Thurii was a powerful Greek city in the same quarter, near to Sybaris, and was founded in B. C. 443 by the remains of the Sybarites and by colonists from all parts of Greece, including many from Athens, and the historian Herodotus. In the Third Century B. C. it fell under the power of Rome.

In Sicily, the Doric city of Agrigentum was very wealthy and populous, till its destruction by the Carthaginians in B. C. 405. It was here that the celebrated Phalaris was "tyrant" in the Sixth Century B. C.—the despot said to have had a brazen bull, in which he roasted his victims alive. But the main interest and importance of Greek history in Sicily are centered in the great city of Syracuse, which was founded in B. C. 734 by a colony of Corinthians and other Dorians, and extended in time from an island, Ortygia, to the mainland opposite, when it consisted of five separate quarters, each with its own fortifications. It had two fine harbors and became a very large and flourishing city. In B. C. 485, after struggles between the aristocratic and democratic parties, Syracuse came under the sovereignty of Gelon, who greatly increased its power. In 480 (the year of Thermopylæ and Salamis) he gained his great victory over the Carthaginians, who had invaded Sicily with an immense force, which was almost destroyed. The career of Syracuse was thus assured, but Gelon, a monarch of excellent character, a model "tyrant" (in the Greek sense of the word), died soon afterwards, in B. C. 478. He was succeeded by his brother, the famous Hieron or Hiero I, who reigned till B. C. 467. Under him Syracuse rose to her greatest prosperity, his chief exploit being a naval victory over the Etruscan fleet near Cumæ, in B. C. 474. Hieron was a great patron of literature, and entertained at his court the poets Æschylus and Pindar, the latter of whom has celebrated in his odes the victories won by the chariots of the Syracusan King at the Olympian contests. Hiero's brother, Thrasybulus, who succeeded, was driven out by the Syracusans for his tyranny (in the modern sense), and a democracy was established which continued for about sixty years. This ended in the triumph of Syracuse in B. C. 413, and in B. C. 405 the state fell under the absolute rule of Dionysius I (the elder), who reigned till B. C. 367.

After conquering several Sicilian cities, Dionysius turned his arms in B. C. 397 against the old enemy of Sicily, the great, commercial Carthage. In 395 his fleet was beaten and he was besieged in Syracuse, but he drove the enemy off and destroyed their fleet, after a plague had reduced their strength. In 392 peace was made between Carthage and Syracuse, and for twenty-five years Dionysius, till his death in B. C. 367, ruled Syracuse as the most powerful of Greek states in that quarter, commanding with her fleets the seas to east and west of Italy. He was a steady encourager of literature and the arts, and erected at Syracuse many fine temples and other buildings. His severe conduct and system of espionage against treachery, in the last part of his reign, have caused him to be denounced as a model of a bad despot, but he unquestionably did much for Syracuse.

His son, Dionysius II (the younger), reigned at Syracuse from B. C. 367-356, and after losing and recovering his power, again from B. C. 346-343. He was a weak and dissolute person, fond of theoretical philosophy and a friend of Plato and other teachers. He was expelled by Timoleon, who was despatched from Corinth, the mother country of Syracuse, with an expedition to relieve Sicily from her troubles of internal dissension and dread of Carthage.

In B. C. 343 Syracuse thus became again a republic, and in B. C. 339 her strength was tested by a formidable Carthaginian invasion. An army of 80,000 men landed from Africa at Lilybæum, but was defeated by Timoleon with a force of one-sixth of that number. This brilliant victory saved Sicily, and Timoleon followed it up by the expulsion of almost all the "tyrants" from the Greek cities in the island, and the establishment of democracies in their stead. Timoleon ruled as virtual head of Syracuse and these other republics till B. C. 337, when he died, greatly regretted by the people. In B. C. 317 a wealthy citizen of Syracuse, named Agathocles, put down the democracy by force and treachery, backed by money, and became master not only of Syracuse, but of much of Sicily. He was a brilliant adventurer, who warred with success against the Carthaginians, defeating their troops in Africa, and reigning till B. C. 289.

In B. C. 270, after factious times with a democracy, Hieron II, a descendant of Gelon, was chosen King, and long reigned with great advantage to his country. In B. C. 263 he made a treaty with Rome, and remained for nearly fifty years her faithful ally, being master of Southeast Sicily, which enjoyed continued peace and prosperity. Hiero helped the Romans after their disasters of the second Punic war, and died, aged ninety-two, in B. C. 216, with the reputation of a wise, just, and moderate ruler. With him ended the prosperity and the freedom of Syracuse.

His young and foolish grandson, Hieronymus, succeeding to his power, joined Carthage against Rome, and the city of Syracuse was taken after the famous siege of two years' duration by the Romans under Marcellus, B. C. 212.   It was on this occasion that Archimedes, the most famous of ancient mathematicians, exerted his inventive mechanical genius in defense of his native city.   His intellectual powers were of the best kind, combining originality, clearness of thought, and the gift of continuous and concentrated application.   His killing by the Roman soldier, ignorant of his illustrious personality and irritated at the indifference of the philosopher to the drawn sword which threatened him, is well known.   Syracuse then became a town of the Roman province of Sicily, and with her fall ends the history of Greek independence in the central Mediterranean.

GRECIAN CIVILIZATION

The importance of a nation is not to be measured by its duration as an independent power amongst the peoples of the world, but by what was effected in it for true freedom and civilization within the limits of time assigned to its political and intellectual workings.   The history of the Greeks as a leading people is brief, compared with that of many other nations, for its grand period lasted only for the Century and a half between the battle of Marathon, B. C. 490, and the subjugation of Greece by Philip, of Macedon, B. C. 338; but the interest belonging to it is enduring and engrossing.   Greece gave to the world the first example of a democracy—the free, self-governing state in which every citizen not only feels a personal interest, but can always take a personal part, in the decision of questions intimately connected with his personal welfare as a member of a political community.

In Oriental empires there was only a master and his subjects: in the Greek commonwealths the people decided and acted for themselves, and were politically responsible to themselves alone for the consequences of their actions. There can be little doubt that this condition of freedom had much to do with the expansion of the human mind and with the progress made in all the arts of civilization; but beyond and apart from that stimulus to improvement, there was in the Greeks a special genius, an inborn spirit. By "the Greek spirit" we mean the moral and intellectual character belonging to the best specimens of the Greek race—the Athenians and the Ionian race in general, though the Spartans, in their courage, military ardour, and resolve to be free from outward domination, claim a high place in the Hellenic world.   In Greek life and Greek religion are seen two great features—the worship of the Beautiful and the worship of the Human.   As regards the first, the Greek mind looked at the world only on its side of beauty.   The Greek called the universe Kosmos, i. e., divine order or regularity.   Greek religion became in its essence "a devotion to the fine arts.   All man's powers were given to producing works of the imagination.   This was the inspiration of the Greeks—the arts became religion, and religion ended in the arts."   As to the Greek worship of Humanity, "the Greek had strong human feelings and sympathies.   He threw his own self into nature —humanized it—gave a human feeling to clouds, forests, rivers, seas.   Rising above the idolatry of Egypt, he worshiped human power, human beauty, human life.   In his conception of a god, he realized a beautiful human being— not merely animal beauty, but the intelligence which informs and shines through beauty.   He thus moulded into the shape of gods the visions of earth, and made a glorious human being into his divinity.   Light, under the conditions of humanity—'the sun in human limbs arrayed'— this was the central object of Greek worship.   The Hindu worshiped God as power: the Egyptian as life: the Greek as physical and intellectual beauty." Thus, with a mind at once observant and creative, from the watching of nature the imaginative Greek developed his mythology, turning natural effects and phenomena—the rising and the setting of the sun, the rude northern blast, the murmuring of the fountains, the rustle of the breeze in the foliage, the roar and movement of ocean, the quivering of the earthquakes, the outburst of the volcano—into the persons and action of the deities concerning whom the poets devised so many graceful and ingenious fictions.

In general the Greeks were distinguished, firstly, by a national pride in the unity of the Hellenic race, as shown in a common language, a common religion, and a special character, superior to that which belonged to other nations, whom they regarded as "barbarian," or non-Hellenic; secondly, by a quickness of sympathy which made them ever ready to laugh at a blunder, and to weep over a misfortune; to be indignant at injustice, and amused at knavery; to be awed by solemnity and tickled by absurdity; and thirdly, by a good taste and reasonable spirit, which made them, as a rule, avoid extremes in their thoughts, words, and actions. The grievous faults which their history shows them to have possessed were connected in a great measure with the excitability of their nature. They were very fond of power, and unscrupulous as to the means of obtaining it; their political jealousy gave rise to sedition and domestic warfare, especially in the minor states, involving unjust proscriptions and bloody revolutions, and brought about the great contest of the Peloponnesian War, which had effects so disastrous to the nation. They were often cruel, and had little regard for truth when any end was to be served by its violation. What they felt and did themselves they attributed also as feelings and actions to the deities whom they worshiped, and, having no high spiritual standard of moral goodness, they degenerated, with the loss of political freedom, into a race of quick-witted, supple, and sensual slaves. The qualities which prevented the Greeks, with all their patriotism, courage, acuteness, activity, enterprise, industry, and taste, from becoming the masters of the world, which the Romans became, were the fickleness and restlessness, and the want of patient and steady resolution, so often found in the artistic nature.

Though the gods of the Greek pantheon were beings that owed their origin to the observed phenomena of nature, they were, to the Greeks, individuals—not abstractions, nor allegories, nor symbols. The earlier divinities of Greece clearly represent natural powers. Among these were Ouranos or Uranus (a name which is simply the Greek for heaven), Ge or Gaia (the earth), Okeanos (ocean), Helios (the sun), Selene (the moon), Cronos (time). Ouranos and Gaia bore a family of gigantic sons and daughters called Titans, who were overthrown by the race of gods, of whom Zeus was the chief—this "War of the gods" being supposed to represent the victory of reason and intelligence over the rude forces of nature.

Zeus, identified with the Roman Jupiter, then appears as the head of the new divinities (the Olympic gods), who embody a spiritual meaning, retaining, however, natural elements and having a fixed relation to the powers of nature. Zeus has his lightnings and clouds. Hera, wife of Zeus, is goddess of maternity (the productive power of nature). Zeus is also the political god, the protector of morals and of hospitality. Poseidon has in his character the wildness of the sea; to him, too, is ascribed the production of the horse—no doubt from the white-crested waves that race on the main. Hades, the

god of the lower world, the abode of the shades or disem-
bodied spirits, was brother of Zeus and Poseidon—all
three being children of Cronos and Rhea (the "Great
Mother" or "Mother of the gods"), also called Cybele.
In the new order of deities Zeus is represented as in a sense
ruler of the other gods, but so that they are left free to
display their own particular characters.

Among the other chief deities were Ares, god of war;
Apollo (Phœbus), god of prophecy, music, and later
identified with the Sun-god (Helios). The worship of
Apollo was really the chief worship of the Greeks, as the
god of poetry, light, and intellectual power. He was the
discerner and declarer of truth, as god of prophecy; the
god of the song and dance, in which men show a free and
joyous soul. In Greek art, Apollo appears in the perfection of manly beauty, as in the famous statue known as
the "Apollo Belvedere" in the Vatican Palace at Rome.
Artemis is the great maiden-goddess, protectress of the
young, devoted to the chase, and later, as twin-sister of
Apollo, identified with the moon. Hermes was the herald
or ambassador of the gods, and so is represented as patron
of eloquence, prudence, shrewdness, and as the promoter
of intercourse, commerce, and wealth. Athena, the great
goddess of Athens, was the embodiment of power and wisdom, the patroness of political communities, and of the
arts that support the state, such as agriculture, weaving,
etc.; the maintainer of law and order; she also was a
maiden-goddess. Demeter was goddess of the earth and
its fruits. Aphrodite, goddess of love and beauty, was
especially worshiped in the Island of Cyprus, Hephæs-
tus, god of fire, was the inventor and patron of artistic
works in the metals. Dionysos, the youthful and handsome god of wine, was held to be the patron of the tragic

drama, which in Greece arose out of the choruses sung at his festivals.

Minor deities included the nine Muses, the three Graces, and an endless variety of Nymphs of the sea, the forests, and the streams and fountains, with monsters hideous, grotesque, and fearful. Among the Greek divinities are Hestia, goddess of the domestic hearth, whose sacred fire burned on an altar in the building called the Prytaneum (the town-hall of a Greek community), kept constantly alight, or, if extinguished, rekindled only by the burning-glass or by friction, in the primitive way, with wood. She was a maiden-goddess, the guardian-deity of hearth and home, and at her altar in the inner part of every house was the shelter and safety of our mediæval sanctuary for strangers, fugitives, and offending slaves.

The deities had temples built in their honor, with the statue of the particular god or goddess placed on a pedestal within a central holy chamber, or shrine. In front of the statue was the altar, for the presentation of free-will offerings, consisting of the fruits of the earth, or of the burnt sacrifice of animals devoted to the worship of that god or goddess. Such offerings were also made to appease the anger of the deity, or in fulfilment of a vow, or at an oracle's command, or for success in any enterprise in hand. Sprinkling of salted meal and pouring out (libation) of wine accompanied the sacrifice, at which the priest wore a wreath made of the foliage of a tree consecrated to the special deity worshipped. Dances and sacred hymns and invocations were also used, according to the nature of the service held.

Greek superstition sought, through soothsayers, the knowledge of the will and purpose of the gods, by observation of the flight and song of birds, and mainly by inspection of the healthy or disordered state of the inward parts of animals that had been slain in sacrifices. A great feature in Greek history is the belief in the revelation of the will of gods by oracles, or divine utterances, delivered at special places where special gods might be consulted through the priests attached to the spot. The great oracles of Greece were those of Apollo at Delphi, in Phocis, and of Zeus at Dodona, in Epirus. Delphi was a town on the southern slope of Mount Parnassus, near to the spot where, from between two peaked cliffs, the limpid spring of Castalia issued. The temple of Apollo was resorted to by messengers sent by cities, nations, tribes, and individuals, anxious to learn futurity, and bringing offerings as a fee for knowledge given.

The priestess of the oracle (called Pythia, from Pytho, ancient name of Delphi) sat on a tripod, over a fissure in the ground at the center of the temple. An intoxicating gas issued from the opening, and caused the priestess, when she breathed it, to rave in dark sayings, which the attendant priests wrote down in verse, and furnished, as Apollo's revelation, to the person sent in consultation. The doubtful meaning of these oracular responses has become proverbial from many instances in Grecian history. The responses at Dodona were founded on the rustling sounds caused by the wind among the foliage of holy trees.

The famous "Eleusinian Mysteries" were celebrated at the town of Eleusis, in Attica, in honor of the goddess Demeter. They were of solemn import, with a secret, awe-inspiring ceremonial, at which mysterious doctrines were taught by priests to the initiated worshippers, including that of an immortal life for the soul of man. The Dionysia at Athens was the great spring festival of Dionysos, resorted to by visitors from every quarter of the

Greek world. The whole city was given up to crowds, processions, and masquerade-attire, with gay and noisy revelry of wine and music. The interest of the modern world in these proceedings comes from the fact that at this festival there were performed, in competition for prizes, in the great theater of Dionysos, those tragedies and comedies of which we have such splendid specimens in the extant Attic literature. The Panathenæa was another famous festival at Athens, in honor of Athene-Pallas, guardian goddess of the state. In this imposing pageant Athenian maidens, bearing a sacred gold-embroidered garment (woven by them for the goddess, and called the Peplus), took a chief part.

Amongst the great special features of Greek life were the four national assemblies, composed of visitors from every part of the Hellenic world, known as the Olympic, Pythian, Nemean, and Isthmian games. These were really great religious festivals, at which the Hellenes met in a common worship, to share in a common amusement. The Olympic festival was celebated in honor of Zeus, at the Plain of Olympia, in Elis, every four years. Greek chronology begins in B. C. 776, the year in which a man of Elis, named Coræbus, gained the victory in the foot-race at these games. The Pythian festival was in Apollo's honor, held near Delphi, in the third year of each Olympiad. The Nemean, in honor of Zeus, was held every second year, in the valley of Nemea, in Argolis. The Isthmian, in honor of Poseidon, took place also every second year, at the Isthmus of Corinth. At these national contests prizes were given to the victorious competitors in running, leaping, wrestling, boxing, and chariot-racing, and also (in the Pythian, Nemean, and Isthmian) for music and poetry. The prize was a simple wreath, placed on the victor's head, and made of the special sacred plant or tree belonging to the god—at the Olympian games, of olive; at the Pythian, of bay; at the Nemean, of parsley; at the Isthmian, of pine. The honor of this wreath was great, bringing fame to the victor's native city, and renown, through sculptor and through poet, to himself.

These great gatherings of people of Hellenic race were of a nature and importance peculiar to the nation and its culture. The arts and the graces of civilization were all concerned in them, and "to the sacred ground flocked all the power, and the rank, and the wealth, and the intellect of Greece." Apart from the athletic sports of the occasion, the meeting did for Greece what, in the modern world, is done by the art exhibition, the scientific congress, the publisher, and the platform. Works of the chisel and the brush were shown, ideas exchanged, theories discussed, poems recited, and philosophers heard. The people met in one grand intellectual, social, artistic, and gymnastic assembly, which had great use in fostering a common national pride, a sound physical training, intellectual vigor and emulation, and a healthy desire for success in every kind of competition, where the reward consisted chiefly in the high opinions won from fellow-men.

The literature of Greece is the chief treasure which has come down to us from ancient times, apart from the Hebrew writings of the Old Testament and from the New Testament Books. In original power, and in richness, beauty, and force, it far surpasses that of Rome, to whose writers, indeed, their Greek predecessors served, in some styles, as incomparable models of literary art. The literature of Egypt, Assyria, Babylonia, and Phœnicia has all but perished—the Zend-Avesta, containing the sacred books of Persia, has little merit; the Hindu books called Vedas, in the old Sanskrit tongue, are wanting in general interest. The Sanskrit epic poems called the Ramayana and the Mahabharata have beautiful and striking episodes: the lyric and the proverbial poetry of the ancient Hindus show much true, tender sentiment, some beautiful descriptions of nature, and not a little depth of wisdom. The Hindu drama has much merit, but is not to be named with the productions of modern Europe and of ancient Greece. But, at their best, the literary products of the Hindu mind differ, not merely in degree, but in kind, not only in form but in essence, from those consummate works, those perfect specimens of thought and style, to which the Hellenic intellect gave birth.

The Greeks were the first people who gave their minds to thinking out a subject on a systematic plan. Greek taste—in its acute perception of true elegance and beauty, its hatred of extremes, its instinctive love of symmetry and fitness, its clear simplicity and avoidance of false ornament and color—gave to Greek thought that form and finish in expression which the best moderns can rarely attain to, and can never hope to surpass. For the thought of Greek writers it is enough to say that what they did, in some great branches, such as history, logic, and ethics, forms the foundation still for modern treatment of those topics. The language—wondrous for beauty, wealth, precision, power, and grace—which the Hellenic genius moulded into the finest instrument of human utterance that the world has ever known, enabled this most creative and original of nations to give to its conceptions the fittest garb of literary art.

The two great Homeric poems—the "Iliad" and the "Odyssey"—are, of European literature, the first in time, and of all literature the highest in merit, among compositions in epic style. They were productions of Greek intellect, dating perhaps from B. C. 800 or 900, handed down orally in public recitation, changed in transmission, and

first written, in their present form, under Pisistratus at
Athens in the Sixth Century B. C. They represent, in
language, Ionian Greek, with a slight mixture of Æolic,
as it was spoken and written about B. C. 600. In Greece
these writings were the foundation of poetical literature,
and were taught in every school; for all time since they
have been, in their full, fresh beauty, stores of poetic
imagery, models of epic art. Another school of epic
poetry began with Hesiod, born at the village of Ascra,
in Bœotia, about the middle of the Eighth Century B. C.
His poem, "Works and Days," is a didactic, homely composition, dealing with daily life, religious lore, and moral
precepts. This is in striking contrast to the Homeric
epic, whose themes are chiefly deeds of gods and heroes,
lit up with all the splendor of imaginative power.

New styles of poetry came into existence between the
Eighth and the Sixth Centuries B. C., as the Hellenic
world passed from the monarchy of the times that epic
poetry represented to the republics where democracies or
oligarchs held sway. The verse called Elegy expressed,
in ancient Greece, the poet's views on home and foreign
politics, or social life, or gave his feelings vent in joy or
grief for what was passing in the world around him. Its
chief exponents were the Ionian Tyrtæus, who lived and
wrote at Sparta about B. C. 680, urging the Spartans, in
lays of which some parts remain, to war against her foe-
men of Messene; Mimnermus, of Smyrna (B. C. 630-
600), a poet of the doleful side of elegy; Solon, the great
Athenian (B. C. 640-560), who wrote poetry, sportive
and sober, both before and after his grand political
achievement; Theognis, of Megara (flourished about B. C.
540), a writer of political and festive verse; and Simonides, of Ceos, who lived at Athens and at Syracuse (with
Hiero I) about B. C. 520-470. He wrote the elegy on

W. KRAY, PINX

SAPPHO'S REVERIE

those who fell at Marathon, and the epigrams upon the tomb of the Spartans at Thermopylæ, and was renowned for sweetness and for finish in his style. Most of the elegiac, as of the lyric and iambic, poetry of old Greece was lost in the destruction of the great library at Alexandria in the Seventh Century A. D.

Iambic verse was used for satirical poems, and those of weightier and sharper thought than elegy embodied. In this style Archilochus, of Paros (about B. C. 710-680), was noted for the bitterness and power of his invective; Solon employed it in political discussion.

The lyric poetry of old Greece—the verse expressing human passion, and, with the Greeks, invariably sung to the music of the lyre—this was one of the greatest glories of her literary art, and its almost total loss is, perhaps, the one most to be lamented in the history of letters. Of verse in this style the chief singers were Alcman, Sappho, Alcæus, Anacreon, Simonides of Ceos, and Pindar — all save the last, known to us only in mere fragments or by Roman imitations. Of these, Alcman of Sparta (about B. C. 660), wrote hymns and love-songs, marriage odes, and verse for festival processions; Sappho of Lesbos, flourished about B. C. 600, has given her name to the stanza (Sapphic) familiar to us in the odes of Horace, and has the highest fame for passion, energy, and music in her poetry; Alcæus, of Mitylene (in Lesbos), wrote about B. C. 610-580, gave his name to the well-known Alcaic stanza of Horace's odes, and wrote on war, love, drinking, politics, and gods, with free and graceful gaiety and force; Anacreon of Teos (on the Ionian coast of Asia Minor), lived about B. C. 520, and wrote with easy grace and sweetness on love, and wine, and music; Simonides of Ceos was very popular in lyric strains for hymns and dirges, and odes on victors in the games.

Pindar, who lived from about B. C. 520-440, has reached us in a fairly complete form as regards one portion of his poems—the Epinicia, or triumphal odes written for victors in the Olympian, Pythian, Nemean, and Isthmian games. This great poet was born near Thebes, trained for his art at Athens, and accepted by all Greece as a national writer of the lyric school. It is impossible for modern readers of his difficult writing to judge fairly of his merits as a poet, destitute as we are of the music which gave full effect to the words, and of his poetry in other lyric forms.

The Greek drama is regarded by many as the highest expression of Attic literary genius. The plays, very different from ours, were exhibited in immense structures open to the air, and in the daytime; and at Athens the expense of the performance was borne by some wealthy man. It was the worship of Dionysos that gave rise both to tragedy and comedy. From the hymns sung in chorus at his festivals arose the drama, or "poetry of action," when the leader of the chorus assumed the character of Dionysos, and described with gestures some exploit of the god, or enacted the part of any person engaged in the adventure which his words described. The exclamations and remarks of the chorus would, with the leader's utterances, form dialogues, and here is found the germ of what we call a play. Thespis, the father of Greek tragedy, at a festival of the year B. C. 535, introduced an independent actor, with whom the leader of the chorus held a dialogue during the pauses of the choral song.

Phrynichus (flourished about B. C. 510-480) is regarded by many as the real inventor of tragedy, from his improvements in the character of the subjects treated. Instead of the stories, often of a ludicrous turn, about Dionysos, he selected as his theme some story of the heroic

PINDAR AT THE OLYMPIAN GAMES
Painting by G. Sciutti

age of Greece, or some event of recent times. The introduction by the poet Æschylus, born B. C. 525, of a second actor, making the dialogue entirely independent of the
chorus, gave its true lasting form to the dramatic art.
Action could now be represented in completeness before
the eye, accompanied by speech, and this is the drama as
it has been in Europe ever since the age of Pericles in
Greece. The works of Thespis and of Phrynichus are
lost, and the grand Greek tragedy survives in a few of
probably the best plays of its chief authors, Æschylus,
Sophocles, and Euripides, who succeeded each other in the
order given, Sophocles being born in B. C. 495, and Euripides in B. C. 480. Æschylus had grandeur, Sophocles
grace, and Euripides subtlety and pathos. The word
tragedy means goat-song, as connected with the offering
of a goat (an animal injurious to vines) to Dionysos
before the singing of the choral hymn. From rude beginnings Attic genius thus carried the dramatic art, within
half a century's space, to the highest point of its development in ancient times.

Greek comedy (meaning the village-song, from the
hymn sung and the jokes made at the rustic festivals of
Dionysos) sprang from the same worship of the god of
wine as tragedy. The comic drama began earlier, and
was longer in arriving at perfection than the tragic. The
farces of Susarion of Megara were introduced into Attica
about B. C. 580, but the first great writer in Athenian
comedy is Cratinus (his first play appearing B. C. 454),
who used that style of drama as a means of personal satire,
and for the censure of political shortcomings. He was
followed by Eupolis (his first play appearing about B. C.
430), who is declared to have been great in elegance of
style and bitterness of satire. The works of these two
dramatists are lost, but we have the means of personally

judging of the Attic comedy in the eleven extant plays of one of its greatest authors, Aristophanes. He flourished between about B. C. 425 and 388, and his plays are marked by fanciful extravagance, delicate humor, keen satire, beautiful poetry, and gross expression—a medley of incongruous display, pervaded by a serious purpose, and directed by genius of a high and very peculiar order. Thus far the Attic comedy is known as the "Old Comedy," consisting of plays which were mainly vehicles of political satire and personal attack, and of this alone have we any complete specimens left. The "Middle Comedy," which flourished from about B. C. 390-320, dealt rather in criticism on literature and philosophy, and was succeeded by the "New Comedy," most nearly answering to the modern comic drama, or the "comedy of manners." The best writers of this school came between about B. C. 320 and 250, and of one of them, Menander, we can partly judge in the plays of his Roman imitator or translator, Terence. He is credited with great elegance of style and with abundant humor. Menander died at Athens in B. C. 291. Diphilus and Philemon, contemporary with him, were also eminent writers in his vein.

Poetry, with the Greeks, had reached perfection before real literary prose appeared at all. The first great historian, Herodotus, was born at the Dorian city of Halicarnassus, in the southwest of Asia Minor, in B. C. 484. He was, at any rate in culture and in language, an Ionian Greek, and lived at Athens for some years about B. C. 445, in the best part of the age of Pericles. His great work, in nine books, on the wars between the Greeks and Persians, contains a geographical, social, and historical account of much of the civilized world of Europe, Africa, and Asia, through which the author traveled during many years. The style of Herodotus is charming in its clearness, liveliness, and grace, and modern research has constantly confirmed what he relates on matters subject to his personal observation. Thucydides, the Athenian, one of the greatest of all historians, was born in B. C. 471, and wrote in eight books (the last unfinished) an account of much of the great Peloponnesian War, which occurred in his own time. He is renowned for the accuracy of his statements, the depth and acuteness of his philosophical remarks, and the brevity, vigor, and energy of his style. Xenophon, the Athenian, lived from about B. C. 430-350, and has a pleasing, perspicuous, and easy method of writing on historical and other subjects. His Hellenica ("Greek Events") takes up the history where Thucydides ends, and brings it down to the battle of Mantinea, B. C. 362. The Cyropædia ("training of Cyrus") is a political romance about Cyrus, founder of the Persian monarchy. Xenophon's most famous and attractive work is the Anabasis, an account in seven books of the expedition of the 10,000 Greeks in Asia, B. C. 401-399. The Memorabilia contains an account of Socrates and his teaching, exhibited in conversations between the philosopher and various hearers.

From history we pass to oratory, which reached in Pericles a height that we can judge of now only by fragments reported by Thucydides and others. The names of the great Attic orators are Antiphon, Andocides, Lysias, Isocrates, Isæus, Hypereides, Æschines, and Demosthenes, the last being esteemed one of the greatest masters of the art that men have ever heard.

The two great philosophical writers of Greece are Plato and Aristotle. Plato, the Athenian, the greatest pupil of Socrates, flourished for fifty years, from about B. C. 400-350, and is the finest artist in the handling of dialogue for philosophical discussion that has ever lived.

His style is a poetic prose of wondrous beauty, ease, and grace. Aristotle, of Stagira, in Thrace, lived from B. C. 384-322; he was the private tutor of Alexander the Great. He lived at Athens for over ten years in the last part of his life, and there wrote the extensive works which have come down to us under his name. Of all the writings of antiquity those of Aristotle have most directly and extensively influenced the thought of the modern world. He discussed nearly every subject known to mankind as the world was then. He wrote on rhetoric, ethics, politics, poetry, and natural history, and was the founder of logic, or the science of reasoning, and inventor of the syllogistic process in discussion. His system of philosophy maintained its ground in Europe until the last half of the Sixteenth Century A. D. For twenty years (B. C. 367-347, the year of Plato's death) in the early part of his life Aristotle lived at Athens, and was the greatest of the pupils of Plato.*

The Ionian, Thales of Miletus, on the southwest coast of Asia Minor, one of the "Seven Wise Men" of Greece, lived from about B. C. 630-540. He was a founder in Greece of the study of philosophy and mathematics, and is said to have visited Egypt, and to have derived thence some of his mathematical knowledge. In explaining the origin of the universe he taught that water was the element from which all things originated, and into which all would be finally resolved. Anaximander of Miletus (lived B. C. 610-547) succeeded Thales in the Ionian school of philosophy. He was a great observer of nature, and devoted to mathematics, astronomy, and geography. Pythagoras of Samos flourished about B. C. 540-510. He is credited with geometrical discoveries, undoubtedly held the doctrine of the transmigration of souls, and was a man of

*See volume of World's Great Philosophers.

great powers.   The blind belief of his followers in all that
he asserted passed into the famous proverb, "Ipse dixit"
(himself said it).   Hippocrates of Cos (lived about B. C.
460-360) was the greatest physician of ancient times.
The writings extant under his name were mostly composed
by his disciples.   He was a man of deep thought and
extensive experience, whose medical theories contain much
good sense and truth.   The famous saying, "Life is short
and Art is long," is one of his maxims.

The Ionian, Anaxagoras of Clazomenæ lived from
B. C. 500-428, and passed, from an early manhood to
middle age, thirty years at Athens as the close friend and
the instructor of Pericles, Euripides, and others.   The
great advance made by Anaxagoras in seeking out the
origin of things was this—that whereas his predecessors
referred all things to some pre-existing form of matter
(as Thales did to water), he sought the final cause in
Mind (Greek nous), Intelligence, or Thought.   For thus
advancing what was much like the idea of the One God,
Anaxagoras was accused at Athens of atheism, or refusal
of belief in any god; his offense really being, in Athenian
eyes, his denial of the Sun-god, Apollo.   He was condemned to death in B. C. 450, but, through the eloquent
intercession of Pericles, the sentence was commuted to a
fine and banishment from Athens.

Socrates,* the great Athenian philosopher, lived from
B. C. 469-399, a period covering much of the age of Pericles, and the whole time of the Peloponnesian War.   No
man of ancient times is better known to us in his person,
character, and teaching, though he left nothing written,
and what we know is derived from the affectionate regard
of his illustrious pupil, Plato, and his devoted admirer,
Xenophon.

*See volume of World's Great Philosophers.

In the later period of the history of Greece we find established four chief schools or systems of philosophy. These were the Academic, the Epicurean, the Stoic, the Peripatetic.*   The famous sect of the Cynic philosophers, which was founded at Athens about B. C. 390 by a disciple of Socrates named Antisthenes, as is also the most celebrated adherent of this unamiable system of the Cynics, Diogenes of Sinope, both fully treated in the volume World's Great Philosophers.

The four fine arts are architecture, sculpture, painting, and music.   Of Greek music we know little: of Greek painting we read much, but have no remains: of Greek architecture and sculpture we have remains, and know this—that the ancient Greeks were and are the greatest artists that have ever lived.   The buildings in which the Greek mind and taste effected their chief architectural results were the temples of the gods, and here we find three chief styles—the Doric, Ionic, and Corinthian—distinguished chiefly by the columns and their capitals.   The great examples still surviving in the Doric order are the Temple of Pæstum (near Salerno, in Italy), built in the pure Doric style about the Sixth Century B. C., and the Parthenon (i. e., "house of the virgin-goddess," Athena, from parthenos, a virgin), in the Acropolis or citadel at Athens, finished, under the rule of Pericles, in B. C. 438. It was built of pure white marble from the quarry of Mount Pentelicus, near the city, and its front was adorned with the sculptures of Phidias, of which portions are now in the British Museum.   The Parthenon is proverbial as a model of beauty, unequaled as an instance of what can be effected by the application of intellect to stone for the production of an appropriate and tasteful building.   The architects of this grand work were Ictinus and Callicrates.

* For description of which, see Vol. World's Great Philosophers.

The chief Ionic temple was that of Artemis at Ephesus, built in the Sixth Century B. C., and burned in B. C. 356. The richly-ornamented Corinthian order is illustrated in the "Monument of Lysicrates," and in the great temple of Zeus Olympius at Athens.

If there be one art in which, beyond what they achieved in other ways, this wonderful people, the ancient Greeks, attained pre-eminent perfection, it was in the noble art of sculpture—the reproduction, in the pure marble of their land, of the forms of the lower animals and man, and the representation of their gods, goddesses, and other beings imagined in their infinite and fanciful mythology. Among the Greeks the human form, as represented in sculptures still existing, reached the perfection of beauty and symmetry. Oliver Wendell Holmes says: "The Greek young men were of supreme beauty. Their close curls, their elegantly-set heads, column-like necks, straight noses, short, curled lips, firm chins, deep chests, light flanks, large muscles, small joints, were finer than anything we ever see. It may be questioned whether the human shape will ever present itself again in a race of such perfect symmetry." Such were the almost godlike forms that Greek sculptors, with unrivaled skill, set themselves to reproduce in marble for the honor of their deities and the delectation of the eyes of men. Phidias was the main agent in what was then effected for the glory of the gods and of the art to which Athens was devoted as part of her religion and her life. Within the Parthenon was Phidias' great statue of the goddess Athena, over forty feet in height, with face, neck, arms, hands, and feet of ivory, set off with painting, and her drapery constructed of small plates of pure gold. The sculptures which adorned the fabric of the Parthenon were designed by Phidias, and, in their mutilated state, display much of their original loveliness and power. On

the Acropolis were two other statues of Athena from the
hand of Phidias—one of bronze, considered his best work
by some ancient critics; the other a colossal statue, also of
bronze, called the Athena Promachos (i. e., "the cham-
pion-goddess," as defender of Athens), of which the
helmet-crest and spear-point could be discerned from far,
away at sea.   This statue represented the goddess as
holding up both spear and shield in a fighting attitude,
and was made of the spoils of Marathon.   Another renowned work of Phidias was his colossal figure of Zeus,
in the temple of the chief Olympian god in the sacred grove
of Elis (Peloponnesus).   This was composed of ivory
and gold—the face, feet, and body of ivory, the hair and
beard of pure gold, the eyes of precious flaming jewels.
The drapery was of beaten gold, enameled with figures of
animals and flowers.   The god was seated on a sculptured
throne of cedar, inlaid with gold, ivory, ebony, and jewels,
and the figure was sixty feet in height.   Upon the head
was a chaplet of olive; in the right hand an image of Nike
(the winged goddess of victory), also of ivory and gold;
in the left a polished sceptre, inlaid with several metals,
and bearing an eagle (the symbol of Zeus) on the top.
The throne, and the pedestal of the whole, were adorned
with the elaborate and beautiful sculptures of mythological
subjects.   This marvelous effort of genius was removed
to Constantinople, and perished there by fire in A. D.
475.

The sculptor and architect, Polycletus, of Sicyon, who
flourished about B. C. 452-412, was one of the greatest
artists of that great age.   He was unsurpassed in the
human figure, as Phidias was in the images of the gods.
In the temple of Hera, near Argos, was his famous statue
of the goddess, in ivory and gold, executed in rivalry of
Phidias' works.   One of the statues of Polycletus was that

of a manly youth holding a spear, and was so symmetrical that it became the standard of proportion, and was called the Canon, as being a "rule" or model of form. The Bœotian sculptor Myron, who worked about B. C. 430, was wonderful in bronze representations of animals and of the human figure in difficult and momentary attitudes. The famous "Discobolus" ("quoit-thrower") in the museums of art, is a reproduction in marble of one of Myron's figures; and his lowing Cow is celebrated in the Greek epigrams as a perfect work of the kind. In a later time than that of Phidias came Praxiteles, of Athens (about B. C. 350), famous for the human form, especially the female, in exquisite beauty and grace of execution. His greatest work was his statue of Aphrodite in her temple at Cnidus, in Caria (southwest coast of Asia Minor). Travelers went thither from all parts of the world expressly to see this masterpiece of sculptured loveliness. This also perished by fire at Constantinople in the Sixth Century A. D. Scopas of Paros (the island in the Cyclades famous for the marble used by many of these ancient sculptors) flourished about B. C. 380, and was a rival of Praxiteles in this second period of perfect Greek art. He was employed on the bas-reliefs of the Mausoleum at Halicarnassus, of which a portion is to be seen in the British Museum. A famous group of Scopas represents the destruction of the children of Niobe; a part of this work is in the gallery at Florence. Lysippus of Sicyon, in the time of Alexander the Great—worked chiefly in bronze, and made many statues of Alexander, who would allow no other artist to represent him in sculpture.

Of Greek painting we have no specimens, but they attained great excellence in the art. As in Egypt, this mode of decoration originally accompanied sculpture and architecture in the temples and statues of the gods. Among the earlier Greek painters was Micon of Athens (about B. C. 460) and Polygnotus of Thasos, who was also an Athenian citizen, and flourished at Athens from about B. C. 463-430.   His subjects were mostly Homeric, and were painted on wooden panels, afterward inserted into the walls which they adorned.   Apollodorus of Athens (flourished about B. C. 410) greatly improved the art in coloring and by knowledge of light and shade. Zeuxis of Heraclea (probably the city so named in Bithynia, on the Euxine Sea) lived about B. C. 424-400. He painted a wonderful picture of Helen of Troy for the temple of Juno at Croton, and, in realistic art, is the hero of the story about the grapes so naturally painted that the birds flew at the fruit to peck.   His rival, Parrhasius of Ephesus, who flourished about B. C. 400, and chiefly painted at Athens, brought the proportion of his figures to a perfection which all subsequent artists made their model.   He is said, in the imitative line, to have painted a curtain, apparently drawn in front of a picture, so as to deceive Zeuxis, who desired him "to draw it that he might see the picture."   Timanthes, of Sicyon, also painted at about B. C. 400, and was the artist of the celebrated picture of the Sacrifice of Iphigeneia, in which her father, Agamemnon, was painted with his face hidden in his robe. The greatest of Greek painters is said to have been Apelles, of Ionia, the friend of Alexander the Great, who would allow none other to paint his portrait.   He was especially skillful in and devoted to drawing, his diligence in which gave rise to the proverb, Nulla dies sine linea ("No day without at least a line").   He painted Alexander wielding a thunderbolt, and the famous "Aphrodite Anadyomene ("Aphrodite rising up," i. e., out of the sea-foam, according to the poets' legend as to her creation), in which the goddess was shown wringing her hair, while the falling drops made a translucent silvery veil around her. Protogenes of Caria flourished from B. C. 332 to 300, and resided chiefly at Rhodes, though he also visited Athens. He was brought into notice by Apelles, and was famous for the elaboration bestowed on his admirable pictures. Nicias of Athens worked there about B. C. 320, and was a distinguished painter in encaustic, a style in which the colors were burned into the panel by the application of heat in some form. His master Euphranor flourished at Athens about B. C. 336, and was excellent in proportion and colorings, being also a distinguished sculptor. Pausias of Sicyon (flourished about B. C. 360-330) was great at encaustic painting, and executed beautiful panel-pictures on a small scale, representing children, animals, and flowers.

In the Homeric poems there is mention of the lyre (originally a three-stringed instrument, as in Egypt), the flute, and the Pan-pipe. The father of Greek music is said to have been Terpander of Lesbos, who lived between B. C. 700 and B. C. 650. He established at Sparta the first musical school that existed in Greece. To the four-stringed lyre, as he found it, Terpander added three strings, and the music of this improved instrument became highly popular. He was succeeded by Thaletas of Crete, who also founded a musical school at Sparta, and had great influence there, derived from the power of his art over the minds of the citizens in a time of factious strife. There were musical contests at the great national festivals, and the poet Archilochus of Paros (as Terpander also did) carried off prizes for music at the Pythian games. Timotheus of Miletus (lived B. C. 446-357) was a celebrated musician, and added four strings to the lyre, making it an eleven-stringed instrument. He greatly changed instrumental music, which became highly artificial and intricate under his treatment. At Athens, in the time of Pericles, music was a necessary part of education, and ignorance of the art was held to be a disgrace. Pericles encouraged it by erecting the Odeum, a building for rehearsals of the choral music before the theatrical performances. Flute-playing became very fashionable at that epoch, and large sums were given for a single noted instrument. So elaborate, difficult, and artificial did the execution in flute-playing become, as to arouse the hostility of Aristotle against music generally. We have no materials on which to ground any judgment as to the scientific character of the Greek harmony; we can only conclude that a people so ingenious and artistic in other ways, so devoted to poetry, and having in their religious rites and social meetings so many fit occasions for the practice of the musical art, must have made great advances therein.

In the age of Pericles, at Athens, the Greek mode of life was marked by a dignified and elegant simplicity of tone. Every free citizen was one of the rulers of the state through his vote in the assembly and the law courts; and though there was an aristocracy of birth and long descent in certain families who traced their lineage back to heroic times, there was little exclusiveness in social life. An Athenian might be poor, but if he had general ability, wit, or artistic skill, he was welcome in the best houses of Athens. The only occupations worthy of a freeman were held to be agriculture, arms, gymnastics, the fine arts, and state-duties, retail trade and handicrafts being mainly in the hands of foreigners (who were heavily taxed by the state) and of slaves. The poorer citizens, who took their fees, amounting to about ten cents per day, for their discharge of public duty as jurors, looked down on the mechanic and tradesman. Almost the whole range of social pleasures was mixed up with the religion of the people. The worship consisted of the songs and dances, processions, festivals, dramatic and athletic contests, and the people in general were satisfied with the belief in the recognized deities, along with the gratifications involved in the observance of the state-religion. Moral and religious problems were left to be settled by the philosophers and the serious-minded minority who followed them.

The Athenian citizen was a very sociable person. He rose early, took a slight meal of bread and wine, and went off to make morning-calls, or to attend to public business in the assembly or the law court. A mid-day breakfast was eaten, and then came gossip in the colonnades, the gymnasia, the agora (market-place), and the studios of artists, or a stroll down to the harbor called Piræus, four miles distant, connected with Athens by the famous Long Walls built under the rule of Pericles. The principal meal of the day was a four-o'clock dinner, at which the better classes ate meat (beef, mutton, kid, or pork), fish (especially salt fish), wheaten bread, vegetables, fruit, and sweetmeats, drinking their wine mixed in various proportions with water. Hare was the favorite game, and thrushes among birds; eggs, fowls, olive-oil, and cheese were much used. The guests reclined by twos or threes on couches, using their fingers and spoons for eating, wiping their hands on pieces of dough-cake, and washing them when dinner was over. Wreaths of flowers were worn at dinner-parties, healths drunk, dancing-girls, flute-girls, jugglers, and professional jesters introduced.

The Greek dress was simple, consisting of two garments only, as a rule, for either sex—an under-garment covered by an outer flowing robe. Sandals were worn abroad, bare feet or slippers being the use at home. The poorer class lived on the fruits of the country—figs, grapes, and olives—cheese, garlic, and barleybread, with occasional meat from the public sacrifices. Greek women of the upper class lived, in the main, the secluded life of Eastern harems at the present day, residing in their own apartments, and receiving there the visits only of other ladies, and of their nearest male relatives. Wool-carding, weaving, embroidery, and spinning were their employments; attendance at the great religious festivals, including an occasional tragic play at the Dionysia, were their amusements.

The Athenian boy went to school from seven years of age till sixteen, being attended to his tutor's by a pedagogue, which meant in Greece a trusty elderly slave, who exercised an outdoor supervision, and had nothing to do with his teaching. The schoolmaster was called grammatistes, or teacher of grammata, or learning, in the sense of literature. Grammar (in his own tongue, the only one thought worthy of a Greek's study), arithmetic, and writing were the rudiments; then came the learning by heart of passages from the poets, chiefly Homer, selected with regard to the moral lessons to be derived from them. The higher education was known as mousike (i. e., art over which the Muses presided), and included the literary studies as well as what we call music. The lyre was the favorite instrument, and all the great lyric poems being set to music, there was abundant choice for practice. Gymnastics or athletic exercises formed the third and an important branch of youthful training, practiced between the ages of sixteen and eighteen; this training included running, wrestling, boxing, and military exercises. Thus was the Athenian lad prepared to play his part in manhood as a citizen and a soldier.

The great defect of Greek civilization, according to the modern notions arising from Christianity, was the inferior estimation and treatment awarded to women. There were few Greeks who considered that women possessed any mental power, and the great philosopher Aristotle himself discusses the question as to whether a woman can have any virtues—such as courage, justice and temperance. The Greeks, by this neglect of mankind's better half, were left destitute of the ennobling influence which womankind, properly trained and duly valued, has always been found to exercise on the physically stronger and technically ruling part of the race.

HISTORY OF ROME

The greatness of Roman history lies in the fact that it is, in a large sense, the history of the world from the time of Rome's supremacy down to the present day. Out of the Roman Empire arose the modern state system of Europe, and the Roman language, law, and institutions are still, in changed forms, alive and active in the modern world. The influence of Palestine on our religion and of Greece on our art and literature, have to a great extent been wrought on us through Rome, which preserved and transmitted those great elements of our civilization. In Rome, as she established her power, all ancient history is lost; and out of Rome all modern history comes. In the history of Rome we see how the power of a single small town grew into that of a moderate-sized territory, from that into a country, from a country into a world. It was the mission of Rome in history thus to bring all the civilized peoples of the West, including Western Asia, under one dominion and one bondage; and, this being a political condition which could only end in conquest from without, the culture which she had gathered up into one vast reservoir was given off in streams that, in due season, fertilized the mental soil of rude and restless nations who stepped into Rome's place.

Rome's early history, though of much later date than the early history of Greece, is involved in great obscurity. The burning of Rome by the Gauls in B. C. 390 destroyed almost all the national records, and for our knowledge of the earlier times we are dependent on historians to whom the science of historical criticism was unknown, and who derived their information from legends embodied in lays, and from other untrustworthy sources. The earliest Roman historian, Fabius Pictor, lived during the second Punic War, some 500 years after the reputed foundation of Rome. Little reliance can be placed on the details of Roman history for the first 400 years and more. For about 300 years before the Christian era there are few authentic details, and beyond these, contradictions between which there is no means of deciding.

Italy is the second—from east to west or west to east —of the three great peninsulas of Southern Europe. The coast is not greatly indented, nor surrounded by numerous islands, like that of Greece. One long chain of mountains runs like a backbone through all the country except the wide northern plain, the valley of the Po, called by the Romans Padus. That plain was reckoned by the Romans, until the Christian era, as not being Italian at all, but Gallic, and was called by them Gallia Cisalpina, or "Gaul on-this-side-the-Alps." The mention of Gaul brings us to the olden races. The Gauls, as part of the great Celtic race, were Aryans. South of the Gauls came a people of uncertain origin named the Etruscans, to the west of the Apennines. The occupation of the south of Italy by Greek colonies in historical times has been related in the history of Greece. The Greeks found there and in part civilized and absorbed a people also of uncertain origin (perhaps Pelasgians) called the Iapygians. The main part of the rest of the peninsula, the center, was occupied by the great Italian race, of Aryan stock, and of near kindred, as the language proves, to the Greeks. Of this race there were two great branches—the Latins and the Umbro-Sabellians, also called Oscans. The Oscans or Umbro-Sabellians included the Umbrians, Sabines, Samnites, Æquians, Volscians, Lucanians, and other tribes among and to west of the Apennines. Sicily was inhabited in the west by a race of unknown origin called the Sikanians: the Sikels, who gave their name to the island, were nearly connected in race with the Latins. Sicily was fought for by the Carthaginians and the Greek cities founded in Sicily: in the end the island became almost wholly Greek in speech and usages.

Before relating the origin, so far as it is known, of the early Romans, we will deal with that mysterious people, the Etruscans, who are interesting both in themselves and from the part they seem to have played in the rise and early history of Rome. The Etruscans (called by the Greeks Tyrrheni or Tyrseni, and by themselves Rasena) were a people of uncertain, probably mixed, origin, and became a very powerful nation before Rome existed. In that early time they had extended their dominion as far as the Alps northward, and Mount Vesuvius southward. In the early Roman times their northern and southern conquests had been lost, and they were confined to the limits of the Etruria of the map, forming a confederacy of twelve independent oligarchical republics, in separate cities, of which the chief were named Volaterræ, Volsinii, Clusium, Arretium, Cortona, Falerri, and Veii. In language, manners, and customs they were quite distinct from the Greek and Italian races, and their religion was of a gloomy kind, involving much mysterious worship of infernal deities. Their system of divination became in many points that of the Romans. The civilization of the Etruscans was well developed, and included some skill in statuary, painting, and architecture, and a knowledge of the use of the arch. Many of the religions and political institutions of Rome were of Etruscan origin. They were good at shipbuilding, had a powerful navy in early times, and carried on much commerce with the Greeks.

They were great workers in metal, and famous for mirrors, candelabra, and other works in bronze, as well as for necklaces and other ornaments in gold. The so-called "Etruscan vases," however, are now known to be productions of Greek art.

The Sabines, in a mountainous district of central Italy, were always noted as a people of virtuous and simple habits, deeply religious, faithful to their word, strong lovers of freedom, and brave in its defence.

The ancient Latins, before the existence of Rome, had founded on the west coast of central Italy, south of the Tiber, a confederation or league of thirty towns, of which the town called Alba Longa became the head.

Out of these three nations or tribes—the Latins, Sabines, and Etruscans—the Roman people were originally formed. The principal element was Latin, as the language shows. The next in importance was the Sabine, and the third, in order both of time and of influence, was the Etruscan.

The nominal date of the foundation of Rome is B. C. 753, about which time the Latin town named Alba Longa seems to have established a settlement on the left (south) bank of the river Tiber, about fifteen miles from the sea. The name Roma means probably a march or border, and this Latin settlement would be made as an outpost to guard their march or frontier against the Etruscans on the right (north) side of the Tiber. This Latin town is stated to have been built on a height called the Palatine Hill, and we are to conceive it as a collection of huts inhabited mainly by husbandmen and shepherds. A union was soon made, it seems likely, with the people of a Sabine town called Quirium or Curium, existing on a neighboring hill, called the Quirinal. At an early date, perhaps as a result of warfare partially successful for the

Etruscans, the third, the Etruscan, element was admitted, and the result was Rome. As Freeman, in his "General Sketch of European History," says: "This account sets forth the way in which Rome became the greatest of all cities, namely, by constantly granting her citizenship both to her allies and to her conquered (in the case of the Etruscans we must perhaps read 'conquering') enemies. Step by step the people of Latium, of Italy, and of the whole civilized world, all became Romans. This is what really distinguishes the Roman history from all other history, and is what made the power of Rome so great and lasting."

The sole fact represented by the legends of the "Seven Kings" of Rome is that government began there, as in the early times of Greece, with monarchy, but elective monarchy, not hereditary, as in Greece and in modern times. The King was chosen by an assembly of the chief men, and there was a senate who assisted him to rule. It was probably toward the end of the monarchial period that the Etruscans came into a share of power, and it was owing to the misrule of a King of Etruscan family, it appears, that monarchy at Rome came to an end by his expulsion through a popular hatred so determined that the Romans never afterward could bear even the name of "King," and a republic or commonwealth was established. The date of this may be taken as about B. C. 500, in default of all certainty.

The genius of the Roman people seems to have been shown at a very early period of their history by the organization of the citizens on a military basis, according to which the state was treated, in the person of its grown-up males, as an army, and every man was liable to serve in war. As the city grew in numbers by the immigration of strangers, and the admission of allies or incorporation of subjects, two principal classes of the citizens became developed—the famous Patricians and Plebeians. The Patricians were probably those descended from the original citizens of the united Latin, Sabine, and Etruscan town, and the Plebeians the descendants of those afterward admitted. The internal history of Rome for several hundred years consists mainly of the account of struggles between these two orders—the Patricians and Plebeians. The Patricians alone were at first admissible to the great governing body called the Senate, and they kept in their hands all the high offices of state, the higher degrees of the priesthood, and the ownership of the public lands. The two orders were not allowed to intermarry, and the Plebeians, though they were free and personally independent (with the important exception of compulsory service in war), had no political weight. This was the early state of things in the Roman civil world, and the Plebeians, as might be expected, soon began to strive after a share in the rights exclusively belonging to the Patricians.

In Roman civil history we find three different legislative assemblies, all called Comitia, meaning "comings-together,"—the Comitia Curiata, Comitia Centuriata, and Comitia Tributa. Of these the Comitia Curiata was the earliest, and was a solely patrician assembly, which elected the King, made the laws, and decided in all cases affecting the life of a citizen. The powers of this assembly were soon transferred to the Comitia Centuriata, and it became a mere form long before the end of the republic. The Comitia Centuriata was the second in order of time, and came into existence under the monarchy. In this assembly the Patricians and Plebeians voted together, according to a distribution of power based upon wealth, ascertained by a census, or register of citizens and their property. The institution was a means of admitting a democratic element, while a decided aristocratic preponderance was secured. The Comitia Centuriata was for a time the sovereign assembly of the nation, and received the power of electing the King, and then (under the republic) the higher state officials, of repealing and enacting laws, and of deciding in cases of appeal from a judicial sentence. As time went on these powers remained, with the right of declaring war and making peace, and with the exercise of the highest judicial functions, as in accusations of treason, and in all appeals from Roman citizens on criminal matters. The influence of the Comitia Centuriata in the state was, however, gradually superseded by that of the third, the great popular assembly, the Comitia Tributa. The Comitia Tributa—originally based upon a division of the whole people into local tribes—in time became a solely plebian assembly, voting according to tribes, not man by man. In the course of time the powers of this body became very great, so that it could check all legislation initiated by the senate in the aristocratic Comitia Centuriata, and stop the whole machinery of the constitution.

The most famous part of the Roman constitution—the body which has given its name as a generic term to similar powerful assemblies—was the Senate, or Council of Elders. Founded in the monarchial times, it consisted at first of 300, and then of 600 members, and became the great executive body of the Roman Republic. The members of the Senate were those citizens alone who had held at least one of the five highest offices of the state—the Quæstorship, Ædileship, Prætorship, Censorship, or Consulship. The dignity was held for life, unless expulsion were inflicted by the Censors, who filled up all vacancies in the body every five years from among the past holders of the above five offices. As the people, either in the Comitia Tributa or Centuriata ultimately elected the holders of the above high offices, it is clear that none could be senators who had not both had some experience in public affairs, and enjoyed public confidence. The practical genius of the Roman people is strikingly shown in such an arrangement, theoretically as near perfection as possible for the securing of fit men to administer the government. The powers of this august body were extensive. The Senate controlled legislation by its approval being required for the proposal of a law to the two popular assemblies, while its own decrees, called Senatus-consulta, were valid at once in matters affecting home administration, provincial government, foreign policy, and religion. In foreign affairs the Senate had absolute control, except for declaring war and concluding peace, which were subject to the vote of the Comitia Centuriata. When Rome acquired foreign dominion this great body appointed the provincial governors; in war it exercised control over the conduct of operations, and the appointment and dismissal of generals; in foreign policy the senators alone negotiated, and appointed envoys from their own body. The administration of the finances and all matters of religion were entirely in their hands. Finally, the Senate could suspend the constitution altogether by investing, at its discretion, a consul with absolute power (the famous Dictatorship) in case of imminent danger to the safety of the republic at home or abroad.

On the abolition of monarchy (supposed to have occurred about B. C. 500) the royal power was intrusted to two high officials, elected for one year of office, and called, ultimately, consuls. They were the highest executive officers of the state, both in civil and military affairs. They convoked the Senate, presided over its deliberations, and executed both its decrees and those of the popular assembly. They commanded the armies with the full powers of martial law, and on the expiration of their year of office were appointed (as proconsuls) on occasion, to chief provincial governorships. The office was held in the highest esteem as representing the majesty of the Roman state, and, in monthly turns, each consul was attended abroad by twelve officials called lictors, who marched in front of him, each bearing fasces. These fasces consisted of a bundle of rods encircling an axe, and were symbols of the supreme power, extending in theory to corporal punishment and death. When the lictors appeared in the streets of Rome the axe was removed, as a sign that no magistrate could inflict death on a Roman citizen within the walls.

The censors were also two in number, and their office was, technically, the highest in the state. They were elected every five years, were generally ex-consuls, and wielded very great powers. The censors had a general and arbitrary control over the moral conduct of all citizens, and could inflict political degradation by the expulsion of senators from the Senate, of knights (equites) from their order, and of an ordinary citizen from his tribe, thereby depriving him of his franchise. They also, under the Senate, administered the public finances, farming out the collection of the taxes by auction to those called publicani, and expending the revenue on public buildings, roads, aqueducts, and other important works. The censors, lastly, made the census, or register of the value of the property of every Roman citizen, which affected certain political rights, and was the basis for the assessment of the property-tax.

The prætors were officials who had important functions to perform. Originally there was only one (appointed first in B. C. 366), while subsequently another was appointed. The former, called prætor urbanus, acted as a judge in causes between Roman citizens; the other (prætor peregrinus, added B. C. 246), was judge in cases in which foreigners were engaged. As the foreign dominion of Rome grew, four other prætors were appointed, who acted as governors in Sicily, Sardinia, and the two provinces of Spain, and latterly the number was still further increased.

The curule ædiles, first appointed B. C. 365, had the care of the public buildings, the city drainage, and all matters of police. They also took charge of the celebration of the great public festivals, and at a later period this office became confined to wealthy citizens, as the games had to be held at the private cost of the ædiles. The curule ædileship, in the corrupt age of the republic, thus became a means of bribing the people for election to further high offices, by the exhibition of the costly spectacles in which the citizens took delight.

The quæstors were the paymasters of the republic. They discharged, out of the revenues intrusted to them, the expenses of the civil and military services; their number being originally two for service at Rome, and increased, as foreign dominion extended, and the provincial governors each required such an official to assist him. The first four of these high offices of state were called the curule magistracies, because the holders had the right of sitting upon a state-chair of peculiar form, called the sella curulis, originally an Etruscan sign of royalty.

Rome solved the problem which Athenian statesmen and philosophers failed to solve—how to found an Empire. In studying Roman history we are watching a progress which, in its vast proportions, is quite unique in the annals of the world, the progress of a municipality into a Kingdom and an Empire, the march of an army to universal conquest and dominion. Rome gradually advanced from her position as a rustic fortress on the Palatine Hill to that of an agricultural and commercial community, of an emporium of trade, and of a military town with a regularly fortified wall and a military organization of her citizens. Slowly but surely her internal political unity is cemented by the wisdom of timely concession, though for nearly two centuries the military strength of the young republic was so far crippled by the incessant party-conflicts within her walls that she failed to overpower the neighboring towns and tribes whose inroads still infested her borders.

The year B. C. 366 brings a crisis in her internal history, when the election of the first plebeian consul and the dedication of a temple to Concord announced the fusion of the two rival orders—a fusion whose further progress is traced in the enactments of the Publilian, Ogulnian, Valerian, and Hortensian laws, which did away with the remaining monopolies of the Patricians. By the time these measures were passed Rome had already become lord of Latium. In what was called the "Jus Latii" (or "franchise of Latium")—the species of Roman citizenship to which the conquered Latin population were generally admitted—we may see the secret of Roman dominion, the power of political assimilation and incorporation. The policy of Rome was in this respect always the same. One by one successively, the Sabines (in the earliest days), the Plebeians, the Latins, the Italians, or inhabitants of Italy at large, and latterly the Provincials, were taken up and incorporated with her political life, and the heart of the Imperial city was constantly being nourished with the best blood of the conquerer nations. There is nothing fitful, nothing hesitating, nothing volcanic in the majestic sweep—checked by defeat, but never broken—of the onward march of Rome. In this course of expansion for her Empire Rome had no ideas of the balance of power or of deliberate aggrandizement. She aspired at first simply to be strong, and with that view her enemies were to be made weak. War was from the outset the very condition of her existence. Mars was the national god; the national virtues were the virtues of a soldier; and the greatest of the Cæsars could find no more humiliating rebuke to address to his mutineers than to call them simply "citizens" (Quirites), the name given to Romans in their civil capacity.

Rome's mastery of Latium was followed by her conquest of the Etruscans and the Samnites, which secured for her the command of Northern and Central Italy; then by the defeat of Pyrrhus at Beneventum, which gave Rome Southern Italy; then by Hannibal's discomfiture at Zama, which ended the power of her rival Carthage; then by the victory of Pydna in B. C. 168, which left Rome, at the close of her Macedonian wars, supreme over the Mediterranean world. These were the glorious days of the republic, days when democracy was established by law, while aristocracy was still dear to sentiment.

At this stage the picture of Rome's greatness has another and a darker side. We can see the evil influence of Roman conquest upon Roman morality; we can trace the decline of the old simplicity of life and habits by the influx of debased Greek manners, and the corrosive action of that vast tide of wealth which flowed in upon the victors when the commerce of Carthage and of her dependencies was diverted into Roman ports. Religious reverence and domestic purity decayed; divorce became exceedingly common, and the scandalous and licentious Bacchanalian mysteries were introduced.

Meantime, between the ages of Pyrrhus and of Hannibal, the agricultural system of the peninsula underwent a gradual change, and one pregnant with most important consequences. The small freeholds formerly held by an independent peasantry passed into large estates which were tended by slave-labor and superintended by hired bailiffs, themselves very often slaves. A great proportion of the soil became mere pasture ground, and the increasing population of the idle capital was made dependent on the corn-ships from the fertile Sicily and Africa for its daily food. Thus, neglecting to enforce her agrarian laws, which would have kept land subdivided, and not being a commercial state, Rome possessed no middle class of citizens, without which there can be no permanent liberty; political power came to be placed more and more at the disposal of the lower order of the people, and the genuine Roman character was debased by the constant influx and manumission of slaves.

Latterly the government of provinces, the conduct of wars, with their opportunities for plunder, and the farming of the public revenues, with their openings for extortion, enabled many of the nobility and the knights to acquire immense wealth, with which they purchased from corrupt judges impunity for their crimes, and bought from a thoroughly venal populace the lucrative and influential offices of the state, which their votes threw open to successful candidates. Patriotism gave place to ambition, and the unselfish loyalty that thought only of the Republic was succeeded by the spirit of party rivalry, by the lust for wealth, and by the craving for personal aggrandizement. It is no longer a contest between the Patricians and the Plebeians, for that distinction has long since been effaced. It is a war between the rich and the poor: the nobles harden into an unfeeling oligarchy, while the people degenerate into a mob; the machinery of government suited for a single city cannot be made to serve the purpose of a world-wide dominion, and the time fast approaches when the cry of the commonwealth against the lacerations of civil war, and the cry of the oppressed and plundered provinces against the extortions of their oppressive governors are to be answered by the substitution of one master for many, and by the establishment of that monarchy toward which events had long and steadily been pointing, in place of the Republic which now existed but in memory and in name.

After the triumphs of Pompey in the East, and the conquest of Gaul by Cæsar in the West, we have the collision of the rival conquerors, the thunders of the civil wars, and the consolidation at last of every office and of all power in the state in the hands of Augustus. Then come the enervating influence of Imperialism; the growing servility of the Senate; the death of political activity; the pauperization and dwindling of the people; the demoralizing influence of slavery, of the arena, the circus, and the theater; the rival systems of the Stoic and the Epicurean philosophy, Neo-Platonism, and Christianity; the pompous inanities of expiring superstition; the gradual Orientalization of the Empire. These are the main features in the picture of the culmination and the decline of an Empire around whose frontiers we at last hear the threatening tramp of the barbarian peoples who are assembling for their part in the mighty drama of the death of the Old World and the birth of the New. True it is that Roman history is the history of the world, for into Rome the ancient order dies, and out of her the modern order is born. She persecuted Christianity, but she made Christendom possible by giving it organization and form. Modern liberty was gradually developed upon the basis of the municipal institutions of the queen of cities, and her language and her laws were inextricably interwoven into the progressive fabric of the modern world.

The essential feature of Rome's history is the extension of her power by war, for the carrying out of what was doubtless the unconscious purpose of her existence— the linking the nations together, and preparing the way for a Heaven-sent faith.   We have seen in the panoramic sketch just given what were the achievements of Rome in war, and we are led to inquire to what special causes results so remarkable, so unequaled, were due.   They were due, firstly, to the special character that was inherent in the race, and, in a secondary way, to the special military organization which the genius of the people developed as the fit instrument for effecting the conquest of the world.   The elements out of which the Roman people was formed were Latin, Sabine, and Etruscan, and these must have had a natural adaptation to produce the Roman spirit.

Our ideas of Roman character are derived in some degree from the legends which appear in the earlier part of the Roman story, and which we have rejected from history.   Those legends, however, were universally received as true by the Romans themselves, and therefore they are true to the genius of the times and of the people, true in the lessons of Roman character which they inculcate, true for the practical purpose of teaching us what manner of men those old Romans really were.   Legendary lore possesses, in fact, a formative power in moulding the national character by consecrating traditional types of men for the admiration and imitation of posterity.   The Roman thought of early Rome and of her heroes as his poets and orators had taught him to think, and so from the legends we can understand in a measure the thoughts and actions of those who implicitly believed them.   In Rome, as opposed to the poetry and freedom of spirit among the Greeks, we have stern, constrained, unfeeling, prosaic intelligence.   The character of the people is shown in their religion. The word "religion" means obligation, a binding power, and the religion of the Romans was a feeling of constraint, and their worship a business-like performance involving narrow aspirations, expediency, and profit. They worshiped prosaic abstractions such as Pax, "peace," Tranquillitas, "quietness." They had altars to Plague, Hunger, Mildew (Robigo), Fever. They not only prayed to their gods in time of need, but made solemn vows to them in times of difficulty, and they imported foreign divinities and rites to help them when their home deities appeared to be inefficient. The Roman temples were chiefly built in consequence of vows, and thus arose from necessity and not spontaneously: such a devotion as this was a thoroughly hard, practical, and interested worship. Still the Roman religion was, in one view, high, earnest, and severe, and this resulted in government, as its highest earthly expression.

Duty was the Roman watchword, and therefore law on earth, as a copy of the will of Heaven. The destiny of the Roman seems to have been to stamp on the mind of mankind the ideas of law, government, order. He showed his practical character by what he left behind him —works of public usefulness—noble roads intersecting Empires—huge aqueducts—bridges—excavations for draining cities—and especially that great system of law, the slow growth of ages of experience, which has contributed so largely to the jurisprudence of most European nations. The great Roman poet, Virgil, knew what the Roman's work in life was when he sang, contrasting his countrymen with the Greeks—

> "Others, belike, with happier grace
> From bronze or stone shall call the face,
> Plead doubtful causes, map the skies,
> And tell when planets set or rise;
> But, Roman, thou—do thou control

> The nations far and wide;
> Be this thy genius, to impose
> The rule of Peace on vanished foes,
> Show pity to the humbled soul,
> And crush the sons of pride."

The domestic ties were held sacred by the Romans. Home was sacred, guarded by the deities of the domestic shrine—the Lares and Penates. A Roman's own fireside was nearly the most sacred spot on earth. The battle-cry was "Pro aris et focis," "for our altars and hearths." The fabric of the commonwealth arose out of the family. First the family—then the clan (gens) made up of the family and its dependents (clientes)—then the tribe—last the nation. Thus the Roman state rested on the foundation of the family hearth. Domestic corruption in Rome, the loss of integrity and manliness in her Senate, preceded and led to her ruin. The Roman virtue, when Rome flourished, was manly courage (virtus), manhood. Roman courage was no mere animal daring, but duty, obedience to will, self-surrender to the public good—the courage of the Spartan at his best amongst the Greeks. The Roman legions subdued the world not by discipline alone, nor by strength, nor audacity, but by moral force, contempt of pain, preference of death to dishonor. Unconquerable fidelity to duty was the spell which laid the forces of the world prostrate before her: in that strength she went forth conquering and to conquer. The chief virtues of the old Romans were these—fortitude, temperance, spirit to resist oppression, respect for legitimate authority, ardent patriotism. Of charity and chivalrous generosity—virtues mainly of Christian production and growth—they were generally destitute. They were cruel, hard, and grasping, and often faithless in their dealings with other nations. Among all the qualities which contributed to make Rome supremely great amongst the nations—the one all-con-

A CHARIOT RACE IN THE CIRCUS MAXIMUS

Painting by U. Checa

quering people of the ancient world—the chief was the habit of obedience, of reverence for authority, which was ingrained in the Roman's nature.

Such was the character of the ancient Roman—a character in all its chief features essentially military. To this character accordingly must be mainly attributed the extraordinary success of the Romans in extending their conquests over the world, and in uniting so many different nationalities in one Empire. But as another and almost equally important factor in this result we must regard their military organizations. The constitution of the Roman legion—the great military instrument of Roman conquest —varied at different epochs of history, and underwent successive improvements from men of tactical ability. The main principle of its formation, however, was the same throughout. In the later days of the Republic, when perfected by the great commander Marius, the legion was, in numbers, a brigade; but in form it was a complete small army corps of over 6,000 men, including troops of all arms, cavalry, infantry, and artillery, or the military engines for siege purposes. The cavalry were 300 in number. The infantry, numbering about 6,000, were composed partly of skirmishers, armed with slings or bows and arrows, or light darts, but mainly of armor-clad men using the pilum, an iron-pointed spear (six feet long, and weighing over ten pounds) for hurling at the enemy from a distance of ten to fifteen paces, and (for close quarters) a short, stout, two-edged, pointed, cut-and-thrust sword. The execution done with these weapons by powerful men was terrible, the hurled pilum producing great slaughter and confusion, amidst which the legionaries closed in upon the shaken foe with the short sword, and concluded matters by downright strokes upon the head, or, if that were strongly guarded, by stabs delivered upward below the enemy's shield. The infantry of the legion was divided into ten cohorts, each of 600 men, and, in battle array, stood in two lines (or, in Julius Cæsar's arrangement, in three lines), each line consisting of five cohorts with a space between each. The van, or front line, was composed of the veterans, with the younger soldiers in the rear line, as a reserve. The excellence of the legion's formation consisted in its having both a close array and an organization allowing of division into parts; it combined in itself at once massiveness and capability of dispersion. It was firm and compact at will, and yet could readily expand when it became necessary.

In the best days of Rome every citizen between the ages of seventeen and fifty was liable to military service, unless he was of the lowest class, or had served twenty years in the infantry or ten in the cavalry. The drill was severe, and included running, jumping, swimming in full armor, and marching long distances at a rapid pace. For sieges the Romans used military-engines of Greek invention, such as the ballista for hurling huge stones; the catapult for ponderous beam-like spears; the battering-ram for breaching walls, and the movable tower for pushing close to the enemy's defences so as to overlook them. The Roman entrenched camp was a great feature of the warfare, being admirable for security, with its ditch and solid rampart of earth crowned by a stout wooden palisade. Inside the camp the tents of all the soldiers and officers were ranged in regular order upon a plan common to all the Roman armies.

A triumph, the grand reward of a successful general's achievements, was regarded as the height of military glory, and was the chief object of ambition to every Roman commander. The honor was granted by the Senate, and only to one who, as prætor, consul, or dictator, had gained brilliant and decisive victories, or had by a series of operations permanently and largely added to the foreign territory of Rome. On the conclusion of the war the general and his army returned to Rome, and if a triumph were granted, money was voted by the Senate to defray the expenses, and a special decree of the people assembled in Comitia Tributa suspended the constitution for the one or more days of the triumph so as to enable the successful general to enter the city in his military capacity and with an armed force. Thus jealously were a Roman's civil rights guarded against the military authority conferred by the popular assembly. This authority was called the imperium, and could be held, except by special enactment, only outside the city walls.

A fine poetical description of a triumph is given in Lord Macaulay's Lays of Ancient Rome (Prophecy of Capys). The grand procession entered the city, headed by lictors, clearing the way for the Senate and high officials, who came first. Then followed players upon the pipe and flute, succeeded by the spoils of war—treasures of art, rich plate and pictures, statues and robes of price. All these were borne by bay-crowned soldiers on stands or heads of lances, mingled with products of the conquered country's soil, and with arms and standards taken from the foe. Then came long files of prisoners of war, with vanquished leaders, and it may be a captive King. White oxen with gilded horns were led along accompanied by the priests who were to slay them; and last, preceded by a throng of singers and musicians, came the victorious general standing erect in four-horse car, his body clad in white embroidered robe, an ivory eagle-tipped scepter in his hand, and the triumphal wreath of gold held by a slave above his head. Last came the conqueror's army, and the long pomp marched down the street called "Sacred Way," then through the Forum (the chief square or Place, in continental phrase, of ancient Rome), and up the Capitoline Hill to the temple of "Jupiter of the Capitol," Jupiter Capitolinus, the chief god of Rome.   There the triumphal general laid his golden crown on the lap of the god's statue as an offering of thanksgiving, and the day ended with feasting, revelry, and song.   The Roman character was darkly shown in the usual treatment of conquered foes; the rank and file endured the lot of slaves; the captured general or King passed from the triumphal procession to imprisonment or death.   Jugurtha, King of Numidia, was deliberately starved in prison.   Vercingetorix the ablest and bravest of the Gallic chiefs, was murdered after the triumph of B. C. 45 by order of his conqueror, Julius Cæsar, famed, and that justly, as, toward his fellow-citizens, one of the most generous of Romans.

EVOLUTION OF THE ROMAN CONSTITUTION

When Rome ceased to be under monarchial rule, two high officials called consuls were appointed, to hold a yearly office, and wield the chief executive power in the state. About B. C. 500 began struggles between the Patricians and Plebeians, arising out of the discontent caused by poverty and distress among the inferior class. The Plebeians fought the battles of Rome, and, in order to do so, had to neglect the tillage of the soil by which they lived. Hence came poverty, made worse still by a severe law of debt, and by a high rate of interest extorted by the Patricians who advanced money. The taxation of the state was paid solely by the Plebeians, as the Patricians had ceased to pay their rent to the treasury for the public lands which they held. At the same time, the Plebeians, which body, we must remember, included also many men of birth and wealth, were entirely excluded from public offices, and such a state of things could only end in an outbreak. According to the traditions on which we have to rely for this part of Roman history, such an event occurred in B. C. 493.

The oppression exercised upon the debtors, who were imprisoned and flogged on failure to pay, caused a withdrawal, a secession, of the Plebeians in a body to a hill called Mons Sacer ("Holy Hill") outside the Roman territory, and about three miles from Rome. Their declared purpose was to erect a new town, and dwell apart with equal rights. The Patricians were left helpless against foreign enemies, and as usual in such cases, made concessions when they were forced to terms. It was agreed that two officials should be appointed (to balance the two consuls, who were Patrician magistrates) for the defence of the commoners against the cruel exercise of the law of debtor and creditor. These new magistrates were called Tribuni Plebis ("Tribunes of the Commons"), and the title, in the later development of the office, becomes very famous in aftertime. These Tribunes acted as champions of the subordinate class against all oppression, and pleaded in the law courts on that behalf. The person of a Tribune was sacred and inviolable, and, in the exercise of his yearly office, he could forbid the execution of the order of any official, or of any decree of the Senate; he could pardon offences, and call to account all enemies of the commons under his charge.

In B. C. 486 Spurius Cassius, tried for treason and put to death by the Patricians, is said to have carried the first of the famous Agrarian Laws, for limiting the amount of public land held by the Patricians, compelling them to pay tithe or rent for the land they held, and dividing surplus lands amongst the Plebeians. The law was not acted on, through the violence and injustice of the Patricians. The Plebeians exercised some check from time to time, by the refusal to serve as soldiers. In B. C. 473, however, the Tribune Genucius was murdered by the Patricians, because he had called the consuls to account for not carrying the Agrarian Law into effect. In B. C. 471 a great advance was made by the Plebeians. They succeeded in carrying the famous Publilian Law, proposed by the Tribune Publilius Volero, that the Tribunes should in future be chosen only at the Comitia Tributa, the popular assembly, instead of the Comitia Centuriata, an assembly under Patrician influence. The Comitia Tributa also received the right of deliberating and deciding upon all matters that were open to discussion and settlement in the

Comitia Centuriata. After this the struggle continued, and the commons found it a great disadvantage that there was no written law to control the chief Patrician magistrates, the consuls, in their dealings with the Plebeians.

After violent opposition, and the increase of the number of Tribunes to ten, it was carried by the Plebeians (about B. C. 452) that ten commissioners (the famous Decemviri) should draw up a code of laws which should bind all classes of Romans alike. The ultimate result was the compilation, and engraving on thick sheets of brass, of the first and only code of law in the Roman Republic —the Laws of the Twelve Tables. These laws appear to have made the Comitia Tributa into a really national assembly for legislative purposes, embodying Patricians and Plebeians alike, and having the election of the lower officials—ædiles, quæstors, and tribunes. The Plebeians, however, were still kept out of a share in the lands which they conquered in war, and a time of trouble came in the usurpation and violence of the Decemviri. It is to this period that the well-known story of Virginia and Appius Claudius, told in Macaulay's Lays, belongs. For some years no tribunes were elected, and the commons were subject to wanton tyranny. In B. C. 448, the Plebeians, for the second time, seceded to the Mons Sacer, and the Decemviri were obliged to give way. Tribunes were reappointed, and the new consuls were Valerius and Horatius. By them, in the Comitia Centuriata, the great Valerian and Horatian Laws were passed, which may be regarded as a first great charter of Roman freedom. A great increase of the power of the Plebeians was hereby effected. The assembly of the tribes, Comitia Tributa, was now put on a level with the Comitia Centuriata, so that a Plebiscitum or decree of the people's assembly, had henceforth the same force as one passed by the Comitia

Centuriata, and became law for the whole nation. The struggle between the two orders, Patricians and Plebeians, continued. In B. C. 445 the Lex Canuleia, proposed by the tribune Canuleius, was passed, sanctioning intermarriage (connubium) between Patricians and Plebeians.

Foreseeing that the time would come when the Plebeians must be admitted to the high offices of the state, the Patricians divided the powers of the consulship, and in B. C. 444 caused the appointment of Military Tribunes with consular power (Tribuni Militares Consulari Potestate), officers who might be elected from either order, as commanders of the army, while the civil powers of the consuls were kept by the Patricians in their own hands. In B. C. 443 the office of the Censors was established, with the proviso that they should be appointed only from the Patricians, and only by their assembly, the Comitia Curiata. In this office the Patricians undoubtedly gained an accession of power; the duties of the Censors have been already explained. The power of the Plebeians grew by degrees through the exertion of the prerogatives of the Tribunes, and about B. C. 400 the office of the Military Tribunes became open to the Plebeians, and four out of the six were chosen from that order. After the capture of Rome by the Gauls (B. C. 390) fresh troubles for the Plebeians arose. Their lands near Rome had been laid waste, cattle killed, and implements of agriculture destroyed. Heavy taxes were imposed to make up for the loss of public treasure carried off by the Gauls, and soon the old trouble of debt arose, and consequent oppression by the Patrician creditors. The distress of the Commons increased until a great remedy was found by two patriotic tribunes of the Plebeians, Caius, Licinius Stolo and Lucius Sextius, who are regarded as the civil founders of Rome's greatness, and the authors of the great Roman

Charter of equality and freedom. These able, active, and determined men, after a tremendous struggle, fought with constitutional arms alone—one in which the Romans showed that respect for law and authority which, in their best days, so honorably distinguished them—carried their point in the end. The victory was won through the use of the tribunitian power of stopping the whole machinery of government. Year after year, for ten successive years, Licinius and Sextius were chosen tribunes, and, while the Patricians (a common device afterward) gained over the eight other tribunes, and prevented the popular bills being put to vote in the Comitia, the two tribunes prevented the election of the Consular Tribunes (save in B. C. 371, for a war with the Latins), and other high officials, and would have no troops levied at all.

At last, in B. C. 366, the famous Licinian Laws were carried. Their provisions were these: That the interest already paid the debtors should be deducted from the capital of the debt, and the reduced remainder paid off in three equal annual installments; that no one should hold above 500 jugera (about 280 English acres) of the public land, the surplus to be divided among the poorer Plebeians; that the military tribunate with consular power should be abolished, and the consulship restored, but one Consul, at least, henceforward should be a Plebeian. Sextius was himself elected in B. C. 366 as the first Plebeian Consul. The Plebeians thus acquired perfect equality with the Patricians in the great stronghold of the constitutional offices — the Consulship; and this change was of tne greatest advantage to the state, as the subsequent history shows that among the great men produced by Rome, both as commanders and as statesmen, the Plebeian houses could claim an equal share with the original Patrician nobility.

The idea likely to arise from the modern contemptuous use of the word "plebeian," that the Plebeians, as an order, were composed solely of the mob of Rome, contrasted with the Patricians, as the nobles, must here be guarded against. The distinction of Plebeian and Patrician is here political, and the Plebeians included many wealthy and otherwise influential men, previously excluded by their descent from certain political advantages, just as in England, until the Catholic Emancipation Act was passed in the earlier part of the present Century, a Roman Catholic, though of ducal rank and princely wealth, could take no share in the deliberations of the House of Lords.

In B. C. 339 Publilius Philo, Dictator in that year, carried the Publilian Laws, which put the Plebeians on a thorough practical equality with the Patricians. By these it was enacted: That a Plebiscitum (decree of the Comitia Tributa) should bind as law the whole people: this was a re-enactment of a provision of the Valerian and Horatian laws, which provision had either never been carried into effect, or had become obsolete. That the legislative power of the Comitia Curiata should be, practically, abolished: hitherto that assembly had possessed a right of veto on measures proposed in the other Comitia. That one of the Censors must henceforth be a Plebeian. In B. C. 336 the Prætorship was thrown open to the Plebeians. In B. C. 300 the Lex Ogulnia (carried by two of the Tribuni Plebis, the brothers Quintus and Cnæus Ogulnius) stormed for the Plebeians the stronghold of the state religion, by enacting that four of the eight pontiffs and five of the nine augurs should be taken from that order. The pontiffs and augurs, we may here explain, had charge of the religious ceremonies, and the augurs, who consulted the will of the gods by observation of the flight of birds, and so forth, had much political influence, residing in their power of delaying the progress of measures in the Comitia, by declaring that the day was unpropitious for its meeting, and then no assembly could be held. In the same year, B. C. 300, M. Valerius, as Consul, re-enacted the Lex Valeria (one of the Valerian and Horatian Laws), De Provocatione ("On the right of appeal"), to the effect that every Roman citizen should have a right of appeal to the assembly of the Plebeians, against the sentence of the supreme magistrate. In B. C. 286 Lex Hortensia, carried by Quintus Hortensius, Dictator in that year, confirmed the rights of the Plebeians by solemnly re-enacting the late Publilian Law, that the Plebeians might bind the whole people by laws. The Senate was hereby deprived of its veto on the proceedings of the Comitia Tributa, and that assembly of the Commons became a supreme legislative power.

This enactment followed the third and last secession of the Plebeians, which protest of the order took the form of a retirement to the Janiculan Hill of Rome. Henceforth there is an end of all political distinction between Patricians and Plebeians, and so-called equality of rights for both orders existed. The Comitia Tributa became now, however, the absolute legislative body in the state, the only check on that assembly being the veto of the Tribuni Plebis, and this led afterward to great intrigues on the part of the Patricians, in order to gain over one or more of the ten tribunes, and cause the veto to be exercised.

The general result of all this contest between Patricians and Plebeians was that the constitution of Rome had become a moderate democracy; for the Senate retained the power of taxation, and the chief judicial power, as the judges in the most important civil and criminal cases were taken from the Senatorial order. The

Senate, however, held the general executive administration.   That great body contained the political intelligence and practical statesmanship of the commonwealth, and in consistency and sagacity, in unanimity and patriotism, it was the foremost political combination of all times, an assembly of Kings, which knew how to combine despotic energy with republican self-devotedness.   Such was the end of the legitimate and constitutional development of the Roman state in its civil capacity.

THE CONQUEST OF ITALY

With regard to Rome's gain of territory during the monarchial period, there has been preserved by the historian Polybius a treaty concluded by Rome with Carthage in B. C. 508, which proves that Rome possessed at that time nearly the whole coast of Latium, from the mouth of the Tiber to the town of Anxur or Tarracina. This dominion was soon afterward lost, and it also appears from the legendary accounts that Rome at an uncertain date, perhaps about B. C. 500, was besieged and taken by the Etruscans, who made the Romans redeem their city and some territory around it to the south of the Tiber by an undertaking only to use iron for implements of agriculture, which, of course, implies the disarming of the people. The Etruscans, however, were soon afterward defeated by a united force of the Latins and the Greeks of Cumæ, and driven back to their own territory north of the Tiber.

Rome soon recovered from the check she had received, and, in the times of respite from civil struggles, was engaged in war more or less successful, accounts of which are more or less legendary, with the neighboring cities and peoples, including the Æqui, to the east, the Volsci, to the south, the city of Veii, north of the Tiber, in Etruria, and the Etruscans. What seems certain amidst a chaos of romance is that by about B. C. 400 the power of Etruria had greatly declined, and that the large, wealthy and powerful city of Veii had been taken by Rome and made her permanent possession. The Plebeians received lands in the Veientine territory, and further conquests in Etruria were made, including the city of Falerii.

The Senonian Gauls (Senones) were a powerful Celtic tribe between the Sequana (Seine), and the Ligeris (Loire). A part of this people about B. C. 400 crossed the Alps into Cisalpine Gaul, made settlements in Umbria, and penetrated into Etruria. The Romans sent orders to them to desist from the siege of Clusium, and the Gauls replied by marching on Rome. The result was a total defeat of the Roman army (in B. C. 390) on the "black day of Allia," a little stream to the north of Rome. The day was marked ever afterward in the Roman calendar as a dies nefastus (unholy day), on which no business could be lawfully done, and no sacrifice offered to the gods. Rome was then taken by the Gauls and burnt, the capitol itself being either occupied or bought off by payment of ransom, and the Gauls then retired with a great booty. The result to Rome was disastrous for the moment, but the Gallic invasion seems to have done Rome's work for her in one direction by completely crushing her old enemies, the Æqui, who now disappear as an independent state. Rome then set herself to obtain by intrigue, alliances and arms, the command of the cities of Latium and, on the rebuilding of the city, was engaged in wars as before.

The Roman contests with the Volsci, Etruscans and Latin states were, on the whole, successful for Rome, and by B. C. 375 the south of Etruria (lost by Rome on the Gallic invasion) had become permanently Roman terri- tory. In B. C. 356 the Etruscans were defeated by Rutilus, the first Plebeian censor and dictator, and further attacks by the Gauls were repulsed. Then began (about B. C. 343) a struggle of the rising state against the powerful nation called the Samnites. Rome was for a time in alli- ance with towns of Latium and Campania, and her war with Samnium was really the beginning of the conquest of Italy. Some battles were gained by the Romans, but

C. MACCARI, PINX

PAPIRIUS INSULTED BY THE GAULS

in B. C. 340 a treaty of peace and alliance was concluded with Samnium, and Rome then found herself face to face with a league of the Latins and Campanians.

The Latin War began in B. C. 340, and lasted for three years. The Latin and allied forces were defeated in B. C. 340 near Mount Vesuvius by a Roman army under the consuls Manlius Torquatus and Decius Mus, and after another Roman victory the subjugation of Latium was completed in B. C. 338. The great Latin league of cities came to an end; the lands of Latium were partly allotted to Roman colonies of Plebeians established on the conquered territory as garrisons. Some of the Latins received the Roman citizenship, and some were made mere subjects, so as to divide the interests of the Latins and permanently strengthen the position of Rome. At the same time all the excluded Latins could look forward to acquiring Roman citizenship, and in this politic way the fidelity of all to Rome was secured.

Thus strengthened, Rome began her second Samnite War in B. C. 327, engaging in a struggle for life and death, in which the Samnites fought with the heroic courage of their race, and repeatedly gained great battles over the Romans, but were at last overpowered by Roman perseverance, energy and skill. The chief generals on the Roman side were Papirius Cursor, five times consul and twice dictator, and Fabius Maximus. The great champion of the Samnites was the famous Caius Pontius. In B. C. 321, after some victories, the Romans suffered both disaster and disgrace in the surrender of a whole army to the Samnites, entrapped by them in two narrow mountain passes called the Caudine Forks, on Mount Taburnus, west of Beneventum. The victorious Pontius showed the greatest humanity to the conquered Romans, and released the army on terms, which the Roman government repaid by breaking the conditions of surrender, and refusing to give up conquests and to conclude an alliance. The Romans afterward gained the upper hand, and the second Samnite war ended in B. C. 304 by a temporary submission of Samnium.

The Third Samnite War began in B. C. 298, and the Samnites were now aided, in their last desperate struggle for national independence, by the Etruscans, Umbrians and Senonian Gauls. The Samnite generals, Pontius, one of the great men of ancient days, and Gellius Egnatius, made a brilliant strategical move by marching northward into Etruria and joining their powerful confederates there with their whole force. In B. C. 295 the decisive battle of Sentinum (in Umbria) was fought. There the Romans, under Fabius Maximus, defeated the Samnite confederates with great slaughter and the loss of the leader Egnatius. For five years more the struggle was protracted. In B. C. 292 the gallant Pontius was defeated, taken prisoner, and barbarously executed by the Romans at their general's triumph in Rome. No more disgraceful act stains the annals of Rome than this cruel treatment of the generous and gallant foe who, nearly thirty years before, had spared a Roman army at the Caudine Forks, and had forborne to seek vengeance for the vile treachery with which his mercy was requited. The great modern historian of Rome, Dr. Arnold, a man whose own admirable character lends crushing weight to his deliberate condemnation of wrong, brands this infamous deed by declaring that "it proves but too clearly that, in their dealings with foreigners, the Romans had neither magnanimity, nor humanity, nor justice." After the loss of Pontius the Samnites could only keep up a fitful struggle of detached parties, while the Roman armies marched to and fro, inflicting utter devastation on the land. In B. C. 290 the war ended with the entire submission of exhausted Samnium, and the Romans were now placed, by the conquest of the Samnites and Umbrians, in a position of mastery over Central Italy.

The Romans, in their career of subjugation, had to deal next with the Etruscans, and with the old foe, the Senonian Gauls. In B. C. 283 the great battle of the Vadimonian Lake (in Etruria) was fought, and its results were great. The united army of the Gauls and Etruscans was totally defeated. Etruria's day was done; the Senonian Gauls were "wiped out."

The Romans were now masters of all Northern Italy. In B. C. 282 came the struggle in Southern Italy, with the Lucanians and Tarentines, which brought the Romans into collision—legion against phalanx—for the first time, with Greek methods of warfare. After Roman defeats by Pyrrhus in B. C. 280 (when the Consul Lævinus was beaten at Heraclea, in Lucania, on the river Siris), and in B. C. 279 at Asculum (in Apulia), the war was virtually ended by the rout of Pyrrhus at Beneventum (in Samnium) in B. C. 275. The Roman victor was the renowned consul Curius Dentatus, a fine specimen of the old Roman for courage, determination, and rugged simplicity of character and life. He was of Sabine origin; and soon after the magnificent triumph he retired to his little farm in the Sabine territory, and tilled it with his own hands. The defeat of Pyrrhus was followed by the capture of Tarentum, and the submission of the Lucanians, Bruttians, and all other peoples who had hitherto held out, or risen, encouraged by Pyrrhus, against Roman power in Central and Southern Italy. By the year B. C. 266 the Roman conquest of Italy was completed, and the city on the Tiber was mistress of the whole extent of the land, from the rivers Rubicon (in north of Umbria) and Macra (in northwest of Etruria), on the north (the frontiers of Cisalpine Gaul), to the towns of Rhegium (on southwest coast —the toe), and Brundusium (on the Adriatic Sea—at the heel), in the south of Italy.

Rome had thus become the most compact and powerful state in existence, and she was now to show the genius of her people for government by the method in which the Romans consolidated and organized the territory which they had won. The conquered nations of Italy kept in the main their own laws, languages and administrations, but they looked to Rome as their center and their leader, whom they were bound to follow in war, and in connection with whom alone future advantages were to be acquired.

The whole of Italy now comprised, in a political sense, three classes. These were, first, the Roman citizens (Cives Romani), forming the Roman people in the strict technical sense (populus Romanus), the governing body of the whole state. These citizens belonged to the thirty-five tribes, or wards, or parishes, into which the territory of the city of Rome was divided, north of the Tiber beyond Veii, and south to the river Liris; to Roman colonies established in different parts of Italy; to various municipal towns which had received the Roman franchise. Nearly all of these citizens (the exceptions being the inhabitants of some of the municipal towns) had a right of voting in the Comitia Tributa at Rome.

Second, the Latins (called "Nomen Latinum," or, "the Latin name"). This must be understood in a technical, not in a local, sense (as the towns of Latium were mostly municipalities with the Roman franchise), and applies to those who belonged to towns having the Latin franchise, given originally to the conquered towns of Latium. Any male inhabitant of a town with this "Latin franchise" could, by holding a public office in his own town, become a full Roman citizen of the tribes, if he chose to remove to Rome.

Last, the Socii or Allies (called also Fœderatæ Civitates, or Fœderati); these were all the other communities of Italy, not included in first or second. These "Allied States" really existed in various degrees of subjection to Rome, having no political privileges, and being bound to furnish troops for the Roman armies, but enjoying her powerful protection against foreign enemies. With regard to the Nomen Latinum and the Socii, Rome (the Cives Romani) retained the sovereign rights of making war in which all must join, concluding treaties by which all were bound, and coining money which all must recognize and circulate. In this excellent political system, which "reconciled municipal freedom with the unity and supremacy of the central power," we see the fitness of Rome to govern what she had conquered, and how well she was adapted by the genius of her people to subdue and to form the world into one vast Empire. By the conquest of Italy the wealth of the Roman state was greatly increased in the revenues derived from mines, forests and harbors which she had acquired; the Patricians and Plebeians alike obtained lands to hold and to till; a solid basis of power was obtained, on which to erect the imposing fabric of her vast dominion in the days to come.

Great roads were first made with military purpose of providing a way that should be solid at all seasons of the year, for the march of legions and their heavy baggage through districts subdued by Roman arms. They were wonderful pieces of determined practical engineering, and in order to carry them straight to the points aimed at, marshes and hollows were filled up, or spanned with viaducts; mountains were tunneled, streams were bridged; no labor, time nor money was spared. As they extended their power through Italy, the Romans constructed such roads as these in various directions from the capital, and these great highways in Italy must be understood as representing others which were afterward made, as need arose, in every part of the Roman Empire. First and greatest of the Italian roads was the famous Appian Way (Via Appia, called Regina Viarum, "Queen of Roads"), which was begun by Appius Claudius, censor in B. C. 312. The struggle with the Samnites was at its height when this great causeway, built with large square stones on a raised platform, was made direct from the gates of Rome to Capua, in Campania. The Via Appia was afterward extended, through Samnium and Apulia, to Brundusium, on the lower Adriatic, the port of embarkation for Greece. Parts of the original stonework are existing at this day. Other great roads in Italy were the Via Aurelia—the great coast-road northward, by Genua (Genoa), into Transalpine Gaul;—the Via Flaminia, through Umbria to Ariminum; and the Via Æmilia, from Ariminum, through Cisalpine Gaul, to Placentia.

We here interpose, as a truce between the clash of arms in Rome's conquest of Italy and in her foreign wars, a short account of the Roman gods and worship at the time when an "age of faith" in Paganism still existed. The two original deities of the Roman Pantheon who belonged to it in common with that of the Greeks (with whom, as Aryans, they had a common ancestry), were the great Jupiter (answering to the Greek Zeus), and Vesta (the Greek Hestia). The chief deity of the tribes of Italy was Mars or Mavors, the god of "manliness," and then, by a transition natural with the Romans, the god of war. The Roman gods of similar name to the Greek deities had often very different attributes, and must never be confounded with them. The Roman Hercules was a god of property and commerce, quite distinct from the Greek demigod Heracles, with his heroic exploits and labors. The originally Sabine goddesses, Juno, the type of queenly womanhood, and Minerva, the embodiment of wisdom, were great deities at Rome. Janus, the god of opening and shutting (really a form of the sun-god, who opens the day at his rising, and shuts up light at his setting) is well known from his image with double face, and from the covered passage at Rome (wrongly called a temple), which was left open in war and closed up in peace. Janus is only another form of Dianus (god of day), and his sister was Diana, the moon goddess. We find also, as remnants of the olden worship before Rome existed, certain deities of country life. Saturnus was god of sowing and tillage, in whose honor a great festival in December was celebrated, called the Saturnalia—a time of holiday, feasting, and social freedom for seven days. Ceres was goddess of the corn crops; Pales and Faunus deities of flocks and shepherds. The chief domestic worship was that of Vesta, as goddess of the hearth, at whose rites the Roman father of the household officiated as priest, and only kinsmen could be present; and of the Lares and Penates, the spirits of ancestors and guardians of the home. The mythical king, Romulus, was worshiped under the name of Quirinus.

In order to ascertain the will of the gods in important matters, the Romans employed Augurs to observe the flash of lightning and the flight of birds. This was done before every public act or ceremony—the holding of Comitia and the fighting of a battle; and in taking the auspices, as the mummery of these officials was called, the Augur stood in a space of ground which he had consecrated by a ceremonial for the purpose. Then, facing the south, he watched for a reply to his prayers, beseeching an expression of the divine will. A flight of birds or other sign, appearing on the right hand, was unfavorable; on the left, propitious. The Augur waited till the desired event occurred, and then announced the result. If no Augur were present, signs might be sought from the "sacred chickens," carried about with an army on campaigns: if they ate their food heartily, it was favorable; if not, unlucky. In the first Punic war a Roman consul, who had the chickens with him on shipboard for the purpose of augury, was informed that they would not eat at all—the worst sign possible. "Let them drink then!" he cried, and flung them overboard into the sea. This may be taken as an example of how educated Romans, long before the republic ended, flung away ancestral creeds and superstitions, and became adherents, when they believed in anything, of the Greek philosophers' belief in one divinity of whom they had their various conceptions.

FOREIGN CONQUEST

Rome now engaged in the greatest conflict of her history—that with the powerful maritime and commercial state, Carthage. It was a struggle which when it was fully developed, became for Rome a fight for national existence, in which her enemy was at the height of her power and resources, with Spain and Africa at her back, and with the first general of the age, perhaps of all ages, to command her armies. The interest of the Punic wars (as they are called from the word Punicus, the Latin equivalent of the Greek Phoinikikos—Phœnician, and, in a limited sense, Carthaginian, as used by the Greek historian Polybius) is great and enduring. These wars were fought out "not merely to decide the fate of two cities, or of two Empires; but to determine which of the two races, the Indo-Germanic (otherwise Indo-European or Aryan), or the Semitic, should have the dominion of the world. On the one side— the Aryan—was the genius for war, government, and legislation; on the other—the Semitic— the spirit of industry, navigation, and commerce. The future of Europe and the world depended on the issue of the contest, and the skill and valor, the determination and resource, displayed on both sides, have caused these wars of Rome and Carthage to remain most vividly impressed upon the memories of men."

Carthage had become, by the political and commercial energy of her citizens, the leading Phœnician state, ruling over Utica, Hippo, Leptis, and other cities of Phœnician origin in Northern Africa. The Carthaginians paid also great attention to agriculture, and the whole of their territory was cultivated like a garden, supplying the population with abundance of food. This fact, considered with the wealth derived from her commerce, explains to us how it was that a city with no large extent of territory was enabled to hold out so long against the utmost efforts of Rome, and at one period to bring her, as it seemed, to the verge of ruin. The political constitution of Carthage was that of an oligarchical republic, and her aristocracy is famed for the number of able men that came forth from its ranks. On the other hand, Carthage was weakened by the facts that she was dependent on mercenary troops in her wars, subject to revolts at home among the native populations whom she oppressed, and hampered by the factious spirit prevalent among her leading men. Carthage had a great commercial genius, but no gift for assimilating conquered peoples, or for establishing an Empire on a solid and enduring basis, and therefore, in the end, she succumbed to Rome, whose part it was to bring the nations under one wide long-enduring sway. The struggle of Carthage against Rome became, in fact, the contest of a man of the greatest abilities—Hannibal—against a nation of the utmost energy and determination, and the nation, in the long run, won the day.

The Carthaginians, at this time, held Corsica, Sardinia and various colonies in Spain and possessions in Sicily. It was in Sicily that the cause of quarrel between Rome and Carthage was found, and Rome picked the quarrel by interference in a local matter at Messana. Hiero, King of Syracuse, soon came over to the Romans, who, after defeating the Carthaginian army and taking Agrigentum (B. C. 262), determined to make themselves masters of Sicily. For this a fleet was needed, and with Roman energy they set to work and built one. Twice their squadrons were destroyed, but in B. C. 260 the consul

Duilius gained a great naval victory at Mylæ, on the northeast coast of Sicily, and from this time Rome became more and more nearly a match for Carthage on her special element, the sea. The Romans invaded Africa without success (B. C. 255), but were generally victorious in Sicily. In B. C. 247 the great Hamilcar Barca (father of Hannibal and Hasdrubal) was appointed to the Carthaginian command in Scicily, and maintained himself there with great patience and skill against all the Roman efforts. In B. C. 241, however, the Roman commander Lutatius Catulus utterly defeated the Carthaginian fleet off the Ægates Islands, on the west coast of Sicily, and the Carthaginians then gave in. Sicily thus became (B. C. 241) the first Roman province, the whole island coming into the hands of Rome, except the territory of her faithful ally, Hiero of Syracuse.

The Romans, with gross ill-faith and injustice, took advantage of a revolt against Carthage by her mercenary troops to deprive her of Sardinia and Corsica (B. C. 238), and Sardinia was made into a province. The next exploit of Rome was the conquest of Cisalpine Gaul, which was completed by B. C. 222, and the Roman hold upon the new territory was confirmed by the establishment of military colonies at Placentia and Cremona.

Carthage had resolved upon revenge for past defeats and injuries from Rome, and intrusted her cause to Hamilcar Barca. He formed the bold and ingenious plan of creating for his country a new empire in Spain, which might be used as a fresh base of operations against the foe whom he hated with a deadly hate. From B. C. 237 to 229 (when he fell in battle) he was engaged in reducing a large part of Spain to submission by diplomacy and force. In B. C. 221 his son, the illustrious Hannibal, took up the Spanish command, and he soon brought on a new conflict with Rome by his capture of her ally the city of Saguntum, on the northeast coast of Spain.

The Second Punic War is too well known in every detail to need much description here. The hero of the contest is Hannibal,* one of the purest and noblest characters in history—a man of whom we know nothing save from his foes, and all their wrath and envy have not been able to disfigure the portrait which the facts have forced them to transmit to future ages. Great as a statesman, supremely great as a soldier, beloved by his troops, and justly dreaded by the most warlike people of the ancient world, Hannibal stands forth an object for the highest admiration and esteem. Of his military capacity it is needless to say more than this, that two of the ablest Generals that ever lived, Napoleon and Wellington, both pronounced Hannibal to be the greatest of all commanders.

In B. C. 218 the Carthaginian General crossed the Alps after a five months' march from Spain, and descended with a storm of war upon the Romans. With a force of 20,000 foot and 6,000 horse he encountered the consular armies and defeated them at the Rivers Ticinus and Trebia (B. C. 218), in Cisalpine Gaul, the Thrasymene Lake in Etruria (B. C. 217), and, more decisively than all, and with immense slaughter, at Cannæ, in Apulia, in B. C. 216. For fifteen years (B. C. 218-202) Hannibal maintained his ground in Italy, defeating the Romans again and again, opposed by the cautious Fabius Maximus and the daring Marcellus (the conqueror of Syracuse), but unable to capture Rome, or to subdue Roman steadfastness and courage.

The chief causes of the ultimate failure of Hannibal, besides the doggedness of Rome's resistance, were the faithfulness of many of Rome's allies, especially the

* See volume " World's Famous Warriors."

Latins, in Italy, the success of Roman armies under Publius Scipio in Spain (which was for the time subdued by B. C. 205), and the want of due support by Carthage to her great leader. The crisis came in B. C. 207, when Hannibal's brother, Hasdrubal, crossed the Alps into Italy with a powerful army which, joined with Hannibal's in Southern Italy, would probably have effected the conquest of Rome, now almost exhausted by her efforts and defeats. This was not to be. Hasdrubal was encountered, defeated, and slain by the Romans at the decisive battle of the Metaurus (a river in Umbria), one of the great critical contests in the history of the world. The junction of the forces thus prevented, Rome was saved, and in order to be rid of Hannibal the war was carried now into the enemy's country.

Publius Scipio, who had been so successful in Spain, crossed from Sicily to Africa in B. C. 204, and did so well for Rome that Hannibal was recalled. The Second Punic War ended with the defeat of Hannibal by Scipio at Zama (five days' journey from Carthage) in B. C. 202. The conqueror gained the surname of Africanus. Hannibal lost his army, but not his fame. Rome was made certain now to rule the world. The terms of peace with Carthage made her for the time a mere dependency of Rome. All her foreign possessions were given up; her fleet was reduced to ten ships; she was to make no war without Rome's permission; an enormous war-indemnity was exacted.

In B. C. 213 Rome attacked Philip V, King of Macedon, because he had made a treaty with Carthage, and after concluding an alliance with the Ætolians the Romans gained some successes over Philip in the First Macedonian War, ending in 205. The Second Macedonian War (B. C. 200-197) put an end to Macedon's supremacy in Greece

by the victory of the ex-consul Flamininus at Cynoscephalæ in Thessaly, B. C. 197. Antiochus the Great of
Syria was next attacked. He had irritated Rome by
meddling in the affairs of Greece, which he invaded in B.
C. 192. He was defeated by the Roman armies both in
Greece and Asia Minor, and in B. C. 188 made peace on
terms that left Roman influence supreme in Asia Minor
as far as the borders of Syria.

Hannibal, the great Carthaginian, even after Zama,
had not despaired of himself or of his country. He set
vigorously to work at internal reforms in Carthage with
a view to renewing the contest with Rome; but being
thwarted by jealous and unpatriotic rivals, who also intrigued for his surrender to the Romans, he fled to the
court of Antiochus the Great of Syria in B. C. 194. In
throwing away her greatest man Carthage had lost her
last chance of regaining any real power. Hannibal was
driven from his shelter with Antiochus by the Roman
demand for his surrender, and took refuge with Prusias,
King of Bithynia, for some years; but Roman dread of his
abilities and influence pursued him, and, hopeless of escape,
he poisoned himself about B. C. 183, leaving Rome free at
last to pursue her victorious career without any opponent
likely to arrest it. A third Macedonian War, begun in
B. C. 171, was waged by the Romans against King Perseus, son of Philip V, and ended with a great Roman
victory at Pydna in B. C. 168, and the extinction of Macedon as a kingdom. After a revolt, called the Fourth
Macedonian War, and a war against the forces of the
Achæan League, Corinth was taken by Mummius, and
Macedonia and Greece became Roman provinces (B. C.
147-146).

There was a powerful party in Rome (headed by the
famous and stern censor, Porcius Cato), who relentlessly

insisted on the destruction of Carthage. Her warlike neighbor, Masinissa, King of Numidia, was encouraged by the Romans in harassing attacks, and in B. C. 149 Rome found a pretext for war. Her forces could not be resisted, and Carthage offered a complete submission, seeking the preservation of her commerce and her capital by a surrender of arms, warships, and the internal independence hitherto belonging to her. When Rome insisted on the destruction of the city of Carthage itself, and the removal of the inhabitants to inland abodes, the Carthaginians took counsel of despair, and resolved to stand a siege within their strong fortifications. Scipio Africanus Minor (really a son of Æmilius Paulus, the conqueror of Macedonia, and adopted by a Roman custom into the Scipio family) conducted the three years' siege of the great commercial city and her citadel, and Roman determination as usual carried its point. After fearful house-to-house fighting the remnant of 700,000 people surrendered; the place was set on fire, and burned for seventeen days; the ruins were leveled with the ground, and Carthage the proud city, alike with Carthage the commercial state, had ceased to exist, in B. C. 146, the same year as saw the final conquest of Greece. Part of the territory was given to Masinissa of Numidia, Rome's ally, part became the Roman Province of Africa.

The great peninsula to the west of Italy was inhabited chiefly by people called Iberians (not of Aryan race), and by Celtic tribes, who had made their way into the central part of the land. During the Second Punic War the Carthaginian dominion in Spain had been gained for Rome by the Scipio's; but the inhabitants have always been hard to master thoroughly in war, and even the Romans found the task long and difficult. The north and northwest of the country, indeed, remained independent till the time of the Empire. The Celtiberians, tribes of mixed origin in Central Spain, were conquered by about B. C. 180, after a long resistance. The part of Lusitania (modern Portugal) to the south of the Tagus was mastered after a brave struggle maintained for some years by a gallant leader named Viriathus, with whom the Romans made a treaty, prior to his assassination by their connivance, in B. C. 140. The conquest of the center and south of Spain was completed in the capture and destruction of the strong city of Numantia, near the source of the Douro, by Scipio Africanus Minor (the younger) in B. C. 133. The country had long before been divided by Rome into two provinces, respectively to the east and west of the Iberus or Ebro, called Hispania Citerior and Hispania Ulterior ("hither" and "further" Spain).

The subjugation of Spain, though still incomplete, was an important event in the development of the Roman dominion on the Mediterranean coasts. In subduing Spain, Rome was taking civilization to a land of peoples almost new to the culture of the east and center of the Mediterranean world. The inhabitants were brave, temperate, hardy, warlike, proud, and strongly attached to freedom, and they were now to show themselves, in a marked degree, capable of taking up the new ideas, customs, and language conveyed into their midst by the conquerors. The country was in course of time quite transformed and Romanized; the Latin language was adopted, the literature both of Greece and Rome was taught in the schools, and under the emperors many distinguished authors in the Latin tongue were of Spanish birth. The modern language of the country is so closely derived from Latin that a scholar can readily divine the general meaning without special study. The kingdom of Pergamus became very extensive after the defeat by the Romans of

Antiochus the Great of Syria in B. C. 190. Rome then gave nearly all the south and west of Asia Minor to Eumenes II, King of Pergamus. In B. C. 133, King Attalus III bequeathed the whole of his dominions to the Roman people, and the Province of Asia was formed.

At the beginning of the period now treated of—B. C. 266—Rome possessed only the peninsula of Italy; nor was she mistress of the whole of that, for Liguria, south of Cisalpine Gaul, was not subdued till long after the second Punic War. At the close of this epoch—by B. C. 133—Rome was the one great power of the world—possessor of most that was worth having (save Gaul, Egypt, and Syria) on the Mediterranean shores. In Europe, Asia, Africa, she ruled these territories—Italy, Sicily, Sardinia, Corsica, Cisalpine Gaul, the south and center of Spain, the late territory of Carthage in Africa, Northern and Southern Greece, and most of Asia Minor. Wherever she had not yet carried her conquering arms, the Roman name had become one of fear to the nations who had seen country after country mastered or absorbed by the all-embracing, irresistible Republic. The conquered provinces were governed by ex-consuls and ex-prætors, who went out there with the title of Proconsul or Proprætor, attended by a whole army of officials. The wealthy order in the state known as the Equites (Knights) farmed the taxes and the tribute levied from the provincials, and publicani, or collectors of public revenue (the publicans of Scripture), were scattered over the whole Roman world, and were held in very bad repute. The Proconsuls and Proprætors had the highest military and civil powers in their governments, and their eager desire to return to Rome with abundant means caused gross oppression of the people in the provinces. The grand passion of the Romans at this time was to amass money, whether by plunder in war, usury at home, or speculation and commerce abroad. The provincial governors received gifts from states and kings not yet subdued, bribes for their decisions in law-suits, and a share of the plunder made by extortionate tax-gatherers.

As the Senate alone appointed the provincial governors, and confined the appointments to Senators, it was the chief object of a rising citizen of Rome to become a member of that ruling body. The position could only be reached by holding the high offices in the state, and in order to secure election by the assemblies (Comitia) to these offices, it was needful to get the votes of the people by providing expensive shows in the theater and circus, and, as the degradation deepened, by direct bribes. After passing through the quæstorship, ædileship, prætorship, and consulship on these terms, a man would enter the Senate with an enormous load of debt, and could only hope to pay his creditors and acquire a fortune for himself by the proceeds of his term of office in a province as Proprætor or Proconsul. It is true that a provincial governor was liable to prosecution at Rome on his return, for crimes committed in his public capacity; but the Senatorial judges before whom he would have to appear were as much open to bribes as the voters in the Comitia, and part of the plunder of the provinces was thus devoted to securing impunity at Rome for those who robbed Rome's unhappy subjects.

The old class of Roman citizens, under the military system of universal service and the losses of the Punic and other wars, had greatly diminished in numbers. The soldiers of the armies that went out to the provinces often remained there as military colonists, and Rome and Italy received in exchange millions of foreign slaves. These men, frequently set free, became Roman citizens, and the old race, both in the city and in Italy at large, rapidly degenerated through intermarriages of Italians with these foreigners from all quarters of the Roman world. The lower order in Rome thus became in time a mere mob, living in idleness by the price of its votes, and on the cheap or gratuitous corn from Sicily and Africa, which was distributed by the Senate to appease popular discontents. The original Patricians and Plebeians had become classes of rich men and paupers, with no middle class of yeoman-farmers (or peasant-proprietors) and merchants to hold the political balance, and give stability to the constitutional order of things.

The sudden and vast increase of wealth flowing to Rome from such conquests as those of Carthage, Greece, and Asia, brought with it great luxury and its attendant vices. The newly-enriched Senators and knights, spurning the protests and scorning the example of such men as Cato the Censor, and those who kept to the olden simple style of life, plunged into all the extravagances that Greek and Asiatic fashions prompted, and that Roman want of purity in taste soon carried to a monstrous excess. Money was lavished upon mansions in Rome, decked out with richest furniture and plate; on country houses, pleasure-grounds, and fish-ponds to supply a favorite Roman food; on dancing-girls, musicians, and troops of like artistic or of menial slaves; on foreign wines and dainty dishes; on toadies and buffoons. The old regard for marriage and the sanctity of home declined, and Roman conquests had thus caused evils that were swiftly sapping the very foundations of the free state—the grand old republic of Rome.

A more beneficial use of the new wealth was the employment of it by ambitious men, and by the state officials, on works of public service and adornment. There were buildings at Rome called Basilicæ, which served as courts of law and as places of meeting for men of business. Of these (which were rectangular halls, with rows of columns, and a recess at one end for the tribunal), the Basilica Porcia was erected in B. C. 184, the Basilica Fulvia in 179, and the Basilica Sempronia in 171. The Porticoes (Porticus) were covered with paved walks, open on one side, and supported by columns. The Porticus Metelli was built by the Propraetor Metellus after his triumph over Perseus, King of Macedonia, B. C. 146. Among the most important and celebrated of the public works of ancient Rome were the Aqueducts (Aquæductus or Aquæ), for supplying the city with water from the hills outside. Some of these are still used to supply modern Rome. Of others the stupendous remains are visible in the Campagna di Roma (the undulating district round Rome), and in various countries which were formerly provinces of the Empire. The first of these was the Aqua Appia, begun by the censor Appius Claudius in B. C. 313. The Anio Vetus (or "ancient Anio"), begun in B. C. 273, brought water to Rome from the river Anio, eighteen miles away. It was mostly underground, and the windings of the course taken made the whole work over forty miles in length. The Aqua Marcia, famed for the coldness and purity of the water which it conveyed, was built in B. C. 144, at the public expense, by the prætor Quintus Marcius. It began nearly forty miles from Rome, and was of great height and solidity, proceeding for several miles on arches, of which remains are still visible. In such works as these the Romans displayed their practical character.

The physical might of Rome had subdued Greece, but the mind of Greece mastered Rome. The Greeks became the teachers of their conquerors. The deities of Greece were incorporated into the national faith of Rome. Greek literature became the education of the Roman youth. Greek philosophy was almost the only philosophy the

Romans knew. Rome adopted Grecian arts, and was moulded by contact with Greek life. In name and government the world was Roman, in feeling and civilization it was Greek. The chief works of art at Rome either came from Greece as part of the plunder of war, or were executed there by Greek artists of the later school. Elegance and culture were by nature foreign to the Romans; these they sought from Greece, and large numbers of Greek slaves were brought to Rome. These Greek slaves and freedmen acted as superintendents of factories and teachers of the children. The city population also included large numbers of Greek musicians, teachers of rhetoric, philosophers, secretaries, and copyists (an important class when there was no printing), in many cases inmates of the houses of the great, whom they instructed and amused. The effect of Greek culture and philosophy on the old religious belief is also to be observed. Religion declined into mere expediency, the educated class protecting popular superstitions which they despised themselves.

Roman literature came into existence five centuries after the foundation of the city. The old rude Roman ballads are entirely lost, and the first Roman poet was Livius Andronicus (a native of Magna Græcia), a drama by whom was performed at Rome in the year B. C. 240. He took his comedies and tragedies from the Greek, being master of both tongues. He was followed by Nævius, a Campanian, who adapted, from the Greek, comedies in which he attacked the Patricians. An epic poem of his on the first Punic War furnished matter to Ennius and Virgil. Nævius died about B. C. 200. The founder of Roman literature is generally said to be Ennius, a native of Magna Græcia. He lived between B. C. 239 and 169. Ennius wrote an epic poem, in dactylic hexameters, on the annals of Rome, and this work was the chief epic poem in Latin until Virgil, borrowing largely from his predecessor, surpassed him in his immortal "Æneid." Of these three authors—Andronicus, Nævius, Ennius—we have only the scantiest remains.

The great comic genius, Plautus, wrote between B. C. 225 and 184. Twenty of his plays remain; and modern opinion has ratified the verdict of the Romans, with all classes of whom Plautus was a great favorite. He did not merely translate old Greek comedies, but used their plots and characters for real Roman work as to dialogue and detail. His plays have found imitators among modern writers of the highest order, including the great Frenchman, Moliere., Terence, or to give him his full name, Terentius Afer—"Terence the African," was born at Carthage in B. C. 193, and died in 159. We have six of his comedies, adapted from the Greek, and written in Latin of perfect elegance and purity. The tragic poet, Pacuvius, whose works are lost, flourished about B. C. 160. He is said to have been an accomplished and vigorous writer. Another tragedian, named Accius, was somewhat later than Pacuvius. Roman tragedy, like Roman comedy, was largely imitated from the Greek.

During and after the Second Punic War (B. C. 218-202) the historical writers Fabius Pictor and Cincius Alimentus, occur; they wrote (in Greek) an account of that struggle. The famous censor Porcius Cato (died B. C. 149) wrote a historical work on events from Rome's foundation till his own time; it was called "Origines" (as giving the origins of Italian towns), and is the first prose work in Latin of which we have any considerable remains.

DECLINE AND FALL OF THE REPUBLIC

The "burning question" and chief grievance with the mass of the people in Italy was the land question. The Licinian Law of B. C. 366, limiting the amount of public land to be held by Patricians, and providing for the distribution of the surplus among the Plebeians, had not been carried out, and the former corn-lands of Italy were now turned into pasture-land held by the rich in vast domains, while the old race of peasant-proprietors had become almost extinct. The people had not only lost the land, but the love of labor, and were crowded into the towns, where they lived on the largesses and bribes of the wealthy, and were degraded constantly and increasingly by association and intermarriage with the slave population that now flooded Italy.

Tiberius Gracchus, a son of the famous Cornelia (a daughter of Scipio Africanus, the victor at Zama) [see volume "Famous Women of the World"], became a Tribune (Tribunus Plebis) in B. C. 133, and at once took up the cause of his poor and oppressed fellow-citizens. His object was to give a share of land (the public land, which belonged to the state, and therefore to the people) to each free citizen, and so to people Italy once more with citizens instead of slaves, and to restore agriculture, which had vanished into pasturage. He therefore proposed a bill to enforce the Licinian Law, and on the death of Attalus, King of Pergamus (bequeathing his kingdom and property to the Roman people) Gracchus proposed that this property should be distributed so as to allow the new class of small landowners to stock their little farms. If these measures had been carried out, a new middle class would have been created, which would have done much to avert ruin from the republic.   The jealous and avaricious nobles rose, and with their own hands and those of their retainers murdered Tiberius Gracchus in the Forum during the voting for his second tribunate in B. C. 132.   His brother, Caius Gracchus, was tribune in B. C. 123 and 122, and carried several laws in favor of the poor; but he also was driven to death by the Senatorial party in 121, during a furious outbreak, which ended in the wholesale murder of his adherents in Rome.   The treatment of the Gracchi by the Patricians was of itself sufficient to show that the old Roman respect for law—the basis, the essence, the very life of a free state—had now vanished away.   The legislation of the Gracchi was ultimately, and most of it immediately, neglected or repealed, and the last chance of saving the republic was lost.

The internal history of Rome—almost everything apart from foreign conquest—becomes now a history of the struggles and domination of individuals, and the principle at work is mainly the ascendency of physical force. The contests waged involve an aristocratic and a popular side—a party striving to maintain the privileges of the existing Roman citizens and the predominance of the Senate, and a party determined to make free citizens of all the inhabitants of Italy, and to break down the remaining power of the aristocracy.

At this time the Roman Senate consisted, not of the able and patriotic statesmen of the past, but of short-sighted, selfish oligarchs, who cared for little besides the power wielded in the consulship, the vanity gratified in a "Triumph," and the greed glutted in a provincial government.   On his return from abroad the Roman proconsul or proprætor generally gave himself up to ease and luxury for the rest of his days, and let politics alone when they had given him all he cared for. The Senate had thus become quite unfit to rule at a time when firm and wise control was more than ever needed.

Between B. C. 125 and 120 the Allobroges and other tribes in the south of Gaul were subdued, the colony of Aquæ Sextiæ (the modern Aix) was founded there, and a Roman province was made in B. C. 120, called by the Romans "Provincia" or "the Province," as opposed to the rest of Gallia; hence comes the modern name of that district—Provence. Jugurtha, King of Numidia (northwest of Africa), was grandson of Masinissa, who was a thorn in the side of Carthage at the close of the second Punic War. His connection with Rome is remarkable for the gross corruption thereby revealed in the Roman Senate, members of which Jugurtha bribed to connive at his intrigues and crimes for the possession of the throne of Numidia. The war between Rome and Jugurtha lasted from B. C. 112 to 106, and in the course of it Jugurtha corrupted by bribes two Roman commanders, and defeated another. The great Roman general, Marius, ended it by defeating and capturing Jugurtha (B. C. 106), who was thrown into a dungeon and starved to death after his conqueror's triumph in 104. Numidia became a Roman province about sixty years later. The celebrated Marius, who was seven times consul, was born at Arpinum (birthplace also of the great orator Cicero) in Latium. He appears in the civil struggles as champion of the popular element against the Roman aristocracy. He was one of the ablest generals that Rome produced, but claims no higher place in politics than that of a bold, rude, unscrupulous, and arrogant soldier immersed in civil strife. The Cimbri were a Celtic people in the northwest of Germany; the Teutones (or Teutons) were a German (Teutonic) tribe on the Baltic coast. These tribes, to the number of 300,000 fighting men, with their wives and children, moved southward through Gaul, and, as they neared Italy, defeated several Roman armies with great slaughter between B. Ç. 113 and 105. After an unsuccessful attack on Spain they returned to the Provincia (south of Gaul), and there Marius saved the Roman Empire from being prematurely overwhelmed by northern barbarians. In B. C. 102 he annihilated the Teutones in a great battle near Aquæ Sextiæ (Aix), on a spot where the modern village of Pourrieres still preserves the name of Campi Putridi ("putrefied fields"), given to the battle-ground from the number of decaying bodies. In B. C. 101 Marius destroyed the Cimbri at the battle of Vercellæ in Cisalpine Gaul.

The Social or Marsic War was one of the great contests of Rome in the field of battle. The Italian tribes— the chief who took part in the war being the Marsi, Picentes, Peligni, Samnites, Apuli, and Lucani—were now claiming the full Roman citizenship, just as the Plebeians had done in the old struggles with the Patricians. Rome had given up her old wise policy of making new citizens out of subjects, and she was now to suffer for it in a tremendous and dangerous conflict with the brave and indignant Italians. The Latin colonies were faithful to Rome, and this alone saved her from ruin. The war continued during two years, B. C. 90-89, and was of the most sanguinary and desperate character. In B. C. 89 Asculum in Picenum was taken by the Romans and destroyed. The Romans had already detached some of their enemies by passing the Lex Julia, giving the Roman franchise to the Latin colonies, and to such of the Italian allies as gave up the contest; and after further Roman successes the matter ended in Rome's granting all the

RECONSTRUCTION OF "ROMA IMMORTALIS," AUGUSTAN AGE

Theater of Marcellus

Temple of Jupiter Capitolinus

Circus Maximus

Tabularium

The Palatine and the Palace of the Emperors

Forum Romanum

Coliseum

demands of the Italian confederates, when 300,000 brave men had fallen on both sides. The Lex Julia was extended to the citizens of all towns in alliance with Rome throughout Italy, that is to the Socii, and on compliance with certain formalities the Roman franchise was thus carried to the borders of Cisalpine Gaul.

Mithridates, King of Pontus, on the Euxine Sea (a realm originally formed by a satrap's revolt from the old Persian empire), was a man of boundless energy and great ability, who in B. C. 88 attacked the neighboring countries Phrygia and Galatia, and became master of the Roman province of Asia, where he carried out a general massacre of the Roman residents to the number of scores of thousands. In the first Mithridatic War (B. C. 88-84) Sulla, an able general, and leader of the Senatorial party at Rome, defeated the troops of Mithridates in Greece, and brought him to terms—Mithridates giving up his conquests and paying a large indemnity. The second Mithridatic War lasted from B. C. 74 to 63, and arose out of a claim to the possession of Bithynia, bequeathed by its late King, Nicomedes, to the Romans. The chief generals on the side of Rome were Lucullus and the famous Pompeius Magnus (Pompey the Great, the future antagonist of Julius Cæsar), Mithridates being assisted by his son-in-law, Tigranes, King of Armenia. The power of Rome prevailed of course in the end, and Mithridates, driven from his throne by her arms and by domestic rebellion, died in B. C. 63 in what is now the Crimea.

Meanwhile Rome had been plunged into a civil war. This sanguinary contest lasted from B. C. 88 to 82, and presents a dreary scene of massacre and plunder. It began in a rivalry as to the command in the first Mithridatic War, and Sulla, having ready an army to which the Senate had appointed him, marched on Rome and drove Marius into exile, B. C. 88. It was then that Marius was seen "sitting on the ruins of Carthage," according to the well-known story. In B. C. 87 Cinna, a supporter of Marius (after Sulla had gone to Greece against Mithridates), roused the party and recalled Marius. Rome was forced to yield, and a fearful massacre took place of the Senatorial and other enemies of Marius, who died in B. C. 86. In B. C. 82 Sulla returned to Italy, and defeated the partisans of Marius (who were supported by a Samnite army) in a terrific battle outside the Colline Gate of Rome (B. C. 82). A general slaughter of the opposite faction throughout Italy now followed, proscriptions or lists of the doomed being regularly published. In B. C. 82 Sulla was made "dictator" by the Senate, and his soldiers, and the supporters of the Senatorial party were rewarded by the plunder derived from the confiscated wealth of nearly three thousand slain Equites (the rich tax-farming class), and of such Senators as were of the Marian faction. Sulla now effected an aristocratic revolution, undoing the popular legislation of past times, reducing the power of the Tribuni Plebis, and abolishing the powers of the Comitia Tributa. He also established many military colonies throughout Italy, dividing the lands amongst his old soldiers. In B. C. 79 Sulla suddenly resigned his power, and died in B. C. 78. The changes he made in the constitution were of little moment really, as the free state was virtually dead, and greater men than Marius and Sulla were coming to the front to contest the sovereignty of the Roman world.

Cneius Pompeius was one of the ablest generals produced by ancient Rome. He was born in B. C. 106, and fought with great distinction on Sulla's side in the civil war with Marius. He succeeded Sulla as head of the

aristocratic (Senatorial) party. After some successes
against Roman revolt in Spain (B. C. 76-71) Pompey
became consul in B. C. 70, and now figured as the popular
hero, undoing some of Sulla's legislation. In B. C. 67
the famous Gabinian Law (giving special powers for the
object in view, and carried by the tribune Gabinius), gave
Pompey a grand opportunity, which he used with consummate ability. The Mediterranean Sea was at this time
infested by pirates so numerous and bold that they plundered cities on the Greek and Asiatic coasts, threatened
Rome with starvation by cutting off the corn-ships coming
from Africa and Egypt, and seized persons for ransom
not far from Rome itself. In three months, by skillful
arrangements, wise choice of subordinates, and determined
action, Pompey swept the great central sea clear of these
rebels and marauders from end to end, and, pursuing the
chief body to their nests and strongholds on the coast of
Cilicia, drove them to death or to surrender.

This exploit was followed by his successes in Asia
against Mithridates and Tigranes. Pontus was thus
made a Roman province in B. C. 65. In B. C. 64
Pompey made Syria a province by deposing the King
Antiochus. In 63 he subdued Phœnicia and Palestine,
capturing Jerusalem and returning (with a splendid triumph) to Rome in B. C. 61. Three other prominent men,
one supremely great, had now arisen in Rome : these were
Cicero, Crassus, and Julius Cæsar.

Marcus Tullius Cicero (often called "Tully" in old
English authors) is one of those men of olden time whose
moral portraits are most familiar to the moderns. We
know him not only from contemporary history, but from
his numerous letters to friends, which, besides supplying
a large part of that history, depict the man himself in vivid

colors.   Cicero was born at Arpinum, in Latium, in B. C.
107, and after a studious youth and early manhood spent
on law, philosophy, and rhetoric, became a distinguished
orator about B. C. 76.   He addressed assemblies on public questions in the forum at Rome, and also practiced as
an advocate in the law-courts.   After passing through
the regular gradation of state-offices as quæstor, curule
ædile, and prætor, he became consul in B. C. 63.   His
exploit in this capacity (which Cicero himself never for-
got, nor allowed the world to forget) was the crushing
of Catiline's conspiracy, for which the great orator received from the Senate the title of "Pater Patriæ" (father
of the fatherland).   Cicero's political position was that
of a general supporter of the aristocratic or Senatorial
party.   As an orator Cicero was supremely great; as an
accomplished man of letters he was a master of style, and
had a great variety of attainments; as a statesman he was
patriotic, shrewd, weak, and vacillating; as a man he was
vain, honest, and amiable.

Marcus Crassus was a man of great political influence
in Rome, because he was by far the richest man there—
the possessor of mines, estates, mansions let at high rents,
and hosts of slaves, who were taught to work at handicrafts which brought in large gains to their owner.   In
B. C. 70 Crassus became consul, and feasted all Rome at
ten thousand tables, besides giving out corn enough to
keep every citizen and his household for three months.
His wealth and his zealous courting of the citizens by
studied affability, and by service rendered in the law-courts
to those who needed an advocate, gave him much pop-
ularity: he had half the Senate in his debt, and he could
afford to bribe all judges whom eloquence could not reach.
He was no statesman, and could only have acquired such
weight as he did in so corrupt a condition of things as he

found existing in Rome. He was one of the leaders of the aristocratic party.

Caius Julius Cæsar* is universally admitted to be the foremost man in all the world's history for varied and, in almost all departments, consummate ability. Naturally good-hearted, keenly intelligent, brave as a lion, charmingly and weightily eloquent, endued with a marvelous memory for things and persons, boundless in generosity, cool in anger, gracious in manner, the favorite of the people, the best-beloved courtier of Roman ladies, one of the purest and most forcible of writers, highly accomplished in all the arts of a man of fashion and of a statesman and a man of action—he presents a dazzling picture in the union of many qualities and attainments, some one or two of which suffice to make a man distinguished among ordinary men. In person he is described in Froude's "Cæsar" as "tall, slight, handsome; with dark, piercing eyes, sallow complexion, large nose, lips full, features refined and intellectual, neck sinewy and thick . . . his dress of studied negligence." He was a noble of the highest position, as born in one of the best of the old Roman families, but he became in a sense the popular champion as leader of the Marian party a good many years (about fifteen) after the death of Marius; and, filled with the determination of making himself ultimately master of the Roman world, he used all men and every means with the greatest skill to bring about the preordained result. Cæsar was a man who could thoroughly "appreciate the wants of the moment and the problems of the future;" he was also one who could make instruments for his work out of the ideas, the circumstances, and the politicians of his day, and so he commanded and achieved, in the end, complete and brilliant success. He was one of those world-historical

* See volume " World's Famous Warriors."

men who possess at once an insight into the requirements of the time, a perfect knowledge of what is ripe for development, and the heroic qualities of courage, patience and endurance needed by him who is to create a new world out of the disordered elements of existing decay, and to raise the imposing fabric of imperialism on the ruins of a republic. Julius Cæsar was born in B. C. 100, and gained early distinction as a soldier and an orator. After being Quæstor, Ædile, and Prætor, he warred successfully in Spain (as Proprætor) in B. C. 61, returning to Rome in the following year. This brings us to the remarkable coalition known as the "First Triumvirate."

In B. C. 60 the three chief men of Rome—Cæsar the statesman, Pompey the general, and Crassus the capitalist —made an arrangement for the division amongst themselves of all the real power in the state. The command of money gave them the possession at will of armies of those soldiers who had now become mercenaries instead of Roman citizens, owing obedience to the constitution; and in Pompey and Cæsar was found abundant skill to direct the military force which would at any moment put the Senate and its supporters at their mercy. Cicero held aloof when Cæsar wished him to join the league, and vainly hoped to be able yet to preserve the commonwealth. It was clear that a struggle for supreme power in the hands of one must sooner or later arise. In B. C. 59 Cæsar was consul, and carried a land bill, dividing the rich soil of Campania in allotments amongst the poorer citizens. On the close of his year of office he was appointed Proconsul of the provinces of Cisalpine Gaul, Illyricum, and Transalpine Gaul for the term of five years, with the command of four legions, about 25,000 men. It is surmised that Cæsar sought this important and difficult provincial government with the express object of gaining military fame, and of forging (in the training of an army devoted to his service) the weapon which would be needed in the contest that was sure to come. During Cæsar's campaigns in Gaul, where his government was prolonged for a second five-year term, one of the members of the Triumvirate disappeared from the scene. Crassus, after holding the consulship with Pompey in B. C. 55, went out as Proconsul to the province of Syria in 54. His greed of wealth and desire for the military fame which he envied in Cæsar and Pompey, brought him to ruin when he was induced to attack the Kingdom of Parthia.

Parthia enjoys in history the rare distinction of being a country the prowess of whose warriors baffled the efforts of Rome for her subjection. The Parthian Kingdom lay to the southeast of the Caspian Sea, and came into existence about B. C. 250 by revolt from the Seleucidæ, the monarchs of Syria, which became a powerful realm after the death of Alexander the Great. The Kingdom of Parthia included Parthia proper, Hyrcania, and afterward, by conquest about B. C. 130, Bactria, so that at last her dominions stretched from the Euphrates to the Indus, and from the river Oxus to the Indian Ocean. The inhabitants of Parthia proper (the Parthi) were a people of Scythian origin, and were noted in war for the skill and bravery of their armor-clad horse-archers, who enveloped an enemy on all sides, and poured in their missiles, and then swiftly retired, firing backwards with great and proverbial effect. The ruling dynasty was called the Arsacidæ, from the name of Arsaces, the founder. The formidable repute of the Parthian warriors was increased by the war with Syria in B. C. 131, when they annihilated the Syrian army sent against them. The policy of the Parthian rulers was very exclusive; strangers were not admitted to their dominions, and commerce was sacrificed to their watchful jealousy. Their establishment in the old Persian Empire caused a great change in the lines of commerce between the Eastern and Western world. The East India trade, stopped in its passage through Babylonia, began to shape its course through Northern Arabia and the Red Sea. To this change the wealth and splendor obtained by the great commercial cities Palmyra and Alexandria must be chiefly attributed. The Parthians adopted the Greek religion, manners and customs, which had been introduced into that part of Asia by Alexander's conquests.

It was the downfall of the Kingdoms of Mithridates and Tigranes in Asia Minor that brought Parthia into conflict with the Roman Empire. The conquest of Armenia brought Rome's frontier close to Parthia, and the ambition of Crassus did the rest. Crassus crossed the Euphrates in B. C. 53, and was attacked by the Parthians in the plains of Mesopotamia. The Roman infantry could do nothing against the peculiar tactics of the foe, and Crassus retreated, after great slaughter of his troops, to a place called Charræ. Then, in a helpless situation, he held parley with the Parthian general, Surenas, and was murdered at the interview. The head of Crassus was cut off and sent to the Parthian King, Orodes, who caused melted gold to be poured into the mouth, in mockery of its late owner's love for the precious metal. The Roman standards (the famous "eagles," worshiped as gods by the Roman troops) had been taken by the Parthians, and the remnant of the Roman army became prisoners of war, and settled in the East. A more complete disaster, a more burning disgrace, never befell the arms of Rome.

The subsequent history of Parthia may be interesting. The renowned cavalry seem to have been all-powerful only on their own soil, for their invasions of the Roman province of Syria in B. C. 39 and 38 were utterly defeated,

while the invasion of Parthia by the great Roman general
and Triumvir, Antonius, in 36, was repulsed with the loss
of a great part of his army. In B. C. 20 the Parthian
King, Phraates, restored, chiefly as a friendly concession,
the standards and prisoners taken from Crassus and Antonius, and this is the event commemorated by the Roman
poets of the day as equivalent to a submission by Parthia.
Under the Roman Emperors the Parthians sometimes
courted and were sometimes at war with Rome, and were
partially conquered for a time under Trajan. The Parthian Kings seem to have encouraged Christianity. In
A. D. 226 a revolt of the Persians put an end to the Parthian Kingdom, revived the religion of Zoroaster, stopped
the eastward progress of Christianity in Asia, and began
modern history in Persia.

Cæsar's eight campaigns in Gaul (B. C. 58-50) are
described, mainly by himself, in his admirable Commentaries. Gaul was bounded by the Rhine, the Alps, the
Pyrenees, the Atlantic, and the sea now called "the channel." The southern part (Provence) had been conquered
by the Romans (B. C. 125), and the Roman territory was
gradually extended as far north as Geneva, and as far
west as Tolosa (Toulouse). The Belgæ, a race of German
origin, held the north; the southwest of the country was
occupied by Iberians, a non-Aryan race, the center being
mainly occupied by Celts, the same race as the Irish, who
strongly resemble the old Gauls in character—humorous,
poetical, pious, credulous, shrewd, patriotic, clannish,
brave, undisciplined, indolent, amiable, clever and imprac-
ticable. The greatest hero of the war on the side of the
Gauls was the noble, knightly Vercingetorix, who (in B.
C. 52) most bravely resisted Cæsar at Alesia (close to the
source of the Seine) and was put to death, with true
Roman barbarity, after his conqueror's triumph at Rome,

in B. C. 45. The chief incidents of Cæsar's great contest in Gaul are his dispersion of the emigrant hosts of the Helvetii and the expulsion of the Germans, who had invaded Gaul under Ariovistus in B. C. 58; his conquest of the Belgæ and the Aquitani in 57 and 56; his invasions of Britain in 55 and 54, and his subduing of Gallic revolts, including the great rising of Vercingetorix, between B. C. 53 and 51, when Gallia Transalpina was finally and wholly subdued, and the Roman dominion was extended to the Rhine and the Channel.

In his treatment of the conquered Gauls Cæsar showed, on several occasions, the inhuman cruelty and the perfidy which marked the dealings of Romans with their foes. In the means which Cæsar employed to subdue the Gauls he displayed powers of mind which rank him among the greatest generals of all history. With little previous experience of war, he now adapted means to ends with the utmost skill, showed wonderful foresight and swiftness of movement, and trained for its future work an army of such excellence as has rarely indeed followed a general into the field—an army like unto that with which Wellington crossed the Pyrenees triumphant into France; a force of which he said himself, though he was no boaster, that "it could go anywhere and do anything." The importance of the conquest of Gaul in the history of the world is that it brought the old world of Southern Europe, of which Rome was the head, into contact with the lands and nations which were to play the greatest part in later times, with Gaul, Germany, and Britain. The importance of the conquest of Gaul in the career of Julius Cæsar is that it gave him, in his splendid and victorious army, the lever with which he revolutionized the Roman commonwealth; for these legions afterward conquered Pompey and the

Senate, and the Gallic campaigns made Cæsar the idol of the soldiery of Rome.

Cæsar's brilliant and solid successes in Gaul had aroused a strong jealousy in Pompey, and an indignant fear in the Senate, who now brought Pompey over to their views, and made him again their champion. The greatest enmity soon existed between the rivals, and only an occasion for outbreak into civil war was needed. This occasion arose when Cæsar was ordered by the Senate, at Pompey's instance, to lay down his proconsular command, B. C. 50 (Cæsar being then, after the pacification of Gaul, in Gallia Cisalpina, south of the Alps), and to return as a private citizen to Rome. This was in reply to Cæsar's request to be allowed to stand for the consulship (of B. C. 48) without coming to Rome, as his (second) term of command over Gaul had still a year to run. The object of the Senate and of Pompey was simply this—to get Cæsar into their hands; in which case he would have probably died after a mock trial. Julius Cæsar was scarcely the man to be caught in this way, and he replied in a decisive way to the Senate's order, either to disband his army or to be accounted a public foe. A little river called the Rubicon flowed into the Adriatic Sea, at the frontier-line between Italy and Cisalpine Gaul. To pass that stream with an armed force, from his province into Italy, would be an act of open defiance to the Senate, and (in constitutional law, if there had been any constitution left to violate) an act of treason to the state, and a declaration of civil war. In the early days of B. C. 49 Cæsar settled the matter, with the resolution that belonged to him, by crossing the Rubicon at the head of his devoted and well-disciplined troops.

Cæsar swept onward with a vigor that at once drove

Pompey and the Senate over the narrow sea to Greece, and made the invader master of all Italy within sixty days. On entering Rome, Cæsar was appointed consul for B. C. 48, and turned his first attention, in the summer of 49, to Spain, where he defeated the Pompeiian armies under Afranius and Petreius, making the west safe before going eastward to encounter Pompey. Cæsar crossed over into Greece early in 48, and found Pompey established there with a powerful army. At Dyrrhachium, in Illyria, Pompey defeated Cæsar, who had attacked his fortified position, and then followed him into Thessaly.

There, on the plains of Pharsalia, a decisive battle, fought in August, B. C. 48, ended in the total defeat of Pompey. He fled to Egypt, and was murdered there before Cæsar could arrive to save him, by order of the ministers of the King of Egypt. Cæsar shed tears of genuine sorrow at the sight of his slain rival's head, and promptly executed the assassins. It is important to observe that there is in existence documentary evidence which amply proves that, if the senatorial party had been successful, a fearful and widespread "proscription" (as under Sulla) would have taken place, and the Roman Empire would have become the prey of a few abandoned nobles. From such horrors the victory of Cæsar saved the Roman world.

On his arrival in Egypt, Cæsar became involved in a quarrel which the famous Cleopatra* induced him to take up on her behalf. She was co-sovereign of Egypt along with her brother, Ptolemy, and, having been expelled by his party, was seeking to force her way back with an army raised in Syria. Cæsar had only a small force with him, and the contest (called the "Alexandrine War," from the city where the fighting occurred) waged by him with the

* See volume " Famous Women of the World."

King's troops was of a desperate character. Cæsar was besieged in Alexandria, and had to fight for his life; the Egyptian fleet was burnt, and along with it a large part of the famous library, with its invaluable manuscripts. In March, B. C. 47, the struggle ended in Cæsar's favor, and he made his way back to Rome through Syria and Asia Minor, arriving at the capital in September.

During Cæsar's absence in the East, the Pompeian party had rallied in Africa, and in September, B. C. 47, he sailed to encounter his enemies there. Cato the younger (surnamed Uticensis or "of Utica," from the place of his death), a descendant of the famous Cato the Censor, had gathered a large army of Italians and Numidians, which Cæsar routed, in April, B. C. 46, at the battle of Thapsus, a town on the coast, westward from Malta. At Utica, northwest from the site of Carthage, Cato killed himself in stoical despair of the republic, and the capture of Utica ended the war in Africa.

Cæsar returned to Rome in July, 46, and had four splendid triumphs for his victories in Gaul, Egypt, Pontus (where he had defeated Pharnaces, son of Mithridates, on his way back from Egypt), and Africa. His position was secure, and one of the brightest features of his character, his clemency toward beaten fellow citizens, was displayed in the use he made of his victory. There was no vengeance, no "proscription," no difference made between victors and vanquished. The Roman Republic was at an end, and the Roman monarchy had virtually begun.

Pompey's two sons, Cneius and Sextus, had gathered a powerful army in Spain, and Cæsar proceeded thither late in B. C. 46. In March, 45, at Munda, the Pompeian army was defeated, after one of Cæsar's hardest-fought engagements.

The new constitution established by Cæsar had this

essential principle—that the sovereign authority over the provinces and the direction of public policy resided ultimately in one man. The Senate survived as a council of state; the magistrates administered their old functions; the Imperator (meaning commander-in-chief, from which the word "Emperor" is derived) was the real executive, and the legions were the instruments of rule. The republic, under which crime had been licensed, justice publicly sold, and the provinces used as a gold-mine for profligate nobles, had become impossible, and monarchy, under republican forms and names, was the substitute made for it. When Cæsar returned to Rome from Spain in September, B. C. 45, he was appointed Dictator and Imperator for life, his effigy was to be struck on coins; the month formerly called Quintilis, was named Julius (our July) in his honor, and the senate took an oath of allegiance and devotion to his person.

As master of the Roman dominions, Cæsar did enough to prove that he was as capable of ruling as of winning an Empire; of benefiting as of conquering mankind. In B. C. 46 he had effected the important work of reforming the calendar, which, from inaccurate reckoning, had fallen into confusion, so that the real time was three months behind the nominal. A Greek astronomer was called in to rectify matters, and the Julian calendar remained in use till A. D. 1582. He formed great plans for the public good. If Cæsar had been allowed to live, the still malarious Pomptine (or Pontine) Marshes, on the coast of Latium, would have been drained and turned into healthful, profitable land; and the river Tiber, still mischievous from inundations, would have flowed in a deeper and safer channel. Among his beneficent designs were the codification of the Roman law, the establishment of public libraries, the cutting of a canal through the Isthmus of Corinth, and the development of trade by the enlargement of the harbor at Ostia. A genius so universal, backed by a spirit so enlightened, might at once have restored the decayed agriculture of Italy, and extended and secured the boundaries of the Empire on the Danube and in the East —for these things, with divers other schemes, had entered into his all-embracing mind. All was cut short and rendered vain by the lowest baseness of human envy, and the worst foolishness of human folly. Cæsar had been fully accepted by the great mass of the Romans as their one possible, their one peaceful ruler, when his career was brought to the sudden and tragical end known to all the world.

There is no need to dwell on the crime of the probably sincere and fanatical Brutus, and the assuredly malignant and ungrateful Cassius, who were the prime movers in the plot that slew Julius Cæsar. On the Ides (15th) of March, B. C. 44, in the Senate-house at Rome, called "Curia Pompeii," the greatest man in history died by the daggers of assassins.* He fell, bleeding from many wounds, at the foot of the statue of Pompey, whom he had pursued with intent only to spare, whose fate he had bewailed, whose friends he had first conquered and then forgiven, only to be murdered by their hands at last. Julius Cæsar was in the fifty-sixth year of his age when he died, and left his work unfinished, and his power as a prize for the victor in another inevitable civil war.

Marcus Antonius the Triumvir (known in old English authors as "Mark Antony," and generally as "Antony") was born about B. C. 83, and gained early distinction as a General, serving under Cæsar in Gaul, commanding the left wing of the victorious army at Pharsalia, and acting usually as Cæsar's representative in

* See volume "World's Famous Warriors."

his absence, and his chief supporter in Rome. At the time of the assassination he was Consul along with Cæsar, and his eloquence roused the people, and drove Brutus, Cassius, and their faction among the Senators to seek safety in flight from Rome. Antony's object was to succeed to Cæsar's power, but there was a rival in the way. This was Cæsar's great-nephew and adopted son, Caius Octavius (better known by his imperial title of "Augustus Cæsar"), whose legal name (after adoption) was Caius Julius Cæsar Octavianus. The Senate at first sided with Octavianus, and afterward veered round to Antony. The result was a coalition known as the "Second Triumvirate."

Antony, Octavius, and Lepidus (an insignificant person, from lack either of ability or of energy) arranged, in B. C. 43, to divide the supreme power amongst themselves. The first step needed was to crush their enemies, and this Octavius and Antony did with a cruelty more disgraceful than that shown in the proscriptions of Marius and Sulla. Slaughter lists were made out, and bands of murderers and plunderers let loose on the victims. Hundreds of Senators, thousands of knights (the " Equites "), and many thousands of citizens were slain, and their property plundered. The most illustrious of the victims was the great orator Cicero, who had provoked the rage of Antony by denouncing him in the speeches known as "Cicero's Philippics." The triumvirs then turned against Brutus and Cassius, who had raised a large army in the East, and taken up their position in Thrace. In November, B. C. 42, Antony and Octavius utterly defeated them at the two battles of Philippi, in the east of Macedonia, and Brutus and Cassius died by self-murder. The attempt to galvanize the dead republic into life had signally and finally failed.

The Roman world was now divided amongst the victors. Antony took the portion eastward from Italy, Octavianus the west, and Lepidus had Africa assigned to him. A confused period of conflicts and quarrels between the triumvirs ensued. In B. C. 40 the peace of Brundusium reconciled Antony and Octavianus for a time; in B. C. 36 Lepidus was expelled from the league, and returned from his province to live quietly at Rome. The conduct of Antonius with Cleopatra, the fascinating Queen of Egypt, at last occasioned the certain rupture between him and Octavianus. Antony had married Octavia, his rival's sister, and then divorced her in order to marry Cleopatra. With her at Alexandria he assumed the pomp and lived the life of an Eastern despot, and his doings had disgusted many of his own supporters. The wary, cool, and hypocritical Octavianus had meanwhile been strengthening his position in Italy and the West by rewarding veterans with lands, and cementing the attachment of his legions to his person; by successful warfare in Illyria and Pannonia (northeast of Adriatic Sea), and by the general contrast of his actions with those of the reckless Antony. In B. C. 32 the Senate declared war against Cleopatra, and this meant that Octavius and Antonius were to meet in a decisive struggle.

Antony had gathered his fleet (aided by Cleopatra in person with sixty galleys) and his army at Actium on the Ambracian Gulf, south of Epirus, and there Octavius encountered him in the first days of September, B. C. 31. The contest was decided by a naval battle, in the midst of which Cleopatra fled with the Egyptian squadron, and was ignominiously followed by Antony, whose ships and army then surrendered to his foe. In the following year (B. C. 30) Octavianus followed Antony and Cleopatra to Alexandria, where the unhappy pair committed suicide—he with his sword, she with a poisonous snake, the asp—rather than fall into the hands of the cold-blooded conqueror, who would have killed the one and kept the other to grace a Roman triumph, as a captive, with her charms. Egypt, in B. C. 30, thus became a Roman Province, and Rome's dominion in the Mediterranean basin now became formally, as it had long been virtually, complete.

The Roman Empire, replacing the Roman Republic, had become a fact, being founded by Julius Cæsar, after the battle of Pharsalia, and now to be consolidated by Octavianus, after Actium. The conqueror in the last civil strife was at the head of a vast military force, devoted to his service. The provinces, long oppressed by the proconsuls and proprætors of the commonwealth, hailed the accession to power of a single absolute ruler, who would, it was hoped, put an end to all tyranny of petty Governors. The people of Rome, rejoicing in the humiliation of the aristocracy, and desiring only to be fed with imported corn, and amused by the spectacles of the circus and the theater, were equally ready to submit to the monarch who would supply them with both. All citizens of wealth and culture, desiring ease and quiet as the greatest of earthly blessings, rejoiced in the prospect of relief from the blood and violence of the past. The Republican faction had perished either on the field of battle or by the murders of the proscription. The Senate had lost authority and dignity alike, having been largely increased in numbers by the admission of Gauls and other provincials under Julius Cæsar's brief tenure of power, and was prepared to give its formal sanction to all that a master should ordain.

In B. C. 29 Octavianus returned to Rome and celebrated three triumphs for his successes in Dalmatia, and over Antonius, and for the addition of Egypt to the Roman dominion. The so-called "Temple" of Janus was shut in token of general peace. Secure in power as he was, he sought for no more victims, and acted with conspicuous moderation and prudence. The great historian Gibbon describes him as having "a cool head, an unfeeling heart, and a cowardly disposition," and as wearing throughout his life the mask of hypocrisy. The truth seems to be that he was a man who, with no innate cruelty, and with a perfect self-command, adapted means to ends throughout his career, and, filled with "an austere and passionless ambition," struck down his enemies with pitiless severity when he deemed it needful for his safety, and, once safe, sheathed the no longer needed sword forevermore. In B. C. 27 the Senate conferred upon Octavianus for ten years the Imperatorship, which was the symbol of absolute power, and saluted him with the title of "Augustus," by which name he is best known in history.

"The Latin literature of the Republican period which has come down to us (Macaulay's Lays, Preface) consists almost exclusively of works fashioned on Greek models. The Latin meters, heroic, elegiac, lyric, and dramatic, are of Greek origin. The best Latin epic poetry is the feeble echo of the Iliad and Odyssey. The best Latin eclogues are imitations of Theocritus. The plan of the most finished didactic poem (the Georgics) in the Latin tongue was taken from Hesiod. The Latin tragedies are bad copies of the masterpieces of Sophocles and Euripides. The Latin comedies are free translations from Demophilus, Menander, and Apollodorus. The Latin philosophy was borrowed without alteration from the 'Portico' and the 'Academy,' and the great Latin orators constantly proposed to themselves as patterns the speeches of Demosthenes and Lysias."

Macaulay observes: "Satire is the only sort of composition in which the Latin poets, whose works have come down to us, were not mere imitators of foreign models; and it is therefore the only sort of composition in which they have never been rivaled." Satire sprang, in truth, naturally from the Constitution of the Roman Government, and from the spirit of the Roman people." The origin of the Satire (a word meaning "mixture" or "medley") was the Fescennine Songs (a name derived from an Etruscan town), a rude style of extempore dialogues, in which the country people "chaffed" each other at their festivals. The founder of Roman satire, as a poetical composition, is held to have been Lucilius (B. C. 149-103), who wrote in rough-and-ready hexameter verses against the vices and follies both of individuals and of mankind at large. The fragments which remain of his writings show a coarse and stinging pleasantry and personality. No other Roman satirists occur till the period of the Empire.

Among the greatest of Roman poets was Lucretius (B. C. 96-52). He has left a philosophical poem in hexameter verse, called De Rerum Natura ("on the nature of things"), in which he maintains the "atomic theory" of the origin of the universe. The work is admitted to be the greatest of all didactic poems for the clearness and stateliness of its style and the beauty and power of its descriptions and episodes. It is a truly grand and original effort of Roman literary genius. Another great Roman poet was Catullus (B. C. 82 to about 40). His writings are lyrical, elegiac, and epigrammatic, partly imitated from the Greek, but adorned with much originality and grace of invention and expression. One poem, called "Atys," on a Greek myth of a shepherd beloved by the goddess Cybele, is full of passion and power.

Varro (B. C. 116-28) was the most learned man of Republican Rome. Cæsar employed him to superintend the collection and arrangement of the great public library which he instituted. Only two of his very numerous works are extant, and one only in a perfect form— a work on agriculture, the other being a treatise on the Latin language, which has preserved much valuable information on Roman usages. Sallust (B. C. 86-34) is well known for his two vigorous historical treatises on the Jugurthine War and Catiline's Conspiracy. Cicero (B. C. 107-43) is renowned as an orator, essayist, and letter-writer, his style being esteemed the perfection of Latin prose. At his favorite villa (country-house) at Tusculum, a few miles distant from Rome, he received his literary friends, and had a splendid library, constantly enlarged by the labors of the Greek slaves whom he employed as copyists of the works of the Greek writers.

Oratory was one of the chief pursuits of educated Romans. Antonius "the orator" (B. C. 143-87) is named by Cicero as one of the most distinguished speakers of that earlier time. Hortensius (B. C. 114-50) was the greatest orator of his day until Cicero surpassed him, and was noted for his florid style and graceful and elaborate gestures.

ROME AS AN EMPIRE

The system of rule established by Augustus Cæsar, when he became master of the Roman world at the age of thirty-six (in B. C. 27), was such as accorded with the prudence and moderation of his character. As Gibbon says: "He was sensible that mankind is governed by names, and expected, as he found, that the Senate and people would submit to slavery, provided they were respectfully assured that they still enjoyed their ancient freedom." Accordingly, the Republican offices were still retained, but the one person who was invested with them all, or who dictated the election to them all, was the Imperator, the head of the State. His power was secured by the military establishment, of which he was the permanent head; to him every soldier swore personal fidelity; by him every officer was directly appointed. The legionaries and the aristocracy were thus alike devoted to his will "by the restraints of discipline, the allurements of honor, and the ideas of military devotion." The imperial system was, in fact, a military despotism under Republican forms, the names of the ancient free State being retained as a veil to cover the fact of autocratic rule.

The provinces were divided, as to their administration, between the Senate and the Emperor, in such a manner that those in which regular armies were stationed belonged to Augustus, while the rest were assigned to the Senate and the people. The Governors of the Senatorial provinces held their office, according to the ancient custom, only for one year, while the Lieutenant-Gov-

ernors appointed by the Emperor kept their posts for
various terms. The dignity of the Senate was outwardly
maintained by a deference to its decision on the most
important question of peace and war; in civil and criminal matters it was the highest judicial court; in legislation it was held to be supreme as representing the
Roman people. The debates were conducted with much
show of freedom, and the Emperor sat and voted as a
Senator among his equals, or, at the most, as a leader in
the Assembly. No outward show, as of sovereignty,
was assumed by the real ruler of the State; and in this
way all popular jealousy as to "kingship," which was so
hateful an idea to Romans, was avoided.

The boundaries of the Roman Empire in the time of
Augustus were as follows: On the north the English
Channel, the Rhine, the Danube (Ister), and the Black
Sea; on the east the Euphrates and the Syrian Desert;
on the south the great African Desert (the Sahara), and
on the west the Atlantic Ocean. In round numbers,
this great dominion was about 2,700 miles from east to
west, with an average breadth of 1,000 miles. A great
military force was kept on the frontiers at the Rhine, the
Danube, and in Syria, and the commerce of the Mediterranean was protected by two permanent fleets, with
stations at Ravenna on the Adriatic, and at Misenum in
the Bay of Naples. The imposing size of the Roman
Empire is seen at once by a mention of the modern countries whose territory it included at this time, these being
—Portugal, Spain, France, Belgium, part of Holland,
Rhenish Prussia, parts of Bavaria, Baden, and Würtem-
berg, Switzerland, Italy, the Tyrol, Austria proper, part
of Hungary, Croatia, Slavonia, Servia, Turkey in
Europe, Greece, Asia Minor, Syria, Palestine, Egypt,
Tripoli, Tunis, Algeria, and most of Morocco. The

population of the Empire under Augustus is supposed to have been about one hundred millions, of whom one-half were slaves.

In this view we have the Western (or European) provinces, the Eastern (or Asiatic), and the Southern (or African). In the west, the civilization became mainly Roman, so that in Gaul, Spain, and Africa the Latin language and Roman customs were adopted. In the east, from the Adriatic Sea to Mount Taurus (in south-east of Asia Minor), the civilization remained Greek in language and manners. In the east, beyond Mount Taurus, and southward to and including Egypt, the civilization remained largely Oriental, though at Alexandria and some other great cities the Greek language and culture had become established by the Macedonian conquest.

Of this vast empire the capital was Rome, the population of which may have been a million and a half. It was after the conquest of Carthage and of Greece that Rome began to be truly splendid in its public buildings and private houses, and very great additions and improvements were made under Augustus. The city had long since extended beyond the ancient walls, and was practically unfortified. Augustus divided the whole city, for purposes of police, into fourteen districts (Regiones), containing two classes of dwellings, called domus ("mansions") and insulæ (literally islands, meaning here, detached piles of buildings, or blocks). The domus were the abodes of the nobles, and the insulæ were divided into sets of apartments and single rooms, as the dwellings of the middle and the lower classes.

The successors of Augustus added largely to the number. The magnificence of the city in imperial times can best be described by mentioning Fora (paved spaces surrounded by buildings), Campi (recreation grounds, like our parks), temples (by hundreds, including the small shrines), theaters, amphitheaters, Thermæ (large and splendid buildings, which included baths, gymnastic grounds, porticoes for loungers, libraries, sculptures, fountains, and shady walks), triumphal arches, Curiæ (or Senate houses), Castra (or barracks), palaces, Horti (public or private gardens, adorned with works of art), mausoleums, columns, and obelisks.

The period of Augustus is the most brilliant in the history of Roman literature, whether as regards poetry or prose. Hence, from being originally applied to this period, "Augustan age" has come to be a proverbial expression for a period of literary fruitfulness and vigor in the history of any civilized country. Augustus himself was a liberal patron of literary men, and his age has been made illustrious by the number and eminence of the writers who appeared in it.

Virgil's name alone is sufficient to crown the Augustan age with greatness. He was the first of the famous Latin poets, the greatest in the history of Rome and admittedly one of the half dozen greatest the world has seen. Publius Vergilus Maro was his name, and he was born near Mantua, in Cisalpine Gaul, and lived from B. C. 70 to 19. His father was a moderately wealthy farmer, who was rich enough to send his son to Rome, where he studied rhetoric and philosophy under the best teachers of his time. Virgil's farm was confiscated during the civil wars of the period, but his rising fame as a poet brought him to the attention of the Governor of his Province, and afterward to that of the powerful Minister, Mæcenas, who added him to the circle of court poets which made the age famous. His eclogues, or pastoral poems, published in B. C. 37, were received with enthusiasm. Mæcenas gave him a villa near Naples and a country house near Nola, where he lived seven years and composed the Georgics, or Art of Husbandry, a poem in four books, which deals with tillage and pasturage, the breeding of horses and cattle, and other bucolic subjects, but which, on their appearance in B. C. 30, for their poetic merit made him admittedly by his contemporaries the greatest poet of his day. The remaining eleven years of his life were devoted to the writing of the Æneid, the famous national epic of the Romans, which described the wanderings of Æneas, the Trojan, the legendary founder of the Roman Nation and the Julian family, from the fall of Troy to his arrival in Italy, his wars and alliances with the native Italian races, and his final establishment of his new kingdom. Virgil spent three years in revising the Æneid, and at his death ordered that it be burnt, because it had not been polished sufficiently. But Augustus refused, and it was published as we now know it. Virgil was shy, silent, and reserved in manner, and was never married. His sincerity and sweetness of temper won even the praise of Horace, who is not lavish of praise; and the fastidious purity of his life in an age of very lax morality gained him the name of "lady." The supremacy of Virgil in Latin poetry was immediate and almost unquestioned. His works became classics among his countrymen and have been studied in the schools in all Europe since as models of Latin style. Critics say that the Georgics are his greatest poems, because of their elegant finish and masterly verse. The Æneid has passages of equal grace, but is more uneven. His dramatic power, finished beauty of language, and his imaginative insight, with his intricate and rich harmonies, have given his work a secure place in literature, where it ranks as one of the greatest names. All other Latin

A. LELOIR, PINX

HORACE AT TIBUR

poetry is estimated by the degree in which it falls short of his.

Horace wooed the lyric muse in his verse. He was born at Venusia, in Apulia, and lived from B. C. 65 to 8. He went to school at Rome and afterward at Athens, but losing his property was forced to write verses, as he says, for a living. His earliest were chiefly satires and personal lampoons, but it was probably through some of his first lyrics that he became known to Virgil, who introduced him to Mæcenas, to whose gift Horace owed the celebrated farm among the Sabine hills. Horace was the poet-laureate of his age, and wrote odes to order in honor of various events. His Epistles are distinguished for grace, ease, good sense, and wit. His Satires, his earliest publication, which appeared about 35 B. C., are satires more of manners and follies than of vice or impiety. Horace was always a man of the world, as was shown clearly in his Odes, his greatest work, which appeared in B. C. 19, when he was forty-six years of age. These are terse, melodious, and exquisite in finish—the delight of scholars in all ages. Horace's historical position in Latin literature is this: On the one hand he carried on and perfected the native Roman growth and satire from the ruder essays of Lucilius, so to make Roman life live anew under his pen; and on the other hand he naturalized the meters and manners of the Greek lyric poets. His poems are of great value as a picture of life during his times.

Tibullus (lived from about B. C. 55 to 18) has left some books of elegiac poems distinguished by pure taste and graceful language. Propertius (B. C. 51-16) left elegiac poems of considerable beauty and power, ranked by the ancient critics with those of Tibullus.

Ovid's poems are marked by richness of fancy and by

variety and beauty of phrase. His Latin name was Publius Ovidius Naso. He was born at Sulmo, in the country of the Peligni (a tribe in Central Italy), and lived from B. C. 43 to A. D. 18. His Metamorphoses are legends or fables on heaven-wrought "transformations" of men and women, in the mythical age, into other creatures; the Fasti is a sort of calendar in verse, introducing the Roman festivals and the mythological origin of the same. His amatory poems (Amores, or "loves," Ars Amatoria, or "Art of Love," and Remedia Amoris, or "Remedies for Love") are clever and licentious; the Epistolæ Heroidum ("Letters of the Heroines") are letters in verse, purporting to have been written to absent lovers or husbands by women famous in olden legend. Phædrus is believed to have been a freedman of Augustus, and has left, in iambic verse, Latin adaptations of the Greek Æsop's Fables, expressed with clearness and conciseness.

The historian Livy (in Latin, Titus Livius) was born at Patavium (now Padua), and lived from B. C. 59 to A. D. 17. He wrote a history of Rome from the foundation of the city to B. C. 9, in 142 books, of which 35 have come down to our time. The "lost books of Livy" is an expression which testifies to the regret of the moderns for perished treasures, leaving one of the greatest gaps in the literature of the world. The existing books are: I-X, giving the history from Rome's foundation to B. C. 294; XXI-XXX, giving the history from B. C. 219 to 201, and including, happily, the Second Punic War; XXXI-XLV, containing the history from B. C. 201 to 167, and including Roman wars in Cisalpine Gaul, Macedonia, Greece, and Asia Minor. As a critical historian, in the modern sense of one who tests authorities and aims at the transmission of indubitable fact, so far as he can ascertain it, Livy is lacking; as a writer of historical narrative he stands among the foremost masters of style in the world—becoming, as occasion requires, simple, rich, picturesque, and vivid, and remaining always calm, clear, and strong.

Velleius Paterculus (lived about B. C. 19 to A. D. 31) wrote (in a clear, concise, and vigorous style, much like that of Sallust) a compendium of universal history, chiefly as connected with Rome. Seneca, the philosopher (Lucius Annæus Seneca), was born about B. C. 5, at Corduba (Cordova), in Spain, and lived till A. D. 65. He was first tutor, and afterward one of the chief Ministers of the Emperor Nero, but being accused of conspiring against the tyrant he was sentenced to death, and was forced to commit suicide. The writings of Seneca (a Stoic philosopher) are chiefly moral treatises containing much good, sound thought, clearly and vigorously expressed. He has left also ten tragedies, mostly on Greek mythological subjects.

Pliny the Elder (Caius Plinius Secundus) lived from A. D. 23 to 79, and has left a voluminous work called Historia Naturalis ("Natural History"), which, besides treating of natural history proper, deals also with geography, astronomy, human inventions, and institutions, the fine arts, etc., furnishing a wonderful but ill-digested and uncritical proof of his industry and learning. This enthusiastic scholar died by suffocation from poisonous gases emitted in the first recorded eruption of Mount Vesuvius (A. D. 79, as above), having too closely approached the scene of action in his eagerness for observation. He was at the time in command of the Roman fleet stationed at Misenum.

This eruption was the one which buried the city of Herculaneum (from 70 to 100 feet deep) under showers

of ashes, sand, and rock. It has been partially excavated, having been accidentally discovered in A. D. 1720
by the sinking of a well. At the same time the city of
Pompeii was overwhelmed by ashes, over which a soil
was gradually formed, and the excavations made since
A. D. 1721 have uncovered about half the place, and
revealed most valuable and interesting facts as to ancient
Roman life.

Persius, born in Etruria, lived from A. D. 34 to 62,
and has left six short Satires in verse, remarkable for
their difficulty, and containing some fine passages.
Lucan (in Latin, Marcus Annæus Lucanus) was born at
Corduba (Cordova), in Spain, and lived from A. D. 39
to 65. He wrote the famous extant heroic poem called
Pharsalia, giving an account of the struggle between
Julius Cæsar and Pompey. This is an unequal work,
having finely imaginative and vigorous passages, with
much that is overwrought and inartistic. Martial (Marcus Valerius Martialis) was born in Spain, and lived from
A. D. 43 to about 105. He is the well-known writer of
epigrams (short, witty poems), of which we have fourteen books, and has never been surpassed in that style
for wit and happiness of expression.

Pliny the Younger (Caius Plinius Cæcilius Secundus,
nephew of the elder Pliny) was born in Cisalpine Gaul,
and lived from A. D. 61 till after 115. He has left ten
books of interesting and valuable letters, including two of
great celebrity (one addressed by Pliny to the Emperor
Trajan, the other, Trajan's reply), concerning the conduct of the early Christians and their treatment by the
Roman civil magistrates. Quintilian (Marcus Fabius
Quintilianus) (42-120) born in Spain, left a famous work
on rhetoric, which contains the opinions of a most accomplished instructor on the proper training for the art of

oratory in its highest development. The matter and style of this great treatise are alike admirable.

Two of the greatest writers, not only in Roman, but in any literature, were, first, the renowned satirist Juvenal (Decimus Junius Juvenalis), who wrote about A. D. 80-100, and has left sixteen satires in verse (if the last fragmentary one be really his), aimed mainly at the grosser vices of his day. The Sixth Satire (against the Roman ladies, then shockingly depraved) and the Tenth (on the vanity of human wishes) are the most vigorous of this powerful writer's denunciations. The second, the historian Tacitus (Caius Cornelius Tacitus), who lived from about 55 to 117. Distinguished in his own day as an orator, and will be ever famous as a historian of peculiar powers of perception and expression. His insinuation of motives for the human actions which he records is impressive and masterly; his method of using the Latin tongue gives it a wonderful power for compression of much meaning into few words. His extant works are : A life of Agricola, his father-in-law, Roman Governor of Britain, one of the finest biographies ever written; four books of Histories (part of a larger work), giving an account of the important events which occurred in A. D. 69, 70; some books of his greatest work, the Annals, which contained the history of the Empire from A. D. 14 to 68, and a treatise on the Germanic Nations.

Suetonius, the historian, lived from about A. D. 72 to 140, and has left (besides some minor works of a biographical nature) a valuable book called "Lives of the Twelve Cæsars," including Julius Cæsar and Domitian; it is the matter, not the style, which makes the work precious.

Under the rule of Augustus the greatest event of the

world's spiritual history occurred in Bethlehem of Judæa
—the birth of Jesus Christ.   This really took place in
the year 4 B. C., but the erroneous calculation has, for
the sake of convenience, been allowed to stand, and the
chronology passes from B. C. ("before Christ") to A. D.
(anno Domini, "in the year of the Lord"), when Augustus had held sway, according to the wrong reckoning,
for twenty-seven years.

The great secular fact of Rome's history under
Augustus Cæsar was the destruction of the Roman General, Varus, and his legions by the celebrated Arminius
in Germany.   Arminius is the Latin form of the Teutonic Herman, the great National hero in whose honor a
colossal statue has been erected in the northwest part
of Germany, near the scene of his patriotic and momentous achievement—one which decisively affected the
whole future of the world's history.   He was the chief of
the Cherusci, a powerful tribe dwelling on both sides of
the River Visurgis (Weser), and closely akin in race to the
Angles and Saxons who conquered England, and gave
to Englishmen their being, their language, their free
spirit, and the germ of the laws and institutions which
they enjoy.   If Arminius had not done what he did
against Rome, Germany might have been thoroughly
subdued; the Latin language might have extinguished
the Teutonic as it had the Gallic and the Spanish; the
Teutonic tribes might have been overwhelmed; the Teutonic influence in molding modern Europe, in creating
the English race, might never have been exerted, and it
is clear that Europe and the world would have had a
widely different development from that which they have
actually undergone.

To Arminius belongs the glory of successfully defy-
ing the power to which Hannibal in Africa, Mithridates

NERO AND HIS MOTHER, AGRIPPINA

Painting by Fred. Klein-Chevalier

in Asia, and Vercingetorix in Gaul, had finally and disastrously succumbed. Under the rule of Augustus the Roman arms had been extending the dominion of the all-conquering Empire. The north of Spain had been subdued; the Roman frontier had been pushed from the Alps to the Danube, and much of southern Germany had been annexed. The Roman eagles had been carried even to the Elbe, and it seemed that the Germanic tribes, who had, under the Republic, threatened the very existence of Rome, were now, under the Empire, to be deprived of freedom, fame, and future. The contest, however, was really one between Rome in her decline and Germany in her rude and ancient best, when to courage she added truthfulness, to truthfulness a manly independence and a love of freedom, and to these a purity of life, a practice of domestic virtues, which had become rare indeed in Rome degenerate and decayed. Arminius, as chief of the Cherusci, headed a confederacy of German tribes who were determined, if they could, to expel from northern Germany the invaders and partial conquerors of the Fatherland. The Roman Governor, Quintilius Varus, and his officers and troops, had provoked the German outbreak by their licentious behavior toward German women, and the vengeance wreaked on the offenders was complete in itself, and effectual for the preservation of German freedom against the future efforts of Roman armies. The German hero, when his plans were formed, tempted Varus and his three legions by a revolt of the tribes near the Weser and the Ems to march into the difficult country now called the Teutoburger Wald, a woody and hilly region near the sources of the Lippe and the Ems. When the Roman force was thoroughly entangled amidst the forests, glens, and hills, and had been further imperiled by the rashness of Varus (who was as incompetent in military command as he was insolent and oppressive in his rule) as to his order of march—then, and not till then, Arminius and his Germans fell on the hated foe. Front, flanks, and rear were assailed at once with fierce shouts, thick-hurled darts, and broadswords keen of edge. The Roman column was pierced and disarranged; the Roman cavalry fled, but was pursued and utterly destroyed. Varus slew himself in despair. The infantry of Rome, still steady, stubborn, disciplined, and brave, was overpowered and slain almost to the last man. All efforts of Rome thereafter never gave her a secure and permanent foothold on German soil. This great deliverance of Germany, so momentous in European history, was wrought in A. D. 9. Augustus, cool and impassive as he was, was often heard to wail aloud for his lost legions, and Roman dominion in this quarter was henceforth virtually bounded by the Rhine until the time came when Germans were, with their conquering swords, to aid in carving the provinces of imperial Rome into the kingdoms of modern Europe.

Augustus died in A. D. 14, leaving behind him, as the result of his efforts dealing with the materials bequeathed to him by Julius Cæsar, an Empire thoroughly organized on a system of centralization, having a vast standing army, a host of officials, a uniform taxation; an Empire in which the old Roman liberty had withered away and been replaced by servility and stoicism. The imperial system was, in fact, a concentration of military force for the defense of the Empire against foreign foes, and the benefit conferred by it was that for two centuries the world was in the main at peace. If republican liberty was extinguished, material happiness was increased. The chief fact of the time is that freedom was dead, and for several centuries Europe became like a scene of Asiatic despotism. That effeminacy came upon men which always infects them when they live for a long time under the rule of an all-powerful soldiery.

Such was the material upon which Christianity was in due time to work with its transforming and transcendent influence and power.

During the period after Augustus, the Roman Empire, in spite of some rebellions of conquered nationalities, and contests between rival claimants of the imperial power, was mainly in a condition of peace and material prosperity. The frontier of the Roman dominion was not only maintained against the attacks of barbarians, but was at some points greatly, if transiently, extended. In the west, in Gaul and Spain, the Roman civilization was thoroughly established. In the center and east of the Mediterranean shores in Europe the Greek language and culture were supreme, and Greek philosophy was the religion of the cultivated classes at Rome. In the Asiatic part of the Empire the Oriental ways of thought were preserved, and the East in the end gave a religion to its conquerors and masters. The political distinction of the Roman citizenship was still existent, and the Empire might fairly be called "Roman" in the old sense, though the provincials were more and more freely admitted to the possession of the coveted honor of being "cives Romani." The Senate was still invested with an outward dignity, being composed, in the latter part of this period, of distinguished men chosen by the Emperor from the whole Empire, and resident in Italy for the purpose of engaging in actual, if formal, deliberations. The best of the Emperors during this period, however absolute their actual power might be, assumed only the character of life-presidents of the body whose coöperation in government they sought and encouraged.

The "Claudian Emperors" derive their name from Tiberius, adopted son and successor of Augustus, belonging to the noble family of the Claudii, and owing his power to being recognized by the Senate as the appropriate possessor of the imperial dignity. The name of "Cæsar" became soon a species of title attached as a surname to all the holders of imperial power, being in the four earlier instances acquired under the law of adoption. The Claudian Emperors were four in number—Tiberius (ruled A. D. 14-37), Caligula (37-41), Claudius (41-54), and Nero (54-68), in whom the family of the great Julius Cæsar became extinct.

Of these, Tiberius had shown himself an able general during the rule of Augustus. As Emperor he was a gloomy, suspicious, hypocritical, lustful, and in every way hateful tyrant, whose character has been drawn with consummate skill and branded with ineffaceable infamy by the historian Tactitus. A reign of terror existed for all citizens who were conspicuous in ability or virtue, while a host of informers used an elastic law of treason for their destruction at the prompting of the Emperor. His wicked minister, Sejanus, commander of the Prætorian Guards, was put to death in 31. Tiberius lived the last ten years of his life at the island of Capreæ (Capri), on the coast of Campania, and was then murdered by smothering almost as he drew the last breath of old age and disease.

Caligula was a madman of a wicked and malignant type, and was murdered by a Tribune. Claudius was a weak ruler. His wife, Messalina, is proverbial for immorality. In his reign the conquest of Britain was begun (A. D. 43).

C. MACCARI, PINX

BLIND APPIUS CLAUDIUS LED INTO THE SENATE

Nero was a monster of vice and tyranny. In his reign the British insurrection under Boadicea took place. He was at last deposed by the Senate, and died by his own hand. Among the crimes of Nero were the murder of his mother, Agrippina, and the persecution of the Christians in Rome on the false charge of causing the great fire there in A. D. 65. Claudius had been really made Emperor by the choice of the soldiers, which the Senate confirmed, and this evil precedent was often followed afterward. The rule of the empire was sometimes at the disposal of the famous "Prætorian Guard," the headquarters in Rome of the military force, and the armies also in different parts of the Empire chose their own Generals as Emperors in the two years of confusion that succeeded the suicide of Nero in A. D. 68.

The disorders of these calamitous years arose from a cause to which the military system and vast extension of the Empire rendered it peculiarly liable—the rebellion of great officers and viceroys entrusted with the defense of the frontier. The Legati (lieutenant-governors, with full military and civil control) of the Rhine, of the Danube, and of Syria, held the power of independent sovereigns, and under weak Emperors or in case of disputed succession to the supreme sway, were tempted to revolt.

Thus in A. D. 68, Galba, Governor of Spain, revolted against Nero, and on his arrival at Rome, after Nero's death, was acknowledged as Emperor. Galba had been an able and successful Governor in Gaul and in Africa, but his day was now done (at seventy-one years of age), and, becoming unpopular with his troops through his severity and avarice, and with the people from the doings of unworthy favorites, he was murdered (January, 69) in a military rebellion under Otho, who had been a vicious adherent of Nero's.

Otho thus became Emperor for three months.   At this very time Vitellius, noted for nothing but his gluttony, being Governor in part of Germany, was proclaimed Emperor by his soldiers at Colonia Agrippinensis (Cologne).   His generals, Valens and Cæcina, marched into Italy and defeated Otho at Bedriacum in Cisalpine Gaul (between Cremona and Verona).   Otho killed himself, and Vitellius reached Rome and was accepted as Emperor in July, 69.   Meanwhile, early in the same month, Vespasianus, Commander of the Roman army in Judæa, was proclaimed Emperor at Alexandria, and acknowledged throughout the East, his cause being also supported by the army of the Danube.   The troops of Vitellius were defeated in the north of Italy; the legions from Illyricum seized Rome for Vespasian; the Capitol was burnt in the civil war that raged in the city; the palace of Vitellius was stormed, and the Emperor dragged out, slain, and hurled into the Tiber.   Amidst these horrors, Vespasian, to the joy of all good citizens, became Emperor of Rome, arriving at the city in A. D. 69.

The Flavian Emperors, deriving their name from Flavius Vespasianus, were three in number—Vespasian, A. D. 69-79; Titus, 79-81, and Domitian, 81-96.

Vespasian was a man of high character, whose rule was an unmixed blessing to the Empire.   Born in a low class, of the fine old Sabine stock, he had the abilities and virtues of a Roman of the antique type—skill and bravery in war, strictness of rule, simplicity and frugality of life, moderation and dignity of character.   The chief event of his reign was the complete suppression of the Jewish revolt (begun in 66) in the capture and destruction of Jerusalem by his son Titus, A. D. 70.   The dreadful incidents of the siege of Jerusalem are well known.   The great eruption of Vesuvius, A. D. 79, causing the destruction of the towns of Herculaneum, Pompeii, and Stabiæ, near the foot of the mountain, occurred two months after the death of Vespasian, June, 79, who was succeeded by his elder son, Titus. His brief reign (two years) was marked by his care for the public good, and by the completion of the great amphitheater called the Colosseum.

Domitian, younger son of Vespasian, became a cruel tyrant, under whom the informers of the reign of Tiberius were again rampant with their false charges of treason. The conquest of Britain was completed in this reign by the great and good Agricola, and a new enemy for Rome appeared in the Dacians, dwelling to the north of the Danube, in the territory now comprising Transylvania, Roumania, and part of Hungary. This warlike people had long troubled the Danubian frontier by their inroads, and in the years A. D. 86-90, under their King Decebalus, they had such success against the Roman armies that Domitian disgraced the Empire by consenting to pay tribute to Dacia for freedom from harassing attacks. Domitian was murdered by a conspiracy of court officials in 96.

In the reigns of the five "good Emperors," we come to the happiest time of Rome's imperial sway. They succeeded each other in adoption as sons by their predecessors.

Nerva, 96-98, a cautious, feeble, humane, and virtuous man, reigned but fifteen months, wisely choosing an able and vigorous successor.

Trajan, A. D. 98-117, reckoned the greatest of Roman Emperors, was born in Spain in A. D. 52, being the first foreigner that attained the imperial position. In physical strength and demeanor, moral excellence, and intellectual capacity, Trajan was thoroughly fit to rule. His successes in war extended the Roman dominion beyond all former limits. Between A. D. 100 and 106 Dacia was subdued and made a Roman province, the Column of

Trajan at Rome being erected to commemorate the Emperor's victories in that quarter. Arabia Petræa was conquered, Armenia and Parthia were humbled, and the Persian Gulf, for the first and last time in Rome's history, was navigated by a Roman commander.

Hadrian, A. D. 117-138, was an active ruler, who visited the various provinces of the Empire, in order to inspect their management and remedy disorders. In Britain he erected the famous wall from the Solway Firth to the mouth of the Tyne. He was an excellent Greek scholar, residing for three years at Athens, and greatly favoring its people. He subdued the desperate revolt of the Jews. A. D. 131-136, under Barcochab, after which the great dispersion of the nation took place, and the city of Jerusalem was rebuilt as a Roman military colony under the name of Ælia Capitolina. Hadrian did much for the administration of justice and for the science of jurisprudence, in which the Romans were so great and so beneficial to future ages. A fixed code of laws, called the Edictum Perpetuum, "Permanent Decree," founded on the decisions and rules of the judges, was drawn up by the eminent jurist Salvius Julianus, and promulgated by the Emperor.

The last two of the "good Emperors" have given a name to the period called "the age of the Antonines," in some respects the happiest time during the whole duration of the Roman Empire. Antoninus Pius, A. D. 138-161, was one of the best Princes, as a ruler and as a man, that ever governed a State. His life was perfectly pure, and all his powers were devoted to promoting the happiness of his subjects. Order and tranquillity reigned in his days.

Marcus Aurelius, surnamed "the Philosopher," and also called Antoninus, after his adoption by the preceding Emperor, reigned from A. D. 161 to 180. He was a man of spotless virtue, devoted to literature and philosophy, and was the best product of Stoicism, to which he was a lifelong adherent. His "Meditations," written in the Greek tongue, is an extant work, registering his ideas and feelings on moral and religious points, and giving us the philosophy of heathenism in its noblest form. It was a little before this time that the great Stoic teacher Epictetus had put new life into that form of philosophy which he professed, as made known to us in the writings of his pupil Arrian, who was to him what Xenophon was to Socrates. In the reign of Aurelius the barbarian nations on the northern frontier of the Roman Empire began to be restless, and gave great trouble during most of his time. The Marcomannic War takes its name from the powerful people (Marcomanni, i. e., men of the march or border) in the territory now known as Bohemia and Bavaria. Along with other German tribes they fought the Romans with varying success, and Aurelius died in March, A. D. 180, in the midst of the struggle.

The Slavonic tribes of the Northeast began to drive the Germans into Roman territory, where many of them were allowed to settle, or were taken into the Roman military service. The barbarizing of the Roman world had thus begun. In the time of Aurelius the Oriental plague appeared, A. D. 166, and scourged the Roman world from Persia to Gaul. A majority of the people is said to have been carried off, and this visitation was followed during, the next century by many others of the same kind.

The old beliefs of Rome were now in a declining state; the old ideas were growing constantly more obsolete; the old sacrifices were attended with constantly less devotion. The populace cared for nothing but to be fed by the fleets of corn-ships from Africa and Egypt, and to be amused with the cruel spectacles of the amphitheaters. The Greek author Lucian, born in Syria early in the Second Century, wrote under Aurelius, and in his amusing "Dialogues of the Gods" and other works pours contempt on the old theology, and aims at spreading universal scepticism. The attitude of the noble-minded Stoic, Aurelius himself, toward the ancient creed was that of entire disbelief in the heathen gods, while in his life and writings he cherished and practiced a piety worthy of a far different age. The most cultivated men of the time believed in the ancient gods as little as Aurelius himself did.

The last "good Emperor," Marcus Aurelius, was succeeded by his son Commodus, A. D. 180-192. This man was a cruel and depraved wretch, a mere disgrace to human nature. In his time the Prætorian Guards assumed the full ascendency which they so long maintained. Commodus was poisoned by his favorite mistress, Martia, in 192, and by her act the history of Rome passed into a new phase.

An age of revolution now began, during which the imperial system was struggling for its life, and underwent a transformation which had important effects on its vitality for the rest of its career. The history of Europe presents no more disastrous time than this Third Century of the Empire of Rome. We have a succession of tyrannies, revolutions, and calamities, all of the worst kind— including the ravages of pestilence and the mischiefs wrought by a mutinous, omnipotent, and half-barbaric soldiery. Mention need only be made of a few of the more important persons and events.

Septimius Severus, 191-211, gained victories over the Parthians in the East, and, having visited Britain in 208, fought against the Caledonians, and died at Eboracum (York).

Caracalla, 211-217, son of Severus, was a savage tyrant, in whose reign the old political distinction between

Romans and provincials wholly disappeared. All the free inhabitants of the Roman Empire were henceforth Roman citizens, and many of the best Emperors hereafter sprang from nations previously regarded as "barbarian." Caracalla was murdered by his successor, Opilius (217), who, beheaded in a mutiny, was succeeded by Heliogabalus. The latter is notorious as one of the most debauched men who ever lived, and he was put to death for his enormities.

Alexander Severus, 222-235, was a just, wise, and virtuous ruler. The only important event during his reign is the disappearance of the Parthian Kingdom from history. A revolt of the Persians established the Persian Kingdom of the dynasty called the Sassanidæ, which reigned until A. D. 651.

Maximinus, 235-238, was of Gothic parentage on his father's side, and had a German woman for his mother. At various times there were several so-called Emperors ruling at once in different parts of the Empire, sometimes acknowledged as colleagues by others, sometimes rival claimants for the supreme sway. The different armies, in all these cases, were the authorities appointing the ruler.

In the reign of Decius, A. D. 249-251, the Goths appeared in force, and defeated and slew the Emperor. This powerful German people, destined to do much hereafter in overthrowing the Empire of Rome, had migrated from the Baltic coasts to those of the Black Sea, and overrun a large part of the Roman province of Dacia.

Under Valerian, A. D. 253-260, the Roman frontier was broken into at several points. The Franks (a confederacy of German tribes on the Lower Rhine, replacing the league of the Cherusci of the time of Arminius), invaded Gaul; the Alemanni (another German confederacy of peoples between the Danube and the Rhine) were moving south and west; the Goths attacked Greece and Asia Minor.   The Persians invaded Syria, and Valerian's reign ended in his defeat and capture by the Persian King, Sapor, who skinned the Emperor alive.   It seemed as if the Roman Empire would be broken up by outward force; but the end was not yet to be.

A change came with the brilliant deeds of the brave Emperor Aurelian, 270-275, a Pannonian of low birth. He drove the Goths and Vandals (another German confederacy of tribes) out of Pannonia (Modern Hungary and countries northeast of the Adriatic); he drove the Alemanni and other German invaders out of Italy; he recovered Gaul, Spain, and Britain from a rival claimant to the Empire.   In order to secure the frontier on the Danube, Aurelian wisely surrendered Dacia to the Goths. In the East he defeated and brought captive to Rome the famous Zenobia, Queen of Palmyra, who was aiming at the sovereignty of the Eastern world.   She had succeeded to the power of her husband, Odenathus, who had driven the Persians out of Syria after the defeat of Valerian, and had been allowed by the Emperor Gallienus, A. D. 260-268, to set up a "Kingdom of Palmyra."   At Zenobia's court lived the famous Greek philosopher and grammarian Longinus, a man of great ability and extensive learning, still widely known by his admirable work "On the Sublime."   There were at this time thirty generals who claimed the title of Emperor.

The Emperor Probus, 276-282, also a native of Pannonia, did much glorious work in restoring the military supremacy of Rome.   He put down rebellions, defeated the barbarians on the Danubian and Rhenish frontiers, and was at last killed by mutinous and dissolute troops, who objected to the useful labor imposed upon them in the public works.

The revolutionary period ended in the establishment of a new system of government, consisting in a division of the Empire, for administrative purposes, into four parts. This important change was made by Diocletian, a Dalmatian of low rank, established as Emperor by the troops in A. D. 284. The adjustment which he made in the relations between the Emperor and the Viceroys and the army saved the Empire from partition. Power in the purely military state which the Roman Empire had now become, was divided amongst four rulers. There was a co-Emperor name Maximian, and in 292 a ruler, with the title of "Cæsar," was appointed under each of the Emperors. The city of Rome lost its importance, as the four rulers resided mainly on the frontiers for purposes of defense against barbarian foes. Under this new arrangement, if one of the Emperors died he was to be succeeded by his subordinate "Cæsar," so as to deprive the army of the appointment of rulers. The Empire was now ruled from four centers—Nicomedia, in Bithynia (Asia Minor); Milan, in Italy; Antioch, in Syria; and Treves, or Trier, on the Moselle, in Gallia Belgica. After Diocletian, a firm and wise ruler, this arrangement did not work; but it paved the way for other improvements made by Constantine.

At the end of the Third Century, by A. D. 300, great changes had passed over the Roman Empire. In population the Empire had become, to a large extent, barbarized; the armies contained great numbers of Goths, Vandals, and Sarmatians, a people in territory now the west and south of Russia. The Goths and Vandals were Germans, and Germans were the nationality that was spread through the Empire more than any other. The former distinction as to Roman citizenship had been lost, and that between the

"Roman legions" and the "allies" effaced, and the last visible record of Rome's conquest was obliterated.

The political system of the Roman Empire had become half Oriental and half barbaric; and the great city of Rome itself, whence men had issued in olden time for the conquest of the world, had become a provincial town on the banks of the Tiber. The Roman Senate, as a political body, as an organ of public opinion, practically disappears, and the Emperor becomes virtually a Sultan, ruling with thoroughly despotic power in the stately splendor of an Eastern Monarch. Human free-will vanishes away, and sovereignty becomes a thing regarded with awful reverence, a species of divinity, to which the subject yields, not only without resistance, but without a thought of opposition to irresistible decrees. Eastern cruelty and disregard of human life become manifest, and the Emperor's right of naming his successor had ruinous effects when that successor proved weak and incompetent for the vast burden of government laid upon his shoulders. From this principle of quasi-hereditary sovereignty, succeeded by the actually hereditary development, Europe was to suffer at intervals, until the French Revolution taught the Continental world that Kings exist for Nations, and not Nations for Kings. In the later Roman Empire the evils of this state of political superstition and degradation, in which the subjects had no rights and the sovereign no responsibility, were often mitigated by the accession of really able and vigorous rulers. An enormous army of civil and military officials was spread over the Empire for administrative purposes, and extravagant expense led to oppressive taxation, which ruined the people, and contributed to the downfall of the whole system before the encroachments and assaults of barbarian nations. "Rome, the representative of European civilization, the inventor of civilized jurisprudence, and the inheritor of Greek philosophy, descends to the level of an Asiatic state."

The beneficent encroachments of Christianity were now to cause a change in men's minds, an uprising and growth of new ideas, a vehemence of opinions, a conflict of beliefs, and an outburst of enthusiasms, which revolutionized the spiritual world at the very time when mankind was politically dead. The Church had arisen within the State, and within this citadel, generally undisturbed by the political despotism, civilization took refuge, and a large share of a new freedom for mankind was secured. An age of faith had come, and men were busied about the acceptance of new beliefs or the revival of old ones, in order to satisfy the cravings of awakened souls.

Jesus Christ was crucified in the nineteenth year of the reign of Tiberius, A. D. 33. At Antioch, in Syria, where Paul and Barnabas taught the faith, the disciples were first, as a term of reproach, called "Christians." St. Paul, in his journeys, carried the new religion through Asia Minor and Greece, and then to Rome, where he died in the reign of Nero. The Christian religion was thus silently but surely spread, first among the Jews, then among the Greeks, or Eastern, and lastly among the Latin, or Western heathen. Nero was the first Roman Emperor who openly persecuted the Christians, with whom the Jews were at first frequently confounded. The reason why even good Emperors like Trajan and Aurelius harassed the Christians was that the religion of Rome was a part of the State system, and the denial of the Roman gods by the Christians was regarded as political hostility and disloyalty. The Christians were a sect, and not a nation; and the Roman government, which tolerated all national faiths, looked with suspicion on the votaries of a creed which had a new and unknown God, and taught that all other deities were non-existent or else powers of evil.

Severe persecutions also occurred during the reigns of Decius and Valerian, and the struggle between the old faiths and the new culminated in the decree of Diocletian (A. D. 303), ordering the destruction of all Christian places of worship and of all the holy books, and the removal of all Christians from official posts of dignity and power. For eight years a cruel persecution raged throughout the Empire, except in Britain, Gaul, and Spain, but it ended in permission being given (A. D. 311) for the Christians to worship God as they pleased. Henceforward Christianity was safe from external foes.

Diocletian's resignation of his power in A. D. 305 was followed by a period of confusion and civil war, which ended in the establishment of Constantine as sole Emperor in A. D. 323. He was son of one of the co-Emperors and of a Christian woman named Helena. Constantine made an important change in the government of the Empire by dividing the military power from the civil authority. The influence of the Legati of provincial viceroys was thus reduced, and the Emperor alone had both civil and military power in his hands, a fact which gave him a great predominance.

In A. D. 324 Christianity was established by Constantine as the religion of the State, and in 330 he made Byzantium the capital of the Empire. This town, on the Thracian Bosporus, founded by Greek colonists in B. C. 658, had early become a great commercial center. After being held successively by the Athenians, Lacedæmonians, and Macedonians, it came into Roman possession, and the new city now built there, or the enlarged and reconstructed Byzantium, was afterward called Constantinopolis ("City of Constantine," from Greek *polis*, city), and remained the capital of the Eastern Empire of Rome till A. D. 1453.

In religion, Constantine seems to have been a strange compound of Paganism and Christianity. He was an able general and statesman, whose real character has been obscured by historical excesses, both of panegyric and of detraction, and around whose name, in connection with Christianity, ridiculous fables have gathered. Constantine embraced the new religion because he thought it expedient for his own interest so to do, and not from any miraculous apparition or divine command. He died in 337, leaving the Empire to confusion and civil war under his sons.

Apart from its effects upon the morals, the new religion greatly and beneficially stirred the mind of the age. Political speculation and discussion were impossible under a despotism, and active minds turned to theology, and soon showed that the intellectual power of the time was to be found within the ranks of Christianity. Amongst these early writers and rulers of the Church known as the "Christian Fathers" the following are the chief: Tertullian, Ambrose, Cyprian, Lactantius, Jerome and Augustine, being Latin Fathers; Origen, Gregory, Basil, Chrysostom, Athanasius, being Greek Fathers.

Julian, surnamed the Apostate, or deserter from the faith, was Emperor from A. D. 360 to 363. He was a descendant of Constantine, and a man of great abilities and attainments, distinguished at Athens in the study of Greek literature and philosophy. He fought with great success, before he became Emperor, against the Franks and the Alemanni, German Confederacies who

had invaded Gaul. Brought up as a Christian, he declared himself a Pagan when he was made Emperor by
the troops in 360, and did what he could to root out
Christianity. In 363 he invaded Persia, but was compelled to retreat by the climate and want of supplies,
and being then attacked by the Persians, was killed in
one of the battles that covered the Roman army's retirement beyond the Euphrates. Julian was a man of extraordinary character: virtuous in life; energetic, just,
and wise in administration; a diligent and thoughtful
writer, who has left, in a pure Greek style, letters, orations, and satirical works of considerable interest and
humor. Christianity was restored by Jovian, his successor.

Under the joint Emperors Valentinian I and Valens
(364-375) the wars with the German barbarians continued. Valentinian was an able and vigorous ruler and general, and drove the Alemanni out of Gaul, which they had
again invaded.

The Goths become at this time very prominent in
the history of the decaying Empire of Rome. Of this
great nation there were two divisions, the Ostrogoths,
or Eastern Goths, and the Visigoths, or Western Goths.
The nation as a whole extended through central Europe
from the Baltic to the Black Sea. In the latter half of
this Century there was a compact and powerful Gothic
Kingdom, under a ruler named Hermanaric, extending
over what is now Hungary and Poland. The Goths had
to some extent become Christians through the teaching
of their devoted countryman, Bishop Wulfilas, or
Ulphilas, who appears to have also invented an alphabet
for them, based upon the Greek alphabet.

A most formidable Asiatic race had already made its
appearance in Europe, moving westward from the Cas-

pian and the Ural Mountains with irresistible ferocity and strength. They were Tartars, originally coming from the northeast of Asia, where they had made inroads upon China. About A. D. 374 these Huns crossed the Volga and the Don, and fell upon the Gothic Kingdom. The Ostogoths partly submitted and partly sought a refuge among the Visigoths.

By permission of Valens (Emperor of the eastern part of the Empire, A. D. 364-378), large numbers of Goths were allowed to settle south of the Danube. The newcomers soon attacked the Romans, and Valens was defeated and killed in a great battle near Adrianople in 378. This great settlement of Goths to the south of the Danube was a considerable step toward the breaking up of the Roman Empire. They spread themselves westward to the Adriatic Sea and the borders of Italy, and, entering the Roman army and acquiring Roman civilization, became prepared to play their destined part in the coming change.

Theodosius, who reigned over the whole Empire only from 392 to 395, being previously Emperor of the eastern division, restored matters for a time. He put down in battle the Goths who had entered the Empire, and made peace with them in 382. The rising power of the Christian Church was shown in the treatment of this Emperor by St. Ambrose, Bishop of Milan. Theodosius, in 390, had caused a cruel massacre of the people of Thessalonica, in Macedonia, in punishment for a riotous outbreak, and St. Ambrose induced him humbly and publicly to acknowledge his guilt. The formal end of Paganism took place at this time, in the decrees of Theodosius which prohibited, under severe penalties, the worship of the old heathen gods. He was the last Emperor who ruled over the whole undivided Empire.

DIVISION OF THE EMPIRE

The Empire was now (A. D. 395) divided between the two sons of Theodosius, but its main defender against the barbarians was the brave and able Stilicho, a Vandal by birth, who was the real ruler of the Western Empire, comprising Italy, Africa, Spain, Gaul, and Britain. The Eastern Empire has henceforth a career of its own, to be noticed hereafter, and we pursue the history of the Western down to the time of its extinction. Stilicho maintained the northern frontier of Britain against the Picts and Scots, and the Rhine frontier of Gaul against the German tribes called Suevi and Alemanni.

A formidable enemy now appears on the scene, Alaric, King of the Visigoths. Under him the Goths settled within the Danube had already overrun Macedonia and Greece, and in A. D. 402 Alaric attacked Italy in great force. Stilicho hurried to the rescue, and drove out the Visigoths, gaining decisive victories in two desperate battles (403). After his general's success Honorius, the Emperor, celebrated at Rome the last triumph ever seen there, the event being sung in stirring verse by Claudian, the last of the Latin classic poets, a writer of pure style and real genius.

In A. D. 405 a leader named Radagaisus invaded Italy with a vast host of barbarians from the interior of Germany—Suevi and Alemanni, Alani and Vandals, Goths and Huns. At Fæsulæ, near Florence (in 406), Stilicho encountered and defeated the enemy. Stilicho was put to death in 408 on a charge of aspiring to the Empire.

In A. D. 408 Alaric came again into Italy, this time with an irresistible force, and after extorting an enormous ransom on condition of sparing Rome, captured the city in 410, and gave it up to a six days' plunder by his warriors, without any cruel slaughter of the people. This was exactly 800 years after the taking of Rome by the Gauls under Brennus. Alaric died shortly afterward.

Early in the Fifth Century the Roman forces were withdrawn from Britain, which was left open to conquest by the Angles and their kinsmen from northwest Germany. Soon after Alaric's time the Visigoths established themselves in the south of Gaul and the north of Spain, while hordes of Suevi and Alani, Vandals and Burgundians, a German nation akin to the Goths, swarmed over the rest of both those great provinces. In 429 Genseric, King of the Vandals, passed over from Spain into Africa, and made himself master of the whole northwest of Rome's dominions there. His fleet swept the Mediterranean, conveying troops who conquered the chief islands, and made descents on the shores of Italy and Greece. The Western Empire was thus gradually absorbed and repeopled by swarms of new inhabitants, many years before its formal and final extinction as a political fact.

The reappearance of the savage and formidable Huns, under the most famous of Barbarian conquerors, Attila, styled by himself "the Scourage of God," as the slayer and plunderer of mankind in his wide and erratic course of conquest. When this mighty warrior turned his arms against Gaul, in A. D. 450, a crisis in the history of the world had come, like unto that which had been decided by Greece on the plain of Marathon more than nine hundred years before. The race of Rome was run, and the questions now to be settled were these: What races of mankind should inherit the civilization which she had received from Greece; and what should be the fate of the laws, institutions, and Christian faith which had grown up within the Roman Empire, and had been already accepted in part by the Germanic nations that had occupied most of her territories? Were the Aryan races of Europe to be overcome and extinguished by Tartars from Asia? Was the civilization of modern Europe to include the great Teutonic element which has given it so much of its peculiar power and grandeur? Was there, in a word, to be at all any such modern Europe as we know? or, was the worst barbarism of the northern and uncivilized part of Asia to stifle classic culture on its way to our times, and crush the Christian creeds and institutions in the vigor of their youth? These questions were answered with a glad and glorious issue for mankind in the last victory won by the arms of Imperial Rome.

The Germanic tribes of Europe were remarkable for two things—reverence for the purity of woman and love of personal and political liberty. From these noble elements of character, when they were inspired by vital Christianity, were to issue the brightness of chivalry, and the grand reality of freedom for the greatest races of mankind. Since half Europe, all North America, and, in the British colonies, many other smaller portions of the earth are, in the wide sense, German (or Teutonic, as including the Angles and the Saxons, and the Scandinavian nations) in race, in institutions, and in language, it is easy to see how the future history of the world was affected by the issue of the great conflict between the pagan Huns of Attila and the Christianized hosts of Aëtius and Theodoric.

Attila was in person a short, sinewy, huge-headed, keen-eyed, flat-nosed, swarthy Mongol; in character he was brave, just, temperate, prudent, and sagacious; he waged war with great skill; he was ruthless to all who resisted his advance. Between A. D. 445 and 450 he had ravaged the Eastern Empire, between the Euxine and the Adriatic Seas, and had acquired a large territory south of the Danube, in addition to his dominions north of the Danube and the Euxine. The force which he could bring into the field has been estimated at half a million of warriors, and in A. D. 450 he set out for the conquest of Western Europe, and crossed the Rhine, near Strasburg, into Gaul, where he proceeded to attack Orleans.

The Roman General Aëtius, in conjunction with Theodoric, King of the Visigoths, was the hero of this occasion. On the approach of their united armies Attila retreated to the plains round Châlons-sur-Marne, which were adapted to the movements of his cavalry. In the battle which ensued (A. D. 451) between the immense rival hosts, Theodoric was killed, and Attila's army was defeated, though not routed, by the efforts of Aëtius. The great enterprise of Attila was, however, completely baffled, and, after an invasion of Italy which took him to the gates of Rome, he died in 453. The Empire founded by his genius then fell to pieces, and the danger of Europe's conquest by Huns had passed away.

In A. D. 455, Genseric, the Vandal conqueror in Africa, invaded Italy, took Rome, and gave the city up to pillage for fourteen days. The Vandals carried off on their ships most of the metal statues of the temples and the Forum, and the precious trophies in the Capitol and the Temple of Peace, including the Golden Candle-stick from the Temple of Jerusalem. This sacred relic was recovered a century afterward from Africa, taken to Constantinople, and then replaced in Jerusalem, where it vanishes from history for evermore.

The Emperors of this last period were insignificant personages, and in 472 the Suevian, Ricimer, who had served under Aëtius, and had for some time been virtual master in Italy, took and plundered Rome again.

The immediate cause of the fall of Rome's Empire in the West was that it had proved unequal to repelling in war the encroachments and inroads of the barbaric world beyond the frontier. But why had Rome's power thus succumbed to outward pressure after so many centuries of conquest and victorious repulse or utter destruction of Gallic and German assailants from the north? Why did the Romans prove at last inferior in force to the Barbarians? The first answer is, that the Barbaric world had grown stronger than of old. The confederations of Germans in the Third Century of the Roman Empire show that the Barbarians had learned the secret of strength in union. They had also improved in intelligence and military skill. They were, moreover, impelled in aggressive force against the Roman frontiers by the irresistible pressure wrought on themselves by the newcomers from Asia—the Huns. The second answer is, that not only had Rome failed to increase or to maintain her power, but that power had positively and largely declined. Rome had ceased to conquer, and this was only because she had reached the limit of her resources. When Hadrian gave up the Parthian conquests of Trajan, and when Aurelian abandoned Dacia—when the boundaries of the Empire were thus deliberately

HUNNIC WARRIORS PLUNDERING A ROMAN VILLA

Painting by C. Rochegrosse

narrowed by able and energetic rulers—it is certain that Rome was becoming weak and exhausted, and that these rulers knew it, and wisely acted on their knowledge. It was no moral degeneracy, caused by luxury and success, that could account for this. The Roman armies were not affected by the doings of a brutal and effeminate aristocracy; the discipline was what it had ever been; the Generals were as capable as most of those who commanded under the Republic. The successes of Julian against the Alemanni, of Theodosius against the Goths, of Stilicho against Alaric, and of Aëtius against the Huns of Attila, prove that the armies of Rome could still fight and win. It was from physical causes, not moral, that Rome fell.

The Empire perished for want of men. The Roman armies had become mainly composed of Barbarian troops, and thus the citadel of Rome's strength was occupied by defenders whose very presence was a proof that power had passed into other hands. The dominion of Rome was thus absorbed rather than conquered; the former population of the Empire was replaced by a new set of men. For lack of people to till the lands within the frontier of Rome, whole tribes of barbarians had been peacefully admitted, and Vandals, Goths, and Franks had settled within the borders in a continual stream of barbaric immigration. The older races of the Roman Empire had for some centuries ceased to increase materially in numbers by the natural means, and in such a case, while the barbarian world was ever growing, the Roman population, if even it remained positively stationary, was relatively in a condition of rapid and alarming decay. The Roman civilization was simply military, and not industrial.

The wealth of Rome was gained by war, and not by

manufactures or by commerce, and thus, when conquest
ceased, the acquirement of wealth came to an end, and
lack of money, as of men, made Rome more helpless
still. The series of visitations of disease—the Oriental
plague—which came upon the Roman world between
the reigns of Aurelius and Diocletian, was a calamity
from which Rome never recovered, and existing and
ever-growing weakness was made incurable by the incessant demands of an oppressive and irrational system of
taxation. Thus, by slow degrees, from causes gradually
working with an ever-growing effect, faded away the
power of that great Rome which had known how to conquer the nations, and to acquire a vast Empire including
many races and conditions of men; how to create a cen-
tralized government of great stability and efficiency,
but not how to thwart the subtle working of physical
and financial maladies which were inherent in the constitution of her whole system of society; which were fed
by deeply-seated moral mischiefs, and were not to be
remedied by any pagan philosophy or any statesmanship
known to the Roman world.

The conquest by Rome of all the countries on the
shores of the Mediterranean had a great and beneficial
effect upon the commerce of the inland sea, round
which was gathered all civilization in the later
period of the ancient world, and upon the development of that civilization itself. When Pompeius
Magnus performed his great achievement of sweeping piracy away, the work was one of permanent
benefit, and the power of Rome's consolidated Empire
secured for ages the peaceful traffic which could
not fail to result in material and moral good to the peoples thus brought together. In the West, especially, a
great growth of prosperity ensued. The African prov-

inces supplied half the Mediterranean world with grain. The eastern coast of Spain sent forth from its harbors corn and wool, and wine and oil, receiving in return the products of other regions. The Spanish cities in that quarter were many and populous; the arts and literature were sedulously cultivated, and some of the leading authors in Latin letters were of Spanish origin and training. In Gaul, the southern region had already received civilization from Greek settlers, and the Roman conquest carried material and intellectual culture to the center and north of the land, and across the narrow sea to Britain, where Roman supremacy secured for the people three centuries of peace and prosperity. There can be no doubt that human happiness was largely increased in these regions of the world by a dominion which put an end to intertribal conflicts, and gave men the prime blessing of orderly and systematic rule.

But the chief benefits derived by the world from Rome's imperial sway were the spread of the Greek culture and the clear course made for the progress of Christianity. To Rome's controlling power we owe the preservation of Greek ideas in Greek literature, and the transmission to our times of some of the greatest productions of the Greek mind—works which Roman imitation took as the highest models of excellence, and which Roman admiration preserved, by multiplication of copies, for the good of future ages. As to Christianity, the spread of Greek philosophy over the world after the conquests of Alexander the Great had prepared the higher class of men for the reception of still nobler lessons, and the free intercourse among the nations which Roman supremacy secured carried the teachers and preachers of the new religion to many a region which must have been otherwise inaccessible to their efforts and their devotion.   It was thus that, long before the official establishment of the faith by Constantine, the surviving strongholds of Paganism were steadily and imperceptibly sapped, and, without formal assault or vigorous shock, crumbled into noiseless and irreparable ruin.

As to art, the Romans were not originally an art-loving people, but used the abilities of those whom they had subdued by their arms.   They derived the use of the arch and the architecture of their earliest buildings from the Etruscans, and the early statues in the city of Rome, made of terra-cotta and of bronze, were also Etruscan work.   The conquest of Macedon brought Grecian influence to bear, and at the triumph of Æmilius Paulus in B. C. 167 there was a magnificent display of costly armor, vases, paintings, and statues, which showed the people of Rome what Greece could furnish in the way of models of artistic work.   The "triumphs" of Mummius over Greece and of Pompey over Mithridates brought to Rome numerous pictures, statues in marble, engraved gems, pearls, specimens of chased and embossed plate, figures and vessels of Corinthian brass, and splendid works in gold.   As wealth and luxury grew, the works of statuary, mosaic, painting, and architecture, executed by Greek artists, became countless, and many of these are now in the museums of Europe. Medals, coins, and cameos of fine execution were produced under the Empire, the age of Hadrian and that of the Antonines being flourishing times for art.

The profuse ornamentation of the triumphal arches and pillars in Rome has been of great antiquarian value for our knowledge of armor, costume, and military engines.   The devastations of barbarians in both the western and the eastern Empires caused irreparable losses; the

HISTORY OF ROME

four bronze horses now at Venice are specimens of later and inferior Greek art, saved from destruction wrought at Constantinople in the Thirteenth Century. The chief collections of ancient sculpture are in the Vatican and the Capitol museums at Rome, the Museo Borbonico at Naples, the Villa Borghese and the Villa Albani at Rome, the Gallery of Florence, the Louvre in Paris, the British Museum in London, several private collections (Woburn Abbey and Lansdowne House) in England, and the Sculpture Gallery at Munich. In the Greek and Roman Courts of the Crystal Palace at Sydenham good copies of some of the chief productions of Grecian art in its principal periods may be seen.

The last Roman Emperor of the West was a child, called, as if in derision, Romulus Augustulus, the one name being that of the city's mythical founder, the other, "Augustus the Little," a parody of the style of him who organized the Empire. Augustulus became nominal ruler in A. D. 475, and in 476 was overthrown by the invasion of some German tribes, of which the chief was called the Heruli. Their leader, Odoacer, took the title of "King of Italy," and the Western Empire came thus ignobly to an end, in the displacing of a lad seven years old by the captain of a horde of banditti.

MEDIÆVAL HISTORY

The history of the "Middle Ages" embraces a period of about one thousand years, extending from the close of the Fifth to the end of the Fifteenth Century of the Christian Era. The first half of this period has been some-times called the "Dark Ages," as if the light of ancient learning and culture had been well-nigh extinguished in the occupation of the provinces of the Western Empire of Rome by barbarian peoples. This time of the world's history, however, is more correctly regarded as a time in which the creation of a fresh state of society and of civ-ilization was effected in the blending of the new with the old, in the adoption both of Christianity and of the olden institutions by the new races, mainly of German nation-ality, who appear upon the scene. The development of the German world begins, kindled by a foreign culture, a foreign religion, polity, and legislation. These new elements were taken up by the Teutonic tribes, and amalgamated with their own national life. The Chris-tian religion had already received from the Councils and Fathers of the church a perfected system of doctrine and government; the rulers of the church, moreover, pos-sessed the culture and the philosophy of the Greek and Roman world, and the Latin tongue, in its perfectly developed form, continued for ages to be the language of literature and men of learning. The new system of things was, in this sense, merely a continuation of the old; but there lived in it an entirely new spirit, through which the world was to be politically and socially regen-erated—the spirit of freedom, which was ultimately to reconcile the antagonistic principles of Church and State, and regulate the political life of nations by reason, after the church had failed in her attempt to maintain herself as a theocracy, and the State had passed through the form of feudal to that of constitutional monarchy.

A brief summary of what is included in these thousand years of history will show an abundance of stirring and interesting matter, which should fully rid the period of the character for dullness with which it has sometimes been invested. The close of the Fifth Century shows us the beginnings of England in the first lodgment effected by the Angles and Saxons on the shores of this island. In the Sixth the Latin tongue begins to turn into French, Italian, Spanish, and the Benedictine monks found the first monasteries. The Seventh sees the wondrous career of Mahomet, and the beginnings of Saracen conquest. In the Eighth, Europe is saved for Christianity by Charles Martel's defeat of the Saracens at Tours, and the great Slavonic race (a burning question in modern diplomacy, as it deals with Russia and Bulgaria) begins to be felt in Eastern Europe. The Ninth brings the feudal system and the temporal power of the Popes. In the Tenth Saxon supremacy in England is firmly established and feudality begins. In the Eleventh the German Empire is the great political fact, side by side with Papal supremacy, asserted by Gregory VII, and the capture of Jerusalem by the Turks, which results in the Crusades. In the Twelfth, under fullgrown feudalism, we have the age of chivalry, the great Italian republics, and the beginning of power for France under Philip Augustus. The Thirteenth has the rise of modern towns and the germ of political freedom in municipal institutions. Trade, manufactures, banking, begin to assert their importance. Men dare to doubt the dogmas of the Church, and the Inquisition meets "heresy" by organized torture and murder. The Papal power is at its height, and the Christians of Spain have at last loosened fairly the grip of the Saracens. In the fourteenth, intellectual light is growing, and England, France, Italy, Germany, have the rise of a native literature. The compass makes maritime discovery possible, and the use of gunpowder changes the character of warfare. A Swiss Republic exists. Feudal barons decay as monarchs rise to power. The Fifteenth Century brings the crisis to which the work of a thousand years has been leading mankind, and the new world of geography coincides with a new world of mental and social life due to the invention of printing, the revival of classical learning, the growth of free thought, the rise of a middle class, and the establishment of law and order.

The Aryan migration into Europe from Asia has been dealt with in the first part of this work. The ancient history of Europe has been concerned with the Italic (Latin) and Hellenic races as the ruling and conquering powers of the civilized world. The modern history of Europe has to do partly with races of mixed descent arising from the union of these old historic peoples with barbarian tribes, but mainly with the other great races of the Aryan stock—the Celts, the Teutons, and the Slavs or Slavonians.

At the present day nine-tenths of the people of Europe belong to the Aryan stock; the other tenth, consisting of the Turks, the Magyars (in Hungary), the Finns, and the Laplanders, is Mongolian in race, akin, (though now very different in character and appearance) to the Chinese, Burmese, Siamese, and other peoples in the southeast of the mainland of Asia.

In early historical times the Celts inhabited the British Isles, Gaul, Spain, and the north of Italy; the Teutons occupied the territory known as Sweden, Norway, Denmark, and central Germany; an Aryan people called Lithuanians had settled on the southern coast of the Baltic; the Slavonians were to be found in the great Eastern plain, forming the modern Empire of European Russia.

Of the three great Aryan races—Celts, Teutons, and Slavonians—the Romans came into close contact with two only—the Celts and the Teutons. The Celts of Britain, Gaul, and Spain were conquered by Rome, and those of Gaul and Spain especially took up the Latin language and civilization, receiving the Roman citizenship, and being converted to Christianity before the end of the Western Empire.

The terms Teutonic, Gothic, and Germanic are all used to designate the great race of men that had occupied central and northern Europe, and was destined to work so powerfully in the development of the modern civilization. The chief tribes of this great race were the Goths (divided into the Visigoths and the Ostrogoths), the Vandals, the Franks (i. e., the "Free men," a confederacy of tribes on the Lower Rhine), the Burgundians, the Lombards (in Latin, Langobardi or Longobardi, originally from the banks of the Elbe, then found north of the Danube in the Fifth Century, A. D.), the Angles, the Saxons, and the Scandinavians or Norsemen.

The Vandals invaded Spain (where their name survives in the name of the district Andalusia), and passed over into Africa, where they founded a powerful kingdom. The Ostrogoths, under their King Theodoric the Great, overcame Odoacer in Italy, and Theodoric ruled there as head of a peaceful and prosperous realm from

A. D. 493 to 526. The Roman laws and institutions were maintained, and the age was distinguished by the learning and statesmanship of Cassiodorus, and of the famous Boëthius, who was great in Greek philosophy, and wrote (during his imprisonment by Theodoric for opposing certain oppressive measures), the well-known work, De Consolatione Philosophiæ ("On the comfort of philosophy"). This book is pure in style and of a high tone of thought; its author was the last of the western Romans to study deeply the literature and language of Greece, from which he translated many works of Aristotle and other philosophers. The Visigoths had founded a kingdom which included what is now Spain, Portugal, and southern France, the capital being Tolosa (now Toulouse). This Visigothic Kingdom lasted for two centuries, when it was overthrown by the Saracens, after losing the portion in Gaul through conquest by the Franks from Germany.

In A. D. 486 the Franks, under a King named Clovis (a corrupted form of his German name Chlodwig, and really the same as the modern Louis) invaded and conquered a part of Gaul, and the first or Merovingian dynasty (from Merwig, grandsire of Clovis) of the earlier monarchy of France was established, the name France being derived from the conquering people, as England from the Angles. These tall, blue-eyed, flaxen-haired Germans, armed with heavy swords, battle-axes, and large shields, gradually made their way to the south, and drove out the Visigoths, but settled themselves chiefly in the north of Gaul. Clovis and his people embraced the faith of his wife Clotilda, a Christian Princess of Burgundian race, and the Frank conquerers adopted the language (a corrupted Latin) spoken by the conquered Gauls. Clovis died in A. D. 511, and the division of his dominions among his sons was followed by a period of dreary warfare and crime. The dominion of the Franks extended far to eastward of the Rhine. Thus much of Gaul passed from being a Roman province into the form of a monarchy inaugurated by German barbarians. The Burgundians established a Kingdom in the southeast of Gaul, which disappeared for a time by Frankish conquest, and the boundaries of which varied from time to time according to their successes in war against neighboring states.

The Kingdoms founded by the Lombards and the Scandinavian tribes come later in the history. The Angles and the Saxons belonged to the Low Dutch division of the Teutonic race, being that portion of the German peoples that had not been Christianized or civilized in Roman times, and that dwelt near the sea, by the mouths of the Rhine, Weser, and Elbe. The German tribes with whom we have dealt in connection with the Roman Empire belonged to the High Dutch division, dwelling in central and southern Germany away from the sea. The conquest of Britain by the Angles, Saxons, and Jutes, was completed by the end of the Sixth Century, the English Nation was gradually formed, the land was Christianized by missionaries from Rome under St. Augustine in the Seventh Century, and the people were united into one realm under Egbert early in the Ninth.

From the union of the new Germanic Nations and tongues with those of the conquered Roman Empire of the West sprang the Romance (i. e., Romanized or Latinized) peoples and languages of mediæval and modern Europe. The Latin of literature and of educated speech was corrupted in the common parlance of the people of Gaul, of Spain, and of Italy, and from this corruption

and the admixture of Teutonic words arose the Provençal tongue of southern France, and the French, Spanish,
and Italian languages. In the east of Switzerland and
in Roumania (part of the ancient Dacia) the language
spoken by the people is also of Latin origin. The chief
Latin or Romance Nations of modern Europe are therefore the French, Spanish, and Italian; in the earlier
mediæval times the people of the districts called Provence and Aquitaine, south of the Loire, are to be
regarded as a separate Nation from the French to the
north of that river.

The English language is in the main Teutonic, with a
Romance or Latin element in the Norman-French, Old
French, and Latin words introduced after the conquests
the German nations of central Europe and the people of
Holland have kept their speech free from the influence
of Latin, as also the Scandinavian nations, including the
Danes, Swedes, and Norwegians. The Slavonic races
of Europe (Russians, Poles, etc.) speak languages of
their own, Aryan in origin, but distinct both from the
Romance and Teutonic tongues. The Celtic tongues
(Gaelic, Erse of Ireland, and Manx being included) are
almost extinct, save in Wales and in Brittany, inhabited
by Celtic descendants of the ancient Britons, who still
to a great degree retain the olden speech, and in the
Highlands of Scotland.

The Eastern, Greek, or Byzantine Empire continued
to exist for nearly a thousand years after the downfall
of the Western, and to pass gradually to decay, while the
new nationalities and the new civilization of Europe
were being developed in ever-growing vigor under the
influence of the German spirit that was to regenerate the
world. The Emperors at Constantinople, though they
ruled dominions where the language and civilization

were mainly Greek, still claimed to be Roman Emperors, and under their sway the laws and official forms of Imperial Rome were maintained.   The head of the Christian Church in the East was the Patriarch of Constantinople, as the Bishop of Rome was in the West.

The Byzantine Empire reached its highest point of power and fame in the Sixth Century, during the reign of Justinian, A. D. 527-565.   It was he who built the great Church (now the Mosque in Mahommedan hands) of Saint Sophia at Constantinople.   His chief service to mankind was the codification of the laws of Rome, to which is due the great system of Roman jurisprudence called the Civil Law, forming the basis of so much of the law in European states at the present day.

The Roman law was an active and living principle. It was always open to receive new impressions, and anxious for improvement and development.   It set before itself ideas of humanity and justice which it aimed at accomplishing.   It trained multitudes of keen intellects in the contemplation and pursuit of broad and noble ends.   It constituted in itself a wide and liberal education, and familiarized its students first with the highest philosophy, and afterward with the purest religion of the period.   It had been the constant policy of the Emperors to render the old municipal law of Rome a fitting instrument for the Government of a world-wide Empire.   Ideas of universal equity replaced, under their patronage, the narrow selfishness of the Twelve Tables.   From the time of Augustus the subjects of the conquering city received a long and patient training in the philosophy of jurisprudence.   While the Empire was tottering to its fall they still cherished a conviction of the permanence of the principles on which its social fabric had so long been maintained.   At the end

of the Fourth Century the poet Rutilius could boldly
prophesy that in her legal institutions Rome should yet
be immortal.   In this faith her jurists still persevered,
working bravely for an unknown future.   When the
Theodosian Code or Digest was at last promulgated by
the third Valentinian, Africa was already occupied by
the Vandals, Gaul and Spain had been seized by the
Visigoths and Burgundians; the Franks, the Saxons, the
Ostrogoths, and the Lombards were visibly hovering in
the rear; but preparation had been thus made for placing
all these barbarians under civil restraints, and to these
restraints they for the most part consented to submit.
It was this "noble legacy" of Roman law that Justinian
undertook to put into a practical shape, suited to the
then present and future needs of the whole world.

In A. D. 528-529 a number of commissioners, including the famous Tribonianus, completed the Codex Jus-
tinianus (Justinian's Code), a summary of the imperial
legislation of Rome.   Tribonian, then at the head of
another commission, superintended the compilation,
from the books of the great Roman jurists, of the work
known as the Digest or Pandects (i. e., "arranged matter" or "all-embracing work"), containing authoritative
interpretations and judgments on legal points.   A third
commission, including Tribonian, then prepared a
simple elementary summary called Institutiones ("Institutes," i. e. precepts or principles), based chiefly on the
above-named work of Gaius.   A second revised edition
of the Code was published in 534, and this work, with
the Pandects (or Digest), the Institutes, and a supple-
ment to the Code, known as the Novels (in Latin
"Novellæ Constitutiones," "new enactments"), form the
Corpus Juris Civilis ("Body of Civil Law"), the Roman
law as generally accepted in Europe.

In the East, Justinian's great General, the famous Belisarius, an Illyrian of low birth, fought against the Persian King (one of the greatest monarchs of the later Persian Empire) Chosroes I (or Nushirvan), who reigned A. D. 531-579. Justinian purchased peace by payment of tribute to this Oriental despot, whose Empire extended from the Red Sea to the Indus. In the West, Justinian's arms had great success. In 534 the Vandal Kingdom in Africa was brought to an end by the victories of Belisarius. In 535 Belisarius conquered Sicily, and from 535-540, and again from 541-544, fought with the Goths in Italy, until the jealousy of his master recalled him. His successor in command, Narses, completed the overthrow of the Ostrogothic Kingdom in Italy by his campaigns in 552-553. Under Justinian, the Visigoths were driven out of the south of Spain, so that there was for a time a revived Roman Empire of the West, and the Roman dominion again comprised almost the whole of the Mediterranean coasts. Justinian died in 565, and a speedy change came in Italy.

The warlike German people called Lombards had settled in Pannonia (territory in the south of what is now the Austrian Empire), by Justinian's invitation, about 540. In their new quarters they fought to extermination with the Gothic people called Gepidæ, and in 568 passed over the Alps into the fertile plain of northern Italy which still bears their name. Under their King Alboin, the Lombards subdued all the north and much of the south of Italy (the central part, including the cities of Rome and Ravenna, on the Adriatic, with Sicily, Corsica, and Sardinia, remaining still Roman), and the Lombard Kingdom of Italy thus formed continued for two centuries, until it was conquered by Charlemagne. The growth of Venice dates from the time of this Lombard conquest, when fugitives from their cruel ravages fled for safety to the islands and lagoons at the head of the Adriatic Sea, where a town had been previously founded by fugitives from the Huns. The flourishing period of the Eastern Empire closes for a long time with Heraclius, who died in A. D. 641. The Persians, and the Mongolian race from Asia called the Turks (with their kinsmen the Avars), attacked the Empire in formidable strength. Between 611 and 615 the Persians overran Egypt, Syria, and Asia Minor, remaining encamped for ten years within sight of Constantinople. At last Heraclius arose from his sluggish impotence, and with great ability and courage, between 620 and 627, recovered the whole of the Persian conquests.

On the whole, the Byzantine Empire presents the dreary spectacle of a state possessing the form and the dogmas, with very little of the life, power, and spirit of the Christianity which was the established religion of the realm. The chief interests in religious matters were fierce and endless disputes and conflicts about doctrine and image-worship, and on the appointment to ecclesiastical offices. Murder, conflagration, and plunder resulted from differences of dogma and of worship. In secular affairs, sanguinary encounters arose between the factions of the blue and the green, the distinguishing colors of the different parties of combatants in the gladiatorial games, which cruel spectacles the Christianity of Constantinople had not succeeded in abolishing as a source of popular delight. Greek culture was still preserved in these Eastern provinces, "where the ancient civilization, though slowly fading away under the influence of misgovernment, might still astonish and instruct barbarians; where the court still exhibited the splendor of Diocletian and Constantine; where the public build ings were still adorned with the sculptures of Polycletus and the paintings of Apelles, and where laborious pedants, themselves destitute of taste, sense, and spirit, could still read and interpret the master-pieces of Sophocles, of Demosthenes, and of Plato."

The history of this Byzantine Empire presents, again and again, disgusting pictures of weakness against outward attack, evil passions within, rebellious Generals, Emperors deposed, and often poisoned or otherwise murdered by their own wives and sons, intellectual decay and moral corruption bringing all at last, after periods of revived power and prosperity, to long-delayed and then irretrievable ruin.

Clovis, founder of the Merovingian dynasty, died in A. D. 511, and his descendants kept for nearly two centuries the crown which he had won; but the history of the Frankish Empire during this period is chiefly that of the follies or crimes of weak or wicked Kings, while frequent changes took place in the boundaries of the Kingdom. In 584 the real power passed over to certain officials called Mayors of the Palace. The Minister called Mayor of the Palace was elected by the Frank nobles, and, in command of the army, was the actual sovereign; the stupid slothfulness of the nominal monarchs has given them the title of Rois fainéants or Do-nothing Kings. In 687 a Mayor of the Palace named Pepin (of Heristal, a town on the Meuse) defeated rival Frankish claimants, and, acquiring rule over the whole Frankish dominions, really founded the Second or Carlovingian dynasty, already holding his office of Mayor by hereditary right. His son, Charles Martel, was a vigoros ruler, famous for his victory over the Mussulman invaders of France in 732. In 752 Pepin the Short, son of Charles, became King of the Franks in name as well as in fact, being crowned by the Pope with the title of "King of Francia," while the dynasty of the Merovingian Kings was brought to an end by the formal deposition of the last of the rois fainéants, Childeric III.

In the northwest corner of Europe, aloof from the troubles that harassed the races on the Continent, were what is now known as the British Isles, but which then were reckoned as of a scant importance. To its inhabitants of Celtic origin had come successively tribes of Teutonic origin driven from the Continent by enemies. Rough and uncouth were they when Cæsar's all-conquering armies made a raid in 55 B. C., which Claudius attempted (in A. D. 43) to make a complete conquest, but without entire success. The Britons met their formidable foes with a most tenacious and determined opposition. Vespasian, afterward Emperor of Rome, had all he could do to win for Rome, after many battles, the territory now forming Hampshire and the Isle of Wight. But four years later Roman skill and discipline won their way, and Caractacus being defeated by Ostorius Scapula, the limits of Roman sway were increased. Under Boadicea, a female ruler in the eastern district, the tribes rose in revolt, being wearied by extortions, licentiousness and insults to Druidism, which was the National worship. Led by the Queen herself, the Britons for a time were triumphant, but in the end Suetonius captured the stronghold of the Druids in Mona, cut down the sacred groves of oaks and burned the priests in their own wicker idols. This was the end of the independence of the Kings who ruled the scattered British tribes. Eight years of wise government ended occasion for revolt. Yet all of Briton was never subdued by the Romans, who attempted by great defensive works to exclude from their dominions the still unconquered Celts of the North. With them there was constant warfare.

Three distinct races existed in Britain under the Roman rule. At the North, now known as Scotland, were the Caledonians, Picts, and Scots unsubdued by the Romans. The Scots are known to have been Gaelic immigrants from Ireland—the language spoken by some of the Scotch Highlanders to-day being the same as the Erse tongue spoken by the Irish. The Picts have always been a puzzle to ethnologists, for though they were probably of the Celtic race, their language differed from that of the British and Irish. In the East and South were the Logrians, who had come under the influence of the Roman civilization. At the West, beyond the Severn, were the Cambrians or Welsh, who seemed invincible in their mountain fastnesses. Abandoned by the legions (428), and without defense from the Picts, the Logrians appealed (453) for aid to the Saxons, the Jutes, and the Angles, who were constantly leaving their German and Scandinavian shores to plough the seas. Two Saxon chiefs, Hengist and Horsa, vanquished the Picts and received in recompense the Isle of Thanet, off the shore of Kent. But Hengist, despoiling those who had called him, took possession of the country from the Thames to the Channel and gave himself the title of King of Kent. From this time the ambition of these pirates was to secure a foothold in Britain. In 491 the Kingdom of Sussex was founded, in 516 that of Wessex, in 526 that of Essex. The invasion of the Angles began in 547, and they founded the Kingdoms of Northumberland on the east side of the island, and those of East Anglia (577) and of Mercia (584). This made three English Kingdoms besides the four Saxon ones, being in all seven petty monarchies, which later became a single State. The Saxons formed the basis of the actual population of the country, and England owes her language to them. Long before political union had been reached the unity of the people found expression in a single Christian church. The political union of England was effected during the thirty-six years' rule of Egbert (801-837), King of Wessex, who had seen something of centralization in the court of Charlemagne, whose friend he was.

RISE OF THE SARACENS

Early in the Seventh Century a movement began in the heart of Arabia which was to result in a succession of the most stupendous religious and political revolutions that the world has ever witnessed. The Arabs or Saracens were about to assail, almost at the same time, every Nation and tribe of the Old Roman and Persian world, from India and the borders of China to France and Spain. The term Arabs means "people of the West" (from their position in Asia), and the word Saracens means "people of the East," the name adopted by them after their passage into Africa and Europe, when the former title had become geographically inappropriate. The fact that Islamism is at the present day the hope and the faith of some two hundred millions of the human race gives an enduring interest to the story of the deeds of those who brought about so mighty a result. The Saracens, now attacking Aryan Europe, were of Semitic race, and theirs is the only Semitic power which has played any great part in history since the time of the great dominion of Carthage. Islamism is also the last of three great religions which have come out from among the Semitic nations, and all of which taught men that there is but one God, and bade them to keep from the worship of idols. First came Judaism, then Christianity, and last the religion of Mahomet (or Mohammed).

The secret of the power wielded by the Saracens lay in the religious enthusiasm which is called fanaticism—the reckless fervor of abandonment to the one present passion of the soul. In their poetry, in love, in the warfare by means of which their religion was so widely spread, this enthusiastic devotion is displayed. Hence the extraordinary rapidity of their conquests in forcing the peoples, under the influence of terror, to embrace a faith which, in order to promote the worship of the One God, has no regard to race, or caste, or nation, or political distinction; a religious system, in which it was the highest merit to die on its behalf, with promise of a sure reward in Paradise for him who should fall fighting for the cause.

Their enthusiasm was roused by the founder of a new religion—Mahomet. This extraordinary man was born at the sacred city of Mecca, in Arabia, in the year 569. He came of a noble family among a people who have been described as "the semi-barbarous sons of the Desert, but slightly penetrated with the civilization of city life; a people whose courage was the daring of the robber—a race careless alike of fatigue and danger, lawless in daring, pertinacious of purpose, implacable in revenge, strangers as yet to the enervation that is born of wealth and luxury and power, but not devoid of a rude chivalry of action and an imaginative poetry of feeling—such were the Arabians of the time of Mahomet. When the great religious reformer appeared among the Arabs, the old patriarchal faith, of the time when Job was an Arabian chieftain, had been changed into a degrading idolatry, and in the Kaaba or sacred temple, at Mecca, 360 graven and molten images were standing. In Persia the philosophical and elevating creed of Zoroaster had degenerated into vague mysticism and fire-worship, while in Syria and Egypt Christianity had hidden its face, amid a wild carnival of fantastic speculations, idolatries, and heresies. But the hour and the man had now come.

Over the scattered tribes of Arabia there arose a King,

and over their divided worships a priest and a prophet. "There is no God but God, and Mahomet is His prophet. God is one, Almighty, all-righteous, not a mere cold and remote abstraction, no motionless image graven in stone or marble, but a living God, the King of Kings, and the Lord of Lords. He has chosen you to be the workers of His will and the champions of His truth. He has called you to victory over the infidel in this world, and to an ever-lasting paradise in the next." It needs no great effort of the imagination to picture the effect of such an announce-ment, when once it had succeeded in gaining for itself a hearing. It was at once an appeal to the deepest and truest instincts of a Semitic people, and the gathering cry of an awakened patriotism. It proclaimed to the skeptic a creed, and to the warriors a warfare and a crown. To win the joys of Paradise by the subjugation and conver-sion of the earth was a prospect which might well whet a worldly ambition no less than stimulate a religious zeal, and we wonder not so much at the victories of Islamism as that it left anything unconquered, and that, after the fiercest onslaughts of the Saracen, the incense of Christian worship still went up from the temple of St. Sophia. Such, in its purer beginnings, was the religious system which has endured for twelve hundred years, recognizing and perpetuating the two fatal social evils of polygamy and slavery, stereotyping despotism, and making political progress impossible by the inextricable interweaving of the civil law with the divine in the eternal and immutable Koran.

In 629 Mohammed* captured the holy city, Mecca, completed the conquest of Arabia, and, after calling on the King of Persia (Chosroes II) and the Byzantine Emperor (Heraclius) to embrace Islamism, prepared to march be-

*See volume "World's Famous Foreign Statesmen."

yond the borders of Arabia. At this juncture he died, cut off by a fever at Medina in A. D. 632.

The leaders and rulers of the Arabs who came after Mohammed were called his Caliphs or Successors, and the first of them was his father-in-law, Abubeker. The success of the arms of Islam was generally rapid. The choice offered to mankind lay among three things—the Koran, tribute, or the sword—all must either embrace the new faith, pay tribute for the keeping of their old faith, or die. By the year 639 all Syria and Egypt had been conquered, and the armies started westward through Northern Africa, and swept on northward to Asia Minor, and eastward over Persia. Persia and the east of Asia Minor fell an easy prey; but in Africa, where Christianity was strongly established, a long and stout resistance was made, the conquest not being completed till 709. From Africa the followers of the prophet crossed over into Spain, and by the year 713 the Crescent was triumphant by the Atlantic in the West, and in the Indian province of Sind, (or Scinde) in the East.

In 673 the Saracens were repulsed from Constantinople, and in 718 a formidable crisis came. The ruler of the Eastern Empire was, happily for Europe and the world, a man of vigor and ability, Leo the Isaurian (from Isauria, a district of Asia Minor), and his repulse of the Saracen attacks on Constantinople, and his defeat of the foe beneath her walls, prevented a loss which, at that epoch, would have been most serious for the religion and civilization of Europe. Constantinople was then the head of Christendom, and the law, literature, and theology which she contained and represented might have perished in a Saracen success. The efforts of the Saracens to enter Europe by the east continued at intervals for many years afterward, but they never had any perma-

ENTRY OF MOHAMMED II. INTO CONSTANTINOPLE
Painting by Benjamin Constant

nent success in or beyond the west of Asia Minor, and the faith of the Mussulmans (the words Moslem, Muslim, and Mussulman are derived from Islam, and mean "the Righteous," i. e. "those who are at peace with God through right doing" was to become established at Constantinople by Mongolian instead of by the original Semitic believers.

It was in A. D. 711-713 that the Saracens (or Moors, as the Spanish writers have called them, because they crossed over into Spain from Mauritania, the modern Morocco) overthrew the Kingdom of the Visigoths in Spain. The leader of the Saracen (Moorish) invaders was named Tarik, and the place of his landing derives its name, Gibraltar, from the Arabic words Gebel-al-Tarik, "the rock of Tarik." The town of Tarifa (the most southerly place in Europe, having still the fortifications built by the Moors, and a very ancient Moorish castle), southwest of Gibraltar, preserves the name of the same victorious General. The Visigothic King Roderick, called "the last of the Goths," was decisively defeated at the town north of Cadiz called Xeres de la Frontera, and in the struggle Roderick—a hero of Spanish romance— was killed. In a short time afterward all Spain was subdued by the Saracens, with the exception of a narrow mountainous strip in the north, where the Christians maintained themselves and their faith. The Moorish or Saracenic rule in Spain lasted in whole or in part for 700 years.

The Saracens' invasion of Europe soon crossed the Pyrenees into southern Gaul (a more correct designation than "France" at this period of history) and made a lodgment there. Another great crisis in the history of Europe and the world had come—one in which was to be decided a contest between the Crescent and the

Cross, and which was to issue in the deliverance of European Christendom, save in Spain, from Islam, and in the re-establishment of the old superiority of the Indo-European over the Semitic family of mankind.

A young Prince of Germanic race, Karl Martel (or Charles Martel, in the French form of his name), was the champion of the Christian cause in this great wager of battle, when appeal was made by arms to the one God whom both the combatants acknowledged and adored. It was exactly a Century after the death of Mohammed (A. D. 632) when the deliverance wrought by the battle of Tours thus affected the future welfare of mankind (732).

In the summer of A. D. 732 the great Saracenic leader Abderahman, a brave and skillful General, led a great host of Moslem soldiery—Syrians, Moors, Saracens, Persians, Tartars—across the Pyrenees, and, with his clouds of light cavalry, overran the country as far as the Loire. In October the great seven-days' battle of Moslem horse—white-turbaned warriors of tawny skin —against the fair-haired, stalwart Frankish foot, steel-helmed, and armed with heavy sword, or battle-axe, or mace—was fought upon the plain between the towns of Poitiers and Tours. The end was that the Saracens were utterly defeated, Abderahman was slain, and the attempt of Islam to conquer Europe by the west had signally and finally failed. The Frankish leader, Charles (son of Pepin of Heristal), was surnamed Martel (old French for "Hammer") for the crushing blow thus dealt, as if with the favorite weapon of the war-god (Thor) of his forefathers' pagan creed.

It was only for a short time that the vast dominion acquired by the Saracenic conquests was kept together as a single Empire, over which one Caliph ruled from

India to Spain. In A. D. 755 the Empire was divided into the Eastern and Western Caliphates, the Western Caliph having Spain, with his capital at Cordova; and the Eastern Saracenic Empire including northern Africa and the East, with the capital first at Damascus and then at Bagdad. The Caliph at Bagdad was generally regarded as the head of the world of Islam, as various sects arose, and various parts of the Empire were split off under the pressure of Turkish invasion from the East.

The best known of the Caliphs of Bagdad is Haroun-al-Raschid, who succeeded to power in 786. In the "Arabian Nights" we have a picture of the life led by this monarch and by his people in the capital. After his time, province after province was lost to the Turks, and in A. D. 1258 the Mongols, under the leadership of a grandson of Genghis Khan, conquered the Caliphate of Bagdad, and subverted the dynasty of the Seljukian Turks (from Seljuk, a chieftain of Bokhara in the Ninth Century) which had been established there.

The Mohammedan rule in Spain was at its strongest under the Caliph Abdalrahman, about the middle of the Tenth Century. In 1051 the Moors, who had been summoned from Africa to help the Saracens against the advancing power of the Christians, overthrew the Caliphate of Cordova, and the real Moorish dominion in southern Spain began.

To the Arabs Europe is indebted for many of the arts and sciences. It was no race of rude and savage warriors that secured a foothold in the southern part of the Continent. The Arabs liked and practiced commerce long before the rise of Mohammed, who was originally a camel-driver. The armies prepared the way for caravans in Asia and Africa, and their merchants traveled by roads in every direction. The Arabs became sailors and, already acquainted with the use of a compass, imperfectly borrowed from the Chinese, they voyaged over the Red Sea and the Sea of Oman penetrating as far as Hindustan and Indo-China. African commerce served as a link between the East and West. The ports of Tripoli, Tunis, and Tangiers had inherited the fortune of the vandal Carthage; Egypt wisely governed, preserved her old fertility. Haroun-al-Raschid, Abou-Giafar, and Al-Mamoun, displayed in the Eighth and Ninth Centuries the most wonderful luxury at Bagdad. Palaces ornamented with marble columns, and with rich carpets manufactured in the East, superb gardens, refreshed by marble fountains falling into marble basins, a profusion of silken materials from India and of precious stones, every refinement of luxury, and all the magnificence of the old Oriental monarchies—this scarcely describes the pomp of the Caliphs, who lavished thus the tributes levied from a hundred races. Arab poets do not appear to have exaggerated the wealth of these sovereigns of Bagdad who succeeded to the riches of Egypt and Asia.

The Caliphs of Cordova were not less opulent through the wise administration of Abd-er-Rahman I, of Hischam I, of Abd-er-Hahman II, of Al-Hakkem I, or of Al-Hakkem II. Arab agriculture converted several parts of Spain into vast gardens, where all the most beautiful plants of the southern countries flourished. The ingenuity of the Arabs counteracted the dryness of the climate by skillful irrigation, and aqueducts conveyed the water preserved in artificial ponds. The Arabs introduced rice, cotton, the sugar-cane, and the date-palm into Spain. The most illustrious chiefs were proud in personally cultivating their own gardens. The towns were filled with manufactures of silk, cotton, and cloth. The Arabs introduced the use of indigo and cochineal, or rich porcelain-colored earthenware and linen paper into Spain. They excelled in the art of dyeing. The leathers of Cordova and the well-tempered weapons of Toledo were famous. Spain maintained a large commerce, and the Caliphs of Cordova had at least a thousand ships in their fleets.

The first Caliphs would have liked to confine all learning to reading the Koran, but they were not so barbarous as they were reported to be, and the conflagration of the Alexandrian library was not ordered by Omar. Science and education flourished. Haroun never traveled without a procession of savants and he endeavored to found a free school by the side of each mosque. Al-Mamoun ordered a search made for valuable manuscripts and for their translation he paid their weight in gold. Ten thousand pupils studied in the College of Bagdad alone. The Arabs had poets rich and luxuriant in their images and historians whose narratives are naive. But they were chiefly successful in romances such as those known as "The Arabian Nights." In philosophy they were followers of Aristotle, whom they did not understand. Their greatest service to literature was in translating and preserving the work of the ancients.

In science the Arabs were more successful than in literature. They borrowed Aristotle's "Natural History," but they added much to it. They were excellent physicians, and Christian Princes went to Cordova to be healed. In abstract studies they were pre-eminent. They transmitted, if they did not invent, the numerals which replaced the clumsy Roman signs. The Arabic origin of algebra is indicated by its name. They translated the works of the Greek geometricians and invented new problems in the science. They also studied trigonometry. They devoted themselves to astrology, which led them to astronomy, in which they were far in advance of the rest of the world in their day. They studied geography from globes, and knew the annual movement of the equinoxes, and they estimated the circumference of the earth at 26,000 miles. Chemistry owes its name and its beginnings to the Arabs, and pharmacy was developed by them.

By the middle of the Eighth Century, then, the Visigoths had long disappeared from history through the conquest of their Spanish Kingdom by the Saracens, and the transference of their African dominion, first to the Eastern Empire, and then to the Mohammedan Caliphs. In Italy, the Ostrogoths had disappeared before the revival of the power of the Eastern Empire there, and the incoming of the Lombards. A Frankish (German) Kingdom occupied Gaul and most of west and central Germany, and though for the sake of convenience we have used the term "France," there was as yet no "France" in our modern sense of the word, and we must regard the Princes of the Merovingian dynasty and the founders of the Carlovingian (Pepin of Heristal and Charles Martel) simply as "Kings of the Franks." The Saracen Empire was the greatest in the world for power and extent, and the Eastern or Byzantine Empire included only the west of Asia Minor, Greece (to the Balkans), and part of Italy. The Slavonians were becoming powerful between the Danube and the Baltic, and Mongolian (Tartar) tribes from Asia, called Bulgarians and Magyars, are found northwest and north of the Black Sea. The English are settled in their new home, and the Danes and the Norwegians (or Northmen)—the flower of the Scandinavian branch of the Teutonic race—are beginning to be formidable pirates in northwest Europe. We have now come to the epoch when the Roman Empire of the West was for a time revived by the great man who has been (to the confusion of many minds) called by the French name of Charlemagne, being in birth, and speech, and character, and ways, a thorough German.

EMPIRE OF CHARLEMAGNE

Karl or Charles the Great, son of Pepin the Short, King of the Franks, came to the throne in A. D. 768 as joint King, but assumed sole rule in 771. He is one of the great men of history—distinguished as a soldier, a politician, and a man of intellectual taste and ability. He created a great and powerful monarchy out of the chaos of nations and institutions which he found existing around him, and though his Empire fell to pieces at his death, much of his work had a permanent effect, in that he created a solid Frankish dominion capable of maintaining itself generally against the hordes of Pagans and pirates, which threatened Christian Europe from the East and North. Charlemagne* displayed a wonderful administrative power, and much wisdom, insight, and largeness of view as a legislator. He greatly promoted Christianity, law, order, and learning, showing his ceaseless activity in the reform of the coinage, the founding of schools, the collection of libraries, the settlement even of religious disputes, and in attention to countless details of reform and administration which, after his death, showed that unsettled tribes had been turned into real, regular, and durable communities. The power of the Church was advanced by his enforcement of the regular payment of tithes throughout his dominions, and his assigning a place to Bishops and to Abbots, as well as to Dukes and to Counts, in the feudal system which had already virtually arisen. In the Frankish Empire of Charlemagne, Chris-

* See Volume "World's Famous Foreign Statesmen."

tianity was first consolidated into a political form proceeding from itself, and the principle of hereditary monarchy became established.

The Pagan foes subdued by the Frankish arms under Karl the Great, were the Germanic and Tartar tribes to the North and East of his inherited Kingdom. After many years of intermittent warfare he thoroughly conquered the Saxons on the Weser and the Elbe, and forced them to embrace Christianity. He overcame the Tartar race called Avars, settled in the territory now called Hungary, and the whole of Germany was now for the first time united under one ruler. In Spain, he took from the Saracens the territory as far as the Ebro (A. D. 778); it was in connection with this expedition that the legends arose about the famous hero Roland (the Orlando of Italian poetry), and his exploits in the valley of Roncesvalles. In 773 the German King marched into Italy, to help Pope Adrian I against the attacks of the Lombards. Their King Desiderius was deposed, and Charlemagne was crowned King of Lombardy with the famous iron crown. On Christmas Day, A. D. 800, as he knelt on the steps of the altar at divine service in Rome, in the basilica of St. Peter, on the spot where now the great cathedral stands, Pope Leo III placed on the brow of Karl the Great the diadem of the Cæsars, and saluted him as "Emperor of the West" by the title of Charles I, Cæsar Augustus. Bryce in his "Holy Roman Empire," says: "Modern history begins with this union, so long in preparation, so mighty in its consequences, of the Roman and the Teuton, of the memories and the civilization of the South with the fresh energy of the North." Rome now became the capital of the Western Empire in the South, as Aachen (Aix-la-Chapelle) was in the north, and Italy and Rome were henceforth entirely cut off from the Eastern Empire, whose capital was Constantinople.

The great Charles made no effort to wield the despotic rule of the old Roman Emperors. Each nation in his dominions was allowed to retain its own laws, hereditary chiefs, and free assemblies, while the control of a central government over the different local functionaries and authorities was kept up by the despatch of royal commissioners from province to province as the sovereign's representatives, to inspect, report, and reform.

Charlemagne's energy and activity were incessant and almost superhuman. Though almost every year found him engaged in some warlike expedition of deliberate conquest, with a distinct and beneficial end in view for the furtherance of civilization and Christianity, he found time to attend to all sorts of matters belonging to the administration and improvement of his great Empire —public works of every kind, and the advancement of learning, even to the collection of ballads and old Frankish poems. He gathered men of letters round him from all quarters, including the English scholar Alcuin, who knew Latin, Greek, and Hebrew, and was Charlemagne's chief instructor and adviser in literary affairs. Under his superintendence many schools were founded in connection with abbeys and monasteries, for the study of grammar, rhetoric, philosophy and science.

Karl the Great was very tall and very strong; simple and frugal in dress, habits, and mode of life; dignified, amiable, kind. One of his favorite modes of pastime and exercise was swimming, for which purpose he constructed magnificent baths at Aachen, his capital. Here Charlemagne died in A. D. 814, after a reign of forty-three years.

The Empire of Charles the Great extended over the

whole territory northeast from the Ebro to the Elbe, and west of a line drawn south from Hamburg to Venice, including also, to east of that line, Bavaria, Bohemia, and most of Austria, except Hungary; in Italy it reached as far south as Gaeta. In other words, it included what is now the northeast of Spain, the whole of France and of northern and central Germany (except eastern Prussia), much of Austria, and all northern and central Italy, with the Island of Corsica.

Charlemagne's Empire bore only a fictitious resemblance to the Empire he claimed to have restored. No doubt its unity was maintained by the formidable conqueror's iron hand, but it was badly secured by an incoherent administration, that was but a confused imitation of the ingenious mechanism of the Roman. The different nationalities of which the Empire was composed had submitted to the ascendency of the Franks, but the latter were too few in number to assimilate the conquered nations, even had they thought of doing so. By placing Frank counts in Italy on the marches (frontiers) of Spain, the Elbe and the Danube, and in the valley of the Main, Charlemagne aimed only at insuring obedience. To maintain authority over these turbulent, bellicose populations required a succession of Charlemagnes. Pepin's family seemed exhausted and the Empire of Charlemagne lasted only during his life. Many other causes contributed to the dissolution of the Empire that outwardly seemed so strong. But though it fell, its effects remained. Charlemagne would not occupy the place in history that posterity has accorded to him if he had been only a successful conqueror. Charlemagne created Germany and bequeathed to its ruler the title of Roman Emperor. Charlemagne disciplined the new populations who settled in the Empire, forced them to adopt agricultural life; and throughout central Europe he planted bishoprics and abbeys that became the centers of civilization. In a word his powerful hands kneaded together the materials of modern Europe. His Empire was dismembered, but the pieces formed nations, the development of which astonishes us even now.

BEGINNINGS OF MODERN NATIONS

Charles the Great's son, Louis le Debonnaire ("the gentle"), became the second Frankish Emperor, but had not the force of character necessary to maintain a position so difficult, and even during his lifetime parts of the Empire were lost to him. The truth was that a reaction was taking place, on the part of particular nationalities, against the universal sovereignty of the Franks, and, after much contention among the three sons of Louis, the Empire was divided, in A. D. 843, by the Treaty of Verdun. The name of the King of the central and southern portion (Lothar) survives in the province of Lorraine (in German, Lothringen). The eastern and western parts correspond roughly to modern Germany and France.

There were frequent changes of boundary by which the Kingdoms formed began gradually to roughly correspond to real divisions of language and nations. By the year 930 the Kingdom of Burgundy had arisen, including what is now Switzerland and the southeast of France, with the capital at Arles; about 1030 this State became part of the German Empire. A Duchy of Burgundy, corresponding nearly to the modern French province, continued independent or semi-independent till the Seventeenth Century.

In 887 a final separation took place between the Kingdoms of the East and West Franks, answering to Germany and France. Germany first became great under the Saxon line of Kings, and afterward Emperors, beginning in A. D. 918 with Henry I, or Henry the Fowler, elected to be King by certain German Princes. He was a prudent and active ruler, who forced Suabia, Bavaria, and Lorraine to submit, and fought with great success against the Magyars or Hungarians, who were striving to make their way into Germany from the East. His son Otto (or Otho) the Great, ruled from 936 to 973, and was a brave, honest, and able monarch. Under him the Western (Roman or German) Empire was restored in a new form, by which it was attached to the chief Frankish Kingdom (which Ger: many had now become), so that whoever was chosen, by the Princes of Germany, King of Germany, had alone a right to the title of Emperor. By marriage with the King of Italy's widow, Otho became King of Lombardy in 951; he was crowned Emperor by the Pope in 962. This line of Emperors, the Saxon, ended in A. D. 1024.

Under Conrad II, who began the line of Franconian Emperors, so called because its Princes belonged to Franconia or Eastern Francia, the eastern or German part of the old Kingdom of the Franks, the Kingdom of Burgundy was annexed to the Empire. Conrad's son, Henry III, reigned from A. D. 1039 to 1056, and was one of the greatest of the German sovereigns—bold, energetic, and enlightened. He did much to maintain order and religion both in Italy and Germany, assuming great authority in the appointment and control of the Popes, and keeping down the great feudal nobles of his realm. Henry III also promoted art, science, and literature, founding many schools in connection with the monasteries. Under his successors, serious and frequent quarrels arose between Popes and Emperors, causing great disorders of rebellion and civil war in Italy and Germany. It was Henry IV of Germany who was compelled, by excommunication absolving his subjects from allegiance, to submit to the famous Pope Hildebrand, Gregory VII * in 1077. The Emperor went to see Gregory in his residence at the

* See volume "World's Famous Foreign Statesmen."

mountain castle of Canossa, near Modena, in north Italy, and was only admitted to an audience after waiting in the courtyard for three successive days in the depth of winter, clad in a penitential dress.   This famous episode has made "going to Canossa" a proverbial phrase for abject submission to a powerful foe.   The Franconian line of Emperors ended in A. D. 1125.

The Carlovingian dynasty in France, or Karlings, the proper German name of these Frankish Kings, ruled during part of the time between A. D. 750 and 980, their tenure being interrupted by the election to power, as Duke of France, in 887, of Eudes, or Odo, whose family may be looked upon as French, since they spoke an early form of the Romance language thus called.   The capital of this Duchy of France was Paris, and the power of its rulers did not extend south of the Loire.   At this period, Ninth and Tenth centuries, in what we now call France the territory and rule were divided amongst a number of independent or quasi-independent Dukes and Counts, such as the Dukes of Guienne or Aquitaine and of Gascony in the south; the Duke of Burgundy in the east, with his capital at Dijon; the Count of Toulouse in the south; the Count of Flanders in the north; the Duke of Brittany in the northwest, and the Duke of Normandy in the north.

At last, in A. D. 987, an end came to this perplexing record and to the Carlovingian dynasty, by the election as King of France of Hugh Capet, whose dynasty ruled for nearly 350 years, and whose descendants, except during revolutionary and Napoleonic periods, were Kings of France till 1848.   With Hugh Capet, then, in 987 begins a Kingdom of France with Paris as its capital, destined to grow to its full size and strength by the reduction of the power of the petty sovereigns and feudal lords.   Capet, eldest son of a Duke of France, was chosen King by the great feudal lords, and the power which he possessed was simply that of a feudal superior. The barons were constantly engaged in wars with each other and in oppression of the peasantry, and the influence of the church was beneficially used in some quarters by causing the conclusion of a "God's peace" or "Truce of God," prohibiting all warfare and tyranny.

About the middle of the Tenth Century, Otho of Germany had become King of northern Italy. The south of Italy still belonged to the Byzantine (Eastern) Empire. The temporal power of the Popes had become established in central Italy. About the middle of the Eleventh Century the Normans conquered Apulia, in the southeast of Italy, and also Sicily, under the leadership of Robert Guiscard, so that the Eastern Empire lost most of its Italian possessions.

In Spain the Saracens gradually lost power by divisions amongst themselves, and the Christians began to gain ground. In the north a Christian Kingdom, that of Navarre, had risen about A. D. 843. In 1031 the Western Caliphate came to an end, and the Saracen dominion in Spain was cut up into several small States. The Spanish Kingdoms of Aragon, Castile, Leon, and Asturias were founded in the Eleventh Century, and these successes caused the Saracens to call in the aid of the Moors from Africa, and the Moorish Kingdom in southern Spain maintained the Mohammedan cause firmly for some time longer.

From the south inroads were made by the Magyars, or Hungarians. This people, of Asiatic origin, became Christianized and settled in a Kingdom still bearing their name, before the end of the Tenth Century. To the north of them Slavonic States were founded in Bohemia and Poland, and a Duchy of Austria arose as

a border State between Germany and the Hungarians.
Before the Eleventh Century Russia, under her King
Vladimir, had made a beginning in Christianity and civ-
ilization, derived from intercourse with the Byzantine
Empire.

Of the three invasions from the north, south, and
east which brought about the dissolution of the Carlovingian Empire, that of the Northmen has been the most
important in its effect upon history. They were the
dwellers in Scandinavia and on the northern Baltic
coasts. All the territories now called Denmark, Sweden,
and Norway supplied these dreaded invaders, but England was chiefly assailed by men from Denmark, while
the Norwegians made their descent on France, Scotland,
and Ireland. The Danes were closely allied to the English and Saxons. They were sea-warriors and pirates,
distinguished by strength, courage, merciless ferocity,
and hatred of the Christian name and religion. England was the chief sufferer, because of her exposed position west of the North Sea, nor was any part of the land
so far distant from the sea as to be secure from attack.
The Northmen had pillaged the coasts of France even
during the lifetime of the great Charles, and once in the
south of his Empire, as he gazed from a port on the
Mediterranean upon some Norman cruisers, he had
shed prophetic tears over the coming fate of his peoples. These formidable foes, destined to make two
successive conquests of England, came at first only for
pillage, to the estuaries of France and the British isles.
In a few years the Dane, or Northman, came to both
lands for territory, and his efforts were crowned with
success. The great point of difference between the invaded and the invaders lay in the maritime skill of the
Danes. It is believed that the younger sons of the

Scandinavian chiefs were driven to sea robbery for a livelihood by the law of primogeniture, under which the eldest son inherited all of the property. The term King, or Viking (applied to the leaders of the pirates or to the whole body), means men of the bays and creeks, in reference to the countless fiords or inlets on the west coast of Norway. The English had by this time, in their devotion to a life of tillage and pasture, lost their olden love for maritime pursuits, and were thus unprepared with a fleet to meet their foes on the seas. The French had never had any maritime skill. The pirates bore as their national flag the effigy of a black raven woven on a blood-red ground, and were armed with long, heavy swords and battle-axes of formidable keenness and weight. The Northmen kept both to the worship of Odin and their life of roving and robbery, and had great contempt for those who tilled the soil and had adopted the worship of the Christian God.

The first footholds upon foreign soil secured by the Northmen were to the south of the continent, where they met less resistance than they had received in England and Scotland. They seized the Walcheren Islands at the mouth of the Scheldt, Betau in the Rhine, the Wahal and the Lech in the Seine, and Noirmoutier at the mouth of the Loire. In 840 they burned Rouen and in 843 they sacked Nantes, Saintes, and Bordeaux and entered the Mediterranean. They besieged the walls of Paris repeatedly, once at a memorable siege in 885, and sacked Tours, Orleans, and Toulouse. They ascended the Rhine and the Meuse in 851 and devastated their shores. Then a royal edict ordered the Counts and vassals of the King to repair old castles and build new ones, and soon the country was fortified and the invaders, halted at each point, wished to settle in some place secure and arable, rather than continue the warfare. Neustria was given them in 911. Their devastations, continuing for three-fourths of a century, had prepared for the rise of feudalism.

The Northmen robbed France and the Netherlands of both safety and a part of their wealth. In England they took away independence as well. The Saxon heptarchy in 827 was a single monarchy under Egbert the Great, who repulsed the first Danes attacking his shores. After his reign the Danes occupied North-umberland, East Anglia, and Mercia. For seven years Alfred the Great, on the throne of Wessex, carried on a deadly struggle with the entrenched Danes, and at length concluded a treaty of partition at the peace of Wedmore (878), surrendering to the Danes the north and east of England, to be held by them as vassals of the Saxon King. The supremacy of Wessex was thus secured and ripened in the following reigns into some-thing like imperial authority. The main features of the organization given the Kingdom by Alfred have been preserved. These are: division of the country into counties; justice rendered by twelve—a jury of twelve freeholders; general affairs decided by the Witenage-mot, an assemblage of wise men aided by a King, half hereditary and half elective. The development of the power of the English King was such that Edward the Elder was recognized not only as overlord of Mercia and Northumbria, but the Welsh Kings swore allegiance and the Kings of Scotland and Strathclyde acknow-ledged him as their father and lord. Edward treated on equal terms and contracted alliances with the great-est Princes in Europe. Under Athelstan the Saxon monarchy was at the height of its power; it was he who dealt a death-blow to all opponents by the battle of

Brunanburg in 937 and drove the Danes from England. But they soon returned under the leadership of Olaf, King of Norway, and Sweyn, King of Denmark, who carried away enormous booty. Gold not succeeding in buying them off, Ethelred attempted a vast counter-plot. All the Danes in England were massacred on St. Brice's Day (1002). Sweyn avenged his compatriots by dethroning Ethelred, and in 1013 he assumed the title of King of England. Edmund II, known as Iron-sides, renewed the struggle against Canute heroically but futilely (1017). Gradually all of the country sub-mitted to the rule of the Danes. At first Canute was cruel, but became a milder monarch, and by marrying Emma, widow of Ethelred, he united conquerers and conquered. He made wise laws or restored those of Alfred the Great, prevented the Danes from oppressing the English, sent Saxon missionaries to Scandinavia to aid in the fall of decadent paganism, and in 1027 made a pilgrimage to Rome, where he promised in the name of England to pay an annual tax, known as St. Peter's pence, annually to the Pope.

Thus in France the Northmen had taken only a province. In England they took a Kingdom. For the rest on both sides of the channel these robbers showed the same aptitude for civilization, and these ferocious pagans became excellent Christians. In Normandy, Rollo made a severe judge, and Canute deserved the name of Great.

GROWTH OF THE PAPAL POWER

We have seen how Christianity became the religion of the Roman Empire. The Catholic Church in the Western Empire had for its head the Bishop of Rome, to whose authority disputants appealed for decision, and oppressed persons for advocacy and protection. This influential position of the hierarch of Rome grew by degrees into a spiritual ascendency unequaled in the history of the world, and still flourishing in full vigor. Macaulay has declared that "there is not, and there never was on this earth, a work of human policy so well deserving of examination as the Roman Catholic Church. The history of that church joins together the two great ages of human civilization. No other institution is left standing which carries the mind back to the times when the smoke of sacrifice rose from the Pantheon, and when camelopards and tigers bounded in the Flavian amphitheater. . . . The Church of Rome saw the commencement of all the governments and of all the ecclesiastical establishments that now exist in the world, and we feel no assurance that she is not destined to see the end of them all. She was great and respected before the Saxon had set foot in Britain, before the Frank had passed the Rhine, when Grecian eloquence still flourished in Antioch, when idols were still worshiped in the temple of Mecca."

It was the fall of the Western Empire that first gave a virtually political standing to the Bishop of Rome. A decree of the Emperor Valentinian III in A. D. 445 had acknowledged the Bishop of Rome as primate, and as the last tribunal of appeal from the other bishops, though the Eastern Church always resisted this claim of the See of Rome. Still the Bishop of Rome was the leading personage in that city which had been the capital of the world, and when, under Justinian, the Eastern Empire gained dominion over Italy, the seat of government was not at Rome, but at Ravenna, and the moral influence of the Roman Bishop continued to grow.

From the title Pontifex Maximus (the chief official of the old Pagan religion of Rome) he came to be called Pontiff; while the word Pope is derived from Papa, "Father," being appropriated to the Roman Pontiff (having previously been given to all bishops) by a decree of Gregory VII (Pope 1073-1085) with the prefixed epithet sanctus, "holy," whence the modern phrase "His Holiness the Pope." The spiritual authority of the Popes was increased in the establishment of new churches in Britain and Germany by missionaries sent forth from Rome, and both the spiritual and political influence of the See grew through the personal ascendency of such Popes as Leo the Great in the Fifth Century, the zealous, good, and able Gregory the Great in the Sixth, and Leo III in the Eighth.

The temporal power of the Papacy really began about the middle of the Eighth Century, when Pepin the Short (son of Charles Martel) was crowned "King of the Franks," or "King of Francia," by Pope Stephen III in 753. Pepin, on his side, helped the Pope against the Lombards, and, after checking the progress of their arms, bestowed on the Pope the territory known as the Exarchate of Ravenna, exarch having been the title given by Justinian to the official who governed central Italy as a province of the Eastern Empire. This transaction, which founded the temporal authority of the

Church of Rome, is famous in history as the "Donation of Pepin." This gift of Pepin's was confirmed to the Popes by his son Charles the Great, who overthrew the Lombard Kingdom in Italy, and was crowned King of Italy and then Emperor of the West in A. D. 800.

During the period of confusion which followed the death of the great Karl, the power of the Papacy was growing, and the Popes exercised a great influence in political affairs, especially through the spiritual terrors of excommunication which they wielded against sovereigns and their subjects. In 865 Pope Nicholas I enforced an edict, in a matter of divorce, against Lothaire, King of Lorraine; in 875 Pope John VIII, in conferring the imperial crown on Charles the Bald, made him acknowledge the independence of the Roman See. A period of weakness and anarchy for the Papacy followed, owing to the violence of feudal lords in Italy, who appointed and deposed Popes at will. The Emperor Otho the Great (ruled 936 to 973) put the imperial power for a time above the Papal by deposing Pope John XII, causing his successor Leo VIII to swear obedience and fidelity, and putting down effectually the resistance made by the Roman nobility and clergy. At a later period the Popes asserted themselves with success against the Emperors, and after many bitter disputes and fluctuations of superiority from Pope to Emperor and Emperor to Pope, a crisis came in the papacy of the famous Hildebrand, who became Pope Gregory VII in A. D. 1073.

Gregory VII was one of the greatest men of the Middle Ages, and the greatest Pope in the history of the See of Rome. It was the chief object of his life to make the ecclesiastical power entirely independent of the temporal. Of humble birth, by his ability and energy he rose to be Cardinal in 1049. From this time Hildebrand was the ruling spirit of the papacy. Under Pope Nicholas II (1058-1061) he brought about a change in the mode of election of the Pontiffs, so that the cardinals alone could nominate, and the clergy and people of Rome were deprived of their votes. When Cardinal Hildebrand became Pope Gregory VII in 1073, he set to work at carrying out his idea of a theocracy in which the Pope should be the chief temporal, as well as ecclesiastical, ruler of the world. In order to concentrate the energies of the clergy upon their sacred duties and the interests of the church, he prohibited the marriage of priests. He then took from the sovereign Princes their right of investiture—that is, the right of investing with their offices the higher clergy in their dominions—the right of conferring the title and the church lands upon bishops and abbots, by the giving of a crozier and a ring.

This latter decree (issued in 1075) at once brought Gregory VII into conflict with the Emperor Henry IV of Germany. Henry supported several German bishops whom Gregory had deposed, and was summoned to appear before a council at Rome. Henry called a council at Worms and had a sentence of deposition passed against Gregory, who retorted by excommunicating the Emperor, and releasing his subjects and vassals from their oath of allegiance. Henry IV found himself helpless, and in 1077 made his humiliating submission at Canossa. The Emperor's friends then gained the upper hand, and Gregory, driven from Rome, died at Salerno in 1085.

The quarrel about investitures—really involving the right of temporal sovereigns to be supreme in ecclesiastical appointments within their own dominions—long survived both Gregory and Henry, and, as far as Germany was concerned, ended in 1122 by the Emperor Henry V surrendering his claim of investiture to the Pope, so far as the ecclesiastical office was concerned, while the bishops were to receive the temporalities (church lands and revenues) from the hands of the Emperor as the feudal superior. The history of England contains one of these Papal claims in the quarrel between Pope Innocent III and King John. As usual in these conflicts between the higher powers, it was the people who suffered. The minor Princes of the Empire and their feudal subjects were distracted between their civil duty to the Emperor and their religious fear of the Pope, and, after infinite disorder and suffering, neither side was really victor in a strife which, if a wise discrimination had been exercised, would never have begun. Innocent III (Pope 1198-1216) is held to have made the Papacy more powerful than at any other time. He constituted himself feudal lord of Rome and the surrounding territory; and, in compelling the submission of John of England, showed forth the See of Rome as possessed of a supreme sovereignty.

The crusade against the heretics called Albigenses is a striking proof of the power wielded by the Popes in that age. Toward the close of the Twelfth Century a sect of early Protestants existed in the County of Toulouse. They were called Albigenses, from the town of Alby, northeast of the city of Toulouse. The region in which they dwelt was at that time the most civilized and flourishing part of western Europe, the fruitful and well-cultivated Languedoc, abounding in corn fields and vineyards, rich cities, and stately castles. The civilization of Languedoc was distinguished by freedom of thought, which permitted friendly intercourse with the

Moors of Spain, and brought to the north of the Pyrenees the mathematical and medical science of the schools of Granada and Cordova. A flourishing trade was carried on by merchants from the Eastern Empire at Toulouse and at Narbonne, and these traders appear to have introduced, along with their wares, doctrines resembling those of modern Protestantism, and regarded as deadly heresy by the Papal See. Pope Innocent III resolved to meet the evil with the sword, and called the warriors of northern France to his aid. The Spanish monk Dominic (the famous founder of the order of the Dominicans) was employed to preach a "crusade" against the Albigenses, and Simon de Montfort (father of the great Earl of Leicester) headed the expedition against the heretics. Raymond VI, Count of Toulouse, refused at first to join in the extirpation of heresy by the slaughter of his best subjects, but was induced to submit and to take part in the attack upon the strongholds of the new faith. The war began in 1209; town after town was taken and burnt by the crusaders, and fire and slaughter sped throughout the land. Peace was not made until 1229, when heresy was extinguished by the killing of nearly all the heretics, and the power of the feudal lords in that region was ended by annexation to the dominions of the crown of France.

It was in connection with these events that the famous Inquisition had its rise, the institution being started by Innocent III and St. Dominic, for the seeking out of adherents of false doctrines. The Dominican and Franciscan monks were the first instruments employed for this purpose. The power of the Papacy reached its height during the two generations which followed the Albigensian crusade.

THE CRUSADES

During two hundred years—including the whole of the Twelfth and the Thirteenth centuries—European history is greatly concerned with the series of expeditions known as the Crusades. The word crusade means "war of the cross," from the French croisade (Provençal crozada, from croz, Latin crux, a cross). The main object of the enterprise thus undertaken by the western nations of Europe was to recover the Holy Land—Palestine—from the Saracens and Turks. A craving seems to have arisen in Christendom at the end of the Eleventh Century, for the possession of those sacred places in Palestine where Christ, whose vicar on earth the Pope claimed and was held to be, might be regarded as more especially present to believers. Pilgrims in crowds had resorted to those holy places, but the hallowed spots themselves were in the hands of infidels, and it was felt as a reproach to Christendom that the sepulcher of Christ, in particular, was not in possession of the church. We must, as a preliminary to some account of the Crusades, glance at the position of the Eastern Empire and of the Mohammedans in the East at this time.

Toward the end of the Ninth Century much of its former power was recovered by the Eastern Empire under Emperors of the Macedonian or Basilian dynasty, founded in 867 by Basilius, a Macedonian of low birth and great ability, who had worked his way to the throne by a series of crimes. The city of Antioch and other important places were recovered from the now divided Saracens, and a large part of the west of Asia was again under the control of the Emperors at Constantinople.

A change came in the middle of the Eleventh Century, when the Turks, under the rule of the house of Seljuk, began to be formidable. A conqueror named Alp Arslan, leader of the Seljukian Turks, defeated the Byzantine forces in 1071 at the battle of Manzikert so decisively, as to become master of most of Asia Minor. Here, in 1092, was established the Sultanate of Roum (Rome), with its capital first at Nicæa in Bithynia, and then at Iconium. The seat of the Seljukian dynasty of Roum was thus planted only 100 miles from Constantinople, and the divinity of Christ was denied and derided in the same temple in which it had been solemnly declared by the First General Council (of Nice, whence our Nicene creed) of the Catholic Church. The Christian city of Antioch was soon afterward betrayed to the Mohammedans, and a still more important acquisition of the Seljukian Turks was to follow. This was the conquest of Syria and Palestine from the Caliph who had ruled there with mildness and tolerance, and the holy city of Jerusalem now fell into the hands of those who insulted the resident Christian clergy and the faith of the Western world. At this, as Gibbon says (now that "a new spirit had arisen of religious chivalry and papal dominion"), " a nerve was touched of exquisite feeling, and the sensation vibrated to the heart of Europe."

A French monk of Amiens, famous forevermore as "Peter the Hermit," kindled the scattered sparks of religious and chivalric enthusiasm into a wide-spread raging flame. This man, like St. Paul, was of small stature and contemptible presence, but he had a fiery eye and vehement speech, well fitted to rouse mankind to action. He went to Jerusalem a pilgrim; he saw the state of the Holy City; he felt the cruel treatment of the Turks; he returned to Europe a complete and irrepressible fanatic.

Pope Urban the Second encouraged Peter in his project of delivering the Holy Land, and the hermit sped through Italy and France, everywhere preaching a crusade for the rescue of the sepulchre of Christ from the hands of the infidels. With head bare, feet naked, and lean body clad in coarsest robe, riding an ass, and bearing a massive crucifix, he preached to crowds in streets and highways, calling all to repentance and to arms. He was welcome alike to castle and to cottage; his picture of the pilgrims' woes melted all souls to pity and filled all eyes with tears or hearts with wrath. The ready fuel of religious zeal was soon everywhere kindled—the time of the Crusades, in a word, had fully come. The feudal warriors of the age were eager to draw the sword for the defense of their brethren in Palestine and the rescue of their Savior's tomb from desecration; and all that was now needed was to organize and direct the mighty force which had been called forth to battle with the infidels in the distant East.

At the end of the year 1095 the Pope (Urban II) summoned a great council at Clermont, in the south of France. This was attended by the Cardinals, hundreds of Prelates, and a great train of lords and knights, whom the Pope addressed in a stirring speech, which found an instant response. When from the thousands of hearers the cry arose "God wills it," uttered in the corrupted Latin (Dieux el volt and Deus lo volt) of Northern and Provençal France, the orator cried out, "It is indeed the will of God, and let this memorable word be forever adopted as your cry of battle to animate the devotion and courage of the champions of Christ. His cross is the symbol of your salvation; wear it, a red, a bloody cross, as an external mark on your breasts or shoulders, as a pledge of your sacred and irrevocable engagement." The suggestion was adopted, and the red cross of the Crusaders was soon everywhere seen. The time for the starting of the great expedition to the East was fixed for the festival of the Assumption—August 15th in the following year, A. D. 1096.

At the Council of Clermont, Pope Urban II had proclaimed for those who should enlist under the banner of the Cross forgiveness of all sins, and a full freedom from all penances due to the church. War and enterprise being the prevailing passions of the age, the people were now enjoined, as a penance, to gratify those passions, to visit distant lands, and to draw their swords against the nations of the East.

The impatience of the ruder classes anticipated the appointed time, and in the early spring of A. D. 1096, nearly 250,000 pilgrims, including men, women and children, gathered round Peter the Hermit in the east of France, and called upon him to take the command. Before sweeping through Germany along the banks of the Rhine and Danube, this horde of fanatics and ruffians attacked the colonies of wealthy Jews in the trading towns on the Moselle and the Rhine. This roused against them the native ferocity of the Hungarians and Bulgarians, and only a remnant of the whole body crossed the Bosphorus at Constantinople, and that to be destroyed by the Turks of Asia Minor. Hundreds of thousands of persons had thus perished without the slightest result as to the real object of the Crusade.

The practical Crusaders were of a very different class, and went to work after due and careful preparations. None of the great sovereigns of Europe took part in this First Crusade. The leaders were the feudal princes of the second order. The first rank both in war and council is to be given to the famous hero Godfrey of Bouillon. This brave and accomplished soldier was a descendant of Charles the Great in the female line, and was a worthy representative of such an ancestor. His valor was tempered by prudence. His piety was sincere; his life virtuous; his aim, in joining the expedition, single and disinterested. His character and fame brought under his banners, from France, Lorraine, and Germany, an army of 80,000 foot and 10,000 horse.

Among the other chiefs were Robert, Duke of Normandy, Count Hugh of Vermandois (in French Flanders), Count Robert of Flanders, and Stephen, Count of Chartres. These were the leaders of the French, the Normans, and some Crusaders from the British Isles. Count Raymond of Toulouse headed an army of 100,000 horse and foot from Languedoc, Provence, Burgundy, and Lombardy. From Southern Italy Bohemond, son of the famous Norman chief Robert Guiscard, Duke of Apulia, ed 10,000 horse and 20,000 foot, and that model of Christian knighthood, the great Tancred, the hero of Tasso's poem Gerusalemme Liberata (" Jerusalem Delivered "), accompanied his cousin Bohemond. In all, six armies, numbering 600,000 men, started by different routes for Constantinople.

After various obstacles, and losses by land and sea, and difficulties with the Greek Emperor Alexius Comnenus, who feared for himself as to the possible doings of the Western Princes, a great host of Crusaders arrived in Asia Minor in the spring of 1097. The main strength of the army consisted in the mail-clad horsemen, said to have numbered 100,000—the flower of European chivalry, knights, esquires, and men-at-arms, protected by helmet and shield, and chain and scale-armor, and armed with lance, sword, battle-axe, and heavy mace or club. The footmen consisted chiefly of archers, provided with the long bow and the cross-bow. The body of cavalry, on which the Crusaders relied to overcome the Turks, was of the most formidable force and the most splendid appearance. The horses were of a large and heavy breed, and when the rider, fixing his long lance in the rest, spurred his steed onward at full pace, the light Eastern horse could not stand against the weight of such a charge. The followers of each feudal chieftain were distinguished by his banner, his armorial coat, and his special war-cry, and the armor of the leaders was bright with gold, gems, and color.

The first work of the Crusaders was to attack the Turkish capital, Nice, or Nicæa (Nikaia), in the northwest of Asia Minor. The Turkish Sultan, Soliman, kept watch from the hills with a large force of cavalry, while the Crusaders for seven weeks (May and June, 1097) assailed the town with the old Roman engines and methods—the battering-ram and mine, movable tower, catapult, balista, and sling—with the more modern inventions of artificial fire and the cross-bow. The famous Greek fire was a composition invented by a Greek in the Seventh Century A. D. It was used, wrapped in flax, attached to arrows and javelins, to fire buildings, and was very difficult to extinguish. When Nice was fully invested by the Crusaders, the city surrendered to the Greek Emperor, Alexius, who treated the infidels with a generosity displeasing to the fanatical Crusaders.

When the invading army began its march southeastward through Asia Minor, on its way to the Syrian frontier, Soliman called round him all his allies, and attacked the Crusaders with an immense force of his light cavalry, armed with the javelin, the crooked sabre, and the long Tartar bow. The battle of Dorylæum, in Phrygia, fought in July, 1097, ended at last, after a great effort of valor on both sides, in the complete defeat of the infidels. The weight of the Crusaders' horses and equipments was more than a match for Asiatic quickness and skill, and the re-

ENTRY OF GODFREY OF BOUILLON INTO JERUSALEM
Painting by Karl von Piloty

sults of the victory were the taking of Soliman's camp with a great booty, and his abandonment of the Kingdom of Roum, leaving the way open into Syria.

Retreating before the advancing columns of Crusaders, Soliman laid all the country waste, so that the invaders, as they passed through Phrygia, Pisidia, and Pamphylia, suffered fearfully from hunger, thirst, and toil. They thus lost thousands of the men as well as a large part of the horses which bore the mail-clad warriors, forced now to stagger onward on unwonted weary feet.

The Crusaders at last arrived (October, 1097) before the city of Antioch, the great and populous capital of Syria, defended by the river Orontes, by marshes, hilly ground, and a solid stately wall. For seven months the place was beleaguered in vain by the crusading host, destitute alike of the implements and of the skill for besieging (which at Nicæa had been supplied by the Greek Emperor's assistance), and the losses of the army by desertion, famine, and fatigue were very serious. Their cavalry had almost disappeared from loss of horses, and little progress had been made in the enterprise, when Bohemond the Norman managed to effect an entrance by surprise, assisted by treachery within the walls. Antioch was taken thus one dark and stormy night in June, 1098.

The captors of Antioch were then besieged in turn by a great host of infidels dispatched to aid the cause of Islam by a Persian Sultan. Famine within the walls was rife, for the Crusaders, in spite of their religious aims, had lived for months outside the walls in luxury and waste and riot, expiated now by pestilence and hunger. Despair at last gave strength to starved and sickly men, and superstition lent her aid in the opportune discovery, within the walls of Antioch, of the famous Holy Lance, a spear-head stated to be that which pierced the side of Christ. With this sacred relic in their midst, and headed by the truly noble Godfrey of Bouillon, the chivalrous Tancred, and the brave and able, if ambitious, Bohemond, the Crusaders made a sortie, and by determined fighting drove the besiegers from the ground, and cleared the way for a march upon the holy city.

The hundreds of thousands of invading Christians who had been present at the siege of Nicæa were now, in July, 1098, reduced to a few hundreds of cavalry, and about 20,000 foot. This was the work of war, disease, and famine; this the result of desertion, and of the detachment of large forces from the main army by the action of self-interested leaders. Of these one, named Baldwin, had gone eastward to found at Edessa, in Mesopotamia, a Christian Kingdom which lasted until 1151. Bohemond the Norman stayed behind as possessor and Prince of Antioch; Count Raymond of Toulouse had gone off on a foray into the interior of Syria. It was not until May, 1099, that the scanty force just named, with a crowd of camp followers and pilgrims, started from Antioch for the object of the whole expedition—the goal to win which such enormous efforts had been spent—the holy city.

The path of the Crusaders lay along the shore of Syria, between Mount Lebanon and the sea, on which they were attended by the coasting traders from Genoa and Pisa. Through Sidon, Tyre, Acre, and Cæsarea, they passed amidst the relics of old Phœnician glory, and then turned inland for Jerusalem, by Lydda, Emmaus, and other scenes of sacred history and legend. Early in June, 1099, they came in sight of what so many had desired and striven to behold, but so few were left to gaze on with delighted eyes. In full view of the sacred site (then covered, after a period of desolation, by the buildings erected since the great rebellion against Hadrian in A. D. 131) of that Jerusalem of old, where things so wondrous and so awful had been done in sight of earth and heaven, the enthusiasm of the foot-sore soldiers of the cross burst out in cries and even tears of joy, from men prostrated to their knees in worship and thanksgiving.

The holy city was at this time in possession, not of the Turks, but of the Saracens of Egypt, whose Caliph had conquered Palestine three years before. With a powerful garrison the Caliph's Governor was ready for a stout defense. The Crusaders attacked the northern and western sides of the city, Godfrey of Bouillon's standard floating from the lower slope of Calvary. After the repulse of a rash assault, some suffering from thirst, and a siege of forty days in all, the moving tower of Godfrey was successfully used against the walls. "The archers in the turret cleared the rampart of the foe, the drawbridge was let down, and on a Friday afternoon at three o'clock, Godfrey of Bouillon stood victorious on the walls," and the Crusaders then stormed the place on every side. Thus was Jerusalem recaptured by the Christians 463 years after its seizure by the Mohammedans under the Arabian Caliph Omar in 636. This great result was due, along with the valor of the gallant Godfrey, to the energy of Tancred in providing wood for the tower, the skill and industry of the Genoese engineers who built it, and the ferocious courage of the enthusiastic Crusaders. In a three days' massacre, during which 70,000 Moslems perished, and the Jews of the place were burnt alive in their synagogues, the victors showed their zeal for their religion, and then did homage to the God of Christians at the Holy Sepulchre.

The city thus recovered for Christianity was made, together with territory to the north and south thereof, into the Christian Kingdom of Jerusalem. The chiefs of the Crusaders elected Godfrey of Bouillon as the first sovereign of the new dominion, but he declined the title and insignia of royalty, and styled himself simply, "Defender and Baron of the Holy Sepulchre." This worthiest of all Crusaders lived for less than a year, beloved and honored in his office. In August, 1099, Godfrey utterly defeated the Sultan of Egypt at the battle of Ascalon, and thus established firmly the newly-founded kingdom, which continued for nearly a century.

Other Latin principalities in the East existed at Antioch and at Edessa, and between the new kingdom and Antioch arose the County of Tripoli. The laws and language, the manners and titles, of the French Nation and the Latin Church, were introduced, and a military force was maintained as a defense, constantly needed, against the surrounding swarms of Saracens and Turks.

In connection with the new Kingdom of Jerusalem, and as its chief defenders, now arose the great orders of religious knights, as the Knights Hospitallers, or Knights of St. John of Jerusalem, and the Knights Templars. These orders had their origin in the peculiar chivalric spirit diffused through Europe as the result of the Crusade. According to the view of Hegel, the German philosopher, "The ferocity and savage valor of the barbarian, pacified already by civilization and social life, was now elevated by religion and kindled to a noble enthusiasm through contact with the boundless magnanimity of Oriental prowess. These orders of knighthood were founded on a basis similar to that of the monastic fraternities. They had the same vow of renunciation of the world. At the same time they undertook the defense of the pilgrims to the Holy Land as they passed through Europe. The first duty was the display of knightly bravery, afterward they were pledged to sustain and to care for the poor and the sick. Their members sacrificed themselves with reckless bravery for a common interest, and formed a network of fraternal coalition all over Europe."

An immediate result of the First Crusade was a great extension of the territory belonging to the Eastern Empire. The victory of Dorylæum gave back to the Comnenian dynasty of Constantinople (reigned 1057 to 1204) all the west, and a strip in the northwest, of Asia Minor, and a considerable district in the southeast, and forced the Sultan of Roum to have his capital at Iconium, in the south of the peninsula, instead of at Nicæa (now belonging to the Greek Emperor), where he had been a constant threat to Constantinople. The First Crusade, beyond doubt, prevented the fall of the declining Empire of the East, and gave it a new lease of life.

For about half a century the Christian dominion in the East maintained itself against the attacks of the surrounding Mohammedans. Then a time of danger came, when strong help from Europe was needed, and the Second Crusade took place. The Christian principality of Edessa, in Mesopotamia, was seized by the Turks in 1145, and the Christians were put to death. This roused much feeling in Europe, and the Second Crusade was organized by Conrad III, Emperor of Germany, and Louis VII of France, the chief sovereigns of the time. The Preacher of this Crusade (as Peter the Hermit had been of the First Crusade) was one of the greatest ecclesiastics of the Middle Ages, the holy and earnest St. Bernard, Abbot of Clairvaux, near Langres, in the east of France.

A force of over 300,000 men, horse and foot, took the same route to Constantinople (in 1147) as the earlier Crusaders. Conrad was first in the field, accompanied by the Kings of Poland and Bohemia and many feudal lords, with a cloud of light-armed troops, women and children, priests and monks. The Greek Emperor,

Manuel Comnenus, behaved with gross treachery to the forces of Conrad, hampering their movements, supplying bad food in exchange for good money, giving intelligence of their coming to the Turks, and furnishing guides who misled their march.   The army of Conrad, when he arrived in Asia Minor, was almost destroyed by fighting in the interior of the country, and by the hardships undergone, and a small remnant only returned to Nicæa.   There the French advancing army, under Louis VII, met them, and the march through Asia Minor began.   The result was a total failure.   The Turks, in overwhelming numbers, crushed the Christian columns in detail, only a handful of the great host at last reached Jerusalem, and there was nothing to be done except to return ingloriously to Europe.

Forty years passed between the Second and Third Crusades.   During this time the power of the Mohammedans in the East had been growing under Nureddin, whose Empire at last extended from the Tigris to the Nile.   A new power had also arisen in Egypt.   A Kurdish chieftain named Saladin, sprung from the hardy, strong savage, plundering, and independent tribes in the hilly country of Kurdistan, beyond the Tigris, had made himself master of Egypt by sheer force of genius and character in 1171, and on the death of Nureddin in 1174, Saladin began to acquire his dominions.   The invasion of Palestine in 1187 was soon followed by the capture of Jerusalem, and the work accomplished by the First Crusade—the Christian possession of the Holy City—was thus completely undone.

Saladin was the greatest Mohammedan ruler of his time, and one of the greatest and noblest characters in the whole history of Islam.   Master of Egypt, Syria, and Arabia, he ruled at last, in power and wisdom, an

Empire extending from the African Tripoli to the Tigris, and from the mountains of Armenia to the Indian Ocean. Pure in life, rigid in the Mohammedan faith and practice, just in judgment, courteous in demeanor, boundless in liberality, brave as a lion in the field, Saladin shines forth as the brightest example of Oriental knighthood.

This Third Crusade belongs to English history, from the distinguished part played in the expedition by Richard I, the chivalrous foe and admirer (one might almost say—the friend) of the great Saladin, who was well worthy of the steel of the foremost knight of Christendom. The news of the fall of Jerusalem aroused the fanaticism of Europe, and three monarchs prepared to take the field in A. D. 1189. These were the Emperor of Germany, Frederick Barbarossa; Philip Augustus of France, and Richard Cœur de Lion of England.

Frederick I of Germany was a veteran soldier, and marched overland for the East with a great army of horse and foot, reaching Asia Minor early in 1190. His army was then attacked by immense bodies of Turks, who made the Crusaders fight all the way during a march of twenty days, when they reached and stormed the capital, Iconium. The way to Jerusalem was open, but great losses had been incurred, and the German expedition was virtually brought to an end by the accidental drowning of the Emperor in a mountain stream of Cilicia.

The French and English Crusaders went by sea, and their doings are familiar to the English-speaking race through the career of Richard Cœur de Lion. This brilliant but fruitless crusade is described in the article on its hero in the volume, "World's Famous Warriors."

It ended in a three years' truce (concluded in 1192)

by which the honor of the English King was saved by stipulation that Acre, Jaffa, and other seaports should remain in Christian hands and pilgrims should be unmolested in their visits to Jerusalem.

The Fourth Crusade has an importance of its own, not for what it effected against the Mohammedans (for the expedition never went to Palestine at all), but for what occurred at Constantinople. The Greek and the Latin churches had been long at issue on theological points, and the enmity of the Christians in the East and the West of Europe had been increased during the first three Crusades, though one result of the fighting of the Western warriors had been the partial restoration of the Greek dominion in Asia Minor. The existing hostility came to a head in 1203, when the Crusaders of the fourth expedition, headed by Baldwin, Count of Flanders, and the Marquis of Montferrat (in Italy) interfered in the dynastic arrangements of the Greek Empire. This was resented by the Greeks, who deposed and killed the rulers set over them by the Crusaders, and the end of it all was the storming of Constantinople in 1204 by a combined force of French and Venetians.

The Eastern Empire was now broken up for a time. The Venetians got Crete and the islands in the south of the Ægean Sea (the Archipelago). There was a Greek Empire still round Nicæa or Nice in the northwest of Asia Minor, and another, called the Empire of Trebizond, along the southern shore of the Black Sea. The Greek dominion also included Greece and Epirus. The Latin Kingdom at Constantinople lasted till 1261, when Constantinople was won back by the Nicæan Emperor, and the Eastern Empire continued till its final overthrow by the Ottoman Turks at the end of this period of history.

There were other crusades of less importance. In 1218 a large force from western Europe went to Egypt, and captured Damietta after a long siege, but the enterprise ended in total failure. In 1228 Frederick II, Emperor of Germany, assumed the cross (as the phrase was), and started for Palestine with a powerful armament from the harbors of Sicily and Apulia. On his arrival in the Holy Land Frederick entered Jerusalem, and the Mohammedan ruler surrendered that and some other cities to the Christians; this state of things lasted only till 1243, when Palestine was overwhelmed by an invasion of fresh hordes of Turks from the Caspian; Jerusalem has never since been a Christian possession. The Seventh and Eighth Crusades were undertaken by Louis IX of France. In A. D. 1249 this virtuous and fanatical sovereign went with a great force against Egypt, hoping to win his way thence up to Jerusalem. Damietta was at once captured, but sickness, famine, and the Mohammedan foe proved too strong at last, and Louis was taken prisoner and obliged to pay ransom. In 1270 St. Louis undertook the last of the Crusades, one in which English warriors joined. On the way to Palestine the French King turned aside to attack the Mohammedans of Tunis, and died before the walls, of disease. Prince Edward (Edward I) of England made his way to Palestine, and returned after some slight successes. In 1268 Antioch was finally taken by the Sultan of Egypt and Syria; this loss was followed by the capture of many other towns, and the Christian hold on Palestine was reduced to the possession of Acre, then a strong fortress and a place of great trade. A quarrel with the Sultan of Syria led to the capture of Acre in May, 1291, by a great force of Moslems; the remnant of the Knights Templars went to Cyprus, and all dominion of Christians in Palestine came to an end.

The religious enthusiasm aroused by these Wars of the Cross increased, both directly and indirectly, the authority of the Popes and of the Western (Latin) Church throughout Europe. It was by Papal exhortation or command that the European sovereigns, in many instances, undertook the expeditions to the East; with the papal blessing the warriors started on the long and dangerous enterprise; to support the expenses of these wars, the Popes assumed the right of taxation to some extent, and so acquired authority and further recognition as to secular affairs in the European States. The church was enriched by succeeding to lands bequeathed to her by Crusaders who might die, and often did die, without heirs, and by endowments made by such as shirked the duty of personal service in the cause of the Cross.

There is no stronger bond of communion than that which unites those who have fought and bled on the same battle-fields, shared the same adventures, and encountered the same dangers, trials, and misfortunes. The journeying to and from the Holy Land, and the deeds done there against the infidels, were the common simultaneous work of various Western nations, who thereby came to know each other better, to have a fellow-feeling and a mutual respect, and to cast away the prejudices born of ignorance and isolation. Enlightenment in this way came to Europe, in no small degree, from the Crusades.

The power of the feudal aristocracy was lessened in many quarters through the encumbering of estates with debt in meeting the heavy expenses of an expedition to the East. One consequence of this was that land was acquired by members of the rich trading class that had begun to arise, and so a new aristocracy of wealth gained by enterprise and skill, instead of by rapine and extortion, was by slow degrees created. The edifice of feudalism was undermined in the alienation of the estates of proud, martial, and oppressive barons, and in the frequent extinction even of their race by death in war. As Gibbon says: "Their poverty extorted from their pride those charters of freedom which unlocked the fetters of the slave, secured the farm of the peasant and the shop of the artificer, and gradually restored a substance and a soul to the most numerous and useful part of the community. The conflagration which destroyed the tall and barren trees of the forest gave air and scope to the vegetation of the smaller and nutritive plants of the soil." In other words, modern society is indebted to the Crusades for the beginnings of its best constituent, the great middle class.

The commercial republics of Italy received much benefit from the Crusades. The large number of troops that went to Palestine wholly or partially by sea were borne in transport vessels supplied by these maritime States, which also did a great trade in provisions and supplies for warlike purposes. The ships returned on the homeward voyage filled up with products of the East before unknown or little used in Europe, and new markets for commerce became established at many points upon the eastern coasts of the great inland sea. New arts and processes in manufactures were also introduced to Europe.

The mental stir aroused by the experience of an adventurous change of scene could not but have the happiest effect upon the stagnation and stolidity engendered among those who never move from home. The men of Western Europe went forth into the East, and found there, in the foes whom they encountered on the field of battle, not only warriors as gallant as themselves, but their superiors in knowledge, industry, and art. The nations of the west of Europe had abundant energy of character, and an active, imitative spirit, and thus derived essential good from intercourse with the Arabians and Greeks, who then possessed the highest culture of the world. It was at a later period, indeed, that learning thoroughly revived, and the Latin conquerors of Constantinople, early in the Thirteenth Century, were still too rude to understand and master the treasures of literature existing in her libraries and schools. But rudiments of learning, in mathematical and medical science especially, were at any rate acquired in the East, and the way for better things was smoothed. A revival of thought, a growth of liberal ideas, arose out of the expeditions which were due, in the beginning, to a spirit of fanatical enthusiasm, but in the end did much to lessen religious bigotry and prejudice concerning those whom Christian knights found to be as brave, as generous, as truly chivalrous as themselves. Among the minor benefits conferred by the East upon the West during the times of the crusades may be recounted windmills, invented first in Asia Minor, and introduced to Normandy in 1105, and such luxuries as silk and sugar, brought from Greece and Egypt into Italy by the traders of the great commercial states.

ENGLAND'S RISE AS A NATION

After the death of Hardicanute (1042) the English people had been under foreign domination for a quarter of a century. The glories of the ancient race had vanished among intestine conflicts, exhausting war, payment of tributes to rapacious foes and subjection to Danish rulers. The memories of Alfred and Athelstan were preserved in their race, traditions, and songs and so the general voice of the people was for the elevation to the throne of Edward, son of Ethelred, and his second wife, the Norman Princess Emma. His mild religious character, for he was more fitted to be a monk than a monarch, led to his being called the Confessor. Educated in Normandy, he surrounded himself with foreign friends and filled the high places of the Kingdom with Normans. The Saxons were jealous and their leader, the powerful Earl Godwin, succeeded in expelling the Frenchmen. Harold, son of the Earl, was elected successor to Edward by the Witenagemot, which thus for the first time violated the well-established custom of not going outside of the royal family for a monarch. William, Duke of Normandy, demanded the throne as next of kin. When the news of Harold's accession reached William at Rouen he was moved to the deepest wrath. None dared speak to him as he clenched his teeth, strode up and down the palace hall with unequal and hurried steps and half-drew his sword from his sheath. William had good reason for anger, as while on a visit to Normandy he had made Harold prisoner and wrung from him an oath that he would aid the Norman to secure the throne after Edward's death. Accusing Harold of perjury, William undertook the conquest of England with the approval of the Pope, who was angered because Peter's pence had not been paid. Harold was opposed by some of his countrymen and mustered only a meager force to meet William at the battle of Hastings, which resulted in the Saxon's death. William had little difficulty in securing his election by the Witanagemot. Yet many of the Saxons continued for years to resist the conqueror and lived like outlaws in the woods.

The Northmen or Normans were the very pick and flower of the Scandinavian peoples. What the Aryans were to the primitive races of mankind on the plateau of Central Asia, what the Hellenes were to the Pelasgic tribes in olden Greece, were the Normans to their brethren on the coast of the Northern Sea. They had in their best form all the qualities inherent in their race. They were foremost in courage, military discipline, and skill and in the power of embracing and improving on the culture with which their conquests made them familiar. They were the descendants of the men who, under Rollo, had threatened Paris and won French territory. The hardy Northmen, established in a fertile region, under a warmer sky than that of their former home, adopted at last the speech, usages, and faith of those whom they had subdued. They gained and absorbed all the knowledge which they found existing in their new home. They were safe by their courage and arms from all foreign assailants, and so a tribe of pirates became a Nation of civilized people, devoted to tillage, handicrafts, trade, letters, and the arts, but skilled also and courageous in war and full of the chivalrous spirit which has worked with such power and effect on the morals and manners and politics of Europe. The pride and magnificence of life in this formidable Nation were shown by their nobles in large, strong and stately castles, fiery steeds, choice falcons and hawks for the chase, and in the mimic contests of armored knights, where warriors and courtiers strove in tourney for the smiles of graceful dames. Though chiefly renowned for their military exploits, the Normans were famed for their polished manners, winning demeanor, and diplomatic skill.

These traits were found in William, who was one of the most polished knights and skillful warriors of his day. He began by treating the Saxon nobles with kindness. Peace and order were restored, trade resumed its activity and no change in the laws and customs of the realm was made. But William had no idea of assuming the position of a chief among equals which was the feudalistic idea of a King. Nor would he subordinate his power to that of the Church. He found in the organization of the conquered Kingdom principles which enabled him, while using feudal language, to be in fact an absolute King and to set such limits to the power of Rome as to keep the Church virtually in subordination. An administrative system centered in the crown and working chiefly through the exchequer, went far to centralize the Government. Triumphant suppression of insurrection enabled them to get rid of the baronage of the conquest. Gradually a new nobility of administrative origin took the place of the Saxon Earls, England being divided by William among his comrades. The secular and ecclesiastical lands of the Saxons were occupied by the conquerors and those who had been cowherds and weavers or simple priests on the Continent, became lords and bishops in England. Between 1080 and 1086, a register of all the properties occupied was drawn up. This was known as the Doomsday book in England. Thus was established the most thorough feudal system in Europe. There were 600 barons and under them 60,000 knights, while over them all was the King, who took for his own use 1,462 manors and the principal cities, and by requiring direct oath from the chevaliers, bound every vassal personally to himself. The whole history of England depends upon this partition, for when the royalty became oppressive the barons, in self-defense, were able to unite with burgesses, and the nobles saved their rights only by securing those of their humble allies. English public liberty thus came about by agreement between the burgher middle class and the nobles. Another cause was that chivalry was never really dominant in England. For the man unassisted by birth to rise was harder in some ages than others, but there has been no age in England where it was wholly impossible.

The fusion of the two races was so speedy that a writer a little more than a hundred years after the conquest (the author of the famous Dialogues de Scaccario) could say that among the free population it was impossible to tell who was of Norman and who of English birth. That is to say, the great nobles must have been all but purely Normans; the lowest classes must have been all but purely English; in the intermediate classes, among the townsmen and the smaller landowners, the two races were so intermixed and they had so modified one another that the distinction between them had been forgotten.

The greatest of the outward changes which were caused by the Norman conquest was its effect on the language and literature of England. In the matter of language, as in other matters, the conquest itself wrought no formal change; whatever change happened was the gradual result of the state of things which the conquest brought about. The French language was never substituted for English by any formal act. Documents were written in English long after the conquest. As it was with institutions, so it was with language. The old language was neither proscribed nor forgotten, but a new language came in by the side of it. At first there were two languages spoken, the Norman being the fashionable tongue and the Saxon the common speech; but all the nobles, even William himself, learned Saxon. Slowly as the two peoples combined, the two languages coalesced, forming, with the evolution of subsequent centuries, the English language as we know it to-day.

William the Conqueror died in 1087, while on an expedition against the King of France, Philip I. William II Rufus, his second son, succeeded him in England, and Robert, the elder son, in Normandy. Robert tried to take England away from his younger brother, but failing in the attempt went on a crusade. He was still absent when William Rufus died on a hunting excursion. Their younger brother, Henry I, surnamed Beauclerc, seized the crown, and when Robert wished to claim his rights, defeated him at Tenchebray (1106), reunited Normandy to England, and conquered Louis the Fat, who had attempted to secure at least the succession of the duchy for William Cliton, Robert's son (1119). When Henry I died he left his throne by will to Matilda, his daughter, widow of the Emperor Henry V, and wife of Geoffrey, Count of Anjou. Henry charged his nephew, Stephen of Blois, to protect the Empress. Stephen seized the crown and defeated this plot, and vanquished the Scotch, Matilda's allies, at the battle of the Standard. Less successful against her, he

was taken prisoner.   A compromise was made by which
he remained King during his life and was succeeded by
Henry of Anjou, son of the Empress.

Normandy and Maine were acquired by Henry II
through the renunciation of his mother, Matilda, and
from his father he inherited Anjou and Touraine.
Marrying Eleanor, the divorced wife of Louis the
Young, she brought him as dowry Poitiers, Bordeaux,
Agin, and Limoges, together with sovereignty of Au-
vergne, Saintonge, Angoumois, La Marche, and Peri-
gord. Finally, in 1154, at the age of twenty-one,
he ascended the throne of England and afterward
married one of his sons to the heiress of Brittany.
His power was formidable, but Henry used it only
to fight against his clergy and his sons.   The clergy,
from the time of the Roman Empire, had the
privilege of self-judging.   In a case against a clergyman lay tribunals were incompetent and only ecclesiastical jurisdiction could decide.   In England, William the Conqueror had given this privilege, called
"Benefit of Clergy," a wide scope, resulting in numerous abuses and scandalous impunities.   Henry II
wished to put an end to it, and in order to rule the clergy
named as Archbishop of Canterbury his chaplain,
Thomas à Becket, a Saxon, and until then the most brilliant and docile of courtiers.   Becket at once became
another man—austere and inflexible.   In a great assemblage of bishops, abbots, and barons, held at Clarendon (1164), the King passed the constitutions of
Clarendon, which obliged every clergyman accused of a
crime to appear before the ordinary courts of justice,
forbade any ecclesiastic to leave the Kingdom without
royal permit, and intrusted to the King the guardianship
and revenue of every bishopric and benefice vacant.

Thomas à Becket opposed these statutes, and to avoid the anger of his master, fled to France.   Louis VII, having brought about a reconciliation between Henry and Becket, the latter returned to Canterbury, but conceded nothing in ecclesiastical privileges.   So the King let fall words which four knights interpreted as a sentence of death, and slew the archbishop at the foot of the altar (1170).   This crime aroused so great indignation against Henry II that he was obliged to annul the Constitutions of Clarendon and do penance on the tomb of the martyr.   He would not have submitted to this humiliation had he not feared a popular rising and excommunication at the time when he was at war with his three eldest sons, Henry Short-Coat, Duke of Maine and Anjou; Richard Cœur de Lion, Duke of Aquitaine; and Geoffrey, Duke of Brittany.   Even the fourth son, John Lackland, at last joined the others.   Henry II passed his last days in fighting his sons and the King of France, who helped the rebels.   In 1171 he had conquered the east and the south of Ireland.

Henry handed to his son a powerful and well-organized monarchy, in which the feeling of national unity had made great advances.   His system proved strong enough to support the continued absence of Richard in the crusades and in his French dominions; national life even acquired increased strength by the self-government which was thus forced on the administration.   The brave and chivalrous Cœur de Lion* was followed by his brother, John Lackland, a man who seems to have been without a redeeming trait.   Boastful but cowardly, tyrannical but weak, he excited the anger of all classes. He imposed taxes at pleasure, wronged the poor and plundered the rich.   At one time it is said he threw into

*See volume "World's Famous Warriors."

prison a wealthy Jew who refused to give him an enormous sum of money, and pulled out a tooth every day until he paid the required amount. His crime in murdering his brother's son cost him Touraine, Anjou, Maine, Normandy, and Poitou, and he was stripped of all his French possessions, a magnificent territory, greater than that ruled by the King of France himself. He foolishly renewed his father's quarrel with the Papal See, was excommunicated and deposed, whereupon he formally surrendered his crown to the Pope, to whom he acknowledged himself as a vassal. Then he tried to take revenge for his humiliations by forming against France the coalition which was overthrown at the battle of Bouvines. While his allies were defeated in the North John himself was vanquished in Poitou.

When John returned to England he found that the barons, freed from connection with the Continent, and supported by all parties smarting from misgovernment and the shame of disaster, were in revolt. They appeared as the real Government of England, and wrung from the humbled King at Runnymede the Magna Charta (1215), that great charter which secured in the form of a solemn treaty, the foundations of the future liberties of England. This great statute was confirmed no less than thirty-two times, for whenever money was required by the King its renewal was demanded. It now stands on the English statute book as 25 Edward I (1297). Section 29 of this act is the keystone of English history: "No freeman shall be taken or imprisoned, or be disseized of his freeholds, or liberties or free customs, or be outlawed or exiled, or any otherwise be destroyed; nor will we pass upon him nor condemn him, but by lawful judgment of his peers or by the law of the land. We will sell to no man, we will not deny or defer to any man, either justice or right." No class was neglected, but each obtained some cherished right. Personal freedom, security of property, and liberty of movement thus became the essential rights of every Englishman. These rights were not indeed immediately conceded; John himself attempted to tear up the charter and obtained the Pope's sanction to do so. The charter was made a reality, and the orderly development of rights secured under Edward I.

With John and the reign of his son began one of the most important periods in English history. It was the time when the Nation, laws, and languages finally assimilated whatever was to be assimilated of the foreign elements brought in by William the Conqueror, and finally threw off whatever was to be thrown off. During this time most of the things which go to make up the national life of England begin to assume the general outline which has continued with details down to the present time. It was now that the principle of limiting the power of the King began to assert itself. Reverence for the monarch had been destroyed by the acts of the vicious and cowardly John. Henry III (1216-1272) was not such a monarch as to strengthen the respect for kingly power. His reign was a long minority, and in it there was constant weakness, perjury, and acts of violence, and everything which should teach the Nation the necessity of restraining by institutions the royal will that was so little sure of itself. Abroad Henry was defeated by Louis IX (St. Louis) at Taillebourg and Saintes. At home the discontent of the people increased because of repeated violations of the Magna Charta and the favor shown to the relatives of Queen Eleanor of Provence, who caused all the offices to be given to them, and also because of a real invasion of Italian clergy sent by the Pope and who seized the beneficies.

The finances fell into utter decay. At length a demand for money to support, in the interest of Rome, the claim of the King's son to the throne of Sicily brought matters to a crisis, and on June 11, 1258, at the great National Council of Oxford, the first Assembly, to which the name of Parliament was officially given, was held. The barons forced the King to entrust the reforms to twenty-four of themselves, of whom only twelve were appointed by him. These twenty-four delegates published the statutes or provisions of Oxford. The King confirmed the Magna Charta. The twenty-four were to name each year the Lord High Chancellor, the Lord High Treasurer, the Judges, and other public officers, Governors of the castles, etc. It was made a capital crime to oppose their decisions; and ordered that Parliament should be assembled every three years. Henry III protested, and appealed to the arbitration of St. Louis, who decided in his favor. But the barons refused to accept this judgment; attacked the King in arms, under the leadership of a grandson of the conqueror of Albigenses, Simon de Montfort, Earl of Leicester, and took him prisoner, with his son Edward, at the Battle of Lewes (1264). Leicester governed in the name of the King, whom he kept captive; organized the first complete representation of the English Nation by the ordinance of 1265, which prescribed the election to Parliament of two knights for each county and two citizens for each city or borough of each county.

This was the origin of the House of Commons. This summons to Parliament was the first that ever called for representatives of towns. It is true that by the Plantagenet system of rule, local government in the towns as well as in the counties had been already brought to bear on the central administration of affairs, and that the direct summons of delegates chosen by the towns to sit in the great Council of the Realm or the Parliament, was nothing more than a natural extension of the summons of their representatives to meet the royal commissioners of justices on circuit.   The genius of De Monfort is shown in that the thing was natural; it gave no shock to people's minds, and it caused no surprise.   Thus it was that it lived and grew and became a thing abiding as it is now.   Henceforth, in spite of reaction, which ever fades away to naught before the power of real progress, the trader and the merchant were to sit along with the baron, the bishop, and the knight of the shire, and deliberate on measures for the good of all.   All classes in the State were represented and so there was a true and complete Parliament.   It must be understood, however, that there was a gradual development.   Many of the early Parliaments were packed by the King, and Parliaments were of varying strength; some powerful and some weak.   Indeed English history for 500 years became little more than a struggle between King and Parliament, in which Parliament always won when it had the sufficient amount of nerve to insist upon obedience.   Of its development during the Plantagenets it may be said that, armed with the power of taxation, it took advantage of the King's weakness and made good its position as a national council.   In 1309 Parliament stipulated conditions to the voting of taxes, so that royalty, naturally extravagant, would be kept in check and made to respect the laws.   In the course of the Fourteenth Century there was a marked growth in the power and importance of Parliament.   During the first fifty years of the life of the institution since the days of De

Montfort, it became settled that solemn acts of change in the method of rule must be done by this body, and also that Parliament alone could legally enforce the payment of any tax. Under Edward II the Commons are found voting taxes only on conditions of redress, by the King, of grievances which they brought before him. The action of the barons through this period shows, however, that they held the proper sphere of the Commons to be confined to asking for redress and ordering the payment of taxes to the King by the class which they presented; high matters of state, such as the making of peace and war, and important changes in the Government, such as the passing of ordinances, were regarded as belonging only to the nobles of the land.

The Kingdom was increased under Edward I (1272-1307) by the acquisition of Wales. Politically and socially Wales had sunk into seeming barbarism under the evil influence of internal feuds and border warfare with its powerful neighbor. The mass of the people knew nothing of the use of bread, and were wild herdsmen, feeding on the milk and flesh of their flocks, and clothing themselves in skins. They were divided into numerous clans, waging pitiless, revengeful, and treacherous warfare against each other. The only sign of culture lay in the poetry of their bards, whose Celtic nature burst forth in song of real literary merit, expressed in a language which at that early age had reached a definite form and was used with great richness of imagery to manifest the poet's sense of the beauties of nature and to reveal the emotions of the heart. The utterances of the Welsh singers were not confined to the region of romance. The passionate patriotism of their race roused them to fling out in many an ode their people's hatred of the Saxon, and their land was stirred with a new and feverish strength to its last contest with the English invaders. The southern part of the country, in its more level regions along the Bristol Channel, was occupied by Norman barons after the conquest, and Henry I settled as colonists in Pembrokeshire a number of Flemings, who brought with them their habits of industry and their skill in the weaving of cloths. In the last century of Welsh independence some Princes named Llewellyn were in power. The last of these had been in arms against Henry III, but had promised fealty to the King before Prince Edward went on his crusade. Llewellyn had conquered Glamorgan, and in recognition of his strength, he was allowed, in 1267, to take the title of Prince of Wales and to receive homage from the other Welsh chieftains. When summoned as a vassal to do homage at Edward's coronation he refused to do so without a safe conduct. Wars then began, in which the Welsh fought with great bravery, being hunted from one retreat to another. David, the last Prince, was betrayed to the enemy, and tried before Parliament; was put to death as traitor (1283). In April, 1284, the infant son of Edward was born at Canarvon and was invested with the dignity and title of Prince of Wales, since generally given to the English sovereign's eldest son.

Wars with Scotland also marked the reign of Edward I. Chosen as umpire between two claimants for the Scottish throne, Robert Bruce and John Baliol, Edward decided in favor of the latter on condition that he would regard the English King as his feudal lord. Such a condition did not suit the Scots, whose ancestors had refused to yield to either Romans or Northmen, and who, in the reign of Kenneth, son of Malcolm, had acquired Strathclyde from the English. There had been constant border warfare until the century before Edward, when there was scarcely a quarrel. But the Scots could not brook a condition of vassalage and revolted, whereupon Edward took possession of the country as a fortified fief in 1296. Under William Wallace, the Scots arose again, but were defeated, and their leader taken to London and hanged. Another leader was found in Robert Bruce.* Edward marched against him, but died in sight of Scotland. The English soldiers continued the battle and drove Bruce from one hiding place to another. Almost in despair, the patriot lay one day sleepless on his bed, where he watched a spider jumping to attach its thread to a wall. Six times it failed, but succeeded on the seventh. Bruce, encouraged by this experience of the spider, resolved to persevere, and won success. Castle after castle fell into his hands until only Stirling remained. Edward II, going to its relief, met Bruce at Bannockburn (1314). The Scottish army was defended by pits, having sharp stakes at the bottom and covered at the top with stakes and turf. The English knights, galloping to the attack, plunged into these hidden holes. In the midst of the confusion, a body of sutlers appeared on a distant hill, and the dispirited English, mistaking them for reinforcements, fled. In 1328 Scottish independence was acknowledged, and from that period the land was never in danger of being conquered, although there were many wars between Scotland and England. The Scotch were usually allies of the French, and their soldiers were found fighting in the French King's armies.

Ireland had been conquered by Henry II in 1171 and the country was henceforth under English rule, but in a state of disorder. For three hundred years it was

* See Volume "World's Famous Warriors."

the constant scene of battles between the Irish chiefs and the English invaders and their descendants.

It was in Edward's reign that the Jews were banished from England, not to reappear until the days of Cromwell. They had been rigorously treated in accordance with the bigotry of the age before the final step was taken. In 1278 they were seized upon a charge of clipping coin, and a record of the time states that "of the Jews of both sexes 280 were hanged in London and . a very great multitude in the other cities of England." The Christians guilty of the same offenses were only fined. On one occasion all the Jews in the Kingdom, including the women and children, were imprisoned until they paid a heavy fine as ransom. At last, by proclamation of July 27, 1290, all the Jews were banished, to the number of over 16,000.

CONSOLIDATION OF THE FRENCH MONARCHY

The real founder of the French monarchy as a power in Europe was Philip Augustus, who reigned from 1180 to 1223. Under his rule the Kingdom grew to about one-half its present size, a great increase in territorial extent over the petty principality which he inherited. Philip Augustus was shrewd and diplomatic; he exiled and despoiled the Jews in order to make money; he delivered heretics and blasphemers to the church, by which he conciliated the bishops; by allying himself with the rebel Richard, son of Henry II, he added to the embarassments of the English. At the same time he waged little wars that were without peril, but not without profit, as they made him master of Vermandais, Valois, and Amiens. Returning from the third crusade, where he had quarreled with Richard Cœur de Lion, he plotted with John Lackland, brother of the new King of England, to despoil the latter. Richard, on escaping from prison, arrived in England in a rage, and later waged violent war in the south of France. Pope Innocent III interposed and made the Kings sign a truce of five years. Two months later Richard was killed by an arrow at the siege of the castle of Limousin. The crown of England should have reverted by the law of primogeniture to Arthur, son of an elder brother of John Lackland. The uncle usurped it, conquered his nephew and murdered him (1203). Philip Augustus summoned the murderer to appear before his court. John took good care not to come, whereupon Philip, as punishment, declared that he should forfeit his fief in Normandy. This rich province, from which the conquerors of England had come, reverted to the crown, and Brittany also became an immediate fief of the French crown (1204). Poitou, Touraine, and Anjou were also easily occupied. This was the most brilliant conquest a King of France had made. In retaliation John formed an alliance against France with his nephew, the Emperor of Germany, Otto of Brunswick, and the lords of the Netherlands. Philip assembled a great army, wherein the militia of the communes held their place and gained at Bouvines, between Lille and Tournay, a victory whose influence throughout the country was enormous. This was the first national achievement of France (1214). Before his death Philip Augustus had extended the French Kingdom to the Pyrenees and the Mediterranean. The university had been founded, the supremacy of French royal rule concentrated by the verdict of the peers against John, the Kingdom subjected to a regular organization by division for administrative purposes, and Paris was embellished, paved, and surrounded by a wall. France began to be a great nation, inspired with that longing for military glory which has so often proved her bane.

Louis IX of France was remarkable for the virtues least conspicuous in his time and rank—gentleness, meekness, compassion, humility, equity, and public spirit. He was at once handsome in face, accomplished in literature and art, diligent in business, brave in battle, forbearing and even self-sacrificing after victory, munificent in bounty at his own expense and not at his people's charges, strictly just toward the great feudal lords, whose pride and power it was his policy to lower, saintly in life and devoted to the church's real interests, and yet firm in resistance to what he held to be unwarrantable claims. This wonderful union of qualities greatly increased the power of the crown through the moral influence which they exerted. Louis IX ruled from 1226 to 1270. During the early part of his reign the French dominions were extended to the Mediterranean by the cession of the territory of Toulouse. Amongst his other services to France, St. Louis had a code of laws compiled which put an end to the feudal nuisances of private war between barons, and trial by the wager of battle.

Philip the Fair (reigned 1285-1314) was a strong contrast to St. Louis, in his high-handed dealing with his subjects and his foes; but his policy, too, increased greatly the power of France. Under him the rights of the people in the towns were first recognized in the political creation of the Tiers Etat—the Third Estate or political class, the previous two being the nobles and the priests; and in 1302 the first French Parliament or States-General, consisting of nobility, clergy, and burghers (or freemen of the towns) assembled in Paris. Widely different was the fate of this French Parliament proved from that in England, whose powers steadily grew. Philip le Bel waged a fierce contest with Pope Boniface VIII respecting the papal claims, and, after hastening his death by violently seizing him in his palace at Rome, brought the papacy for a time in subjection to France. It was now (1304) that there began, and for seventy years continued, to be Popes at Avignon, in Provence, instead of at Rome, with sometimes a rival Pope also at Rome—a state of things which lowered the position of the papacy before the world. During this reign of Philip the Fair feudalism further declined, and the power of the crown in France grew.

England and France, both strong—one by the progress of royal power, and the other by that of public liberty—found themselves at war for more than a hundred years, from 1328 to 1453. This is the war known as the Hundred Years' War, which the boldness and rashness of the French nobility rendered so glorious for England, but which ended in the acquirement of great power by French Kings and the consolidation of the country into one powerful nation. As grandson of Philip the Fair, Edward III laid claim to the crown of France, for the Salic law did not then have the importance which it gained later. However, on the accession of Philip of Valois, he appeared to abandon it, and rendered feudal homage for the Duchy of Guyenne to the King of France. Nevertheless, Edward cherished a secret hope of supplanting him, and in this he was encouraged by the refugee, Robert of Artois, despoiled of the Earldom of Artois, and by the Flemings, who, having need of English wool for their industries, revolted under Jacques Artveld, the brewer, against their Count, the friend of France, and acknowledged Edward as their legitimate King.

The war was fought as one of attack by England and of defense by France. English expeditions landed on the French coast with varying success. In 1346 the famous battle of Crecy was fought, where the English yeomanry with their long-bows did such valiant work, while the feudal army of the French recoiled before the pitiless storm of English arrows. Calais was captured as a result, and the French, being driven out, it became an English settlement, and for 200 years afforded the English an open door into the heart of France. At the battle of Poitiers (1356), John was made captive, and before the close of the first period after the death of Edward (1377), France was reduced to bankruptcy, the nobility excited to rebellion, and the mass of the people sunk in barbarism. Debasement of the coinage, onerous taxation, and arbitrary conscriptions brought the country to the verge of irretrievable ruin, while the victories of England humbled the sovereign, annihilated the French armies, and cut down the flower of the Nation.

Like the Peloponnesian War, the One Hundred Years' War was not one long struggle, but was rather a series of wars, with truces in which the combatants, worn out by the fighting, prepared for further warfare. One of these truces was due to the ravages of the "Black Death," a terrible plague that swept over Europe. This, the most terrible plague of sickness that has ever ravaged Europe, first appeared in 1346 in India and China, and thence made its way through Asia and into Europe. The habits of an age which knew nothing of the destructive nature of "dirt in the wrong place," or of the merits of pure water and pure air, rendered every street and house in the towns a hot-bed for the propagation of fever in its most deadly form. The visitation of Italy by the pest in 1348 has been vividly described by Boccaccio in his introduction to the Decameron. There was no country in which at least one-third of the inhabitants were not destroyed. The population of England, as far as can be judged, was about 4,000,000, and of these one-half were swept away. The crops were left to rot for want of laborers to cut them, and town and country were full of desolation, mourning, and woe. Travelers in Germany found cities and villages without a living inhabitant. At sea ships were discovered adrift, their entire crews having died of pestilence. The mad passions of men were stayed in the presence of this fearful scourge.

After the plague the long and weak minority of Richard II diverted the English from the prosecution of the groundless claims to the Kingdom of France, but during the minority of Charles VI (1380-1422) the war was renewed with increased vigor on the part of the English,

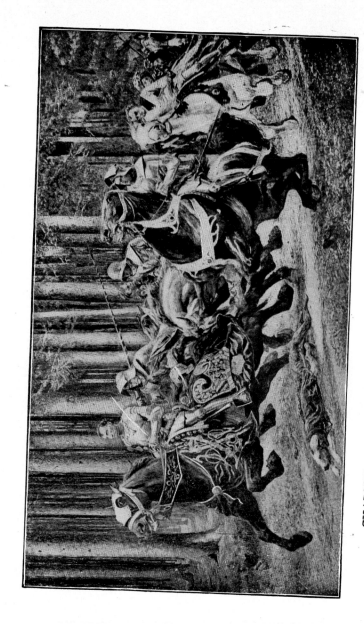

CHARLES THE BOLD'S FLIGHT AFTER THE BATTLE OF MORAT
Painting by E. Burnand

who were stimulated by the daring valor of Henry V. The signal victory won by the English at Agincourt in 1415, the treason and rebellion of the French Princes of the blood, who governed the larger provinces; the ambition of the several regents, the ultimate imbecility of the King, the profligacy of his Queen, and the love of pleasure early evinced by the Dauphin—all these combined to aid Henry in his attempts upon the throne. But the premature death of Henry, the persevering spirit of the people, and the extraordinary influence exercised over her countrymen by Joan of Arc,* concurred in bringing about a thorough reaction. After a period of murder, rapine, and anarchy, Charles VII was crowned at Rheims. He obtained from the States-General a regular tax (taille) for the maintenance of paid soldiers, to keep in check the mercenaries and robbers who pillaged the country. The policy of his successor, Louis XI (1461-83), favored the burgher and trading classes at the expense of the nobles, while he humbled the power of the vassal princes. He was a crafty ruler, who managed the finances well, and succeeded in obtaining for the crown the territories of Maine, Anjou, and Provence, while he made himself master of some portions of the territories of Charles the Bold, Duke of Burgundy. Charles VIII (1483-98), by his marriage with Anne of Brittany, secured that powerful State and consolidated the increasing power of the crown. With him ended the direct male succession of the house of Valois. Louis XII (1498-1515) was the only representative of the Valois-Orleans family. The tendency of his reign was to confirm the regal supremacy, while the general condition of the people was ameliorated.

* See "Famous Women of the World."

PROGRESS OF ROYALTY IN ENGLAND

The national feeling of the English, in abeyance during the political disturbances of Edward II's reign, reasserted itself in the ambitious efforts of Edward III to place himself upon the throne of France, and was strengthened by the brilliant victories which attended them. Though the victories were useless and the war a series of raids rather than a well-planned conquest, the effects at home were of great importance. The continual want of money forced the crown to grant frequent concessions to the Parliament. The practice was now introduced of either house originating statutes under the name of bills and these proposed measures, after being passed or approved by a majority of votes in both lords and commons, were presented to the sovereign for his assent without his alteration of their terms. It was also established that the sovereign should in no way interfere with matters under discussion in Parliament, and that freedom of speech in debate should be enjoyed by members of the commons. Toward the end of this period the judges are found fully recognizing parliamentary rights. The spirit of the people was raised by successes in France, and the life of the soldier played an important part in liberating the lower orders from serfdom. The villanage of early times had been gradually declining, and rent and wages were taking the place of Villain tenure and forced service. The terrible ravages of the Black Death upset for a while the economical arrangement of the country, and the attempt to drive back the liberated serf to his old position caused the great rising of Wat Tyler in 1381. The insurrection was suppressed, but a death blow was practically dealt to serfdom. In close connection with this upheaval of the working classes was the movement in opposition to the Church. The doctrines of Wyclif and the Lollards, so much in harmony with the democratic union, could not fail largely to influence it, and for a while hostility to the Church played a considerable part in parliamentary history.

The completion of constitutional system marked by the accession of Henry IV did not prevent the recurrence of disorder, but during the reign of his son full harmony existed between the King and the people. The disturbance which had broken out in France afforded an opportunity for renewing the war, and Henry V found no difficulty in carrying the people with him in his victorious attack upon that country. A statesman as well as a conqueror, his progress was very different from that of Edward III. The treaty of Troyes seemed to promise the ultimate union of the two Kingdoms, but the work of consolidation was scarcely begun when the great King died, intimating to those who should carry on the work that the occupation of Normandy should be the limit of their aims. The foreign success and domestic harmony was of short duration, for the power of the nobles as feudalists had disappeared. They were still too strong to accept easily the coöperation of the other orders in a national system except from the hands of a powerful ruler. Their strength had been increased by the great position given to the royal princes. The parliamentary establishment of the younger branch upon the throne had opened the door to rival claims of hereditary succession. A strong government was scarcely possible during the infancy of Henry VI, especially as the Council of Regency found in the Duke of Gloucester a man of ill-regulated ambition and an opponent with whom it was difficult to deal. His greater brother, the Duke of Bedford, devoted himself chiefly to the affairs of France, and, though he had succeeded in maintaining some degree of order in England, his early death was the signal for an outbreak with which the Council and subsequently the young King proved unable to cope.

Continual disaster in France still further discredited the government. Richard, Duke of York, believed the moment had come to assert his right to the throne, which was really superior to that of Lancaster, who descended only from the third son of Edward II, while York was the descendant of the second in the female line and of the fourth in the male. He impeached through the House of Commons the King's favorite minister, the Duke of Suffolk. The court having permitted the flight of the accused, he was recaptured on the high seas by an English vessel, whose crew seized him, judged him and beheaded him (1450). At the same time an Irishman, Jack Cade, razed the County of Kent, gathered nearly 60,000 men, and for several days was master of London. The pillage of this mob aroused everyone against them, and an amnesty offered by the King led to their dispersion. Their chief was taken and executed (1459). It was said that he was an agent of the Duke of York. The King, having an attack of sickness, Richard had himself proclaimed Protector (1454) and when the King, restored to health, wished to resume his power, he took arms, aided by the nobility, especially by Warwick, surnamed the Kingmaker, who was rich enough to feed daily on his land 30,000 people. Victorious at St. Albans (1455), the first battle of this war (known as the War of the Roses), and master of the person of the King, Richard had his title of Protector confirmed by the Parliament, and after a second battle in Northampton (1460), had himself declared the legitimate heir to the throne. Margaret protested in the name of her son, and, aided by the Scotch (whom she bought by the cession of Berwick Castle), she defeated and killed Richard at Wakefield. The rebel's head was exposed on the walls of York, ornamented with a paper crown. His young son, the Earl of Rutland, scarcely eighteen years old, was killed in cold blood. Henceforth the massacre of prisoners, the proscription of the vanquished, and the confiscation of their property became the rule of both parties.

Richard, Duke of York, was avenged by his eldest son, who had himself proclaimed King in London under the name of Edward IV. The Lancastrians, victorious at the second battle of St. Albans, experienced that same year (1461), a bloody defeat at Towton. Margaret fled to Scotland, and from thence to France, where Louis XI lent her 2,000 soldiers on her promise to surrender Calais. The battle of Hexam destroyed her hopes, although she was able to regain the continent, while Henry VI, prisoner for the third time, was confined in the Tower of London, where he remained for seven years. The new King offended Warwick, who took arms against him, defeated him at Nottingham (1470), and forced him to flee to the Netherlands to his brother-in-law, Charles of Burgundy. Parliament, always docile to the will of the strongest, reëstablished Henry VI on the throne. This triumph of the Lancastrians was short. Their violence excited great discontent, which permitted Edward to return with a small army, which Charles the Bold had helped him to raise. Warwick surrendered at Barnet, and Margaret was no more fortunate at Tewksbury. This last victory had decisive results. The Prince of Wales had been murdered, Henry VI dead, Margaret in prison, the parti-

sans of the Red Rose killed or outlawed, and Edward IV
remained the peaceable possessor of the throne.   The rest
of his reign was noteworthy for the expedition to France,
which ended in the treaty of Pecquigny (1475), and with
the trial of his brother Clarence, whom he put to death.
As for Edward himself he died a victim of his debauches
in 1483.

Richard of York, Duke of Gloucester, brother of
Edward IV, took advantage of the youth of Edward's
children to supplant them, after which he had them smoth-
ered in the Tower of London.   This usurpation gave rise
to trouble among the Yorkists.   Buckingham revolted and
sent for the Frenchman, Henry Tudor, Earl of Richmond,
the last scion of the female line of the Lancastrian house.
Henry raised in Brittany 2,000 men, landed in Wales,
and defeated Richard III at the battle of Bosworth
(1485), Richard dying on the battlefield.   Henry VII
reunited the two roses by marrying the heiress of York,
son of Edward IV, and founded the Tudor dynasty,
who reigned for 118 years, until the succession of the
Stuarts.   They had only to suppress some obscure revolts
raised by impostors, such as Lambert Simnel and Perkin
Warbeck, and they reigned as masters over the ruins of
the decimated aristocracy.   Eighty persons allied by blood
to the royal family had perished.   Nearly one-fifth of the
lands in the Kingdom had reverted by confiscation to the
domain of the crown.   English royalty found itself then
at the end of the Wars of the Roses with more resources
at its disposition and fewer adversaries to fear.

Henry VII assembled Parliament but rarely, and the
money which he did not wish to ask of them for fear
of placing himself in their power, he procured by forced
loans or benefits, and by confiscations which he multiplied on
all sorts of pretexts.   The Star Chamber became a tribu-

nal devoted to him to strike down those whom the jury system did not permit him to reach. Two measures completed the ruin of the aristocracy: The abolition of the right of maintenance, which permitted the nobles to keep around them an army of servitors with which they ravaged the country, and the abolition of the right of substitution, which prevented the alienation and partition of estates. Henry encouraged commerce and industry, in which the nation engaged with eagerness, by the treaties which he made, by voyages of discovery which he sent out, and by the impetus which he gave to shipping. He prepared the way for the union of Scotland to England by marrying his daughter, Margaret, to James IV of Scotland, the union whence came the rights of the Stuarts to the crown of England, to which they succeeded in 1603. Another marriage, that of his eldest son, and after the death of that young prince, his second son, to Catherine of Aragon, daughter of Ferdinand the Catholic, had graver consequences. Henry VII died in 1506. Perfidious, rapacious and cruel, without grandeur in mind or action to redeem his vices, he founded, like Louis XI in France and Ferdinand the Catholic in Spain, the absolute government which in England had its period of brilliancy under Elizabeth.

DEVELOPMENT OF OTHER EUROPEAN NATIONS

The line of the Hohenstaufen, or Dukes of Suabia, ruled the German Empire from 1138 to 1254, and included some of the greatest sovereigns of German history. Of these, Frederick I (surnamed Barbarossa, or Redbeard) reigned from 1152 to 1190. The principal aim of his political life was to extend and confirm his sway in Italy, where he had much warfare with the powerful and rebellious cities of Lombardy, which had become almost independent commonwealths. In 1162 he destroyed the city of Milan; in 1176 he was defeated by the Lombard League at the battle of Legnano, on the Adige, losing thereby nearly all that he had won; in 1183 Barbarossa made the Treaty of Constance (in Suabia) with the towns of Lombardy, by which they acquired the right of self-government, and acknowledged the emperor's supremacy and a limited right of taxation. In 1190 Frederick Barbarossa perished by drowning, in the Third Crusade. He was proud, brave, and liberal; serene alike in good and evil fortune; of noble mien; a constant friend of literature.

Frederick II ruled the Empire from 1215 to 1250. His high ambition aimed at the subjugation of Lombardy, the mastership of all Italy, and the reduction of the Popes to their old spiritual office as the leading Bishops of Christendom. This led him into constant struggles in Germany and in Italy. In 1237 Frederick II broke the power of the Lombard League by a victory at Corte Nuova, in Lombardy, and his army besieged Rome in 1241. Rebellion in Germany, combined with fierce opposition in Italy and the desertion of old adherents, at last wore down his spirit, and he died in the south of Italy in 1250. Frederick II of Germany was, in person and character, a good specimen of Middle Age sovereigns—courageous, cultured, just; as a man, and toward the church, he is open to the charges of sensuality, irreverence, and scepticism, which have caused Dante, in his "Inferno," to assign to him a fiery grave of punishment. He was "the ablest and most accomplished of the long line of German Cæsars, and had in vain exhausted all the resources of military and political skill in the attempt to defend the rights of the civil power against the encroachments of the church." He was an earnest supporter of literature, the arts, commerce, and agriculture, and in this way greatly benefited his realm. In 1254 the Suabian line of Emperors ended with Frederick's son Conrad. A period of confusion followed, arising from disputed succession, until 1273, and the power of the Empire (which may be called either German or Roman) as the chief State of Europe comes to an end with the loss of dominion in Italy and the rise of France.

Hapsburg is a small place in the present Swiss canton of Aargau (then in Suabia), and in 1273 Rudolph, Count of Hapsburg, was elected Emperor of Germany. He was founder of the present reigning house of Austria. Neither he nor any of his successors for a long time is of much consequence in history. The power of the Empire in Italy was gone, and became ever less in Germany, as the Princes asserted their rights to independence or increased dignity. Many of the so-called Emperors were never crowned at Rome at all. When the Dukes of Austria had become powerful, the electors always chose the Emperor from that house. The long reign of Fred-

erick III (1440-1493) takes us out of the Middle Ages.
The importance of the Empire henceforth is derived from
the power held by its head in States both inside and outside
its olden limits, as Duke of Austria, King of Hungary,
and otherwise.

Early in the Fourteenth Century a gallant little State,
still a free and flourishing Republic, steps forth with honor
to make a first appearance on the stage of history.   The
mountaineers of Switzerland then fought for and won the
beginnings of liberty for their country.   The center of the
land was under the control of the Dukes of Austria, of
the House of Hapsburg, when the three forest cantons of
Uri, Schwyz, and Unterwalden made (in 1291) a league
for the defense of their rights.   In 1315 their forces
gained the great victory of Morgarten (south of Lake of
Zurich) over invading Austrian troops, and in 1318 their
independence of the Hapsburgs was acknowledged.
Other cantons and cities joined them.   The confederation consisted then of eight members till 1481, when
Fribourg and Solothurn joined them, the country of the
league acquiring in time the name of Switzerland, from
the one canton Schwyz, which had taken a leading
part in gaining freedom for the rest.   Further attacks
were victoriously dealt with, as when the Swiss (in 1386)
utterly defeated Leopold III of Austria at Sempach (in
Lucerne), and routed the Austrians again at Näfels (in
north of Glarus) in 1388.   The country still nominally
formed part of the German Empire, but was virtually
independent.

At the end of the Fourteenth Century, Burgundy,
after many changes, had become a powerful Duchy under
a French Prince of the Valois line, with great advantages
of position as a border State between Germany and France.
The Dukes of Burgundy were also rulers of the great

commercial cities of Flanders, and ranked among the wealthiest and most influential Princes of Europe. An invasion of Burgundy by the Swiss, as allies of Louis XI of France, brought them into collision with the famous restless warrior, Charles the Bold, whose ambitious schemes aimed at annexation of territory all round his Duchy. The result was as disastrous to Burgundy as it was fortunate and glorious for Switzerland. In 1476 the Burgundians were beaten in two great fights at Granson, on the southwest shore of Lake of Neufchatel, and at Morat, or Murten, in the north of Fribourg. In 1477 the struggle ended with the defeat and death of Charles the Bold at Nancy, where the Swiss troops fought on the side of the Duke of Lorraine. Henceforth the soldiers of the Swiss confederation possessed for centuries the name for skill, discipline, and valor, which made them sought after by European powers as mercenary troops. Switzerland became formally separated from the Empire in 1499. The Duchy of Burgundy was now joined to the Kingdom of France, and the history of Burgundy as a power in European affairs comes to an end with the close of the Middle Ages. The victories of the Swiss infantry over the chivalry of Burgundy at the close of the Fifteenth Century added conclusive proof to previous signs that a revolution had been taking place in the art of war. The spell of centuries was at last dissolved; the most experienced generals were astounded to find the mountaineers of Switzerland receiving the shock of heavy cavalry on a forest of pikes, which proved to be impenetrable; and from this time the mainstay of Nations in war became their foot, and not their horse.

The cities of Northern Italy rose to greatness and wealth by commerce of the Middle Ages, and a successful struggle was maintained by the Lombard League with the

Emperor Frederick I (Barbarossa), ending with the Treaty of Constance in 1183, which left those cities virtually independent. The Italian cities took a great part in the long contest between the Popes and the Emperors, and it is in connection with this subject that we meet with the names of Guelphs, or Guelfs, and Ghibellines. These names, like the fight between feudalism and freedom, of which they are the symbols, were of German origin. In a contest of the Saxons and others against Conrad III of Germany, the rebels had a leader named Welf (in Italian Guelf), and used his name as a war-cry. Conrad's supporters took the cry of Waiblingen (changed in Italian into Ghibelin or Ghibelline), the name of a village where their leader, Duke Frederick of Suabia, was brought up. Guelfs thus came to mean opponents of the Emperor, and Ghibellines, supporters of the Emperor. When Frederick Barbarossa tried to force back the leagued Italian free cities under feudal government, the popular party in Italy became that of the Guelfs, and the Italian feudal party were the Ghibellines. The Popes, for their own purposes, sided with the Italian free cities against the Emperors, and so the Guelfs mean also the supporters of the Popes, and Ghibellines the partisans of the Emperors, in the long struggle for supremacy in Italy between the church and the Empire, which ended in the success of the ecclesiastical power and its allies, the Guelfs. Between the two parties, the Italian cities themselves became afterward, to their great injury, long divided in rancorous feuds; the Ghibellines contending for the acceptance of imperial rule in the interests of unity and order, the Guelfs insisting on the right of self-government, and jealously watching municipal privileges.

After the downfall of the Western Empire of Rome, when it became overrun by the northern barbarians, Italy had either preserved in a remarkable degree, or had recovered with great rapidity, the blessings of civilization and freedom. In some quarters these seem never to have wholly disappeared, and, when ignorance and feudalism were rampant in other parts of Western Europe, the towns of Northern Italy were marked by a democratic spirit, even when the form of government was monarchical or aristocratic, and in the times of the Crusades, the rising commonwealths of the Adriatic and Tyrrhene Seas— Venice, Genoa, Florence, and Pisa—acquired a large increase of wealth, dominion, and knowledge. Of all these flourishing States, the chief were Venice and Florence.

Venice was not only the leading maritime power of the world in the last part of the Middle Ages, but acquired, in the Fifteenth Century, a large dominion on land in the northeast of Italy. The form of government was that of an oligarchy, in which a few hundred patricians chose a Senate from their own number, and from the Senators a Doge (Venetian dialect for Duke) and Council of Ten were selected, and then the ten chose from their own number a Council of Three. This Council of Ten has become proverbial for a body of secret, dreaded, and irresponsible tyrants. Neither the Senate nor the Doge knew who formed the Council of Three, and a complete system of espionage existed over the actions, words, and very looks of the citizens. The famous "Lions' Mouths" of Venice were two small slits in a wall at the palace, into which were thrust at night the anonymous denunciations written by those who wished to be rid of an enemy through the action of the Council of Three. The members of this fearful tribunal met at night, masked and robed in scarlet cloaks, to judge those accused of political crimes, and there was no appeal from their sentence. The executioner led the condemned across the "Bridge of Sighs" to his dungeon, where he disappeared from human eyes forevermore. Under the sway of the Council of Ten, the Doge himself had little power, and the body of the people had none at all. Nevertheless, the oligarchy succeeded in choosing skillful commanders and statesmen to head the fleets and transact the business of the Republic, and Venice retained her power unimpaired till after the close of the Middle Ages.

Florence—the great example in the Middle Ages of a democratic republic, as Venice was of an aristocratic or oligarchic commonwealth—was the Athens of the mediæval world. In the Fifteenth Century a mercantile family named the Medicis rose to chief power in the State, and Cosmo de' Medici, a princely merchant and popular citizen, came to the head of affairs in 1434. Cosmo is known as the "Father of his country," and he transmitted his power to his descendants for some generations. He is renowned as the liberal and judicious patron of men of learning, philosophers, artists, and lovers of science. He employed agents in all quarters for the collection of manuscripts in Greek, Latin, and the Oriental tongues, and these treasures of literature formed the basis of the famous Laurentian or Medicean Library. Large sums of money were expended by him in adorning Florence with splendid buildings for civil and religious uses. Under the rule of the Medicis, the great Tuscan city became a center of political, intellectual, and commercial life, such as the history of the world has seldom seen. The revenue of the Florentine Republic exceeded that which was yielded annually to Elizabeth by her Kingdoms of England and Ireland. The manufacture of wool employed 30,000 workmen, and the annual sale of cloth amounted, at present values, to two and a half millions sterling. Eighty banks managed the financial business, both of Florence and of merchants in every trading mart of Europe. Edward III of England borrowed large sums of Florentine firms. The schools were flourishing. A rivalry existed amongst the great and wealthy in showing admiration for learning and genius, in collecting books and antiquities, and in encouraging art to produce triumphs of architecture, painting, and sculpture. We go for a moment beyond the assigned limits of the Middle Ages, in order to complete this interesting subject. Under Lorenzo de' Medici, the grandson of Cosmo, knowledge and prosperity at Florence reached their greatest height. Lorenzo ruled from 1469 to 1492, and was a munificent patron of arts and science. Skilled in Greek and Latin literature and in the Platonic philosophy, he cultivated also with much success his own beautiful Tuscan, and wrote poetry with unusual grace of style. To show what Florence was in intellectual greatness during her whole career, there can be nothing more eloquent and convincing than a list of her greatest citizens. In literature, the Tuscan city boasts of Petrarch, Dante, and Boccaccio; in science, of Galileo; in maritime affairs, of Amerigo Vespucci, who was a friend of Columbus; an explorer, though not the discoverer, of America; and the preparer of charts and routes for voyagers to the New World, which soon (with injustice to Columbus not due to Vespucci) received and immortalized his name. In art, Florence has won the highest renown through Michael Angelo, painter, architect, and sculptor; Leonardo da Vinci, an universal genius, at once painter, sculptor, architect, civil and military engineer, scientific inventor, accomplished gentleman, mathematician, and natural philosopher; Andrea del Sarto, the graceful painter; and Benvenuto Cellini, sculptor, engraver, and unrivaled worker in metals, whose exquisite productions fetch immense prices at the present day.   After the time of Lorenzo de' Medici, the political power of the great Italian Republic declined; in 1532 the ancient forms of the free State were abolished, and after being subject to a succession of tyrants, Florence became merged in the Grand-Dukedom of Tuscany.

After the contest between the Christians and Mohammedans in Spain, came the rise, between the Ninth and Eleventh Centuries, of the Christian Kingdoms of Navarre, Aragon, Castile, Leon, and Asturias. In the Eleventh Century Castile became the chief Spanish State.   In the Twelfth Century the Christian power gained much on the Mohammedan, and after the defeat of the Moors at Tolosa in 1212 there remained to the infidels only the Kingdoms of Cordova and Granada. The two Kingdoms of Aragon and Castile were now the chief Christian States of Spain; and in the end they absorbed all the others, Valencia being annexed by Aragon in 1239.   Aragon was the first Christian State in which the people received due recognition in a representative assembly.   The Cortes, made up of members representing the nobility, the clergy, and the towns, exercised for a time an effective control over the sovereign.   In 1412 a Castilian Prince was elected King of Aragon by the Cortes, and his descendants ruled there for some time.   Meanwhile, during the Eleventh, Twelfth, Thirteenth, and Fourteenth Centuries, Castile had waged successful war with the Moors, aided in the Eleventh Century by the bravery of the Cid.   In Castile also (in the Thirteenth Century) a free parliament or Cortes, representing all classes, was established.   At

BOABDIL, THE LAST MOOR OF GRENADA, SURRENDERS HIS POSSESSIONS
TO FERDINAND AND ISABELLA

Painting by F. Pradilla

last, in 1471, the marriage of Isabella, Queen of Castile, with Ferdinand, Infant (or heir to the crown) of Aragon, led to the formation of the one compact Spanish Kingdom. The able minister, Cardinal Ximenes, worked zealously along with Ferdinand and Isabella in bringing all the States into a political and ecclesiastical unity, while they strengthened the royal authority at the expense of the clergy, the feudal aristocracy, and the towns. Order was established throughout the land by the use of a severe police and a strict administration of justice, and the establishment of the Inquisition in Spain in 1481 greatly aided the extension of the power of the crown. But the Mohammedans still had a foothold in the land in their sole remaining realm of Granada, and the Catholic Kings, as Ferdinand and Isabella were styled, could not endure this reproach. A ten years' war (1481-1491) ended in the capture of the beautiful city of Granada, the last stronghold of the Moslem in Western Europe. The Mohammedan rule in Spain had fallen after an existence of about seven and a half centuries; and Spain (except the Kingdom of Navarre) was thus consolidated into one powerful realm, fit to take a leading part in European politics.

Civilization and culture had been attained, with important results to other parts of Europe, by the Jewish and Mohammedan people of Spain. The severities of the Inquisition, directed chiefly against the Jews, had not succeeded in "converting" that ancient and stiff-necked race to Christianity. Accordingly, in 1492, a royal edict was issued for the expulsion from Spain of all Jews who did not submit to be baptized. Nearly the whole race, rather than sacrifice their religion to their worldly welfare, thereupon left the country. The

Moors were included in the sentence of banishment, and with the Jews and Moors departed most of the industry, agricultural skill, manufacturing and commercial enterprise, genius, progressive spirit, and learning of Spain. A blow had been inflicted on the land from which she has not recovered to the present day.

THE FEUDAL SYSTEM

Feudalism, or the feudal system, was the most strongly marked feature of society during the Middle Ages. It was a military institution with a moral and religious character, and it was this combination which gave it such power over the minds and imaginations of men. The church made use of this system of warlike origin to promote the growth of Christianity and civilization. At first very noble efforts to attain moral elevation, religious faith, and knightly courage; in fact, to realize an ideal which would have been noble and lofty in any age. But gradually there came a deterioration, until the feudal chiefs no longer formed an aristocracy, or rather a government of Kings, but were isolated despots, each of whom was a sovereign in his own domains, doing what was right in his own eyes, giving no account of his actions, and asking no opinion as to the nature of his conduct toward his subjects. Under the popular hatred engendered by this abuse of the system, and with the progress of enlightenment and public freedom—in fact, when all the good work it could do was done, and only a tradition and a form remained—feudalism came to a natural and inevitable end.

"The institution," as Dr. Freeman, in his "General Sketch of European history," says, "arose out of the mixture of Roman and Teutonic ideas. It had been common under the Roman Government to grant lands on condition of military service," and this was now "combined with the Teutonic custom of men following a chief as their personal lord." Such chiefs and conquerors as

Charles Martel, in order to reward their victorious officers, divided the conquered land amongst them, to be held on condition of doing military service when required. Most of the land in a Kingdom came at last to be held in this way, so that the great landholders, called feudal lords, held large territories from the crown, which they in turn divided out amongst followers, who owed military service to them.

A fee, feud, or fief, meant a possession, of which the holder (man or vassal, i. e., attendant, companion in war) received the right of use and enjoyment, on condition of fidelity—that is, of affording assistance, avoiding all injurious acts, and performing certain services, while the feudal lord still retained a paramount right. As the son of a vassal commonly devoted himself to his father's lord, he commonly received his father's fief on his father's death, and thus, between the Ninth and Eleventh centuries, fiefs became hereditary. Whatever land was possessed by a man as his very own was called allodial (from *all,* and old German *od,* property—estate held in absolute possession without a feudal superior), and, for security's sake, many allodial owners gave up their land to powerful lords in order to receive it back from them as feudal, held on the usual terms pertaining to the feudal system. The feudal lord is known also by the names of suzerain and liege, and the vassal by those of liegeman or retainer. The system was extended from the laity to the church, bishops and abbots holding fiefs from the King, and letting out their lands in turn to vassals of their own. In return for the services in war and civil affairs rendered by the liegeman to the suzerain, the vassal could claim, in case of attack, protection from the feudal lord, and this caused many powerful Princes to hold their territories as fiefs of the German Empire.

The several orders of vassals thus formed a system of concentric circles, of which each was under the influence of the next, and all moved, in theory, around a common center, the King, as the supreme feudal lord. By the Eleventh Century the whole of France and the German Empire had thus become one vast feudal possession, and the system was well suited to the maintenance of right and privilege against the power of the crown, by insuring to a brave and free nobility, when the people were poor and disunited, the support, in a moment of need, of a powerful military force. The great mass of the people, in feudal times, ultimately consisted of serfs, who were not slaves in our sense of the word, mere chattels to be sold man by man, but were attached as cultivators to particular estates, and passed with the estate into the service of another master. The actual slaves of the Middle Ages were prisoners of war or men condemned to slavery as a punishment for crime. Those called villeins were either freeborn men renting land or serving for wages, or men in the same condition as the serfs.

One of the mischiefs of feudalism was that it ultimately caused the decay of the national assemblies in which, according to the old German constitution, each freeman had a right to appear. When large countries became organized as nations on the feudal basis, which was purely military, the people, trained to arms, trusted to their weapons for the defense of their rights rather than to the legal checks imposed by legislative assemblies, and the representative system was allowed to fall into disuse. Then, when war became first a science and then a trade, the monarchs, whose power had greatly declined through the defiance and rebellion of feudal lords, became the employers and possessors of standing armies, and thus acquired absolute power. In England, owing to its insular situation and general abstinence, after the French wars of the Plantagenet Kings, from interference in continental affairs, standing armies had been unnecessary until such time as a powerful middle class had arisen which had the needful spirit and intelligence to cope with Stuart tyranny. Thus was England narrowly preserved from the fate which befel the continental nations. The great evil of feudalism was the oppression exercised by the feudal barons, protected by their castles, and acting as the sole judges of right and wrong between themselves and their feudal dependents. Appeal to the sovereign was in many cases useless, because the supreme feudal lord did not possess the power of compelling obedience from a member of a great class on which he was himself dependent for the provision and application of military force.

The power of feudalism gave way gradually before the increasing influence of three institutions—the monarch, the free towns, and the church. The King, as the head of the State, became recognized by degrees as the one lord to whom obedience was due in the common interest. Men learned to prefer one tyrant (if tyrant he were, and all Kings are not tyrants) to many, and to appeal to the laws administered under the direction of the one master, the sovereign, rather than dwell under feudalism, where every castle might be a center of capricious violence. The feudal nobles became transformed into officers of State, whose duty it was to execute the decrees of the King and the laws of the realm, and thus royalty waxed, and feudalism waned, dwindled, and died. The power of the sovereign had come to rest ultimately on the support of the great body of the nation, and popular Kings had centered in their own persons the powers of the feudal lords.

The towns also acquired importance and became centers of hostility to feudalism. Many of these communities dated from the Roman times, in which they had been free and self-governing municipalities, and with the growth of intelligence the claims of the citizens awoke to a new life and began to assert themselves. Other towns grew by degrees around the feudal castles and acquired privileges from the lords, sometimes extending to charters which granted the right of self-government by magistrates chosen by the community. Thus the commons, or middle class, was developed, and a powerful agency was brought into operation against the absurdities of feudal superiority.

The church, seeking to gain absolute rule in spiritual affairs, took part with the Kings, as monarchical power grew, rather than with the feudal nobles; and as the clergy themselves owned a large part of the landed property in most European countries, and were themselves feudal lords in many instances, the cause of feudalism in general was greatly weakened by this desertion. In addition to the energetic operation of the above causes, the extension of commerce creating wealth in other forms than land, the invention of gunpowder, making feudal strongholds of no avail, and the internecine conflicts between feudal barons (as in the "Wars of the Roses," which almost destroyed the old nobility) contributed largely to the destruction of feudalism. It was killed, in short was slowly done to death, by the growth of the civilization which, in its own best days, it had helped to foster and to develop.

CHIVALRY

Chivalry had its rise in feudalism, and was the noblest product of that institution. On this subject the great historian Hallam writes: "As the school of moral discipline, the feudal institutions were perhaps most to be valued. Society had sunk for several centuries after the dissolution of the Roman Empire into a condition of utter depravity, where, if any vices could be selected as more eminently characteristic than others, they were falsehood, treachery, and ingratitude. In slowly purging off the lees of this extreme corruption, the feudal spirit exerted its ameliorating influence. Violation of faith stood first in the catalogue of crimes, most repugnant to the very essence of feudal tenure, most severely and promptly avenged, most branded by general infamy. The feudal law-books breathe throughout a spirit of honorable obligation. . . . In the reciprocal services of lord and vassal there was ample scope for magnanimous and disinterested energy. The heart of man, when placed in circumstances which have a tendency to excite them, will seldom be deficient in such sentiments. No occasions could be more favorable than the protection of a faithful supporter, or the defense of a beneficent suzerain, against such powerful aggression as left little prospect except of sharing in his ruin. From these feelings, engendered by the feudal relation, has sprung up the peculiar sentiment of personal reverence and attachment toward a sovereign which we call loyalty, alike distinguishable from the stupid devotion of Eastern slaves and from the abstract respect with which free citizens regard their chief magistrate. . . . In a

moral view, loyalty has scarcely perhaps less tendency to
refine and elevate the heart than patriotism itself." Such
is one view of the spirit of chivalry, so far as it concerned
the maintenance of the peace and order of the social system.

But there is much more than this involved. The feudal
system arose among the Franks, a German people, and
the Teutonic race was always distinguished by its warlike character, and by the great respect shown toward
womankind. Hence we have some of the chief marks
of the age of chivalry—devotion to exploits of arms and
honor paid to the gentler sex. Taking a wider and a deeper
view, the same eminent writer observes that "there are
three powerful spirits which have from time to time moved
over the face of the waters, and given a predominant
impulse to the moral sentiments and energies of mankind. These are the spirits of liberty, of religion, and
of honor. It was the principal business of chivalry to animate and cherish the last of these three.

One of the feudal princes enjoined his knights to
honor, above all, the women, and not to permit any one
to slander them, because from them after God comes all
the honor that men can acquire. It is from the close union
of bravery in knights with this devotion to the fair sex
that the same word—gallantry—has been used to express
both qualities. Like other good things, this was carried
to what appears a ridiculous extreme, when we find the
warriors on each side in serious conflict, bearing over their
armor scarves and devices, as the livery of their mistresses,
and asserting the paramount beauty of her whom they
served, in vaunting challenges toward the enemy.

In the code of morals prevalent during the best part
of the Middle Ages, three virtues were held by mankind
to be essential to the character of a knight—loyalty, cour-

tesy, and munificence. The first of these—loyalty—may be defined, in its original sense, as fidelity to engagements; whether actual promises, or such tacit obligations as bound a vassal to his lord, and a subject to his prince. It was applied also, and in the utmost strictness, to the fidelity of a lover toward the lady whom he served. Breach of faith, and especially of an express promise, was held to be a disgrace that no valor could redeem. "False," "perjured," "disloyal," "recreant," were the epithets which he must be compelled to endure who had swerved from a plighted engagement, even toward an enemy. This is one of the most striking changes produced by chivalry. Treachery, the usual vice of savage as well as of corrupt nations, became infamous during the rigor of that discipline. As personal rather than national feelings actuated its heroes, they never felt that hatred, much less that fear, of their enemies which blind men to the heinousness of ill faith. In the wars of Edward III of England with France, wars originating in no real animosity, the spirit of honorable as well as courteous behavior toward the foe seems to have arrived at its highest point. Though avarice may have been the primary motive of ransoming prisoners instead of putting them to death, their permission to return home on the word of honor in order to procure the stipulated sum—an indulgence never refused—could only be founded on experienced confidence in the principles of chivalry. A knight, then, was held to be unfit to remain a member of the order if he violated his faith. He was ill acquainted with its duties if he proved wanting in courtesy. The word courtesy expressed the most highly refined good breeding, founded less upon a knowledge of ceremonious politeness, though this was not to be omitted, than on the spontaneous modesty, self-denial, and respect for others which ought to spring from the heart. Besides the grace which this beautiful virtue threw over the habits of social life, it softened down the natural roughness of war, and gradually introduced that indulgent treatment of prisoners which was almost unknown to antiquity.

As to munificence, all the romances of chivalry inculcate the duty of a knight's scattering his wealth with profusion, especially toward minstrels, pilgrims, and the poorer members of his own order. The last, who were pretty numerous, had a constant right to succor from the opulent; the castle of every lord who respected the ties of knighthood was open with more than usual hospitality to the traveler whose armor announced his dignity, though it might also conceal his poverty. Valor, loyalty, courtesy, munificence, formed collectively the character of an accomplished knight. Yet something more was required for the perfect idea of chivalry, and was enjoined by its principles: an active sense of justice, an ardent indignation of wrong, a determination of courage to its best end, the prevention or redress of injury. It grew up as a salutary antidote in the midst of poisons, while scarce any law but that of the strongest obtained regard, and the rights of territorial property, which are only right as they conduce to general good, became the means of general oppression.

Chevalry means properly the usages and qualifications of chevaliers or knights, and in the reign of Charlemagne we find a military distinction that appears, in fact as well as in name, to have given birth to the institution. Certain feudal tenants were bound to serve on horseback, equipped with the coat of mail. These persons were called Caballarii (horse-riders, from Latin, caballus, a riding-horse), whence the word Chevalier, a mounted warrior, and then a knight. The truth is that, in the warfare of the Middle

Ages, the strength of armies lay in the cavalry (another form of the word chivalry), and the service of the infantry was assigned to the plebeians; the landed gentry, or feudal tenants of a certain rank, alone could aspire to the name of "miles," soldier, or were "knights" in the technical sense. The dukes and counts, who had usurped the rights of sovereignty, divided the provinces among their faithful barons. The barons distributed among their vassals the fiefs or benefices of their jurisdiction, and these military tenants, the peers of each other and of their lord, composed the noble or knightly order, which disdained to conceive the peasant or burgher as of the same species with themselves. The dignity of their birth was preserved by pure and equal alliances; their sons alone, who could produce four quarters or lines of ancestry, without spot or reproach, might legally pretend to the honor of knighthood; though a valiant plebeian was sometimes enriched and ennobled by the sword, and became the father of a new race. This technical, legal, landed order of knighthood was succeeded, in the time of the Crusades, by the personal chivalry, the order of personal nobility. Knighthood, to be won by merit alone, not claimed as a legal right, became the chief object of ambition with a noble's younger sons, who could derive little or no income from the paternal estate. This knighthood raised such men in the scale of society, making them equal in dress, in arms, and in title to the rich landholders, and, being due only to merit, making them much more than equal to those who had no pretensions but from wealth, so that a territorial knight became at last ashamed to assume the title until he could challenge it by real merit. Thus arose the class of noble and gallant cavaliers, serving indeed for pay. but on the most honorable footing. In the warfare of the Crusades, as no man could be called on to undertake feudal service for the needful length of time, the richer barons took into their pay as many knights as they could afford to maintain. In this way the original connection of knighthood with feudal tenure became forgotten in the splendor and dignity of its new form. Each knight, in his turn, was attended to the field by his faithful squire, a youth of equal birth and similar hopes of plunder, promotion, and renown. He was followed also by his archers and men-at-arms, from four to six soldiers being regarded as the retinue or following of a complete lance.

The warlike character of chivalry had a bad influence in causing the illiterate knight to disdain the arts of industry and peace, to esteem himself the sole judge and avenger of his own injuries, and to neglect, in his pride, the laws of civil society and of military discipline. It is certain, too, that the morals of chivalry, in spite of the religious side of its character, were far from pure. The literature of the Middle Ages, in which chivalry speaks for itself, shows a licentious spirit which only reflects the facts of the life of the times. Brave knights and fair ladies acted, in far too many instances, in accordance with a code of morals very different from that of the Christianity which they professed to believe and to defend. Another evil was that knighthood, as an institution, widened the interval between the different classes of society, and confirmed that aristocratical spirit of high birth by which the large mass of mankind were kept in unjust degradation. At the siege of Calais, for example, Edward III, as a true knight, treated his knightly foes with generous consideration, but displayed a harshness toward the citizens which puts his character, apart from chivalry, in a much less favorable light.

It is a grotesque fact that chivalry, along with the feudalism with which it was so closely connected, owed its final overthrow to a practical application of chemistry —the use of gunpowder in war. Lances and armor could do nothing against guns; personal strength was of no avail against bullets; infantry became, as a military body, the superiors of cavalry; tactics changed; the honors of chivalry became disconnected from a display of prowess in war; the progress of reason and of literature brought ignorance into discredit, and "the ridicule which kills" gave the finishing stroke to that which, in its day, had been so picturesque and glorious, but had degenerated into a fantastic and useless absurdity. The spirit of chivalry left behind it a more valuable successor. The character of knight gradually subsided in that of gentleman, and the one has distinguished society in modern times as much as the other did that of the Middle Ages. A jealous sense of honor, less romantic, but equally elevated, a ceremonious gallantry and politeness, a high pride of birth, a sympathy for martial honor, though more subdued by the habits of civil life—these were the features of character which, in the Sixteenth and Seventeenth Centuries, proved an indisputable descent. The cavaliers of Charles I were genuine successors of Edward III's knights. Time has effaced much also of this gentlemanly, as it did before of the chivalrous, character. Since the latter part of the Seventeenth Century its vigor and purity have undergone a silent decay, and yielded to increasing commercial wealth, to more diffused instruction, to the spirit of general liberty in some, and of servile obsequiousness in others, to the modes of life in great cities, and to the leveling customs of social life. Modern society owes much of the honor, generosity, courtesy, and kind-

ness which are blended in the character of a perfect gentleman, to that exalted institution of past ages whose
soul is a living presence in our midst, though the frame-
work and the system, like the bodies of the gallant knight:
whose tombs remain in many a crypt and shrine, have long
decayed.

CIVILIZATION IN THE MIDDLE AGES

The "Middle Ages" comprise a period of about a thousand years, from the close of the Fifth to the close of the Fifteenth Century. Of this long period the first six centuries, from the end of the Fifth to the end of the Eleventh Century, are usually called the "Dark Ages," from the general lack of knowledge and culture by which they are marked in the history of mankind in Europe since the rise of civilization. Before the territory of the Roman Empire became almost wholly occupied by the barbarian tribes, a general indifference to education and literature had spread amongst the inhabitants of the Roman world. A lethargy existed as to the acquirement of learning, the existence of which was both proved and uselessly combated in the laws enacted by Constantine, Julian, Theodosius, and other Emperors for the encouragement of learned men and the promotion of liberal education. When such enactments as these are required in a society which has once been highly cultivated, the degradation of man's intellect has already reached a low point, and is sure to go lower still. There was even a danger lest the light of learning should be quite extinguished by the destruction or decay of the books existing then only in manuscript, and reproduced at greater cost and trouble than in times when the general love of literature had caused the employment of bodies of rapid and skillful transcribers. One cause of the decay of learning was the general neglect of the pagan literature, containing the highest models of literary art, by the Christian church. Some of the early fathers of the Church were, indeed, men of considerable acquirements in these matters, but there was a general aversion felt among Christians for heathen letters, and a general contempt for physical science, which was held to be opposed to revealed truth. In its earliest stage, more-over, the system of monasticism, founded upon the ascetic enthusiasm of austere recluses, was hostile to literary cul-ture. The temporary ruin of civilization on this literary side was completed in the occupation of Gaul, Italy, and Spain by the untutored barbarians of the Teutonic world. They knew nothing of learning themselves, and they soon reduced nearly all around them to the same level. These intelligent tribes of the central and northern parts of the continent could not fail to observe that the arts of civiliza-tion had not preserved the Roman Empire from corrup-tion in morals or conquest in arms, and they despised all attainments which appeared to be incompatible with suc-cess in war.

The main cause of the almost total extinction of learn-ing was the change that took place in the speech of the inhabitants of Gaul, Italy, and Spain. The original lan-guage of Gaul and Spain was mainly Celtic, resembling the tongues still commonly spoken in Wales and Brittany, and not wholly extinct in Ireland and the Highlands of Scotland. In Gaul and Spain the native speech was, by degrees, first completely superseded by the Latin, and then, as well as in Italy itself, corrupted in pronunciation into a broken Latin called Roman, from which the Italian, French, Spanish, and Portuguese languages were gradu-ally developed—the Romance languages of Europe. The classical Latin still continued, with gradual changes in purity of expression and idiom, to be the written language of such few scholars as were to be found amidst almost universal ignorance. Since written language is the standard by which the ordinary speech of civilized persons is rectified, it follows that ignorance of books will lead to an evergrowing change in speech, and thus, as well as through an influx of foreign words from the Teutonic dialects of the barbarians, the Latin language ceased to be a living tongue, and education in the only language which, for Western Europe, could be said to have a literature, became an impossibility for the mass of the people.

All books were in Latin, which the people could not read, and in their language of everyday life there were no books. The Latin language continued to be taught only in the few schools which, in the course of the Eighth and Ninth Centuries, became attached to monasteries and churches, and the mass of the people were wholly unlettered. Few laymen of any rank could read or write: learning, such as it was, was confined to the clergy, and they had little. France seems to have reached the worst point of darkness by the beginning of the Eighth Century, and England at the middle of the Ninth. Italy was in a degraded condition as to learning during the Tenth Century; in France, after the time of Charlemagne, slow but steady progress was made, and Alfred the Great did much for the revival of letters in England. The state of ignorance in England during the Dark Ages is proved by Alfred's own declaration that he did not know a single priest South of the Thames (the most civilized part of the island) at the time of his accession, who understood the ordinary prayers of the church service, or could translate Latin into the English of his day. A great cause, also, of this general ignorance was the scarcity of books, according to Hallam in his Middle Ages. From the conquest of Alexandria by the Saracens, at the beginning of the Seventh Century, when the Egyptian papyrus almost ceased to be imported into Europe, to the close of the Tenth Century, about which time the art of making paper from cotton rags seems to have been introduced, there were no materials for writing except parchment, a substance too expensive to be readily spared for mere purposes of literature. Hence an unfortunate practice gained ground of erasing a manuscript in order to substitute another on the same skin. This occasioned the loss of many ancient authors, who have made way for the legends of saints or other ecclesiastical matter. Few men of eminent ability or attainments appeared during these Dark Ages, from the Sixth to the Middle of the Eleventh Century. Beda, or Bede (known as the "Venerable Bede") was born near Wearmouth, in Durham, about A. D. 672, and lived till 735. He wrote a history of the English Church—his Ecclesiastical History—virtually a history of England down to the date of its completion in 731. This was written in Latin, and he also completed a translation, from Latin into English, of the Gospel of St. John. Alcuin, another famous Englishman, lived from about 735 to 804, and was educated in the celebrated school attached to the York monastery, where he became afterward the school-master and librarian. He aided Charles the Great in spreading literary culture in his Empire, acting as the Minister of Public Instruction, as Professor Morley, in his First Sketch of English History, styles him. Alcuin was the greatest scholar of his time, and was energetic in causing the multiplication of good books in the scriptorium or writing-room of his monastery. His writings include letters, inscriptions, epigrams, and poems. John Scotus, or Erigena, was a Celt who flourished about the middle of the Ninth Century. He had a knowledge of Greek—a rare accomplishment in Western Europe at that time—and wrote in Latin a philosophical work called De Divisione Naturæ ("On the Division of Nature"), in which he maintained the doctrines of a perfect harmony between reason and revelation, and of the non-eternity of evil. He was a great student of Plato, and endowed with a lively fancy and a bold spirit of speculation. Gerbert (Sylvester II, Pope from A. D. 999 to 1003) was a great promoter of learning, and a man of scientific attainments, which procured for him, in that dull age, a reputation for magic. He wrote on arithmetic and geometry, and constructed with his own hands a clock, a globe, and an astrolabe, the instrument now superseded by the sextant, and used for measuring angles of altitude in observation of the heavenly bodies.

The mental state of these Dark Ages is well exhibited in the superstitious beliefs which prevailed. In the Tenth Century it was believed that the world was to come to an end with the year A. D. 1000. The judgment of Heaven was appealed to in ordeals and judicial combats. Impostors or fanatics raved about Europe, declaring themselves to be divine prophets, and drew many after them into riotous folly. So-called miracles abounded, and had multitudes of believers. The Dark Ages were times when religion was degraded, morals were loose, and lawlessness was rife. Judicial perjury was one of the commonest of crimes. An excessive passion for field-sports caused much oppression of the peasantry by the nobles, and a generally backward state of agriculture, since the leveling of forests, the draining of morasses, and the extirpation of mischievous animals were forbidden by the landed aristocracy, who wanted game-preserves for their pleasure instead of corn-fields for their true and lasting profit. For five or six centuries the finest regions of Europe were unfruitful and desolate. There is no trace of any manufacture beyond what was needed to supply the wants of the immediate neighborhood. In the Ninth Century even Kings had their clothes made by the women upon their

farms. Extended traffic there could be none, amidst the
general ignorance of mutual wants, the peril of robbery in
conveying merchandise, and the certainty of extortion. In
the domains of every feudal lord a toll was to be paid in
passing his bridge, or along his highway, or at his market.
Thus enterprise was stifled in the birth, and trade perished
in the making. The worst of the feudal masters of the
European world were not satisfied with the robberies of
fiscal extortion, but came down openly from their castles
to plunder wealthy travelers, or shared the gains of the
highway robbers whom they protected in their infamous
misdeeds. Travelers were seized and sold as slaves, or
held to ransom, and the Venetians purchased the luxuries
of Asia by supplying the markets of the Saracens with
slaves. The subversion of the Roman Empire of the West
thus led from ignorance to superstition, from superstition
to lawlessness and vice, and thence to general rudeness
and poverty.

   But the Dark Ages were not wholly dark. Though
most of the inhabitants of Europe were chained to the
soil, without freedom, property, or knowledge, and the
nobles and clergy alone deserved the name of citizens and
men, yet mitigations of no mean account existed, and
soothed the miseries of the poor and helpless. It was the
Christian church that did this work, as well as kept alive
in some degree the ancient learning. In Hallam's phrase,
religion made a bridge across the chaos, and linked the
periods of ancient and of modern culture. Three portions
of the religious system then prevailing were concerned in
this beneficial result. These were the papal supremacy,
the monastic institutions, and the use of a Latin liturgy.
It was these that preserved the Latin language, on which
hung the sole hope of a revival of letters. The papal
supremacy kept up a constant intercourse between Rome

and the several nations of Europe. Her laws were received by the bishops, her legates presided in councils, and a common language was preserved, in Latin, as an absolute necessity of the situation. The monastic institutions kept learning alive. The parochial clergy had no literature, and almost every distinguished man belonged either to a cathedral-chapter or to a monastery. There opportunities for study existed, and there books were kept in safety. Without the libraries of the monks we should hardly have had manuscripts at all. The Latin liturgy preserved in tolerable purity that tongue which had ceased to be intelligible to the mass of mankind, and in the Bible called the Vulgate a still more venerable treasure existed. The Latin which kept knowledge from the people in the Dark Ages, preserved knowledge for the people in the dawn of a destined revival of learning.

The first religious order founded in Western Europe was that of the Benedictines. St. Benedict, an Italian of the province of Umbria, introduced a rule of life into his monastery of Monte Cassino, near Naples, in A. D. 529. This system became gradually the rule of all the Western monks, and it included the instruction of youth in reading, writing, ciphering, Christian doctrine, and the mechanical arts. Benedict started a library, for which the aged and infirm brethren were obliged to copy manuscripts, and was thus one of the first who, in the church of Christendom, helped to preserve the literary remains of antiquity. From the Sixth to the Tenth Century almost all the monks in the West might be called Benedictines, as following St. Benedict's rules, which were enforced in the monasteries of Spain and of France, and by the Irish monk St. Columba. A branch of the Benedictines, called the Cluniacs (from the Convent of Clugny, in Burgundy), possessed 2,000 monasteries in the Twelfth Century. In naming some of these orders we shall go beyond the limits of the Dark Ages, but for the sake of convenience bring them together here. The Cistercians arose in a convent near Dijon in 1098, and became a rich order, spread throughout Europe with many hundreds of abbeys. The Franciscans were founded by St. Francis of Assisi (in Italy) in 1210, and are known as the Gray Friars (or Brothers) from the color of their robe. The rule of this order was a life of poverty, devoted to begging and preaching. Afterward, the Franciscan monasteries were allowed to hold property, and the order became very powerful, including members who were the confessors of Princes and virtual rulers of the Christian world, and several who rose to be Popes. To this order belonged the scholars Bonaventura, Duns Scotus, and Roger Bacon. The Dominicans were founded by St. Dominic in A. D. 1215, at Toulouse, in the south of France. The object of their institution was to preach against heretics. They became a very powerful order, and spread over Europe and into Asia, Africa, and America. The scholars Albertus Magnus and Thomas Aquinas belonged to the Dominicans. They were the exclusive managers in Spain, Portugal, and Italy, of the terrible Inquisition, and became great rivals of the Franciscans in political and theological matters. The controversialists on the side of the Dominicans were known as Thomists, from Thomas Aquinas, and of the Franciscans as Scotists, from Duns Scotus.

The monks in the Dark Ages kept alive the virtues of meekness, self-denial, and charity at a time when the laity were little given, indeed, to their practice. The relief of the poor is the outcome of a spirit distinguishing both Christianity and Mohammedanism from the pagan systems of Greece and Rome, which had little of general humanity and sympathy with suffering, and can boast of no public institution for the alleviation of human miseries. At the monastery gate those were fed who must otherwise have starved; by the monkish doctor the sick were tended who must otherwise have perished of disease. Much was also done for agriculture in the reclaiming of waste lands and in improved methods of tillage. Nor did the Christian church fail to fulfill a higher office still in the shelter which she afforded to the fugitive, and the stand which she made against the oppressor. By an established law, founded on very ancient superstition, the precincts of a church afforded sanctuary (a sacred asylum or refuge) to accused persons. With a due administration of justice, this would be simply giving immunity and license to crime; in the Middle Ages, the right of sanctuary was often a protection to innocence.

Between the Eleventh and Fifteenth Centuries we have a time of revival and of recovery from the state of degradation and poverty in Europe. The darkness grows fainter, the twilight comes, the sky reddens, at last the sun bursts forth amidst the lingering mists of prejudice and ignorance and superstition. The rise and growth of important towns are at once the signs of reviving civilization at this period of European history, and the active causes of continued progress. With the advent of the Teutonic nations the Roman towns had decayed, because the new inhabitants of the old Roman world were not fond of the restraints of existence within walled inclosures. As civilization was developed in new forms the old towns recovered some of their former importance, and new towns everywhere arose. Many were founded in Germany by the Emperors of the Saxon

ATTACK BY LORD KITCHENER'S FORCE UPON THE MAHDI
Painting by R. Caton Woodville

dynasty, and the growth of commerce was a powerful agent in the creation and development of new centers of population and wealth. Some of these new or revised cities became powerful and independent commonwealths playing a great part in the history of the Middle Ages.

Towns were in many cases the result of a reaction and protest against feudal violence. As vassals gathered for protection around the castles of feudal lords and around monasteries and churches, towns had their beginnings in hamlets. The inhabitants then became burghers, dependent on the lords of the castles or on the monastic bodies. Unions and confederations also arose among those who were connected in the cultivation of the soil in particular districts. They agreed to render to each other such aid and service as they had been obliged to render to their feudal lord. The first thing was to erect a tower with a bell, to be rung as a signal to meet for defence, and so a kind of rude militia was formed. Then a municipal government was instituted, with magistrates, a common treasury, and the imposition of taxes and tolls. Thus grew the reviving sense of freedom. Then trenches were dug and walls were built for defence, and, along with security, handicrafts found a home. Artisans rose to a higher position than that of tillers of the ground, who were forcibly driven to work; the artisan, moreover, had a skill and an activity of his own. At first artisans required leave from the Liege Lord to sell their work, and earn something for themselves; for this privilege of selling their wares they paid a certain sum, besides giving a part of their gains to the baronial exchequer. In the early days of the new towns the nobility imposed rents for houses, and tolls on imports and exports, and exacted money for safe-conduct from travelers.   As the rising communities grew in wealth and strength, all these feudal rights were bought from the nobles, or the cession of them was extorted by force; by degrees the towns acquired an independent jurisdiction and freed themselves from all taxes, tolls, and rents, and each place was fairly started on a new and prosperous career.   The trading class then divided itself into guilds, with particular rights and obligations.   Thus did cities grow, in many cases, to be independent Republics, in Italy, in the Netherlands, and Germany, and France.

The trade of Northern Europe belonged chiefly to the shores of the Atlantic Ocean, the North Sea (or German Ocean), and the Baltic Sea, on the coasts of Holland, France, England, Germany, Denmark, Norway and Sweden.   The sea, in the middle of the Thirteenth Century, still swarmed with pirates, and the German trade, in particular, suffered greatly from their depredations.   The first trading town erected on the Baltic coast was Lübeck, founded in A. D. 1140, and this town became independent of any sovereign, except the German Emperor, in the Thirteenth Century.   Near to Lübeck, but connected with the North Sea coast, Hamburg (founded by Charles the Great in 808,) became an important center of commerce in the Twelfth Century, and independent of its feudal Lord, the bishop, by purchase of his rights in 1225.   Bremen was established in the Eighth Century, and became a flourishing place. Riga, on the eastern Baltic coast, was founded by a colony from Bremen about 1190.   Dantzic (or Danzig), became great in commerce in the Fourteenth Century, having been founded long before in the Tenth.   Königsberg was founded in 1255, and soon became an important seat of trade.   The chief trading city on the Rhine was Cologne (a Roman colony, Colonia Agrippina of

A. D. 51, annexed to the German Empire in 870), which carried on an extensive commerce by the Eleventh Century in wine, corn, flour, malt, etc.   In Flanders, Bruges (now so fair in her decay)—the Northern Venice, city of canals—was a fortified town by the middle of the Ninth Century, and in the Fourteenth had become one of the greatest commercial cities in all Europe, being the chief entrepôt both for Mediterranean and northern merchandise.   Ghent, also in Flanders, was another city of canals and islands, already famed in the Twelfth Century for her woolen manufacture, and by the end of the Thirteenth it was one of the largest towns in Europe, far surpassing the Paris of that age.   The greatness of Antwerp comes later, dating from early in the Sixteenth Century.   Among these commercial towns, and others such as these, there arose in the Thirteenth Century confederacies for mutual protection against pirates and robbers, and for the furtherance of their common interests.   The chief of these trade alliances was that called (from the old German-Gothic word Hansa, "a league") the Hansa, or Hanseatic League.   This powerful confederacy embraced at last ninety maritime and inland towns, scattered over Holland, England, Norway, Germany, Poland, and Russia.   The head town of the League was Lübeck, being the meeting-place of the deputies from the other towns, and the chief trading centers were Novgorod in Russia, Bruges, London, and Bergen in Norway.   In the Fourteenth Century the Hanseatic League had attained great political importance, which it kept until the Sixteenth Century.

The southern commerce of Europe was found, of course, chiefly upon the shores of the Mediterranean Sea —on the eastern coast of Spain, in Provence and Languedoc, in Italy and Greece, at Constantinople, in Asia

Minor, Syria, and Egypt.   Commercial intercourse between northern and southern Europe began early in the
Fourteenth Century, and we soon find Genoese ships
trading to Flanders and England.   The north of Italy
was the flourishing part of the peninsula, deriving
wealth from the tillage of the rich plains of Lombardy,
which exported large quantities of corn in the Thirteenth
and Fourteenth Centuries, though the country had a large
population of its own to feed.   The Italian cities, beginning with the Eleventh Century, divided most of the land
among them, so that it became "an assemblage of commonwealths, independent of any power but that of the
German Emperor."   Of these cities, Florence became
important early in the Twelfth Century, through the industry and enterprise of her inhabitants.   She had commercial establishments in the Levant, France and other
parts, and her trading-class included money-changers,
money-lenders, jewelers, and goldsmiths.   Pisa (an ancient Etruscan city, and then a Roman colony) became
an independent Republic in A. D. 888, and in the Tenth
Century, by military prowess and commercial enterprise,
took a lead among the Italian States.   The Pisans
greatly distinguished themselves against the Saracens,
driving them from Sardinia in 1025, conquering the Balearic Isles in 1114, and taking a prominent part in the
Crusades.   In the Twelfth and Thirteenth Centuries the
power of Pisa was at its height, her trade was spread
over the whole Mediterranean, and she was supreme in
the Italian Islands, and on the northwest coast of Italy.
Genoa was her great rival, and to her and Florence the
Pisans gradually lost their power.   Genoa (a Ligurian
city, named by Livy as Genua, among Roman allies in
the second Punic war, and then a Roman municipal
town) became a Republic after the time of Charles the

Great, and was noted in the trade with the Levant.   In 1174 Genoa possessed nearly all the coast of Provence, and the Island of Corsica.   She had a long struggle with Pisa for dominion in the west of the Mediterranean, and then with Venice for supremacy in the east of the great inland sea.   The Genoese trade was at its height about the middle of the Thirteenth Century, when Genoa had a large share in the commerce of the Greek Empire, and also control of trade in the Black Sea, obtaining commodities even from India by way of the Caspian Sea.

Venice became firmly seated on her islands in the Ninth Century, and owed much of her subsequent prosperity to the Crusades.   Her shipping was largely and profitably used to convey troops and stores to the East. In 1204 her Doge, Henry Dandolo, aided the French Crusaders to capture Constantinople.   Venice then acquired much territory on the Adriatic coast, and many islands, including Candia (now Crete), her merchants having in their hands all the commerce of the Archipelago.   By the close of the Fifteenth Century Venice was the greatest trading city in Europe, and then her commerce began to decline.   Amalfi (about twenty miles south of Naples) became great in the Ninth Century as a Republic, and was distinguished in exertions against the Saracens.   Before the Crusades she had the chief part of the trade with the Saracenic countries, and was prosperous for nearly three centuries, till she was attacked and plundered by the Norman conqueror Robert Guiscard, in 1075, and again by Pisa in 1130.   After this, Amalfi declined.

In the south of what is now France, Marseilles kept some of her ancient trade.   Narbonne (the first colony founded by the Romans beyond the Alps) was a place of much commerce.   Nismes (or Nimes), famous still for her beautiful Roman remains, had also a flourishing trade. Montpellier was greater still at this epoch, and possessed a university before the end of the Twelfth Century. In Spain Barcelona began to rival the Italian cities, both in trade and in war, at the middle of the Thirteenth Century. Her vessels went to every part of the Mediterranean, and even to the English Channel; she fought, not without success, against the powerful Genoa. The commerce of Barcelona was at its best in the Fifteenth Century. The growth of commerce at this time was closely connected, as usual, with progress in manufactures. One of the earliest and most important of these was the woolen manufacture of Flanders. By the Twelfth Century this had become flourishing, and so great in the Thirteenth that a writer asserts, with evident exaggeration, that all the world was clothed from English wool worked up in Flanders. By the Fourteenth Century Flanders was a market for the traders of the whole civilized world. Merchants from seventeen Kingdoms lived at Bruges, which city, as well as Ghent, was a chief seat of the industry in woolen wares. England became a rival of Flanders in this trade, after Edward III, the father of English commerce, encouraged Flemish weavers to settle there. Wool was at this time the chief English article of export and source of revenue. There was also much making of woolen stuffs in Italy, southern France, and eastern Spain. Robert Guiscard, the Norman, introduced a manufacture of silk at Palermo, in the north of Sicily, about A. D. 1075. About the same time the Genoese derived a knowledge of this from the Moors of Spain. In the last part of the Twelfth Century, silk-producing and silk-weaving became common in northern Italy, and the laws of the cities enforced the cultivation of the mulberry-tree.

The Rhodians of old introduced a code of maritime law, and this was adopted by the Roman Emperors. About the middle of the Thirteenth Century a written code of law had come into existence containing mercantile regulations, and making a good beginning for the law of nations by defining the mutual rights of neutral and belligerent vessels. This code soon acquired a binding force within the limits of the Mediterranean Sea, and the merchant law of modern Europe is mainly founded on its provisions. In the Thirteenth and Fourteenth Centuries piracy was still common, and much trouble was caused through reprisals made by the people of one country on those of another. This half-recognized usage of retaliating upon the innocent for the doings of the guilty citizens of a State was the origin of the modern customs of granting letters of marque for privateering, abolished by a convention of the great powers in 1856.

Throughout the Middle Ages the interest of money was very high, varying from 7 to 20 per cent. The theologians of that day declared usury to be a crime, and the trade of money-lending, as well as much of the general inland commerce, was in the hands of the Jews, not quite unknown in our times for the same occupations, and the cruel persecution connected therewith. The Jews, however, flourished greatly, and in the Twelfth Century are found in Languedoc as possessors of landed property. They were very numerous in Spain, and were protected by Princes for their diligence and skill in money matters. The trade in money was transferred, to a great extent, to other hands early in the Thirteenth Century. At that time, the merchants of Lombardy and of the south of France took up the business of remitting money by bills of exchange, and of making profit upon

loans.   The convenience of the system was found to be
such, that the Lombard usurers established themselves
in every country, from which "Lombard Street," the
locality of banks in the City of London, and the pawn-
brokers' sign of the three golden balls, the arms of Lombardy, is derived.   A bank of deposit is said to have been
established at Barcelona in 1401.

From the Twelfth Century a change begins in the
universal acceptance by mankind, in Western and Central Europe, of the orthodox faith of Rome.   In that age
there broke in upon the Church a flood of heresy which
no persecution was able thoroughly to repress, till it
finally overspread half the surface of Europe.   An erroneous belief (as judged by the accepted standard of the
Scriptures) concerning both the Creator of the world
and the person of Christ had been carried from Armenia,
in Asia Minor, by exiles into Bulgaria.   From this settlement these doctrines spread, by way of the Danube,
through Hungary and Bavaria, and also by way of Lombardy and Switzerland, into Western Europe.   It is not
to be supposed, when we speak of heresy (or false doctrine), that the particular views above mentioned are
intended.   The point is, that men should have begun
to dare to think for themselves in religious matters, to
reject the teaching of the Church, and to protest, as they
did, against the wealth and tyranny (as they called it) of
the clergy.   The existence of such a spirit is the fact to
be borne in mind.   Besides the Albigenses, we find a
sect called the Waldenses, deriving their name from
Peter Waldo, a merchant of Lyons, who headed a con-
gregation of seceders from the Church about the year
1160.   This sect spread rapidly over France and Germany.   They were found chiefly and are still in the
mountain district of the Cottian Alps, southwest of

Turin. The opinions of these people resembled those of the modern Moravians, and were of what is called a Protestant character. The Bible alone was the rule of their faith. They rejected all that was not in accordance with apostolic antiquity. They renounced entirely the usages and traditions of the Roman Church. They suffered persecution along with the Albigenses, and have been thereby confounded with them. It is probable that the effect of the preaching of these and other heretical sectaries was very extensive, since they appear, nearly during the same period, in Lombardy, Germany, Flanders, Spain, France, and England. It was chiefly among the lower class of people that their influence extended.

A letter of Innocent III (Pope, 1198-1216) shows that certain laymen had procured a translation of parts of Scripture into their own tongue (French), and were in the habit of meeting in secret conventicles to read and preach to each other, avoiding the services of the Church altogether. Innocent rebuked these practices in a temperate way. The fact of their existence was, however, more ominous for the power of the papacy than all the defiance of a monarch like King John, whom Innocent took pains to crush and bring to terms. Portions of the Scriptures were translated from time to time, even during the Dark Ages, into the vernacular tongues, and the Council of Toulouse, in 1229, prohibited the laity's possessing the Scriptures. In the Thirteenth and Fourteenth Centuries other sects revolted from the established Church. The doings of Wicklif in England are familiar as well as the persecutions which put down the Lollards. In Bohemia John Huss followed the teaching of Wicklif. Huss began to preach at Prague in 1402, and boldly advocated reforms which would, as he contended, restore the purity and simplicity of Scriptural Christianity.   In consequence of his teaching, a large body of German professors and students, objecting to his views, left Prague and founded the University of Leipsic.   In 1409 Huss became rector of the University of Prague, and attacked in many points the doctrines and practices of the Church.   Summoned to Rome by successive Popes, he declined to appear, appealed to a general council of the Church, and was then excommunicated, Prague being laid under an interdict as long as Huss should remain in it.   Huss then left Prague, and continued his preaching.   In 1414 he decided to attend the Council of Constance in Switzerland, and defend his opinions there before the clergy of all nations.   The Emperor Sigismund of Germany gave Huss letters of safe-conduct, pledging himself for his personal security.   When Huss reached Constance in November, 1414, he was imprisoned, and kept there against the remonstrances of the Bohemian and Moravian nobles.   At a public examination before the council in June, 1415, in presence of the Emperor, Huss refused to withdraw his heresies, and on July 6th was condemned and burned to death, his ashes being thrown into the Rhine.   Such agitations were prophetic of the great revolution in the Sixteenth Century known as the Reformation.

During the Middle Ages, increase of wealth led to greater comfort in the daily life of mankind.   The growth of commerce and manufactures at once supplied improvements in this way, and gave the means of procuring them.   We learn the state of things in Italy, which was superior in refinement to France, Germany, and England, from a writer of about the year 1300.   In speaking of the age of the Emperor Frederick II (reigned 1218 to 1250) he declares that then "the manners of the Italians were rude; that a man and his wife ate off the same plate; no wooden-handled knives, and not more than one or two drinking-cups in a house; candles of wax or tallow unknown, and a servant held a torch during supper.   The clothes of men were of leather unlined; scarcely any gold or silver was seen on their dress.   The common people ate flesh but three times a week, and kept their cold meat for supper.   Many did not drink wine in summer.   A small stock of corn seemed riches.   The portions (dowries in marriage) of women were small; their dress, even after marriage, was simple.   The pride of men was to be well provided with arms and horses.   But now (about A. D. 1300) frugality has been changed for sumptuousness; everything exquisite is sought after in dress; gold, silver, pearls, silks and rich furs.   Foreign wines and rich meats are required."   In 1266 we hear of the Provençal knights with plumed helmets and golden collars, and of a queen's chariot covered with blue velvet, and sprinkled with lilies of gold.   Provence had enjoyed a long tranquillity, the natural source of luxurious magnificance; and Italy, now liberated, under her Republics, from the yoke of the German Empire, soon reaped the same fruit of a condition more easy and peaceful than had been her lot for several ages.   The great poet Dante (lived A. D. 1265 to 1321) speaks of the change of manners at Florence, from simplicity and virtue to refinement and dissoluteness.   In the Fourteenth Century there was a steady progression in England and France of elegance and luxury; the clergy denounced fantastic extravagances of fashion in dress, and sumptuary laws were passed to restrain expensiveness in apparel and food.   In Germany, the growth of freedom and commerce, and the rise of artisans to the condition of free burghers, caused a great improvement in the way of comfort and elegance of life. Competence was diffused over a large class of indus, trious freemen; and, in the Fifteenth Century, an Italian writer dwells on the splendid and well-furnished dwellings, rich apparel, easy and affluent mode of living, security of rights, and equality of laws, to be found in such cities as Spires, Nuremberg, Ratisbon, and Augsburg. The steadiness and frugality of the German character were of great advantage to the working-class.

The improvement in domestic architecture in Europe during the last centuries of the Middle Ages is an indication of the general progress in social life. In England, during the Fourteenth Century, the massive baronial castles, with mere loopholes for windows on the lowest story, and the windows in the upper rooms all looking inward to the court, began to give way to such splendid castle-palaces as those of Windsor, Alnwick, Kenilworth, and Warwick. Large arched windows, like those of cathedrals, were introduced into halls, and this change in architecture bears witness to the cessation of baronial wars and the increasing love of splendor in the reign of Edward III. In the Fifteenth Century came the castellated houses to be seen in Herstmonceux in Sussex, Haddon Hall in Derbyshire, and the older part of Knole in Kent. Early in the Fourteenth Century the art of building with brick, lost since the Roman dominion, was introduced into England, probably from Flanders, and superseded to a great extent the use of stone and of timber of the oak forests. The English gentry at this time, however, were generally lodged in manor-houses of little capacity or convenience. The two chief improvements in domestic architecture during the Middle Ages were things, one of which the civilization even of

Greece and Rome had never devised—chimneys and glass windows. About the middle of the Fourteenth Century the use of chimneys, unknown to the ancients, is mentioned in Italy and England. The art of making glass had been lost in this country, but preserved in France, whence artificers were brought into England to furnish the windows in some new churches as early as the Seventh Century. Glass for domestic use did not come, however, into general use during the Middle Ages. In other matters of domestic comfort, that epoch was in a very inferior condition. The walls of a gentleman's house were commonly bare, without wainscot or plaster; few such abodes had as many as three or four soft beds; no books nor pictures were to be seen; silver plate was rare; chairs, looking-glasses, and carpets were almost unknown even in the great houses. The farm-houses and cottages of that time were much more like what they are at present, save for the modern use of tiles and slates instead of thatch. The architecture of the Middle Ages can boast of durability and grandeur, and in the ecclesiastical way, with which we shall presently deal, has infinite grace and beauty.

During the Middle Ages the power of monarchs became limited over all Western and Central Europe, and in Sweden and Denmark, by some kind of national assembly, representing the different clasess of freemen in the nation—the nobles, the clergy, and the commons (or citizens, in general, of the towns). These assemblies met in each country for the purpose of granting money to the sovereign to defray expenses of government, and also of requiring changes in the laws or other reforms, and the consent of these bodies of representatives was necessary to the validity of some public acts. But these representative assemblies gradually declined before the acquirement of absolute power by the monarchs of Western and Central Europe, save in England alone. There, as money became more than ever necessary to the sovereign for the expenses of civil government, and (in the continental countries) for the support of a regular army, did the Parliament take a firm stand on its constitutional right to give or withhold money, and refuse to supply funds for the support of armies till securities had been provided against despotism. In the Fifteenth Century, in Spain, the Kingdoms of Castile and of Aragon had constitutions quite as free as that of England; in the Sixteenth Century those free constitutions perished under the attacks of Charles the Fifth and Philip the Second. In France, the power of the Parliament gradually decayed, and died out from sheer lack of the vitality which public spirit and political intelligence in the body of the nation could alone supply. In Italy, with her commonwealths, the history of affairs took a special course, which we shall deal with hereafter. In Denmark and Sweden the Kings became absolute by taking advantage of the quarrels between the nobles and commons, which made both an easy prey to usurpation of their constitutional rights by the crown. In Germany, the national assemblies, called Diets, became gradually subservient to the Emperors, and lost all reality of power.

During the latter part of the Middle Ages a general increase of popular freedom took place in the abolition of the servitude or semi-servitude of the feudal times, as regards the domestic slaves and the serfs attached to the land. This change occurred in various ways, working in deference to the general advance of intelligence and morality. In some instances the feudal masters gave freedom to their serfs at the bidding of the church; in others, freedom was acquired by residence for a certain time in a chartered town. Justice began to be administered more regularly according to fixed laws, and a more effectual police was maintained. The courts of judicature, whether they were guided by the feudal customs or by the Roman law, resolved questions with precision and uniformity, and the public ideas of justice and good faith were thereby amended. By the close of the Middle Ages a great improvement in the general maintenance of order was to be observed. Lawless rapine and the private warfare between feudal barons had almost ceased. A regular police was established in towns for internal security and for defense against marauders outside the walls. The increase of wealth, and of the numbers of those who, in their degree, possessed somewhat to defend, produced the effect usual in free communities, of greater security to property and life. As the mind of Europe began to awake from the sleep of the Dark Ages, the study of civil law was one of the earliest signs of new intellectual life. The system of jurisprudence contained in the code of Justinian, which has been already described, was taught early in the Twelfth Century in a school of civil law at Bologna, in Italy. Rapid progress was made in this new pursuit. Lombardy became rich in learned lawyers, and the Bologna schools were distinguished throughout this century. Universities arose at Naples, Padua, and other places, and the Roman law was there, too, a chief object of study. The municipal freedom of the Italian cities, where matters of dispute were settled by magistrates chosen by the citizens themselves, led to the compilation of a more extensive and accurate code of written laws, based upon the Roman system, and the fame of this renovated jurisprudence spread from Italy over other parts of Europe. Justinian's code was studied in the universities of Montpellier and Toulouse, and the Roman law became the rule of all tribunals in the south of France, in Spain, and in Germany, possessing also much influence in northern France. So justly great have been the renown and authority of the old Roman jurists, that portions of their law have been wrought into the modern codes of France and Prussia, and their sagacity is likely to be a guide to legislators for generations still far distant from our times. Thus grandly durable in its beneficence is some of the work done for mankind by the men of ancient Rome.

The establishment of public schools in France was due to Charles the Great. His two successors, Louis the Debonnaire and Charles the Bald, also encouraged learning, and even in the Ninth Century schools flourished at Lyons, Rheims, and in other cities. The basis of study at this time was, however, very cramped and pedantic; even Alcuin forbade the reading of the Latin poets, and general learning (or all beyond the study of a narrow theology) was discouraged. Early in the Twelfth Century the new ardor for intellectual pursuits began to show itself in Europe. The first university to become distinguished was that of Paris, under the teaching of the famous Abelard, a schoolman or scholastic philosopher of bold and brilliant genius. Abelard was noted in his own day as a grammarian, orator, logician, poet, musician, philosopher, theologian, and mathematician; by a strange fate, he is now celebrated only as the martyr of love, through the letters which passed between him and Heloise, with whom he was miserably and shamefully connected. He began to lecture at Paris on rhetoric, philosophy, and theology about 1104, and had

St. Bernard among his pupils. His own misconduct drove him from Paris, and he was condemned for heresy at a council in 1122, and died in disgrace and misery in 1142. Abelard was almost the first who awakened mankind after the Dark Ages to a sympathy with intellectual excellence, and his life is remarkable amongst those of literary men for success and failure, glory and shame, the admiration and the persecution of mankind. In England the Universities of Oxford and Cambridge arose, that of Oxford being a school of learning before the Norman Conquest, that of Cambridge being founded in the Thirteenth Century. In Germany, the first university was that of Prague, founded in 1350; that of Leipsic (Leipzig) followed in 1409. In Spain, the University of Salamanca was founded about the end of the Twelfth Century, and became famous, flourishing till the Sixteenth Century. The golden age of universities began with the Thirteenth Century, and students from all parts of Europe resorted to them, that of Paris being more frequented than any other. There were also, in France, the Universities of Orleans, Angers, Bourges, and Toulouse. In the Twelfth Century the Jews cultivated the studies of medicine and the Rabbinical literature in their own academy at Montpellier.

The University of Paris was unrivaled for the study of scholastic theology.* A peculiar product of the awakened intellect of mankind in Europe in the Middle Ages was the scholastic philosophy, the great aim of which was to reduce the doctrines of the church to a scientific system.

The two great names in science during the Middle Ages are those of Albertus Magnus and Roger Bacon.

* See the "Scholastics" in Volume "World's Great Philosophers."

Albertus Magnus, a native of Swabia, became in 1222 a monk of the Dominican order, and had the great Thomas Aquinas as his pupil at Cologne, where Albertus became rector in 1249. He rose to be Bishop of Ratisbon in 1260, but soon resigned his charge in order to devote himself to literary and scientific work. He wrote commentaries on Aristotle, and studied the sciences of arithmetic, geometry, optics, music, and astronomy. Albertus Magnus was probably the most learned man of his age, and was so far beyond most of his contemporaries that he was accused of dealing in magical arts, or holding communion with Satan—the penalty of intellectual attainments and originality at that time. Roger Bacon was one of the greatest men that arose during the Middle Ages, and possessed extraordinary genius for scientific research and discovery. Born in 1214, in Somersetshire, he showed an early taste for learning, studied at Oxford and at Paris, and became a Franciscan monk at Oxford in 1240. He was a good scholar in Latin, Hebrew, and Greek—a rare thing in the Thirteenth Century. He was thwarted in his scientific studies both by poverty and by the jealousy of the monks of his order, who denounced his opinions to the Pope, and caused his imprisonment for a time. A new Pope, Clément IV (1265-69), admired Bacon's abilities, and encouraged him to write. This led to the production in 1268-69 of his chief book, the Opus Majus ("Greater Work"), followed by two others. These books of Bacon the Friar laid the foundations of the philosophy of Bacon the Chancellor at a later time. The great Franciscan declared that the four grounds of human ignorance were —"trust in inadequate authority, the force of custom, the opinion of the inexperienced crowd, and the hiding of one's own ignorance with the parading of a superficial wisdom." This teaching is worthy of Socrates himself, and entitles Roger Bacon to the admiration and gratitude of mankind, when we consider the influences by which he was surrounded and the persecution which he fought and endured. He advocated the "free honest questioning of Nature," and urged students to aim at reading books in the original text, especially the Bible and Aristotle. He insisted on mathematics as important, with a particular regard for optics, and on the experimental study of nature, which he believed to be at the root of all sciences, and a basis of religion. In optics this ingenious and original observer understood the refraction of light, and convex and concave lenses, involving the principle of the telescope, which he either invented or improved. He was good at geography and astronomy, and made a corrected calendar, of which the Bodleian Library at Oxford possesses a copy. It is little to his discredit, in such an age, that he believed in the superstitions of astrology and of the philosopher's stone. Roger Bacon (whose invention of gunpowder is a matter of doubt) is a man of whom England may well be proud, as an early forerunner of his illustrious namesake and of Sir Isaac Newton, the prince of all natural philosophers. After being accused of magical arts, and enduring a second imprisonment for ten years, he died about 1293.

Early in the Twelfth Century Arabian writings on geometry and physical science were brought into Europe. A high degree of culture had been reached in Spain by its Mohammedan conquerors as early as the Tenth Century. Schools, libraries, and universities were established, and professors lectured on literature, rhetoric, astronomy, and pure mathematics. The works of Greek philosophy came, through the Arabic, into Latin, and so passed into the possession of the European scholars, few of whom could read the Greek originals. Among the Saracenic scholars

of Spain were Avicenna, a physician and philosopher, who
died in 1037, and Averroes, of Cordova, a famed com-
mentator on Aristotle, who died in 1198. Zoölogy,
botany, chemistry, and especially medicine, were studied,
and to the Moorish civilization we owe the mode of nota-
tion in arithmetic, called the Arabic figures, and the words
algebra, alcohol, alchemy, nadir, zenith, elixir, syrup,
cipher, and many others. The Arabian scholars derived
much of their mathematical knowledge from the Greeks
and the Hindoos. The caliphs of the Saracenic Empire
in Asia had caused translations to be made into Arabic
from Euclid, Archimedes, and other Greek geometers.
The Arabian arithmetic (with its symbols) came from
India; algebra either from the Greeks or Hindoos. A
Saracenic author named Ben Musa wrote on algebra early
in the Ninth Century, and dealt with the subject so far as
to include the solution of quadratic equations. While the
scholars of Rome and Constantinople were declaring the
earth to be flat, the Spanish Moors were teaching geography in their common schools from globes, and the
Arabs were the first to build in Europe observatories for
astronomical research. The tower which the Moors built
at Seville with this end in view was turned, by the Span-
iards who drove them from the land, into a belfry, because
they did not know what else to make of it. The present
condition of Spain is not unconnected with what lies
underneath the surface here. It is a fact that Europe, long
delivered from the ages of darkness and brought out into
a marvelous light, has never to this day made any fitting
acknowledgment of the great debt due to the Mohammedan conquerors of Spain.

Nor must the Jewish learning in the Middle Ages be
forgotten. Astronomy, philosophy, mathematics, and
medicine were eagerly studied by Jews in the Arabian

schools of Spain. In the Twelfth Century lived the great Jewish Rabbi, Maimonides, born at Cordova, a man who studied Jewish and Arabic literature and Greek philosophy (in an Arabic translation of Aristotle), and had much acquaintance with medicine. He became physician to the Sultan of Egypt, and acquired great fame by his abilities, learning, and high character. His theological writings had great influence on Judaism, and in the Thirteenth Century his books were widely circulated in Europe by Latin translations. Maimonides died in Egypt in 1204, and was buried in Palestine.

One of the chief causes of intellectual improvement in the latter part of the Middle Ages was the development of those new languages that sprang out of the corruption of Latin—the Romance tongues. The Provençal poets of chivalry and romance flourished, in the Twelfth and Thirteenth Centuries, in the south of France and the north of Spain. The language which had there grown up, under sunny skies and in a state of greater freedom than was known elsewhere, was noted for sweetness, tenderness, clearness, and wealth. The region where this luscious tongue was spoken was the land of gallantry and song, and of religion mingled with the praise of earthly love. The taste for poetry was general among the nobles and the knights, and greatly encouraged by the princes of the ruling house. In their court, then the most splendid and refined in Europe, was gathered the circle of noble poets called Troubadours (in Italian, Trovatori; in Norman-French, Trouvères or Trouveurs, i.e. the finders or inventors of verses). The poetical compositions of these persons were of no great merit, it would appear, and have mostly perished; but they greatly influenced modern poetry in the way of rhyme and meters. The strains of the Provençal poetry were of that class which is allied to music, and largely dependent upon that for effect.   In the Norman-French dialect of the North, the writers called Trouveurs produced poetical fictions about King Arthur and Charles the Great toward the end of the Twelfth Century, and in the Thirteenth we have the famous Roman de la Rose, a poetical allegory of love and other passions.   In this same tongue—the Langue d'Oil (corrupted from Latin *hoc illud*), as opposed to the Provençal or Langue d'Oc—prose romances, history, and other compositions began to be written in the Thirteenth Century.   In the early Spanish, we have the metrical life of the famous hero, the Cid, Ruy Diaz, probably written about the middle of the Twelfth Century.

In Italian, the Middle Ages produced one of the greatest of all poets, Dante (in full, Durante Alighieri), born at Florence in 1265.   His great poem is called the Divine Comedy, and is a representation of the three kingdoms of futurity, Hell, Purgatory, and Paradise, divided into one hundred cantos, containing about 14,000 lines.   Dante created his country's national poetry, and is one of the most original and powerful of writers—bold and concise, and, as occasion calls, soft, sweet, and terrible in turn. This great genius, but rudely treated in his lifetime, and since half a century after his death regarded with an immense reverence by his countrymen, died at Ravenna in 1321.   His poetry was the first good verse that had appeared in Europe for nearly a thousand years, and he has never been surpassed, if equaled, in epic poetry since. The Italian poet Petrarch (Francesco Petrarch), his country's greatest lyric versifier, lived from 1304 to 1374, and is famous for his sonnets, his love for Laura, and the services which he rendered in the revival of classical learning.   His merits were amply recognized in his lifetime and in 1341 Petrarch was solemnly crowned with a wreath

A. MAIGNAN, PINX

DANTE MEETS MATILDA

of bay, in the capitol of Rome, as the laureate poet, or national singer of Italy.

Chaucer, born about 1340, and who died in 1400, is the first really great name in English literature. He held various offices and went abroad in subordinate capacities on the service of the King, and in Italy was introduced to literature in its noblest mediæval shape, and in one of the noblest shapes it has appeared in any age. He had written poetry before this, but it was the work of the poets Dante, Petrarch, and Boccaccio's prose, that most profoundly impressed him and influenced him, and he borrowed much of their style and grace and occasionally incidents as well. His Canterbury Tales, the most famous of his works, consists of twenty-two tales in verse, with two in prose, told by twenty-three pilgrims out of the twenty-nine who meet at the Tabard Inn in Southwark on their way to the shrine of Thomas à Becket at Canterbury. They follow the lead of Boccaccio in that a series of tales is hung together upon a connecting thread of narrative. In the Tales Chaucer shows a genius akin to Shakespeare's. Not only is there a rare dramatic power manifested clearly, though there was not yet a drama, but he had also the calm sense of highest truth and that kindly breadth of human sentiment without which a power such as Shakespeare's can not be. His Troilus and Cressida are versions of two of the most famous poems written by Boccaccio, and the influence of Dante was shown upon his later work. The House of Fame was a brilliant effort of imaginative power, and the Legend of Good Women showed the high esteem for womanly truth and beauty felt by the poet. John Gower, born about 1325, and dying 1408, was a contemporary and friend of Chaucer, who calls him the "moral Gower," from his grave and sent1tious style, even when treating upon topics which might well be treated in a lively manner, such as his "Confessio Amantis," which is his best known work.

In Germany, the native genius asserted itself in the production of the great epic poem, called the Nibelungen Lied ("Song of the Nibelungen," an ancient Burgundian tribe). The hero of the work is called Siegfried; the heroine is Brunhild, an Icelandic princess; the incidents are those of the Teutonic and Scandinavian mythology; the time of the historical basis of the poem is about 440 A. D., and the scene is on the Rhine, and on the borders of Hungary and Austria. The author is not certainly known; it was written about the middle of the Twelfth Century. The German critics place this great epic, in some respects, above the "Iliad"; it is the work of a true poet, but of a different class from the Homeric.

The chief artistic boast of the Middle Ages is to be found in the architecture, whose noble works men still behold with admiration and delight. In these, art lent her aid to religion, and in the twelfth and following centuries arose the glorious cathedrals and abbeys which adorn the ancient towns and beauteous nooks of France and England, Belgium and Holland, Germany, Italy, and Spain. In these structures sublimity of general composition is united with the beauties of variety and form, and with intricacy of parts, and skillful effects of light and shade—all that can, in architectural effect, charm the eye and elevate the soul. The rounded arch of the Norman style—imitated from the Moorish and the Byzantine buildings—began to give place, about the middle of the Twelfth Century, to the pointed arch of what is called the Gothic architecture. The origin of this style is as obscure as its beauty is apparent. It was accompanied, in many instances, with a great profusion of ornament, such as may be seen in the beautiful cathedral of Amiens, and

THE CRUSADES—THE TRIUMPH OF THE CROSS

Painting by M. S. M. Sedano

many similar productions of France. For three centuries the Gothic style prevailed, and the great cathedrals of Milan and Cologne belong to the Fifteenth Century. Of these the latter has only been lately completed; that of Milan remains unfinished yet, a wondrous dream in white marble, bristling with pinnacles and statues, unrivaled in its kind among all the works of men. It has been said that in these cathedrals of the Middle Ages "the artist used a building as a book on which to express, in powerful language, his own peculiar disposition, his hopes, his sentiments, his thoughts, and his experience." The great awakening of mind at the close of the Middle Ages led to the wildness and exuberance of fancy displayed in the richly varied decoration of the later style; the grotesque carvings plentifully seen in it are illustrations of fables, legends, and romances, as well as the individual expressions of the artist's thoughts and embodiments of his creed.

The introduction of Christianity acted at first as a check upon the art of painting. The Greek and Roman arts had represented the pagan gods abhorred by the early Christians, and painting fell into discredit. By degrees the art came to be used to illustrate the new religion, though its development was again checked by the excesses of the Iconoclasts of the Eighth and Ninth Centuries in the Byzantine Empire, who destroyed many works of art in their zeal against image-worship. The Byzantine school of painting is known by its gilded backgrounds, bright colors, and comparative indifference to truthfulness of representation, beauty of form, and grandeur of conception. This school of art was the parent of the great schools of Italy and of the Rhenish or Old Cologne school in Germany. Early in the Thirteenth Century painting was spread from Constantinople to other parts of Europe.

After the capture of that city by the Venetians and the Latin Crusaders in 1204, many Byzantine painters passed into Italy and Germany. A new civilization had now arisen in Italy, and, under the influences now brought to bear, painting there reached, during the next three centuries, a perfection never attained before or since. In the Fourteenth Century the Italian artists set themselves free from the conventional trammels of the Byzantine style. The chief leaders in this were Cimabue, born at Florence in 1240, and Giotto, born in a Florentine village about 1276, a pupil of Cimabue's. Cimabue forms the link between the ancient and modern schools of painting. Poor in coloring and perspective, he had grandeur of style, accurate drawing, natural expression, noble grouping, and fine disposition of drapery. Giotto is the first really great painter of modern times. His influence spread throughout Italy and into other lands, his human figures having truth, nature, dignity, correctness, life, and freedom previously unattained. For nearly two centuries the Florentine school of art was pre-eminent, reaching its height in the first half of the Sixteenth Century. The Roman, Venetian, Bolognese, Milanese, Parmesan, and Neapolitan schools of painting come after the Middle Ages. The Rhenish—or Old Cologne—school of Germany flourished from the Fourteenth to the Fifteenth Century. The Flemish painters begin with the brothers Van Eyck, of Bruges, early in the Fifteenth Century. The Dutch, French, and Spanish painters come after the Middle Ages, and the English later still. Such were the beginnings and first results of that great reawakening of intelligence and progress of culture which mark the closing centuries of the thousand years of history called the Middle Ages.